Managing Knowledge

The Open University Business School

The Open University Business School offers a three-tier ladder of opportunity for managers at different stages of their careers: the Professional Certificate in Management; the Professional Diploma in Management; and the Master of Business Administration.

This book is an MBA Course Reader for the Managing Knowledge course (B823) at The Open University Business School. Opinions expressed in this Reader are not necessarily those of the Course Team or of The Open University.

Further information on Open University Business School courses may be obtained from OUBS Information Team, The Call Centre, The Open University, PO Box 724, Milton Keynes MK7 6ZS (Telephone: +44 (0) 8700 100311).

Alternatively, much useful course information can be obtained from the Open University Business School's website at http://www.oubs.open.ac.uk

Managing Knowledge

An Essential Reader

Edited by
Stephen Little, Paul Quintas and Tim Ray

THE OPEN UNIVERSITY
in association with

Sage Publications
London • Thousand Oaks • New Delhi

First published 2002

SAGE Publications Ltd
6 Bonhill Street
London EC2A 4PU

SAGE Publications Inc
2455 Teller Road
Thousand Oaks, California 91320

SAGE Publications India Pvt Ltd
32, M-Block Market
Greater Kailash – I
New Delhi 110 048

British Library Cataloguing in Publication data

A catalogue record for this book is available from the British Library

ISBN 0–7619–7212–9
ISBN 0–7619–7213–7 (pb)

Library of Congress Control number available

Typeset by Keystroke, Jacaranda Lodge, Wolverhampton.
Printed in Great Britain by The Cromwell Press Ltd,
Trowbridge, Wiltshire

Contents

CONTENTS

Preface

This book is a contribution to the development of a new interdisciplinary field for management education. It has been prepared as a Reader for the Open University Business School's MBA course *Managing Knowledge* (course code B823), launched in October 1999. The book brings together a selection of articles that represent major themes within the broad scope of the emergent field of knowledge management.

The Open University Business School (OUBS) began the development of *Managing Knowledge* in October 1996 following a series of informal meetings. When these started in 1995 there were no established definitions of knowledge management, the boundaries and composition of the field had not been scoped and no syllabuses for MBA courses existed anywhere. The OUBS was able to begin developing the course at an early point in the emergence of knowledge management because of the existing research base in the School. The *Managing Knowledge* course team had to define the area, devise the syllabus and key themes and then develop a wide range of original interdisciplinary materials and study sessions. Our early approach to this is discussed in Quintas et al. (1997).

The OUBS specializes in supported distance learning for managers. As course Reader this book is a component of the *Managing Knowledge* integrated teaching programme that also includes 13 core course printed units (interactive teaching texts); CD-ROMS; synchronous and asynchronous on-line activities using email, conferencing and web-based groupware; face-to-face tutorials and a residential school. The selection of material in this book is therefore related to other material available to B823 students, and is designed to present examples, arguments and positions that evoke and support critical understanding. The opinions and positions adopted in the readings are not necessarily those of the course team or the OUBS.

Over 850 MBA students studied *Managing Knowledge* in its first presentation, and this Reader goes to press with a similar number studying the second presentation. Though part of the MBA programme, the course may also be studied as a stand alone option. More than 25,000 students in 37 countries study with the OUBS every year, and our MBA Alumni Association has around 8,500 members. If you would like to study *Managing Knowledge* or receive further information about OUBS Certificate, Diploma and MBA courses, please visit our website at http://www.oubs.open.ac.uk or telephone (UK) 08700 100311.

This choice of articles presented in this book is in large part the product of the deliberations of the academic team that developed the Open University Business School's *Managing Knowledge* course, plus those involved in its first presentation. The Editors would like to thank the following colleagues who were or are core course team members and authors: Steven Albert, Jill Alger, Nikki Bolleurs, Eva Johanna Brauner, Simon Buckingham Shum, Ysanne Carlisle, Leslie de Chernatony, Adrian Demaid, Roger Dence, Sheila Evers, Wendy Fowle, Joan Hunt, Geoff Jones, Roland Kaye, Paul Lefrere, Carmel McMahon, Jenny Monk, Susan Mudambi, Carol Pate, Ruth Salter, Terry Schumacher, David Skyrme, John Storey, Colin Thomas, Andrew Thomson, Sheila Tyler, Jeff Waistell and Sue Wright. We are particularly grateful for the key contribution of Professor James Fleck from the University of Edinburgh Management School. We also acknowledge the contribution of the critical readers and developmental testers who helped in the development phase. For the smooth production of this book thanks are due to Shirley Eley, OUBS; Gill Gowans, OU copublishing; and Kiren Shoman and Emma Wildsmith at Sage.

Special acknowledgements must go to the team of Associate Lecturers who have been at the forefront of the presentation of this innovative and challenging new venture; their energy, constructive help and feedback has been invaluable. Finally we should thank the many MBA students who have read and commented on the course and the texts presented here.

Opinions expressed in this book are not necessarily those of any of the individuals whose contribution is acknowledged above.

REFERENCE

Quintas, P., Lefrere, P. and Jones, G. (1997) 'Knowledge management: a strategic agenda', *Long Range Planning*, 30 (3): 385–391.

Acknowledgements

Grateful acknowledgement is made to the following sources for permission to reproduce material in this book:

Chapter 1: The Open University Business School.

Chapter 2: Copyright © 1998 by The Regents of the University of California. Reprinted from the *California Management Review*, Vol. 40, No. 3. By permission of the Regents.

Chapter 3: Reprinted from *Long Range Planning*, Vol. 33, Ikujiro Nonaka, Ryoko Toyama and Noboru Konno, 'SECI, *Ba* and Leadership: A Unified Model of Dynamic Knowledge Creation', 2000, with permission Elsevier Science.

Chapter 4: Reprinted by permission of the Institute for Operations Research and the Management Sciences (INFORMS) from S. D. Noam Cook and John Seely Brown, 'Bridging Epistemologies: The Generative Dance Between Organizational Knowledge and Organizational Knowing' © *Organization Science*, 1999.

Chapter 5: The Open University Business School.

Chapter 6: The Open University Business School.

Chapter 7: Reprinted from *Science, Technology and Human Values*, Vol. 19, No. 4, pp. 425–58. Copyright © 1994 Sage Publications, Inc. Reprinted by permission of Sage Publications, Inc.

Chapter 8: Reprinted from the *Journal of the Market Research Society*, Vol. 38, No. 2, April 1996, The Market Research Society.

Chapter 9: Reprinted from *Proc. HICSS '96: 29th Hawaii International Conference on System Sciences, Vol. III, Collaboration Systems and Technology*. January 1996, IEEE Computer Society Press.

Chapter 10: Reprinted from Condon, J. C. and Yousef, F. S. (1975) *An Introduction to Intercultural Communication*. Bobbs-Merrill. Copyright © 1975 by The Bobbs-Merrill Company, Inc.

Chapter 11: Reprinted from the *Journal of the Market Research Society*, Vol. 38, No. 2, April 1996, The Market Research Society.

Chapter 12: Reprinted from Bickerstaff, G. (ed.) *Financial Times Mastering Management*, Pitman Publishing, a division of Pearson Professional Ltd.

Chapter 13: Reproduced from *Creating the Knowledge-Based Business* by Debra M. Amidon and David J. Skyrme, © Business Intelligence, Third Floor, 22–24 Worple Road, Wimbledon, London, SW19 4DD, www.business-intelligence. co.uk.

Chapter 14: Reprinted from Lloyd, P. and Whitehead, R. (eds) *Transforming Organizations through Groupware*. © Springer-Verlag London Limited, 1996.

Chapter 15: Reprinted from the *Academy of Management Executive*, Vol. 11, No. 4, © Academy of Management Executive.

Chapter 16: Reprinted from *Fortune*, 3 June 1991. Figure p. 304: Aluminium Association; Figure p. 311: MIT Sloan School of Management.

Chapter 17: Reprinted from the *Academy of Management Executive*. Vol. 1, No. 3, copyright © The Academy of Management Executive, 1987. By permission of The Copyright Clearance Center.

Chapter 18: Reprinted by permission of *Harvard Business Review*, March/April 1996. Copyright © 1996 by the President and Fellows of Harvard College. All rights reserved.

Chapter 19: Reprinted from the *Financial Times Marketing Management Review*, Issue 17, October 1998. © John Storey.

Chapter 20: Paper presented at MKIRU Workshop, 'Building and maintaining the capability to innovate workshop', The Open University, Milton Keynes, 30 September 1998. © David Straker.

Chapter 21: The Open University Business School.

1

Managing Knowledge in a New Century

Paul Quintas*

> Knowledge has become the most important factor in economic life. It is the chief ingredient of what we buy and sell, the raw material with which we work. Intellectual capital – not natural resources, machinery, or even financial capital – has become the one indispensable asset of corporations. (Stewart, 1997)

> Capital consists in a great part of knowledge and organization. . . . Knowledge is our most powerful engine of production. (Marshall, 1890)

The above quotation from the economist Alfred Marshall 110 years ago suggests that the importance of *knowledge* as a source of economic wealth is in no sense a new idea. Indeed the close relationship between knowledge and political as well as economic power has been observed for centuries. It is perhaps ironic, then, that the realization that the management of knowledge is a core process within organizations has only recently become widespread. From the mid-1990s there has been a rapid growth of interest across the world in knowledge and how it might be managed within and between organizations. Politicians around the globe now routinely emphasize the contribution of knowledge to economic growth and competitiveness. This widespread interest follows a long history of attention to knowledge from economic and organizational perspectives, attention that has remained on the periphery of management thought and practice until now.

At present, however, the phrase 'knowledge management' describes an aspiration rather than a reality for the majority of organizations. Moreover, the interdisciplinary nature of the emergent field means that there is currently only partial agreement on what the knowledge management project consists of and what its agenda may look like. There are still many interpretations of the boundaries, scope and content of this new area, as well as conflicting views on the dominant disciplinary bases. Contributions come from practitioners, academics, consultants and policy-makers, who often have conflicting views

* The Open University Business School

of the basic assumptions and priorities. Within the management field academic interest is converging on knowledge from a number of different perspectives including information management, organizational learning, strategic management, change management, human resource management, management of innovation, and the measurement and management of intangible assets. This book seeks to make a contribution to this process of developing and refining the field of knowledge management. In doing so we take an interdisciplinary approach, gathering together a range of perspectives and practical approaches that contribute to a comprehensive account of knowledge management.

This opening chapter seeks to scope the territory and the principal components of this emergent field. We bring together both conceptual analysis and practical examples. Discussion of the present is located within an historical context: one key question is why is there a surge of interest in the management of knowledge now? Understanding the dynamics driving the phenomenon helps us to identify its key features and likely future direction. We then identify examples of the types of practical responses and initiatives currently pursued by organizations. Finally in the introduction we identify a number of key themes that form the rationale for the structure of the rest of the book.

WHY KNOWLEDGE MANAGEMENT NOW?

The mid-1990s saw a surge of publications, conferences and consultant activity in the knowledge management area, and many organizations woke up to the challenges of managing their knowledge. The first international conference 'Knowledge: the Strategic Imperative', was held in Houston as recently as September 1995, and the first periodicals on the topic including *Knowledge Management*, *Knowledge Inc.*, *Knowledge Management Review* and the *Journal of Knowledge Management* appeared as recently as 1997. The publication of journal articles on the subject also took off from 1996, as indicated in Figure 1.1.

By 1997 the knowledge management bandwagon was rolling. In 1996–97 there were over 30 conferences on knowledge in the USA and Europe, a whole raft of books and other publications, and an estimated $1.5 billion consulting revenue. Talk of the knowledge economy became widespread, with new posts of chief knowledge officers and directors of intellectual capital being created in many firms.

We should not assume that knowledge management received uniform responses in all countries and cultures. A European survey of 100 European business leaders reported that 89% considered knowledge to be the key to business power (Murray and Myers, 1997). Around 85% of the companies believed a value can be attached to business knowledge and over 90% claimed to have plans to exploit it. However there were some interesting cultural differences in these responses. In France, more than anywhere else in Europe, nearly a quarter of business leaders believe you *can't* create any processes to

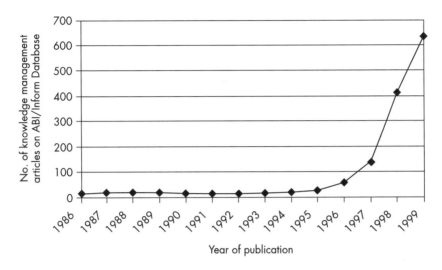

FIGURE 1.1 *Growth in knowledge management literature (Gordon and Grant, 2000)*

help you manage knowledge. It is simply a matter of 'management ability'. In Germany, on the other hand, more than four out of five companies already considered themselves to be good at encouraging staff to share knowledge and bring forward new ideas. In the UK the issue was seen by respondents more as a method of exploiting and controlling the massive amounts of knowledge that companies believe they already have. Almost a quarter of UK firms say creating new knowledge is not a key priority, compared with only 1% in Germany.

As the quotation from Alfred Marshall at the beginning of this chapter suggests, this current surge of interest follows a long history of attention to knowledge from economic and organizational perspectives – and a literature that has lain somewhat dormant for decades. Partly this is a result of the complexity of the subject, as Edith Penrose in her seminal *Theory of the Growth of the Firm* in 1959 observed:

> Economists have, of course, always recognized the dominant role that increasing knowledge plays in economic processes but have, for the most part, found the whole subject of knowledge too slippery to handle. (Penrose, 1959: 77)

The current idea of the knowledge economy also has its roots in Fritz Machlup's heroic attempt to map and measure *The Production and Distribution of Knowledge in the United States* (Machlup, 1962). Peter Drucker wrote in 1969 that knowledge had 'become the central capital, the cost centre and the crucial resource of the economy' (Drucker, 1969: ix). Scholars such as Daniel Bell built on the work of Machlup and others to propose the idea that the developed economies, having moved from agrarian to industrial in the 19th century, moved in the 20th into a service- and knowledge-based *post-industrial* society.

For Bell, knowledge is the 'axial principle' of post-industrial society, and most of the current arguments for a knowledge-based economy were effectively put forward in his 1973 book *The Coming of Post-Industrial Society*.

The key question that emerges from the above is why did knowledge come to the top of the management agenda in the 1990s, some 100 years after Marshall's time? Our analysis suggests that a number of factors have come together at this time. These fall under six headings:

- wealth being demonstrably and increasingly generated from knowledge and intangible assets;
- the rediscovery that people are the locus of much organizational knowledge;
- accelerating change in markets, competition, and technology, making continuous learning essential;
- the recognition that innovation is key to competitiveness, and depends on knowledge creation and application;
- the growing importance of cross-boundary knowledge transactions;
- technology limits and potentials: the limits of information systems and the potentials of communications and knowledge technologies.

We will discuss these drivers in some detail and then go on to look at key knowledge processes that require management attention.

WEALTH BEING DEMONSTRABLY AND INCREASINGLY GENERATED FROM KNOWLEDGE AND INTANGIBLE ASSETS

Company value has come to be increasingly dependent on intangible assets, knowledge assets, intellectual capital and intellectual property. Perhaps the example which created the greatest impact in the early 1990s was when Microsoft, a relatively small company with less than 14,000 employees, was valued by the stock market (in terms of market capitalization) as worth more than IBM, which employed over 300,000 people and had an installed base of computer systems across the world. What was the key to Microsoft's profitability and phenomenal success? They owned an intangible asset – MS.DOS (and Windows) – the *de facto* standard for personal computer operating systems software. The market value of companies that own key intangible assets such as intellectual property rights, a standard or a brand may exceed the value of their conventional assets many times over. In 1996 94% of Microsoft's market value (US$119 billion) came from intangible assets, as did 85% of Intel's (US$113 billion) and 96% of Coca-Cola's market value (148 US$ billion) (Roos et al., 1997).

So too, the value of knowledge and the ability to create it is evidenced in the large scale investments in science based and new technology based companies. Huge investments in biotechnology firms, many of which have no revenue income or show no profits, are based on the assumption that these firms will create knowledge which will lead to new product innovation and therefore competitive advantage.

THE REDISCOVERY THAT PEOPLE ARE THE LOCUS OF MUCH ORGANIZATIONAL KNOWLEDGE

> If NASA wanted to go to the moon again, it would have to start from scratch, having lost not the data, but the human expertise that took it there last time. (Brown and Duguid, 2000: 122)

Ironically, certain negative aspects of human resource strategies in the 1980s and early 1990s have made their contribution to the current interest in managing knowledge. During this period in European and North American economies many organizations underwent programmes of 'downsizing' (e.g. by making employees redundant), 'de-layering' (e.g. by shedding layers of middle management), and 'outsourcing' (removing the capacity to carry out certain business functions, which then have to be bought in). One advocate of 'business process re-engineering' urged organizations 'Don't automate, obliterate!' (Hammer, 1990). The result of these strategies was that many organizations found they no longer retained the ability to react to change or even to fully understand their own markets and business. They had lost their corporate memory and capabilities they didn't know they had or needed.

Following the downsizing, early redundancies and outsourcing of the 1980s, in the 1990s organizations rediscovered the central importance of people. In many cases people who had been made redundant had to be re-hired, often as consultants, because their knowledge was found to be irreplaceable. Once again people were recognized as possessing knowledge and know-how, as having the ability to create knowledge and value, and collectively to retain organizational memory. However, much of this individual knowledge is unknown to others and unmapped. Often knowledge is created within communities of practice who share understandings and experience that is not easily transferable to those outside that community. The relationship between individual, group and organizational knowledge is therefore a central focus for knowledge management.

ACCELERATING CHANGE IN MARKETS, COMPETITION AND TECHNOLOGY, MAKING CONTINUOUS LEARNING ESSENTIAL

The gathering pace of change in most if not all sectors of the economy is a powerful source of anxiety for managers and organizations. Change occurs across several dimensions: changes in markets and industries, new forms of competition and new entrant competitors, globalization in markets and supply chains, and changes in technology which result in product and process innovation, thereby altering cost structures.

Such endemic change demands continuous regeneration and development of organizational knowledge – that is, organizations and the people within them must be continually learning. The need to continually reinvent your organization through learning is a key feature of knowledge management. Knowledge from past experience becomes embedded within systems and technologies and embodied in routines. Continuous change requires the development of organizational routines and an organizational culture that supports the ability to create, absorb and assimilate new knowledge, and to abandon outmoded knowledge and routines. Organizations need to achieve two potentially conflicting objectives: first, to build their knowledge bases cumulatively and learn from past experience; and second, to ensure that they are learning beyond their core areas, generating the capability to assimilate new knowledge in order to be able to respond to change. These are key knowledge management challenges.

THE RECOGNITION THAT INNOVATION IS KEY TO COMPETITIVENESS, AND DEPENDS ON KNOWLEDGE CREATION AND APPLICATION

In many sectors competitive advantage increasingly occurs through innovation, whether in products, processes or services. In turn, innovation, which by definition is concerned with the new, depends on knowledge creation as well as application. Above we noted the value placed on intangible assets, and the recognition that wealth also comes from the ability to create and apply knowledge, as exemplified by the venture capital investments in new industries such as biotechnology. Investment is committed on the expectation that certain companies have the intellectual capabilities to create the knowledge that will lead to innovation and profits. In fast-moving sectors such as telecommunications it is the capability to continuously create new knowledge rather than the possession of knowledge resources or assets that is the key to sustainable advantage, given the threat of innovation in the marketplace. The management of innovation is essentially about the management of knowledge – the creation, reformulation, sharing and bringing together of different types of knowledge.

A central knowledge management dilemma for organizations seeking to innovate focuses on the need to build their knowledge bases cumulatively, share knowledge and learn from past experience, while at the same time to generate variety and untypicality in their knowledge base as the source of novel developments. For all organizations the knowledge management challenges presented by innovation focus on this tension between linear and non-linear processes – i.e. between the predictable and the unpredictable. Innovation therefore is far from safe, and requires eclectic and diverse approaches to the types and sources of knowledge that might be relevant.

Innovation is about diversity, untypicality and uncertainty, and it carries a considerable degree of risk. Innovating organizations must expect, recognize and learn from failure.

THE GROWING IMPORTANCE OF CROSS-BOUNDARY KNOWLEDGE TRANSACTIONS

Arguably no firm has ever been independent in knowledge terms, but it is certainly the case today that all organizations are increasingly dependent on external sources of knowledge. The complexity and pace of change in markets and technologies makes it impossible even for the largest organizations to cover all potential developments and to grow knowledge capabilities across all potentially important fields of research and development. This is exacerbated by the unpredictable nature of change in many sectors, from manufacturing to services.

Cross-boundary knowledge transactions apply to boundaries within organizations, between functional specialisms and between disciplines. Increasingly knowledge is accessed and shared across cultural and national boundaries as organizations and markets become international. Much new knowledge – the vast majority for most firms – is created outside the corporate boundary, so organizations must develop absorptive capacity: the capability to access and assimilate new knowledge from external sources. Knowledge interdependence creates new management challenges resulting from the risks and difficulties of knowledge transactions across boundaries. So too, the development of new products, systems and services increasingly requires the integration of knowledge from many disciplines. The ability to share knowledge across functional and disciplinary boundaries presents particular challenges since different communities and disciplines may have little common ground for shared understandings.

TECHNOLOGY LIMITS AND POTENTIALS: THE LIMITS OF INFORMATION SYSTEMS AND THE POTENTIALS OF COMMUNICATIONS AND KNOWLEDGE TECHNOLOGIES

> In the end, the location of the new economy is not in the technology, be it the microchip or the global telecommunications network. It is in the human mind. (Webber, 1993: 27)

It is ironic that there is a strong tendency for the information technology focus to dominate much of the current writings and conference proceedings on the subject of knowledge management, and indeed products and service offerings marketed under the knowledge management banner. This is ironic because by definition, information technology is concerned with information and not knowledge *per se*. While it may sensibly be argued that codified knowledge is also information, much knowledge cannot be codified and remains inaccessible to information technology. One common delusion underpinning some knowledge management approaches is that we can move seamlessly from data processing to information management and then to knowledge management. As Spender (1996) has pointed out, there is little point in introducing such a complex concept as knowledge into management discourse if we are not to take seriously the characteristics of knowledge that make it special, and distinguishable from information.

There has been an increasing awareness that information systems do not capture the knowledge or even the information that managers use in their daily lives, as noted by the former head of information technology research for Ernst and Young:

> evidence from research conducted since the mid-1960s shows that most managers don't rely on computer-based information to make decisions. . . . managers get two-thirds of their information from face-to-face or telephone conversations; they acquire the remaining third from documents, most of which come from outside the organization and aren't on the computer system. (Davenport, 1994: 121)

This leads to the notion that organizational information systems reached some kind of limit in the early 1990s, and need to go through a step-change in order to support knowledge management. Claims are made for the knowledge management capabilities of current systems, particularly in the area of communications for knowledge sharing, and (in advanced systems) representation of knowledge and knowledge processes.

However technology also has a number of potentials as a medium of knowledge communication, reducing time and distance constraints, and in addition having the potential to add value to communications and knowledge processes. Clearly the World Wide Web provides access to information on a global basis, but we need the knowledge skills of sense-making and learning if the WWW is to contribute to our knowledge resources and processes. We are at a juncture where the limitations of current information systems have emerged, and the potentials for *knowledge* systems have yet to be realized or proven.

KNOWLEDGE MANAGEMENT PRACTICE

We have seen in the previous section that no single factor is responsible for the surge in interest in knowledge management. What appears to have occurred is that a number of factors have come together to place knowledge high on the agenda for all types of organization. Of course these drivers are experienced differently by different organizations and in different sectors and indeed in different global locations. We can see differing priorities in the variety of responses by firms, in terms of the focus of their knowledge management initiatives. There are indications that for the majority of firms in the West, the priorities are the 'capture' of employees' knowledge, exploitation of existing knowledge resources or assets, and improved access to expertise (i.e. improved 'know-who'). Examples of initiatives include Teltech's mapping networks of experts (Davenport, 1997), Ernst and Young's sharing knowledge and best practice (Skyrme and Amidon, 1997), Dow Chemical's leveraging intellectual assets (Davenport and Prusak, 1998) and Skandia's measuring and auditing the value of knowledge and intangible assets (Skandia, 1996). Like many large organizations, the UK Post Office has launched a cluster of knowledge management projects,[1] including:

- knowledge sharing (targeted on communicating, learning, reviewing, capturing and sharing knowledge);
- use of stories to communicate experience (targeted on transferring learning);
- after-action reviews (capturing learning from experience);
- intelligent agents (identifying specific and tailored information or contacts);
- people database (providing access to expertise);
- expert interviews (capturing expertise);
- learning from mistakes (surfacing and capturing learning in a non-blame culture, avoiding costly repetition);
- expert masterclasses (sharing expertise).

Common knowledge initiatives elsewhere focus on capturing and re-using past experience, after-action reviews to capture learning (including from failure), and building and mining knowledge stores. Pharmaceuticals and health care companies such as Glaxo Wellcome and Integra Life Sciences have projects targeted on improved management and exploitation of intellectual property rights (IPR). Recognizing the economic importance of their knowledge or intellectual capital base, organizations in sectors such as the media, retailing and insurance reconceptualize their core business as a knowledge business. Consultancy firms realize they are in a knowledge business and seek to commodify their knowledge as a product. New business opportunities spring up for knowledge brokers and for 'talent' agents who represent knowledge workers in sectors where expertise is in great demand.

Approaches such as those of Xerox and 3M are more generic, seeking to promote better communication, learning and knowledge sharing. These and some other organizations recognize the other half of the knowledge equation – the importance of knowledge creation as the basis for innovation and competitive advantage – and seek to create a culture that supports knowledge creation. The following definition of knowledge management from Xerox indicates a strongly process-oriented account:

> Knowledge management is the discipline of creating a thriving work and learning environment that fosters the continuous creation, aggregation, use and re-use of both organizational and personal knowledge in the pursuit of new business value. (Cross, 1998: 11)

The Xerox definition is action oriented and missionary in its tone. It does not emphasize the notions of intellectual capital or knowledge resources and assets as many definitions and indeed initiatives do. Rather, it focuses on the processes of creating new knowledge and actively doing things with it.

Fundamental to many knowledge management initiatives, and closely related to the latter approach of Xerox and 3M, is the growth of initiatives intended to promote learning within organizations. The notion of organizational learning (or the more prescriptive and ambitious 'learning organization') has become well established over the last decade. Learning is a process of sharing and acquiring knowledge. Many initiatives undertaken to create a learning organization involve steps which are essentially concerned with managing knowledge. Typical approaches include building a knowledge-creating and knowledge-sharing culture, using communications technologies to facilitate learning, giving access to information, and creating learning champions. Moreover, many large organizations in the West have established corporate universities as the core of their organizational learning programme. This is an institutional approach which emphasizes formal structures and processes, discipline-based syllabuses and accreditation, rather than enterprise-wide knowledge sharing based, for example, on practitioner knowledge. One key question for all knowledge management initiatives is whether over-formalization of knowledge processes may not have disadvantages.

EMERGENT THEMES

The previous sections have identified the factors that have driven the significant increase in interest in knowledge management, and some of the current practices and priorities of firms. The drivers that put knowledge management on the map in the 1990s continue to put pressure on organizations and drive the knowledge management agenda in the first decade of the new millennium. Taken together these factors and initiatives present a bewildering array of apparently different dynamics, and therefore potentially conflicting priorities for management practice. However a number of cross-cutting themes are apparent.

First, it is clear that managers and organizations have to develop their understanding of knowledge itself. This means understanding the dynamic process of knowing, and the processes of knowledge creation, sharing, transformation and application. This requires, first, an acknowledgement of the challenges posed by the characteristics of knowledge. Not least, much of the knowledge upon which organizations rely is tacit – it is knowledge that resides within the heads and motor neurone systems of employees and has not been codified or made explicit. Such knowledge is not available to the wider organization, and managers may not be aware of its existence or its importance until employees leave the organization.

Understanding the nature of knowledge, and in particular recognizing the tacit dimension, emerges as a central challenge to managers. However, it is not enough, as many practitioners and consultants do, to focus on the knowledge that already exists within an organization, asking questions such as 'how can we capture the knowledge in the heads of our employees?' This is a preoccupation with resources or assets that already exists. Perhaps the more important consideration is how we create knowledge. The process of knowledge creation is central to a complete account of knowledge management, and for all organizations the ability to create knowledge must be regarded as a core capability. As Nonaka and Takeuchi (1995) point out, the key relationship between knowledge and competitive advantage lies in the potential for knowledge creation to lead to innovation, which in turn provides the basis for competitive advantage. The creation of knowledge, and consideration of knowledge resources and capabilities, emerge as key themes in this book.

It is also clear that *communication* is fundamental to all knowledge management processes. If we are to aspire to manage knowledge we need improved understanding of communications, knowledge sharing and the processes of learning within and between organizations. Communications is a well established field, but its value as a core discipline within management thought and teaching has been somewhat underplayed, particularly in Europe. Advances in our understanding of communication processes as social phenomena suggest an emphasis on the importance of context. Knowledge is created in specific contexts within particular communities and for particular purposes. When we seek to transfer knowledge to another context we must understand the context within which it was created, in order to reinterpret its meaning and decontextualize for a new context. As the discussion of 'drivers' made clear, many knowledge management processes are inherently cross-boundary: boundaries may be functional, disciplinary, physical, cultural, hierarchical, structural, political and national, as well as interpersonal. It is essential to recognize that there are significant differences in the way knowledge is perceived in different countries and cultures.

For example, language plays a major role in our thinking about and discussion of knowledge, and it has often been pointed out that different languages deal with knowledge in quite different ways. The English language is sometimes accused of being deficient in having only the one word – *knowledge* – when, for example, French makes a distinction between *connaître* and *savoir*, and German between *kennen* and *wissen*. The English equivalent is suggested by James (1950) who used the terms 'knowledge about' and 'knowledge of acquaintance' to emphasize the difference between theoretical knowledge and practical knowledge. 'Knowledge about' suggests that the knowledge is the result of systematic thought, rather than mere acquaintance. One view is that differences in language and vocabulary, and indeed in definitions of knowledge, reflect the fact that knowledge itself is different in different contexts, and we should not be seeking universal definitions and vocabularies (Cohen, 1998). Nevertheless, managers and organizations increasingly have to operate across cultural and other boundaries, and an awareness of difference is essential. So too, alternative perspectives provide a rich source of new insights and reconceptualizations of our own thinking. The international and multicultural approach adopted in this book is an attempt to begin to develop a comprehensive account of knowledge management that goes beyond the limitations of a mono-cultural perspective.

A fourth key theme focuses on people and the management of human resources (HR). The observation that people are central to any consideration of knowledge is no surprise. A major practical issue, and conceptual problem, for knowledge management remains the problematic relationship between individual employees' knowledge and the totality of the organization. What *is* an organization, in knowledge terms? The idea that it is the sum of all the individual employees' knowledge added together is flawed since no organization can be aware of, let alone mobilize and exploit, all the knowledge possessed by all employees. Conversely, organizational routines, systems and culture may be said to capture and embed knowledge in a way that transcends and indeed outlasts the employment of individuals, suggesting that organizational knowledge is greater than the sum of currently employed individuals' expertise.

We noted in the 'drivers' discussion that the *re*discovery that employees have skills and knowledge has concentrated managerial minds on the challenges of retaining expertise, and has spawned many attempts to reduce organizational vulnerability by 'capturing' employees' knowledge. Awareness of the importance of knowledge has also led to notions that there are certain forms of work that can be considered 'knowledge work', and even certain types of workers that should be considered 'knowledge workers'. A key question is whether knowledge work is specialist work that requires different human resource strategies from that appropriate for other work, or whether there are 'knowledge workers' requiring special HR treatment. This is particularly apparent in relation to innovation, where the idea that certain workers create knowledge and innovate, often in research and development departments, underpins long-standing structural and cultural segregation of innovation-related work in many Western firms. Human resources management with respect to knowledge can therefore usefully be addressed through consideration of the HR practices relating to the management of innovation.

The remainder of the book consists of four parts followed by a concluding chapter. The parts focus on: knowledge creation; knowledge resources and capabilities; communicating and sharing knowledge; and knowledge, innovation and human resources. Each part has a short introduction. The first addresses the key theme of knowledge creation. In doing so it acknowledges the fact that knowledge is a social phenomenon, and that across different national and ethnic cultures the communities within which individuals and groups create knowledge have very different characteristics and perspectives. In particular, the comparison of Western and Japanese knowledge creation provides important insights into the nature of knowledge and the management practice and organizational cultures that support it.

NOTE

1   The author is grateful to the Post Office, who worked closely with the Open University Business School in the development of the *Managing Knowledge* course, providing insights into their knowledge management programme and access for OUBS researchers.

REFERENCES

Bell, D. (1973) *The Coming of Post-Industrial Society*, London, Heinemann.

Brown, J. S. and Duguid, P. (2000) *The Social Life of Information*, Boston, MA, Harvard Business School Press.

Cohen, D. (1998) 'Towards a knowledge context: report on the first annual UC Berkeley forum on knowledge and the firm', *California Management Review*, 40 (3): 22–39.

Cross, R. (1998) 'Managing for knowledge: managing for growth', *Knowledge Management*, 1 (3): 9–13.

Davenport, T. H. (1994) 'Saving IT's soul: human-centred information management', *Harvard Business Review*, March–April: 119–31.

Davenport, T. H. (1997) 'Ten principles of knowledge management and four case studies', *Knowledge and Process Management*, 4 (3): 187–208.

Davenport, T. H. and Prusak, L. (1998) *Working Knowledge*, Boston, MA, Harvard Business School Press.

Drucker, P. F. (1969) *The Age of Discontinuity: Guidelines to Our Changing Society*, London, Heinemann.

Gordon, R. and Grant, D. (2000) 'Knowledge management or the management of knowledge: why people interested in knowledge management should read Foucault', in Clegg, S., Booth, P, Clarke, T. and Sominan, F. (eds) *Deciphering Knowledge Management*, New York, Springer-Verlag.

Hammer, M. (1990) 'Re-engineering work: don't automate, obliterate', *Harvard Business Review*, July–Aug.: 104–12.

James, W. (1890) *The Principles of Psychology, Vols I and II*, New York, Dover Publications, 1950.

Machlup, F. (1962) *The Production and Distribution of Knowledge in the United States*, Princeton, NJ, Princeton University Press.

Marshall, A. (1972) *Principles of Economics*, 8th edn, first published 1890, London, Macmillan.

Murray, P. and Myers, A. (1997) 'The facts about knowledge', *Information Strategy*, Sept.: 31–3.

Nonaka, I. and Takeuchi, H. (1995) *The Knowledge-Creating Company*, Oxford, Oxford University Press.

Penrose, E. (1959) *The Theory of the Growth of the Firm*, Oxford, Oxford University Press.

Quintas, P., Lefrere, P. and Jones, G. (1997) 'Knowledge management: a strategic agenda', *Long Range Planning*, 30 (3): 385–91.

Roos, J., Roos, G., Edvinsson, L. and Dragonetti, N. (1997) *Intellectual Capital*, Basingstoke, Macmillan Business.

Skandia (1996) *Value Creating Processes*, supplement to 1995 Annual Report.

Skyrme, D. J. and Amidon, D. M. (1997) *Creating the Knowledge-Based Business*, London, Wimbledon, Business Intelligence Ltd.

Spender, J. C. (1996) 'Making knowledge the basis of a dynamic theory of the firm', *Strategic Management Journal*, 17, Winter Special Issue: 45–62.

Stewart, T. (1997) *Intellectual Capital: The New Wealth of Organizations*, London, Nicholas Brealey.

Webber, A. (1993) 'What's so new about the new economy?', *Harvard Business Review*, Jan.–Feb.: 24–32.

Part I Creating Knowledge

Each of the four readings in this section explores different aspects of tacit knowledge and its interaction with wider knowledge-creating processes. Taken together, they reveal essential differences between managing knowledge in Western and Japanese contexts.

In Chapter 2, Brown and Duguid consider the relationship between communities of practice and the problems of organising knowledge in the face of new information and communication technologies that ostensibly threaten the need for traditional firms. Next Nonaka, Toyama and Konno present a unified model of Japanese-style knowledge creation, which is situated in a shared context or *ba* (roughly meaning 'place') and centres on the interplay between tacit and explicit knowledge. In Chapter 4, Cook and Brown argue that the West often undervalues tacit knowledge embodied in individual skills and different 'genres' that represent group-based tacit knowledge, which cannot usefully or meaningfully be reduced to the individual level. They see individual and collective tacit knowledge as 'tools' that exist on an equal footing with individual and collective explicit 'knowledge tools'. All four categories of knowledge tools can be mutually enabling in the process of doing something that they call 'active knowing' or 'the epistemology of practice'. At the end of Part I, Ray considers factors that differentiate knowledge creation in Japan from approaches adopted in its Western counterparts. He highlights the importance of stable organizations that delineate space for mutual understanding amongst permanent employees who spend their careers working together. The relatively fixed boundaries of Japan's organizations make them effective 'social containers' for the accumulated individual and collective tacit knowledge that plays a pivotal role managing Japanese knowledge creation.

THE READINGS

Brown and Duguid argue that, because a great deal of knowledge is produced and held collectively in tightly knit communities of practice, organizational knowledge is inevitably heavily social in character. Shared experience underpins commonly held views about the type of information that warrants attention and what to avoid. It bonds the community and gives meaning to shared information. This 'sticky' knowledge evolves from the interaction of practitioners and (inasmuch as it is difficult for outsiders to understand) does

15

not easily 'leak'. Specialized groups produce specialized knowledge – the 'know-how' that renders 'know what' information meaningful and potentially useful. Information that circulates easily in one community might be of little value to those who lack the background knowledge necessary to render it comprehensible.

While sticky knowledge is relatively easy to protect, it is hard to spread, co-ordinate or change. And it is not commensurate with the 'friction free' information flows implied by Internet transactions. Collectively held social expertise undermines the idea that no organization need or should come between the information-empowered individual and Marshall McLuhan's amorphous global village. Thus, the firm has a future because it produces a distinctive type of knowledge. But the knowledge created by experience-at-work flows more easily amongst *de facto* communities of practice than it does across the firm, which typically draws on expertise from many different types of specialist.

Anyone familiar with disciplinary structure of a university will be aware that progress within a particular subject area tends to foster precepts and attitudes that differentiate it from other disciplines. Research collaboration with like-minded specialists in another country can be easier than with the occupants of adjacent offices who happen to belong to a different discipline. Similar practice in a common field affords effortless exchanges of ideas – allowing specialist knowledge to travel amongst universities while limiting its ability to bridge disciplinary boundaries within the institution.

Western firms rely on hierarchy to reconcile organizational goals with the underlying employee logic of self-interest. As Wenger has noted: 'Our identities are not something we can turn on and off. You don't cease to be a parent because you go to work. You don't cease to be a nurse because you step out of hospital. Multimembership is an inherent aspect of our identities' (Wenger, 2000: 239). Brown and Duguid's approach to this multimembership problem focuses on boundary-spanning processes – translating, knowledge brokering, and the creation of 'boundary objects' (such as contracts, plans and so on) – that enable meaningful information to circulate throughout the organization and thereby glue it together.

The relevance of technology to boundary-spanning activities depends on its ability to evolve in concert with emerging communication needs. Sufficiently motivated members of coherent social networks can easily subvert formal communication policies. Brown and Duguid's conclusion is that communication technology will not sweep away the firm. Contrary to predictions made in the 1930s, the typewriter has not replaced the pencil. And excessive emphasis on discontinuity can obscure the extent to which it is appropriate to think in terms of both 'both/and' rather than simply 'either/or'. Rather than consider whether knowledge resides at the individual or institutional level, it is more instructive to recognize that the two levels are interlaced. Not all actions of human collectives can be reduced to the privacy of individual thoughts. The individual and collective embrace two distinct modes of knowing that are intertwined by *both/and* 'dialectical thinking'.

In Chapter 3, Nonaka, Toyama and Konno extend some of the themes from Nonaka and Takeuchi's much-cited book *The Knowledge Creating Company* (1995), which questioned Western predilections for dealing in explicit knowledge and a taken-for-granted view of the organization as a machine for processing information. The book argued that Japanese companies have been successful because of their skills and expertise in organizational knowledge creation, which they define as: 'the capability of a company as a whole to create new knowledge, disseminate it throughout the organization, and embody it in products, services, and systems' (Nonaka and Takeuchi, 1995: 3). This view resonated with Western interest in 'knowledge management' and drew international attention to Nonaka's studies of knowledge creation in Japanese organizations.

The argument in Chapter 3 uses Nonaka's model of tacit–explicit knowledge interaction – through socialization, externalization, combination and internalization (the SECI model) – as the basis for a unified interpretation of knowledge creation. This creation process is situated in a shared context or *ba* and exploits firm-specific 'knowledge assets' such as trust amongst colleagues. In an earlier paper, Nonaka and Konno adapted *ba* to the interpretation of knowledge creation – explaining that the 'shared space for emerging relationships' (connoted by *ba*) might be physical, virtual (as in email or teleconferencing), mental (e.g., shared experiences, ideals, ideas) or any combination of them (Nonaka and Konno, 1998: 40). *Ba* is a platform for advancing individual and collective knowledge. Chapter 3 considers how *ba* facilitates each of the SECI model's conversion modes according to the level of interaction (individual or collective) and form of communication (face-to-face or virtual).

Rather than top-down leadership, Nonaka, Toyama and Konno argue that Japan's middle managers play a crucial role in marrying grand visions to the realities of front-line operations in a process of middle-up-down management. Hence, the organization – rather than the individual – is empowered by knowledge assets that are nurtured through 'autonomy, creative chaos, redundancy, requisite variety, love, care, trust and commitment' (Chapter 3, p. 60). In conclusion, the authors suggest that their focus on knowledge creation *within the organization* can also be used to accommodate knowledge creation that goes beyond the boundaries of a single company and thereby provides a bottom-up approach to the processes by which companies, government and universities work together to create knowledge.

Chapter 4 further explores the interaction of tacit and explicit knowledge by relating them to individual and group knowing. Cook and Brown's 'Bridging epistemologies: the generative dance between organizational knowledge and organizational knowing' turns upon the distinction between 'knowledge' that individuals and groups possess as tools (the epistemology of possession) and the use of these knowledge tools in the process of doing something (the epistemology of practice), which they call 'knowing'. Although this distinction might appear unduly subtle, it has far reaching implications and demonstrates how the interplay of *knowledge* and *knowing* produces new knowledge in a 'generative dance'.

Cook and Brown argue that the dominant Western epistemology (the nature of knowledge and the presuppositions that it stands upon) over the last three centuries derives from the work of René Descartes. This Cartesian view tends to privilege the individual thinker and explicit knowledge. Although recent years have produced a burgeoning literature that brings tacit knowledge into the literature on organizations and management, there is often an expressed or implied tendency to treat knowledge as if were all of one kind. Tacit knowledge is regarded as an undeveloped form of explicit knowledge, while group knowledge is the sum of what each member knows. Accordingly, tacit/explicit and group/individual comprise four categories of knowledge that appear to exist in some form of convertible currency. The exchange process might be imperfect but, in an appropriate context, conversion amongst categories is assumed to be possible and indeed desirable.

Cook and Brown take a different view. They contend that each of the four categories is distinct and that they all stand on an equal footing – 'none is subordinate to or made up of any other'. However, all four categories represent knowledge tools that can be deployed in the process of active knowing. Moreover, this stance makes it possible to reinterpret the SECI model of knowledge conversion and add to its insights.

The section ends with a chapter by Ray that considers Japanese knowledge creation from a Western point of view. One of the problems is that Western expectations about objective knowledge, explicit criticism and individual accountability do not fit easily in Japan's group-oriented culture, where etiquette stresses the subtle art of indirect communication, together with the significance of what is not said. In contrast to the Cartesian perspective, Japanese knowledge creation relies heavily on individual and collective tacit knowledge. Moreover, Japan's group-oriented culture and the obligations associated with its company-as-family employment system mean that knowledge creation is mainly situated within organizational boundaries. Upper-level organizations maintain stable boundaries and nest within a stable economic structure. Communication between organizations favours the mutual understanding or sticky knowledge that emerges from long-term relationships (such as those that link dependent subcontractors in a supply chain or a distributor to its regular customers). In Japan, the organization rather than the individual is the natural focus for 'steady state' knowledge creation in which new technologies evolve from established companies.

REFERENCES

Nonaka, I. and Konno, N. (1998) 'The concept of *ba*: building a foundation for knowledge creation', *California Management Review*, 40 (3), Spring: 40–54.

Nonaka, I. and Takeuchi, H. (1995) *The Knowledge Creating Company: How Japanese Companies Create the Dynamics of Innovation*, Oxford, Oxford University Press.

Wenger, E. (2000) 'Communities of practice and social learning systems', *Organization*, 7 (2): 225–46.

2

Organizing Knowledge

*John Seely Brown and Paul Duguid**

The firm, taken for granted in the conventional economy, appears to have a doubtful future in the information economy. The new technologies that are helping to define this new economy are simultaneously battering the venerable institutions of the old economy – the press, broadcast media, universities, even governments and nations are all under threat. Enthusiasts suggest that no formal organization need or should come between the empowered individual and Marshall McLuhan's amorphous 'global village'. So it's not surprising to hear that cyberspace has served notice on the firm that its future, at best, may only be virtual.

Many such predictions favor a 'transaction cost' view of the firm. Transaction costs are portrayed as the glue that holds an organization together, and many of these are thought to derive from inefficiencies in communication. Thus, it is easy to conclude that the new communications technologies might drive transaction costs so low that hierarchical firms will dissolve into markets of self-organizing individuals.[1]

Recently, however, through the work of Ikujiro Nonaka and others, a 'knowledge-based' view of the firm has risen to counter the transaction-cost approach. Knowledge-based arguments suggest that organizational knowledge provides a synergistic advantage not replicable in the marketplace. Thus its knowledge, not its transaction costs, holds an organization together.[2] The knowledge-based view provides vital insight into why firms exist (and will continue to exist) and thus why organizing knowledge is a critical part of what firms do.

While knowledge is often thought to be the property of individuals, a great deal of knowledge is both produced and held collectively. Such knowledge is readily generated when people work together in the tightly knit groups known as 'communities of practice'.[3] As such work and such communities are a common feature of organizations, organizational knowledge is inevitably heavily social in character. Because of its social origin, this sort of knowledge is not frictionless. Beyond communities, locally developed knowledge is difficult to organize. The hard work of organizing knowledge is a critical aspect of what firms and other organizations do.

There are those who see the organization as primarily the unintended consequence of individuals acting in isolation and who believe that an organization's central challenge is to discover knowledge. Once found, such arguments tend to assume, knowledge should travel easily. However, organizations are often replete with knowledge (and also deeply embedded in larger fields or 'ecologies' of knowledge). The critical challenge, from this perspective, is to make this knowledge cohere.[4]

It is easy to assume that knowledge-based arguments apply only to what are recognized as 'knowledge' firms. These are firms (in software or biotechnology, for example) whose market value far outstrips their conventional assets and rests instead on intellectual capital. The transaction-cost view, it might seem, still applies to every other form of organization. This, however, is not the case. All firms are in essence knowledge organizations. Their ability to outperform the marketplace rests on the continuous generation and synthesis of collective, organizational knowledge.[5] For all organizations, the cultivation of this knowledge – often an implicit, unreflecting cultivation – is the essence of developing a core competency to maintain the organization and resist its dissolution.

The organizational knowledge that constitutes 'core competency' is more than 'know-what', explicit knowledge which may be shared by several. A core competency requires the more elusive 'know-how' – the particular ability to put know-what into practice.[6] While these two work together, they circulate separately. Know-what circulates with relative ease. Consequently, of course, it is often hard to protect. (Hence the current crisis in intellectual property laws.) Know-how, by contrast, embedded in work practice (usually *collective* work practice) is *sui generis* and thus relatively easy to protect.[7] Conversely, however, it can be hard to spread, co-ordinate, benchmark or change.

The recent vogue for knowledge management must encompass not simply protecting intellectual property in canonical knowledge organizations, but fostering this more complex form of organizational capital. In practice, this sort of fostering is very much what good managers do, but as knowledge production becomes more critical, they will need to do it more reflectively.

ENDS OF ORGANIZATION

Self-organizing systems

Disintermediation, demassification, and disaggregation have become the watchwords of cyberspace. New technologies are apparently breaking collectives down into individual units. (Indeed, it sometimes seems that the only large aggregates needed for the 'third wave' will be very long words.) Any form of coherence and co-ordination beyond the individual, it is predicted, will be the effect of self-organizing systems.[8]

Undoubtedly, in the hands of prominent economists like Kenneth Arrow or Friedrich Hayek, analysis of self-organizing 'catallaxies' has helped reveal the very real limits of formal organization.[9] In particular, it has helped show the folly of planning economies or ignoring markets. They do not, however, necessarily reject planning or nonmarket behavior on a more local scale. Nor do they prove, as some would have us believe, that deliberate organization is somehow vicious, unnatural, and anti-market. As Hayek himself noted, within spontaneous catallaxies, goal-oriented organizational planning is important.

Curiously, many who argue for self-organization often sound less like economists than entomologists: bees, ants, and termites (as well as bats and other small mammals) provide much of the self-organizing case. In a related vein, others draw examples from 'artificial life', whose systems are themselves usually modelled on insect- and animal-like behavior.[10] While these provide forceful models, it's important to notice their limits. Humans and insects show many intriguing similarities, but these should not mask some important differences.

In particular, most champions of complex adaptive systems, particularly those of artificial life, overlook the importance to human behavior of deliberate social organization. It is well known that humans distinguish themselves from most other life forms by the increasingly sophisticated technologies they design. It is less often noted that they also distinguish themselves by designing sophisticated social institutions. To pursue the analogies from entomology or artificial life much further, we would need to know what might happen if bugs decided to form a committee or pass a law or artificial agents organized a strike or joined a firm.

Ants moving across a beach, for example, do exhibit elaborate, collective patterns that emerge as each individual adjusts to the environment. In this way, they reflect important aspects of human behavior – of, for example, the unco-ordinated synchronicity of sunbathers on the same beach seeking the sun or trying to keep the blown sand out of their sandwiches. But, unlike the sunbathers, ants don't construct coastal highways to reach the beach; or beachfront supermarkets to provide food; or farms to supply the supermarket; or coastal commissions to limit highway building, supermarkets, and farming; or supreme courts to rule on the infringement on constitutionally protected private property rights of coastal commissions; or, indeed, constitutions or property rights at all.

Thus, while ants easily fall victim to diminishing provisions of their local ecology, humans do not. By organizing collectively, people have learned to produce more food out of the same areas of land, to extend known energy resources and search for new ones, to establish new regions for human endeavor, and to design the very technologies that are now paradoxically invoked as the end of organization. In all such cases, organization has helped to foster and focus humanity's most valuable resource: its infinitely renewable knowledge base.[11]

But perhaps most significantly of all, humanity has relied on organization not merely to harness advantage, but to ward off disasters produced by the downside of self-organizing behavior. For example, establishing and continually adjusting socially acknowledged property rights have limited the 'tragedy of the commons'. Establishing certain trading regulations has prevented markets from spontaneously imploding. Such institutional constraints help channel self-organizing behavior and knowledge production in productive rather than destructive directions. This ability may be one of humanity's greatest assets.

It is easy to cite the undeniable power of spontaneous organization as a way to damn formal organization. However, it makes no more sense to demonize institutions than it does to demonize self-organizing systems. Rather, each must be deployed to restrain the other's worst excesses. That challenge is profoundly difficult, facing as it must the complex, reflexive feedback loops that social institutions create. These make human organization quite different from that of other species (and consequently make social sciences different from natural sciences).

Institutions and technology

If institutions are endemic to human society, then it seems a mistake to set them in opposition to technologies or economies as some of the cyber-gurus do. Indeed, a glance back to the last great period of technological innovation suggests the importance of institutions. The end of the nineteenth century gave us the telegraph, the train, the car, the telephone, the airplane, the cinema, and much more. Yet it has been argued that the incredible creative energies of the nineteenth century are evident less in industry, engineering, or the arts than in the new kinds of social institutions that developed (among which are the limited liability corporation, the research university, and the union).[12] Moreover, Nobel economist Douglass North suggests that it was the absence of suitable institutions that caused the century-long lag between the dawn of industrial revolution and the late nineteenth century's dramatic technological and economic expansion. Similarly, business historian Alfred Chandler claims that half of this expansion resulted from organizational, not technological innovation.[13]

So, while the changing economy may indeed be suffering from the drag of 'second wave' institutions, as Alvin Toffler suggests, it doesn't necessarily follow (as Toffler's wired disciples often seem to think) that the third wave will not need institutions at all. One clue to today's 'productivity paradox' (which notes that the increasing investment in new technology is not yet showing up in increased national productivity) may well be that society is still struggling to develop third-wave institutions adequate for a new economy.[14]

If nothing else, these examples suggest a complex relationship between organizations and technologies which crude juxtaposition of new technologies and old institutions oversimplifies. It is often pointed out that the arrival of printing technology in the West profoundly destabilized the Catholic Church, the dominant institution of its day. But even here, the direction was not simply against institutions. Printing allowed other institutions, the university in particular (and, in some arguments, the modern state) to flourish. And today, while communications technologies have dispersed power and control in some sectors, leading to disaggregation and empowerment, in others they have clearly led to centralization and concentration. Francis Fukuyama points, for instance, to the extraordinary success of firms like Wal-Mart and Benetton, both of which have used technology to centralize decision making and disempower their peripheries. In other sectors (communication in particular) the trend has also been towards concentration.

More generally, the relationship between improving technologies and shrinking organizations has not been linear. The telegraph, typewriter, and telephone – which launched the communications revolution – allowed the growth and spread of the giant firms of industrial capitalism as well as the proliferation of small businesses.[15] Similarly, today the emergence of small, adaptable firms may not point in any simple way to market disaggregation.

Research into small firms and start-ups highlights the concept of the 'embedded firm'.[16] These arguments indicate that many important relations between firms, let alone *within* firms, are not ultimately self-organizing, market relations. Increasingly, they reflect complex interorganizational networks. Even where interfirm relations are extremely competitive, cross-sector cooperation and agreements are often highly significant. In the cut-throat world of silicon chip manufacture, for example, firms continuously cross-license one another's patents and even engage in joint research through SEMATECH, a supraorganizational body. The classic antithesis between hierarchy (the firm) and market – even when hedged with the notion of 'hybrids' – seems inadequate to describe what is going on. To understand them, we need better insight into what organizations do, and how knowledge plays a key part.

ORGANIZATIONAL ADVANTAGE

The firm has a future because it provides an important means of knowledge generation. In particular, it gives rise to types of knowledge not supported in a marketplace of individuals linked only by market relations. It also plays an important role in the development and circulation of complex knowledge in society – circulation that is too readily assumed to be friction free.

Know-how and the community of practice

Knowledge is usually thought of as the possession of individuals. Something people carry around in their heads and pass between each other. Know-what is to a significant degree like this. Know-how is different.

Know-how embraces the ability to put know-what into practice. It is a disposition, brought out in practice. Thus, know-how is critical in making knowledge actionable and operational. A valuable manager, for example, is not simply one who knows in the abstract how to act in certain circumstances, but one who in practice can recognize the circumstances and act appropriately when they come along. That disposition reveals itself only when those circumstances occur.

Such dispositional knowledge is not only revealed in practice. It is also created out of practice. That is, know-how is to a great extent the product of experience and the tacit insights experience provides. A friend and lawyer once told us that law school – with its research, writing, and moot courts – prepared her for almost everything she encountered in her work. It did not, however, prepare her for what she did most: answer the phone. That ability – the ability to deal in real time with critical situations, demanding clients, and irrevocable commitments, putting the knowledge she had acquired in school to effective use in practice – she was only able to acquire in practice itself. Her own and her colleagues' ongoing practice has created an invaluable reservoir of dispositional knowledge, which she calls on (and improves) all the time.

Experience at work creates its own knowledge. And as most work is a collective, co-operative venture, so most dispositional knowledge is intriguingly collective – less held by individuals than shared by work groups. This view of knowledge as a social property stands at odds with the pervasive ideas of knowledge as individual. Yet the synergistic potential of certain people working in unison – a Gilbert and Sullivan, a Merchant and Ivory, a Young and Rice, or a Pippin and Jordan – is widely acknowledged. In less exalted workplaces, too, the ability of certain groups to outstrip their individual potential when working together is a common feature.

Shared know-how can turn up quite unexpectedly. Julian Orr, a colleague at Xerox, studied the firm's 'tech reps', the technicians who service machines on site. These technicians work most of the time in relative isolation, alone at a customer's office. And they carry with them extensive documentation about the machines they work with. They would seem to be the last people to have collective dispositional knowledge. Yet Orr revealed that despite the individualist character of their work and the large geographical areas they often have to cover, tech reps take great pains to spend time with one another at lunch or over coffee. Here they continuously swap 'war stories' about malfunctioning machines that outstripped the documentation. In the process of telling and analysing such stories, the reps both feed into and draw on the group's collective knowledge.[17]

Orr describes an extraordinary scene in which one technician brought in another to help tackle a machine that had defied all standard diagnostic procedures. Like two jazz players involved in an extended, improvisational riff, they spent an afternoon picking up each other's half-finished sentences and partial insights while taking turns to run the machine and watch it crash until finally and indivisibly they reached a coherent account of why the machine didn't work. They tested the theory. It proved right. And the machine was fixed.

This case and Orr's study as a whole suggest that, even for apparently individual workers armed with extensive know-what, collective know-how can be highly significant. More generally it supports the notion that collective practice leads to forms of collective knowledge, shared sensemaking, and distributed understanding that can't be reduced to the content of individual heads.

A group across which such know-how and sensemaking are shared – the group which needs to work together for its dispositional know-how to be put into practice – has been called a 'community of practice'. In the course of their ongoing practice, the members of such a group will develop into a *de facto* community. (Often, the community, like the knowledge, is implicit. Communities of practice do not necessarily think of themselves as a community in the conventional sense. Equally, conventional communities are not necessarily communities of practice.) Through practice, a community of practice develops a shared understanding of what it does, of how to do it, and how it relates to other communities and their practices – in all, a 'world view'. This changing understanding comprises the community's collective knowledge base. The processes of developing the knowledge and the community are significantly interdependent: the practice develops the understanding, which can reciprocally change the practice and extend the community. In this context, knowledge and practice are intricately involved. (For a related argument, see Nonaka's celebrated 'Knowledge Creation Spiral'.)[18]

This picture of knowledge embedded in practice and communities does not dismiss the idea of personal, private knowledge. What people have by virtue of membership in a community of practice, however, is not so much personal, modular knowledge as shared, partial knowledge.[19] Individual and collective knowledge in this context bear on one another much like the parts of individual performers to a complete musical score, the lines of each actor to a movie script, or the roles of team members to the overall performance of a team and a game. Each player may know his or her part. But on its own, that part doesn't make much sense. Alone it is significantly incomplete: it requires the ensemble to make sense of it.[20]

Communities of practice and organizations

If in many situations, work and knowledge do not readily decompose into the possession of individuals but remain stubbornly group properties, then markets themselves do not readily reduce to *homo economicus*, the idealized individual. Nonmarket organization (the community of practice) may be a salient factor of market activity.

Does this suggest that, if nonmarket organization is needed at all, it is only at the level of community of practice? That everything else can be done in the market? On the contrary, most formal organizations are not single communities of practice but hybrid groups of overlapping and interdependent communities. Such hybrid collectives represent another level in the complex process of knowledge creation. Intercommunal relationships allow the organization to develop collective, coherent, synergistic organizational knowledge out of the potential separate, independent contributions of the individual communities. The outcome is what we think of as organizational knowledge, embracing not just organizational know-what but also organizational know-how.

Cross-community organization is important because it helps to overcome some of the problems communities of practice create for themselves. For instance, as Dorothy Leonard-Barton points out, isolated communities can get stuck in ruts, turning core competencies into core rigidities. When they do, they need external stimuli to propel them forward.[21]

Communities of practice, while powerful sources of knowledge, can easily be blinkered by the limitations of their own world view. In a study of technological innovation, for example, Raghu Garud and Michael A. Rappa show how even the most sophisticated of knowledge workers can fail to recognize quite damning evidence.[22] New knowledge often requires new forms of evaluation, and when the two are produced together, knowledge, belief, and evaluation may only reinforce one another, while evaluation independent of that belief appears irrelevant.

Garud and Rappa's study explores this self-deluding/self-reinforcing social behavior in highly technological communities, where counterevidence is usually assumed to be easily capable of overwhelming belief. Obviously, such problematic interdependence of belief and evaluation is even more likely in areas where what counts as evidence is less clear cut and where beliefs, hunches, predictions, and intimations are all there is to go on – which, of course, is the case in most areas of human behavior.

Markets offer one very powerful way to punish self-deluding/self-reinforcing behavior or core rigidities once these have set in.[23] Such punishment tends, however, to be severe, drastic, and reserved for organizations as a whole. Organizations present an alternative antidote, which works more readily at the community level and is both more incremental and less destructive. By yoking diverse communities – with different belief systems and distinct evaluative practices – together into cohesive hybrids, organizations as a whole challenge the limits of each community's belief. This process generates knowledge through what Hirshhorn calls the 'productive tension' or Leonard-Barton 'creative abrasion', forcing particular communities beyond their own limits and their own evaluative criteria.[24]

Thus while markets punish those who produce bad ideas (or fail to produce at all), organizations work to produce beneficial knowledge out of social (rather than market) relations. The productive side of organizational tension, drawing on the experience of people throughout an organization, produces knowledge that requires systemic, not individual explanation. It adds value to the organization as a whole (and redeems those otherwise intractable battles between designers and engineers, sales and marketing, or accounting and almost any other division).

As most people know from experience, cross-divisional synthesis is itself an achievement. But organizations must reach beyond synthesis to synergy. In so doing, they both draw on and continuously create their unique organizational know-how – their ability to do what their competitors cannot. For this they must produce true, coherent organizational knowledge (which is quite distinct from an organization's knowledge – the scattered, unco-ordinated insights of each individual in its community of practice). Organizations that fail to achieve this particular synthesis are most likely to fall prey to market alternatives.

DIVISIONS OF LABOR AND DIVISIONS OF KNOWLEDGE

Search and retrieval

In many ways the relationship between communities of practice and organizations presents a parallel to that between individuals and communities of practice. Yet there are important differences in the way knowledge moves in each relationship.

Organizing knowledge across hybrid communities is the essential activity of organizational management. It is also difficult, though why is not often appreciated. Certainly, most managers will acknowledge that getting knowledge to move around organizations can be difficult. In general, however, such problems are reduced to issues of information flow. If, as the saying goes, organizations don't always know what they know, the solution is seen to lie primarily in better techniques for search and retrieval. Given the opportunity, information appears to flow readily. Hence the belief that technology, which can shift information efficiently, can render organizations, which shift it inefficiently, obsolete. A great deal of hope (and money) is thus being placed on the value of intranets. Intranets are indeed valuable, but social knowledge suggests that there is more to consider with regard both to search and to retrieval.

The distribution of knowledge in an organization, or in a society as a whole, reflects the social division of labor. As Adam Smith insightfully explained, the division of labor is a great source of dynamism and efficiency. Specialized groups are capable of producing highly specialized knowledge. The tasks undertaken by communities of practice develop particular, local, and highly specialized knowledge within the community.

From the organizational standpoint, however, this knowledge is as divided as the labor that produced it. Moreover, what separates divided knowledge is not only its explicit content but the implicit shared practices and know-how that help produce it. In particular, as Garud and Rappa's example suggests, communities develop their own distinct criteria for what counts as evidence and what provides 'warrants' – the endorsements for knowledge that encourage people to rely on it and hence make it actionable. (Warrants are particularly important in situations in which people confront increasing amounts of information, ideas, and beliefs; warrants show people what to attend to and what to avoid.) The locally embedded nature of these practices and warrants can make knowledge extremely 'sticky', to use Eric von Hippel's apt term.[25]

If the division of labor produces the division of knowledge, then it would seem reasonable to conclude that the market, used to co-ordinate the division of labor, would serve to co-ordinate the division of knowledge. But markets work best with commodities, and this 'sticky' knowledge isn't easily commodified. Within communities, producing, warranting, and propagating knowledge are almost indivisible. Between communities, as these get teased apart, division becomes prominent and problematic. Hence, the knowledge produced doesn't readily turn into something with exchange value or use value elsewhere. It takes organizational work to develop local knowledge for broader use. Development of knowledge in the organization is a process somewhat analogous to the way a film production company takes a story idea and, stage by stage, develops it into a movie.

Thus, ideas of 'retrieving' locally developed knowledge for use elsewhere do not address the whole issue. Furthermore, organizations, while they may help get beyond 'retrieval', present problems with the antecedent problem of search.

Organizational blindness

Organizations, as economists have long realized, offer an alternative to markets. Instead of synchronizing goods and labor through markets, they do it through hierarchy. This allows them to overcome some of the stickiness arising from the indivisibility of know-how and practice. Nonetheless, in the organization of knowledge, hierarchical relations unfortunately introduce their own weaknesses. Hierarchical divisions of labor often distinguish thinkers from doers, mental from manual labor, strategy (the knowledge required at the top of hierarchy) from tactics (the knowledge used at the bottom). Above all, a mental–manual division predisposes organizations to ignore a central asset: the value of the know-how created throughout all its parts.

For example, the Xerox service technicians develop highly insightful knowledge about the situated use (and misuse) of the complex machines they service. As such machines encounter a wide range of locations (some hot, some cold, some dry, some humid) and an inexhaustible range of uses (and abuses), the possible combinations make it impossible to calculate and anticipate all behaviors and problems that might arise. Knowledge about these only emerges in practice. Yet mental–manual divisions tend to make this knowledge invisible to the organization as a whole.

In an analysis of the importance (and anomalous position) of technologists in the modern workplace, Stephen Barley has argued forcefully that the knowledge potential in the practice of such front-line employees must eventually force organizations to reconsider the division of labor and the possible loci of knowledge production. As Henry Chesebrough and David Teece point out, 'some competencies may be on the factory floor, some in the R&D labs, some in the executive suites'. The key to organizational knowledge is to weave it all together. Successful organizational synthesis of knowledge requires discovering knowledge as it emerges in practice. That can't be done if when and where to look are predetermined *ex ante*.[26]

BEYOND SEARCH AND RETRIEVAL

Within and between

Bringing this knowledge into view is only a first step, however. Restricted search paths alone are not the problem, significant though these may be. Organizations that set out to identify useful knowledge often underestimate the challenge of making that knowledge useful elsewhere. Robert Cole's study of Hewlett-Packard's approach to quality, for example, shows how the firm successfully pursued 'best practices' throughout the corporation. The search, however, assumed that, once these practices were identified, the knowledge (and practice) would spread to where it was needed. In the end, HP was quite successful in identifying the practices. It was not, however, so successful in moving them.[27]

Some knowledge moves quite easily. People assume that it is explicit knowledge that moves easily and tacit knowledge that moves with difficulty.[28] It is, rather, socially embedded knowledge that 'sticks', because it is deeply rooted in practice. Within communities, practice helps to generate knowledge and evince collective know-how. The warranting mechanisms – the standards of judgement whereby people distinguish what is worthwhile and valid from what is not – inhere in the knowledge. Consequently, trying to move the knowledge without the practice involves moving the know-what without the know-how.

Due to its social origins, knowledge moves differently *within* communities than it does *between* them. Within communities, knowledge is continuously embedded in practice and thus circulates easily. Members of a community implicitly share a sense of what practice is and what the standards for judgement are, and this supports the spread of knowledge. Without this sharing, the community disintegrates.

Between communities, however, where by definition practice is no longer shared, the know-how, know-what, and warrants embedded in practice must separate out for knowledge to circulate. These divisions become prominent and problematic. Different communities of practice have different standards, different ideas of what is significant, different priorities, and different evaluating criteria. What looks like a best practice in California may not turn out to be the best practice in Singapore (as HP found out).

The divisions between communities tend to encourage local innovation, as Adam Smith recognized, but they also encourage isolation. Anyone who has spent some time on a university campus knows how knowledge-based boundaries can isolate highly productive communities from one another. That it is very hard to get sociologists and mathematicians to learn from one another is obvious. What is sometimes less clear is that biochemists can't always share insights with chemists, economic historians with historians, economists with the business school, and so forth. Different precepts and attitudes, shaped by practice, make interchange between quite similar subjects remarkably difficult, and thus invisibly pressure disciplines to work among themselves rather than to engage in cross-disciplinary research. Over time, disciplines increasingly divide rather than combine.

On the campus, however, work across different communities has been relatively unimportant. In the past, few have expected a campus as a whole to produce synthesized, collective insight. Physicists work on physics problems; historians on history problems; and except when they come to blows over the history of physics the two, like most other departments, lead predominantly independent lives.

Firms, by contrast, cannot afford to work this way. When it gets to the point where it is so loosely connected to other firms that there is no synthesis or synergy of what is produced in their various communities – when, as Teece and colleagues argue, there is no 'coherence' – then a firm has indeed lost its edge over the market. The firm then needs either to work towards synergy or divest until it achieves coherence.[29] Indeed, firms are valuable exactly to the extent that, unlike universities, they make communities of practice that expand their vision and achieve collective coherence. Consequently, the problematic *between* relationship is a critical organizational feature – and one that demands significant organizational investment.

It is a mistake to equate knowledge and information and to assume that difficulties can be overcome with information technologies. New knowledge is continuously being produced and developed in the different communities of practice throughout an organization. The challenge occurs in evaluating it and moving it. New knowledge is not capable of the sorts of friction-free movement usually attributed to information. Moreover, because moving knowledge between communities and synthesizing it takes a great deal of work, deciding what to invest time and effort in as well as determining what to act upon is a critical task for management.

STICKINESS AND LEAKINESS

The 'leakiness' of knowledge out of – and into – organizations, however, presents an interesting contrast to its internal stickiness.[30] Knowledge often travels more easily between organizations than it does within them. For while the division of labor erects boundaries within firms, it also produces extended communities that lie across the external boundaries of firms. Moving knowledge among groups with similar practices and overlapping memberships can thus sometimes be relatively easy compared to the difficulty of moving it among heterogeneous groups within a firm. Similar practices in a common field can allow ideas to flow. Indeed, it's often harder to stop ideas spreading than to spread them.

A study of interorganizational work by Kristen Kreiner and Majken Schultz suggests that the tendency of knowledge to spread easily reflects not suitable technology, but suitable social contexts. They show how many of the disciplinary links between business and academia are informal. They argue that the informal relations between firms and universities are more extensive and probably more significant than the formal ones. Informal relations dominate simply because they are easier, building on established social links. Formal interfirm relations, by contrast, can require tricky intrafirm negotiations between quite diverse communities (senior management, lawyers, and so forth).

Studies of biotechnology support this view. A study by Walter Powell reveals biotechnologists working extensively across the boundaries of organizations. Some articles in this field have more than a hundred authors from different (and different types of) institutions.[31] Their extensive collaboration undoubtedly relies on communications technologies. But these are available to researchers in other fields where such collaboration does not occur. Biotechnology is distinct in that being a relatively young, emerging field, its researchers are significantly linked through personal connections. The field is not as tight as a local community of practice, but nonetheless relations are dense enough and practices sufficiently similar to help knowledge spread. While a field is small and relatively unfragmented, practitioners have a lot in common: their training, their institutional backgrounds, their interests, and in particular the warrants with which they evaluate what is important from what is not.[32]

People connected this way can rely on complex networks of overlapping communities, common backgrounds, and personal relationships to help evaluate and propagate knowledge. In such conditions, practices are fairly similar and consequently the barriers *between* different groups are relatively low.[33] In such knowledge ecologies, knowledge that is sticky within organizations can become remarkably fluid outside of them, causing great difficulties for the intellectual property side of knowledge management. The challenge of plugging these leaks is significant. But cutting off the outflow can also cut off the inflow of knowledge. Living in a knowledge ecology is a reciprocal process, with organizations feeding into each other.

TOWARDS AN ARCHITECTURE FOR ORGANIZATIONAL KNOWLEDGE

The way ecologies spread knowledge helps point to some of the ways that organizations can help to propagate knowledge internally and develop an enabling architecture for organizational knowledge. Social strategies for promoting the spread of knowledge between communities can be described in terms of 'translation', 'brokering', and 'boundary objects' – terms developed by the sociologists Susan Leigh Star and James Griesemer.[34]

Translators

Organizational translators are individuals who can frame the interests of one community in terms of another community's perspective. The role of translator can be quite complex and the translator must be sufficiently knowledgeable about the work of both communities to be able to translate. The powerful position of translator requires trust, since translation is rarely entirely innocent (translators may favor the interests of one group over another deliberately or inadvertently). Yet, participants must be able to rely on translators to carry negotiations in both directions, making them mutually intelligible to the communities involved. The difficulty of doing this makes translators extremely valuable and extremely difficult to find. External mediators and consultants are often called in to provide such translation.

Knowledge brokers

The role of in-firm brokers, in contrast to that of translators, involves participation rather than mediation. They are a feature of overlapping communities, whereas translators work among mutually exclusive ones. In an analysis of the diffusion of knowledge across networks, sociologist Mark Granovetter noted that overlaps are hard to develop in communities with very strong internal ties. These tend to preclude external links. Thus Granovetter argued for the 'strength of weak ties', suggesting that it was often people loosely linked to several communities who facilitated the flow of knowledge among them.[35]

As almost all communities within an organization overlap, those who participate in the practices of several communities may in theory broker knowledge between them. Trust is less of a tendentious issue than with translation. Brokers who truly participate in both worlds, unlike translators, are subject to the consequences of messages they carry, whatever the direction.

Boundary objects

Boundary objects are another way to forge co-ordinating links among communities, bringing them, intentionally or unintentionally, into negotiation. Boundary objects are objects of interest to each community involved but viewed or used differently by each of them. These can be physical objects, technologies, or techniques shared by the communities. Through them, a community can come to understand what is common and what is distinct about another community, its practices, and its world view. Boundary objects not only help to clarify the attitudes of other communities, they can also make a community's own presuppositions apparent to itself, encouraging reflection and 'second-loop' learning.[36]

Contracts are a classic example of boundary objects. They develop as different groups converge, through negotiation, on an agreed meaning that has significance for both. Documents more generally play a similar role, and forms and lists that pass between and co-ordinate different communities make significant boundary objects. Plans and blueprints are another form of boundary object. Architectural plans, for instance, define a common boundary among architects, contractors, engineers, city planners, cost estimators, suppliers and clients. Severally and collectively these groups negotiate their different interests, priorities, and practices around the compelling need to share an interpretation of these important documents.

To help produce intercommunal negotiation, organizations can seed the border between communities with boundary objects. The idea-fomenting metaphors that Nonaka describes draw some of their power from being boundary objects.[37] They work within groups to spark ideas. Once a group has found one metaphor particularly powerful, that metaphor may also serve to foster understanding between groups.

Business processes as boundary objects: enabling and coercive

Business processes can play a similar role. Ideally, processes should allow groups, through negotiation, to align themselves with one another and with the organization as a whole. Business processes can enable productive cross-boundary relations as different groups within an organization negotiate and propagate a shared interpretation. In the right circumstances, the interlocking practices that result from such negotiations should cohere both with one another and with the overall strategy of the company. The processes provide some structure, the negotiations provide room for improvisation and accommodation, and the two together can result in co-ordinated, loosely coupled, but systemic behavior.[38]

Many business processes, however, attempt not to support negotiation but to pre-empt it, trying to impose compliance and conformity through what Geoffrey Bowker and Susan Leigh Star call 'frozen negotiation'. Here Paul Adler and Bryan Borys's discussion of 'enabling' and 'coercive' bureaucracies suggests the importance of enabling and coercive business processes. The first produces fruitful intercommunal relations and, in the best case, widespread strategic alignment; the second is more likely to produce rigid organizations with strong central control but little adaptability.[39]

TECHNOLOGY ISSUES

As noted earlier, the ease or difficulty of moving knowledge is a reflection of its social context. Technologies inevitably have an enormous role to play, but they play it only to the extent that they respond to the social context. The desire to disaggregate, disintermediate, and demassify, however, is more likely to produce socially unresponsive behavior.

A good deal of new technology attends primarily to individuals and the explicit information that passes between them. To support the flow of knowledge, within or between communities and organizations, this focus must expand to encompass communities and the full richness of communication. Successful devices such as the telephone and the fax, like the book and newspaper before them, spread rapidly not simply because they carried information to individuals, but because they were easily embedded in communities.

Supporting the informal

One important issue for technology involves the way the local informality found within communities differs from levels of explicitness and formality often demanded between communities – much as the slang and informal language people use with immediate colleagues differ from the formal language of presentations or contracts. The demands for formality demanded by technologies can disrupt more productive informal relations. For instance, in many situations, asking for explicit permission changes social dynamics quite dramatically – and receiving a direct rejection can change them even further. Consequently, people negotiate many permissions tacitly. A great deal of trust grows up around the ability to work with this sort of implicit negotiation. Direct requests and insistence on rights and duties do not work well.

Technologies thus have to include different degrees of formality and trust.[40] The range will become apparent as different types of 'trusted systems' begin to emerge. At one end are systems that more or less eliminate the need for social trust. They simply prevent people from behaving in ways other than those explicitly negotiated ahead of time and constrained by the technology. Everything must be agreed (and paid for, usually) *ex ante*. For high-security demands, such technologies will be increasingly important. People are glad they can trust bank machines and Internet software servers. But if new technologies ask people to negotiate all their social interrelations like their banking relations, they will leave little room for the informal, the tacit, and the socially embedded – which is where know-how lies and important work gets done.

This choice between formality and informality will have repercussions in the design of complex technologies. But it also has repercussions in the implementation of such things as corporate intranets and mail systems. Increasingly, workplaces seek to control the sorts of interactions and exchanges these are used for. Yet these systems in many ways replace the coffee pot and the water cooler as the site of informal but highly important knowledge diffusion. Limiting their informality is likely to limit their importance.

Reach and reciprocity

As continual chatter about the global information network reminds us, information technology has extensive reach. Markets supported by this technological reach spread further and further daily. However, it is a mistake to conclude that knowledge networks, which require a social context, will spread in the same fashion. Technology to support the spread of new knowledge needs to be able to deal not with the *reach* involved in delivery so much as with the *reciprocity* inherent in shared practice. The ability to support complex, multidirectional, implicit negotiation will become increasingly important.

The Internet provides an interesting example of the way people retrofit information technology to enhance its social capacities. It was designed primarily so that computers could exchange electronic information and computer users could exchange files. Early in its development, though, some insightful programmers at Bolt Beranek and Newman piggy-backed email on the protocol for transferring files. This highly social medium superimposed on the fetch-and-deliver infrastructure planted the seed that would transform this scientific network into the social network that has flourished so dramatically in the last few years. Email still accounts for the bulk of Internet traffic. Similarly, the World Wide Web has been the most recent and dramatic example that further accelerated the social use of the technology. Its designer, Tim Berners-Lee, a programmer at the CERN laboratories in Switzerland, saw that the Internet was much more interesting if used not simply for exchanging information between individuals, but to support 'collaborators . . . in a common project.' That social imperative, quite as much as the technology, has driven the Web's extraordinary evolution.[41]

Interactivity, participation, learning

One of the Net's greatest assets is that it is interactive and thus has the potential to foster reciprocal knowledge and learning. On campuses, conventional classes now regularly increase not so much reach as reciprocity by using web pages and listserves (communal mailing lists) to do this. Well-designed corporate intranets, which supplement more conventional communication, do the same. In particular, these help present and circulate boundary objects. New forms of multicasting, such as the 'M-Bone' or Multi-Cast Backbone, offer yet denser prospects for such interaction.[42]

When simply combined with reach, interactivity is often merely burdensome. To cultivate true reciprocity (rather than babble), people often find it necessary to introduce limits on the reach. Listserves now increasingly restrict participation, web sites demand passwords, and intranets erect firewalls. Imposing limits, however, can prove disadvantageous.

Reciprocity is a feature of what Jean Lave and Etienne Wenger (who developed the notion of 'communities of practice') refer to as 'legitimate peripheral participation'.[43] People learn by taking up a position on the periphery of skilled practice and being allowed (hence the importance of legitimacy) to move slowly from the periphery into the community and the practice involved. New communications technologies provide intriguing forms of peripherality. They allow newcomers to 'lurk' on the side of interactions in which they are not taking part and on the side of communities of which they are not members. Students, for example, lurk on the sides of exchanges among graduate students and faculty. Novices oversee the Net traffic among experts. Lave and Wenger also showed, however, how vibrant training programs die once newcomers are cut off from such experienced practice. Closing lists to lurkers can have the same results. Consequently, the negotiation of access, of reach, and of reciprocity in such circumstances needs to remain a complex socio-technological challenge and not simply a technological one.

The rewards of reciprocity are high. Technologies that can recognize and to some extent parse how relations *within* communities (where reciprocity is inevitable) differ from those *between* communities (where reciprocity must be cultivated) may actually help to extend reach between communities without disrupting reciprocity within. Understanding the challenges of the *between* relation should be a significant issue for new design – of both technologies and organizations.

Technology that supports not merely the diffusion of know-what but the development of know-how allows for knowledge to be shared rather than marketed. Curiously, this highlights a pervasive trajectory in the development of communications software, where explicit design strategies for exchanging information are repeatedly subverted by users who press for a social network.

CONCLUSION: DIALECTICAL THINKING

The propagandists of cyberspace have a tendency to speak in terms of discontinuity. The new, they always insist, will simply sweep away the old, so they confidently predict that hypertext will replace the book. (Here they might do well to pay attention to the *New York Times*'s confident prediction in the 1930s that the typewriter would replace the pencil. The pencil seems to have won that particular struggle.) Or, as in the issue at stake here, the prediction is that communications technology will sweep away the firm.

Undoubtedly, the present technological revolution will sweep many familiar aspects of life away. Nonetheless, sometimes it is useful to think in terms of 'both/and' rather than simply 'either/or'. This seems particularly true when considering the effect of heterogeneous categories on one another, such as the effects of technologies on institutions.

Instead of thinking of individuals vs. institutions, or markets vs. firms, or start-ups vs. large corporations, it may be more instructive to think of how the two are interlaced. From this perspective, it does not seem as though disintermediation, demassification, and disaggregation are the only watchwords of the future. Community, practice, organization, network, and above all organizational knowledge and distributed know-how are equally important.

NOTES

1. The classic statement on transaction costs is R.H. Coase, 'The nature of the firm', *Economica*, 1937: 386–405. For more recent explorations, see, for example, Oliver Williamson and Sidney G. Winter (eds) *The Nature of the Firm: Origins, Evolution, and Development* (New York: Oxford University Press, 1993). For relations between technology and transaction costs, see, for example, Thomas W. Malone, JoAnne Yates, and Robert Benjamin, 'Electronic markets and electronic hierarchies', *Communications of the ACM*, 1987: 484–497 or Claudio U. Ciborra, *Teams, Markets, and Systems: Business Innovation and Information Technology* (New York: Cambridge University Press, 1993). For variants of arguments about the fading boundaries of the firm, see vol. 152 of *Journal of Institutional and Theoretical Economics* (1966). It is interesting to note that Williamson has retreated a little from the totalizing view of transaction costs reflected in many of these works and acknowledged the complementary perspectives that an understanding of embeddedness contributes. See Oliver Williamson, *Transaction Cost Economics: How it Works; Where it is Headed*, Business and Public Working Paper, BPP 67, University of California, Institute of Management, Innovation and Organization, Berkeley, CA, October 1997.

2. See, for example, Ikujiro Nonaka and Hiotaka Takeuchi, *The Knowledge-Creating Company: How Japanese Companies Create the Dynamics of Innovation* (New York: Oxford University Press, 1995); Bruce Kogut and Udo Zander, 'What firms do? Co-ordination, identity, and learning', *Organization Science*, 7 (5), 1996: 502–518; R.M. Grant, 'Toward a knowledge-based theory of the firm', *Strategic Management Journal*, 17 (1996): 109–122; J.C. Spender, 'Making knowledge the basis of a dynamic theory of the firm', *Strategic Management Journal*, 17 (1966): 45–62; Dorothy Leonard-Barton, *Wellsprings of Knowledge: Building and Sustaining the Sources of Innovation* (Cambridge, MA: Harvard Business School Press, 1995). For a dissenting voice, see Nicolai J. Foss, 'Knowledge-based approaches to the theory of the firm: some critical comments', *Organization Science*, 7 (5), 1996: 470–476. It might be argued that knowledge production simply imposes another transaction cost, so the knowledge-based view is merely part of the transaction-cost argument. We argue, however, that some important knowledge is only produced through social, nonmarket relations. Thus the transaction cost for individuals in market relations would be infinite. To embrace infinite transaction costs as part of the transaction-cost argument trivializes the very important contribution of transaction-cost analysis to understanding organizations.

3. For 'communities of practice' see Jean Lave and Etienne Wenger, *Situated Learning: Legitimate Peripheral Participation* (New York: Cambridge University Press, 1993); John Seely Brown and Paul Duguid, 'Organizational learning and communities of practice: towards a unified view of working, learning, and innovation', *Organization Science*, 2 (1991): 40–57.

4. It might be possible to reach such a conclusion from Mark Casson, *Information and Organization: A New Perspective on the Theory of the Firm* (Oxford: Clarendon Press, 1997). It is important, however, not to elide information, Casson's main topic, and knowledge, though we do not expand on this problem here. See John Seely Brown and Paul Duguid, *The Knowledge Continuum*, Cambridge, MA: Harvard Business School Press, forthcoming.

5. See, for example, Leonard-Barton's portrayal of the 'learning organization' and her example of Chaparral Steel. Leonard-Barton, op. cit.

6. The distinction between know-what and know-how and the notion of 'dispositional knowledge' comes from Gilbert Ryle, *The Concept of Mind* (London: Hutchinson, 1954). Know-how may appear to be little more than so-called 'physical' skills, such as catching a ball or riding a bicycle. It is much more, however. For any student to 'know' Newton's second law in any meaningful way requires having the skill to deploy the law in an analysis of colliding objects. This sort of knowledge, a disposition as well as a possession, emerges when called upon. It is evident, for instance, in such complex skills as talking, writing, and thinking or in negotiating with clients, overseeing employees, controlling production processes, developing strategy, conducting scientific experiments, fixing complex machines, cooking a meal, or writing computer programs. For the importance of dispositional knowledge, see S. Noam Cook and John Seely Brown, 'Bridging epistemologies: the generative dance between organizational knowledge and organizational knowing', *Organization Science*, 10 (4), 1999: 381–400.

7. As the CEO of Chaparral Steel told Leonard-Barton, 'He can tour competitors through the plant, show them almost "everything and we will be giving away nothing because they can't take it home with them"'. Leonard-Barton, op cit., p. 7.

8. See, for example, George Gilder, *Life after Television* (New York: W.W. Norton, 1994) for disintermediation; Alvin Toffler, *The Third Wave* (New York: Morrow, 1980) for demassification; Nicholas Negroponte, *Being Digital* (New York: Alfred A. Knopf, 1996) for disaggregation.

9. Friedrich Hayek, *The Fatal Conceit: The Errors of Socialism* (Chicago: University of Chicago Press, 1988). See, also, Friedrich Hayek, 'The use of knowledge in society', *American Economic Review*, 35, September 1945: 519–530; Kenneth J. Arrow, *The Limits of Organization* (New York: W.W. Norton, 1974).

10. See, for example, Kevin Kelly, *Out of Control: The New Biology of Machines, Social Systems, and the Economic World* (New York: Addison-Wesley, 1994) for bees; Andy Clark, *Being There: Putting Brain, Body, and World Together Again* (Cambridge, MA: MIT Press, 1997) for termites; Richard Dawkins, *The Blind Watchmaker* (New York: W.W. Norton, 1986) and Sherry Turkle, *Life on the Screen: Identity in the Age of the Internet* (New York: Simon and Schuster, 1996) for artificial life.

11. See Douglass C. North, *Structure and Change in Economic History* (New York: W.W. Norton, 1981).

12. Raymond Williams, *The Long Revolution* (New York: Columbia University Press, 1961).

13. Douglass C. North, *Institutions, Institutional Change, and Economic Performance* (New York: Cambridge University Press, 1990); Alfred D. Chandler, *The Visible Hand: The Managerial Revolution in American Business* (Cambridge, MA: Harvard University Press, 1977).

14. Though for a qualified view of this argument, see Daniel E. Sichel, *The Computer Revolution: An Economic Perspective* (Washington, DC: Brookings Institutions Press, 1997).

15. Francis Fukuyama, 'Social networks and digital networks', in preparation. For an analysis of the complex relationship between communications technology and institutions see the classic study by Harold Innis, *The Bias of Communication* (Toronto: University of Toronto Press, 1951).

16. See Mark Granovetter, 'Economic action and social structure: the problem of embeddedness', *American Journal of Sociology*, 91, 1985: 481–510; Gordon Walker, Bruce Kogut, and Weijian Shan, 'Social capital, structural holes and the formation of an industry network', *Organization Science*, 8, 1997: 109–112; Martin Kenney and

Urs von Burg, 'Bringing technology back in: explaining the divergence between Silicon Valley and Route 128', *Industrial and Corporate Change*, 8 (1), 1999: 67–103; AnnaLee Saxenian, *Regional Advantage: Culture and Competition in Silicon Valley and Route 128* (Cambridge, MA: Harvard University Press, 1996); Gernot Grabher, *The Embedded Firm: On the Socioeconomics of Industrial Networks* (London: Routledge, 1993).

17. Julian E. Orr, *Talking about Machines: an Ethnography of a Modern Job* (Ithaca, New York: ILR Press, 1996).
18. Nonaka and Takeuchi, op. cit., p. 72; Ikujiro Nonaka and Noboru Konno, 'The concept of *ba*: building a foundation for knowledge creation', *California Management Review*, 40 (3), Spring, 1998.
19. For views of personal knowledge, see M. Polanyi, *The Tacit Dimension: The Terry Lectures* (Garden City, NJ: Doubleday, 1966); Ludwig Wittgenstein, *Philosophical Investigations*, trans. G.E.M. Anscombe (New York: Macmillan, 1953); David Bloor, *Wittgenstein: a Social Theory of Knowledge* (New York: Columbia University Press, 1983); Thomas Nagel, *The Last Word* (New York: New York University Press, 1997).
20. For a discussion of collective sensemaking, see Karl Weick, *Sensemaking in Organizations* (Beverly Hills, CA: Sage, 1995); Karl Weick and K. Roberts, 'Collective mind in organizations', *Administrative Science Quarterly*, 38 (3), September 1993: 357–381.
21. Leonard-Barton, op. cit., especially Chapter 2.
22. Raghu Garud and Michael A. Rappa, 'A socio-cognitive model of technology evolution: the case of cochlear implants', *Organization Science*, 5, 1994: 344–362.
23. Garud and Rappa argue that in such cases, markets are actually quite inefficient means to challenge the interdependence of belief and evaluation – in part because markets, too, rely on evaluations provided by the blinkered technologies. Ibid., p. 358.
24. Larry Hirschhorn, *Reworking Authority: Leading and Following in the Post-Modern Organization* (Cambridge, MA: MIT Press, 1997); Leonard-Barton attributes 'creative abrasion' to Gerald Hirshberg of Nissan Design International. Leonard-Barton, op. cit., p. 63. See also Karl Jaspers, *The Idea of the University*, trans. H. Reiche and T. Vanderschmidt (Boston, MA: Beacon Press, 1959) for the notion of 'creative tension'.
25. Eric von Hippel, '"Sticky information" and the locus of problem solving: implications for innovation', *Management Science*, 40, 1994: 429–439.
26. Stephen R. Barley, 'Technicians in the workplace: ethnographic evidence for bringing work into organization studies', *Administrative Science Quarterly*, 41, 1966: 401–444; Henry W. Chesebrough and David J. Teece, 'When is virtual virtuous? Organizing for innovation', *Harvard Business Review*, 74 (1), 1996: 65–73.
27. Robert Cole, *The Quest for Quality Improvement: How American Business Met the Challenge* (New York: Oxford University Press, forthcoming).
28. Polanyi, op. cit.
29. David Teece, Richard Rumelt, Giovanni Dosi, and Sidney Winter, 'Understanding corporate coherence: theory and evidence', *Journal of Economic Behavior and Organization*, 23 (1), 1994: 1–30.
30. For the notion of leakiness, see R.M. Grant and J. C. Spender, 'Knowledge and the firm: overview', *Strategic Management Journal*, 17, 1996: 5–9.
31. Walter W. Powell, 'Inter-organizational collaboration in the biotechnology industry', *Journal of Institutional and Theoretical Economics*, 152, 1996: 197–215;

Kristen Kreiner and Majken Schultz, 'Informal collaboration in R&D: the formation of networks across organizations', *Organization Science*, 14, 1993: 189–209.

32. To some degree, such fields resemble 'social worlds'. See Anselm Strauss, 'A social world perspective', *Studies in Symbolic Interaction*, 1, 1978: 119–128.

33. See Brown and Duguid, *The Knowledge Continuum*, Cambridge, MA: Harvard Business School Press, forthcoming.

34. Susan Leigh Star and James R. Griesemer, 'Institutional ecology, "translations" and boundary objects: amateurs and professionals in Berkeley's Museum of Vertebrate Zoology, 1907–39', *Social Studies of Science*, 19, 1989: 387–420.

35. Mark Granovetter, 'The strength of weak ties', *American Journal of Sociology*, 78 (6), 1973: 1360–1380; Granovetter's argument presupposes that for knowledge to spread, groups cannot simply be related as isolated individuals connected by market; they (and, indeed, markets) must be embedded in complex social systems. This argument appears more forcefully in his critique of transaction costs cited above.

36. Chris Argyris and Donald Schon, *Organizational Learning* (Reading, MA: Addison-Wesley, 1978).

37. Ikujiro Nonaka, 'The knowledge creating company', *Harvard Business Review*, 69 (6), Nov./Dec. 1991: 96–104.

38. For the notion of 'loosely coupled' systems, see Karl E. Weick, 'Organizational culture as a source of high reliability', *California Management Review*, 29 (2), Winter 1987: 112–127; J. Douglas Orton and Karl E. Weick, 'Loosely coupled systems: a reconceptualization', *Academy of Management Review*, 15 (2), April 1990: 203–223.

39. Geoffrey Bowker and Susan Leigh Star, 'Knowledge and infrastructure in international information management: problems of classification and coding', in Lisa Bud-Frierman (ed.) *Information Acumen: the Understanding and Use of Knowledge in Modern Business* (London: Routledge, 1994), pp. 187–213; Paul Adler and Bryan Borys, 'Two types of bureaucracy: enabling and coercive', *Administrative Science Quarterly*, 41, 1996: 61–89.

40. For an insightful view of the interplay of the formal and the informal in the creation of trust, see Sim B. Sitkin, 'On the positive effect of legalization on trust', *Research on Negotiation in Organizations* (Greenwich, CT: JAI Press, 1995), pp. 185–217.

41. Time Berners-Lee, 'The World Wide Web: past, present, and future' [available online]: http://www.w3.org/People/Berners-Lee/1996/ppf.html.

42. See John Seely Brown and Paul Duguid, 'The university in the digital age', *Change*, 28, 1996: 10–15; John Seely Brown and Paul Duguid, 'The social life of documents', *Release 1.0*, October 1995: 1–12.

43. Lave and Wenger, op. cit.

3

SECI, *Ba* and Leadership: a Unified Model of Dynamic Knowledge Creation

*I. Nonaka, R. Toyama and N. Konno**

As Alvin Toffler said, we are now living in a 'knowledge-based society, where knowledge is the source of the highest quality power.[1] In a world where markets, products, technologies, competitors, regulations and even societies change rapidly, continuous innovation and the knowledge that enables such innovation have become important sources of sustainable competitive advantage. Hence, management scholars today consider knowledge and the capability to create and utilize knowledge to be the most important source of a firm's sustainable competitive advantage.[2] The *raison d'être* of a firm is to continuously create knowledge. Yet, in spite of all the talk about 'knowledge-based management' and in spite of the recognition of the need for a new knowledge-based theory that differs 'in some fundamental way'[3] from the existing economics and organizational theory, there is very little understanding of how organizations actually create and manage knowledge.

This is partly because we lack a general understanding of knowledge and the knowledge-creating process. The 'knowledge management' that academics and businesspeople talk about often means just 'information management'. In the long tradition of Western management, the organization has been viewed as an information processing machine that takes and processes information from the environment to solve a problem and adapts to the environment based on a given goal. This static and passive view of the organization fails to capture the dynamic process of knowledge creation.

Instead of merely solving problems, organizations create and define problems, develop and apply new knowledge to solve the problems, and then further develop new knowledge through the action of problem solving. The organization is not merely an information processing machine, but an entity that creates knowledge through action and interaction.[4] It interacts with its environment, and reshapes the environment and even itself through the process of knowledge creation. Hence, the most important aspect of understanding a firm's capability concerning knowledge is the dynamic capability to continuously create new knowledge out of existing firm-specific capabilities,

* Reprinted from *Long Range Planning*, Vol. 33, Ikujiro Nonaka, Ryoko Toyama and Noboru Konno, 'SECI, *Ba* and Leadership: A Unified Model of Dynamic Knowledge Creation', 2000, with permission Elsevier Science.

rather than the stock of knowledge (such as a particular technology) that a firm possesses at one point in time.[5]

With this view of an organization as an entity that creates knowledge continuously, we need to re-examine our theories of the firm, in terms of how it is organized and managed, how it interacts with its environment and how its members interact with each other. Our goal in this chapter is to understand the dynamic process in which an organization creates, maintains and exploits knowledge. The following sections discuss basic concepts related to the organizational knowledge-creating process, how such a process is managed, and how one can lead such a knowledge-creating process. Knowledge is created in the spiral that goes through two seemingly antithetical concepts such as order and chaos, micro and macro, part and whole, mind and body, tacit and explicit, self and other, deduction and induction, and creativity and control. We argue that the key in leading the knowledge-creating process is dialectical thinking, which transcends and synthesizes such contradictions (see Figure 3.1).

WHAT IS KNOWLEDGE?

In our theory of the knowledge-creating process, we adopt the traditional definition of knowledge as 'justified true belief'. However, our focus is on the 'justified' rather than the 'true' aspect of belief. In traditional Western epistemology (the theory of knowledge), 'truthfulness' is the essential attribute of knowledge. It is the absolute, static and non-human view of knowledge. This view, however, fails to address the relative, dynamic and humanistic dimensions of knowledge.

Knowledge is dynamic, since it is created in social interactions amongst individuals and organizations. Knowledge is context-specific, as it depends on a particular time and space.[6] Without being put into a context, it is just information, not knowledge. For example, '1234 ABC Street' is just information. Without context, it does not mean anything. However, when put into a context,

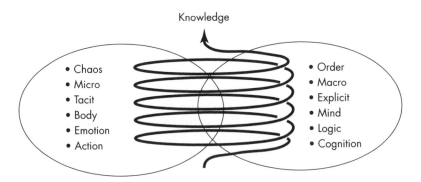

FIGURE 3.1 *Knowledge created through a spiral*

it becomes knowledge: 'My friend David lives at 1234 ABC Street, which is next to the library.' Knowledge is also humanistic, as it is essentially related to human action. Knowledge has the active and subjective nature represented by such terms as 'commitment' and 'belief' that is deeply rooted in individuals' value systems. Information becomes knowledge when it is interpreted by individuals and given a context and anchored in the beliefs and commitments of individuals. Hence, knowledge is relational: such things as 'truth', 'goodness' and 'beauty' are in the eye of the beholder. As Alfred North Whitehead stated, 'there are no whole truths; all truths are half-truths'.[7] In this study, we consider knowledge to be 'a dynamic human process of justifying personal belief toward the "truth"'.[8]

There are two types of knowledge: explicit knowledge and tacit knowledge. Explicit knowledge can be expressed in formal and systematic language and shared in the form of data, scientific formulae, specifications, manuals and suchlike. It can be processed, transmitted and stored relatively easily. In contrast, tacit knowledge is highly personal and hard to formalize. Subjective insights, intuitions and hunches fall into this category of knowledge. Tacit knowledge is deeply rooted in action, procedures, routines, commitment, ideals, values and emotions.[9] It 'indwells' in a comprehensive cognizance of the human mind and body.[10] It is difficult to communicate tacit knowledge to others, since it is an analogue process that requires a kind of 'simultaneous processing'.

Western epistemology has traditionally viewed knowledge as explicit. However, to understand the true nature of knowledge and knowledge creation, we need to recognize that tacit and explicit knowledge are complementary, and that both types of knowledge are essential to knowledge creation. Explicit knowledge without tacit insight quickly loses its meaning. Written speech is possible only after internal speech is well developed.[11] Knowledge is created through interactions between tacit and explicit knowledge, rather than from tacit or explicit knowledge alone.

THE KNOWLEDGE-CREATING PROCESS

Knowledge creation is a continuous, self-transcending process through which one transcends the boundary of the old self into a new self by acquiring a new context, a new view of the world, and new knowledge. In short, it is a journey '*from* being to becoming'.[12] One also transcends the boundary between self and other, as knowledge is created through the interactions amongst individuals or between individuals and their environment. In knowledge creation, micro and macro interact with each other, and changes occur at both the micro and the macro level: an individual (micro) influences and is influenced by the environment (macro) with which he or she interacts.

To understand how organizations create knowledge dynamically, we propose a model of knowledge creation consisting of three elements: (1) the SECI process, the process of knowledge creation through conversion between

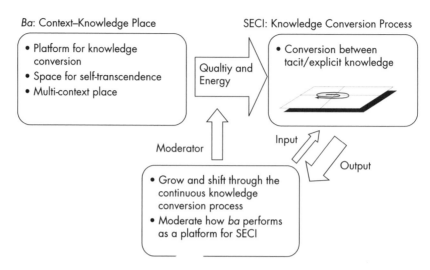

Ba: Context–Knowledge Place

- Platform for knowledge conversion
- Space for self-transcendence
- Multi-context place

Qualtiy and Energy

SECI: Knowledge Conversion Process

- Conversion between tacit/explicit knowledge

Moderator

Input

Output

- Grow and shift through the continuous knowledge conversion process
- Moderate how *ba* performs as a platform for SECI

FIGURE 3.2 *Three elements of the kn̖   ͓reating process*

tacit and explicit knowledge; (2) *ba*, the shared context for knowledge creation; and (3) knowledge assets – the inputs, outputs, and moderator of the knowledge-creating process. The three elements of knowledge creation have to interact with each other to form the knowledge spiral that creates knowledge (see Figure 3.2). In the following sections, we discuss each of these three elements.

The SECI process: four modes of knowledge conversion

An organization creates knowledge through the interactions between explicit knowledge and tacit knowledge. We call the interaction between the two types of knowledge 'knowledge conversion'. Through the conversion process, tacit and explicit knowledge expands in both quality and quantity.[13] There are four modes of knowledge conversion. They are: (1) socialization (from tacit knowledge to tacit knowledge); (2) externalization (from tacit knowledge to explicit knowledge); (3) combination (from explicit knowledge to explicit knowledge); and (4) internalization (from explicit knowledge to tacit knowledge).

Socialization   Socialization is the process of converting new tacit knowledge through shared experiences. Since tacit knowledge is difficult to formalize and often time- and space-specific, tacit knowledge can be acquired only through shared experience, such as spending time together or living in the same environment. Socialization typically occurs in a traditional apprenticeship, where apprentices learn the tacit knowledge needed in their craft through hands-on experience, rather than from written manuals or textbooks. Socialization may also occur in informal social meetings outside of the workplace, where tacit knowledge such as world views, mental models and mutual trust can be created and shared. Socialization also occurs beyond organizational boundaries. Firms often acquire and take advantage of the tacit knowledge embedded in customers or suppliers by interacting with them.

Externalization   Externalization is the process of articulating tacit knowledge into explicit knowledge. When tacit knowledge is made explicit, knowledge is crystallized, thus allowing it to be shared by others, and it becomes the basis of new knowledge. Concept creation in new product development is an example of this conversion process. Another example is a quality control circle, which allows employees to make improvements on the manufacturing process by articulating the tacit knowledge accumulated on the shop floor over years on the job. The successful conversion of tacit knowledge into explicit knowledge depends on the sequential use of metaphor, analogy and model.

Combination   Combination is the process of converting explicit knowledge into more complex and systematic sets of explicit knowledge. Explicit knowledge is collected from inside or outside the organization and then combined, edited or processed to form new knowledge. The new explicit knowledge is then disseminated among the members of the organization. Creative use of computerized communication networks and large-scale databases can facilitate this mode of knowledge conversion. When the comptroller of a company collects information from throughout the organization and puts it together in a context to make a financial report, that report is new knowledge in the sense that it synthesizes knowledge from many different sources in one context. The combination mode of knowledge conversion can also include the 'breakdown' of concepts. Breaking down a concept such as a corporate vision into operationalized business or product concepts also creates systemic, explicit knowledge.

Internalization   Internalization is the process of embodying explicit knowledge into tacit knowledge. Through internalization, explicit knowledge created is shared throughout an organization and converted into tacit knowledge by individuals. Internalization is closely related to 'learning by doing'. Explicit knowledge, such as the product concepts or the manufacturing procedures, has to be actualized through action and practice. For example, training programmes can help trainees to understand an organization and themselves. By reading documents or manuals about their jobs and the organization, and by reflecting upon them, trainees can internalize the explicit knowledge written in such documents to enrich their tacit knowledge base. Explicit knowledge can also be embodied through simulations or experiments that trigger learning by doing.

When knowledge is internalized to become part of individuals' tacit knowledge bases in the form of shared mental models or technical know-how, it becomes a valuable asset. This tacit knowledge accumulated at the individual level can then set off a new spiral of knowledge creation when it is shared with others through socialization.

The following list summarizes the factors that characterize the four knowledge conversion modes.[14]

Factors that constitute the knowledge-conversion process
Socialization: from tacit to tacit:

- Tacit knowledge accumulation: managers gather information from sales and production sites, share experiences with suppliers and customers and engage in dialogue with competitors.
- Extra-firm social information collection (wandering outside): managers engage in bodily experience through management by wandering about, and get ideas for corporate strategy from daily social life, interaction with external experts and informal meetings with competitors outside the firm.
- Intrafirm social information collection (wandering inside): managers find new strategies and market opportunities by wandering inside the firm.
- Transfer of tacit knowledge: managers create a work environment that allows peers to understand craftsmanship and expertise through practice and demonstrations by a master.

Externalization: from tacit to explicit:

- Managers facilitate creative and essential dialogue, the use of 'abductive thinking', the use of metaphors in dialogue for concept creation, and the involvement of the industrial designers in project teams.

Combination: from explicit to explicit:

- Acquisition and integration: managers are engaged in planning strategies and operations, assembling internal and external data by using published literature, computer simulation and forecasting.
- Synthesis and processing: managers build and create manuals, documents and databases on products and services and build up material by gathering management figures or technical information from all over the company.
- Dissemination: managers engage in the planning and implementation of presentations to transmit newly created concepts.

Internalization: from explicit to tacit:

- Personal experience; real world knowledge acquisition: managers engage in 'enactive liaising' activities with functional departments through cross-functional development teams and overlapping product development. They search for and share new values and thoughts, and share and try to understand management visions and values through communications with fellow members of the organization.
- Simulation and experimentation; virtual world knowledge acquisition: managers engage in facilitating prototyping and benchmarking and

facilitate a challenging spirit within the organization. Managers form teams as a model and conduct experiments and share results with the entire department.

As stated above, knowledge creation is a continuous process of dynamic interactions between tacit and explicit knowledge. Such interactions are shaped by shifts between different modes of knowledge conversion, not just through one mode of interaction. Knowledge created through each of the four modes of knowledge conversion interacts in the spiral of knowledge creation. Figure 3.3 shows the four modes of knowledge conversion and the evolving spiral movement of knowledge through the SECI (Socialization, Externalization, Combination, Internalization) process.

It is important to note that the movement through the four modes of knowledge conversion forms a *spiral*, not a circle. In the spiral of knowledge creation, the interaction between tacit and explicit knowledge is amplified through the four modes of knowledge conversion. The spiral becomes larger in scale as it moves up through the ontological levels. Knowledge created through the SECI process can trigger a new spiral of knowledge creation, expanding horizontally and vertically across organizations. It is a dynamic process, starting at the individual level and expanding as it moves through communities of interaction that transcend sectional, departmental, divisional and even organizational boundaries. Organizational knowledge creation is a never-ending process that upgrades itself continuously.

This interactive spiral process takes place both intra- and inter-organizationally. Knowledge is transferred beyond organizational boundaries, and knowledge from different organizations interacts to create new knowledge.[15] Through dynamic interaction, knowledge created by the organization can trigger the mobilization of knowledge held by outside constituents such as consumers, affiliated companies, universities or distributors. For example, an innovative manufacturing process may bring about changes in the

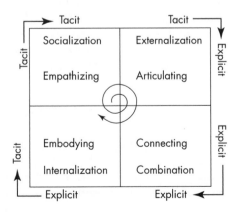

FIGURE 3.3 *The SECI process*

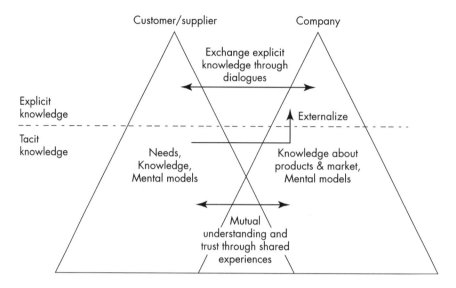

FIGURE 3.4 *Creating knowledge with outside constituents*

suppliers' manufacturing process, which in turn triggers a new round of product and process innovation at the organization. Another example is the articulation of tacit knowledge possessed by customers that they themselves have not been able to articulate. A product works as the trigger to elicit tacit knowledge when customers give meaning to the product by purchasing, adapting, using, or not purchasing it. Their actions are then reflected in the innovation process of the organization, and a new spiral of organizational knowledge creation starts again. Figure 3.4 shows how the organization interacts with outside constituents to create knowledge.

It should also be noted that knowledge creation is a self-transcending process, in which one reaches out beyond the boundaries of one's own existence.[16] In knowledge creation, one transcends the boundary between self and other, inside and outside, past and present. In socialization, self-transcendence is fundamental because tacit knowledge can only be shared through direct experiences which go beyond individuals.[17] For example, in the socialization process people empathize with their colleagues and customers, which diminishes barriers between individuals. In externalization, an individual transcends the inner and outer boundaries of the self by committing to the group and becoming one with the group. Here, the sum of the individuals' intentions and ideas fuse and become integrated with the group's mental world. In combination, new knowledge generated through externalization transcends the group in analogue or digital signals. In internalization, individuals access the knowledge realm of the group and the entire organization. This again requires self-transcendence, as one has to find oneself in a larger entity.

Ba: *shared context in motion for knowledge creation*

Knowledge needs a context to be created. Contrary to the Cartesian view of knowledge, which emphasizes the absolute and context-free nature of knowledge, the knowledge-creating process is necessarily context-specific in terms of who participates and how they participate. Knowledge needs a physical context to be created: 'there is no creation without place'.[18] *Ba* (which roughly means 'place') offers such a context. Based on a concept that was originally proposed by the Japanese philosopher Kitaro Nishida[19] and was further developed by Shimizu,[20] *ba* is here defined as a shared context in which knowledge is shared, created and utilized. In knowledge creation, generation and regeneration of *ba* is the key, as *ba* provides the energy, quality and place to perform the individual conversions and to move along the knowledge spiral.[21]

In knowledge creation, one cannot be free from context. Social, cultural and historical contexts are important for individuals, as such contexts provide the basis for one to interpret information to create meanings. As Friedrich Nietzsche argued, 'there are no facts, only interpretations'. *Ba* is a place where information is interpreted to become knowledge.

Ba does not necessarily mean a physical space. The Japanese word *ba* means not just a physical space, but a specific time and space. *Ba* is a time–space nexus, or as Heidegger expressed it, a locationality that simultaneously includes space and time. It is a concept that unifies physical space such as an office space, virtual space such as email, and mental space such as shared ideals.

The key concept in understanding *ba* is 'interaction'. Some of the research on knowledge creation focuses mainly on individuals, based on the assumption that individuals are the primary driving forces of creation. For example, quoting Simon's 'All learning takes place inside individual human heads', Grant claims that knowledge creation is an individual activity and that the primary role of firms is to apply existing knowledge.[22] However, such an argument is based on a view of knowledge and human beings as static and inhuman. As stated above, knowledge creation is a dynamic human process that transcends existing boundaries. Knowledge is created through the interactions amongst individuals or between individuals and their environments, rather than by an individual operating alone. *Ba* is the context shared by those who interact with each other, and through such interactions, those who participate in *ba* and the context itself evolve through self-transcendence to create knowledge (see Figure 3.5). Participants of *ba* cannot be mere onlookers. Instead, they are committed to *ba* through action and interaction.

Ba has a complex and ever-changing nature. *Ba* sets a boundary for interactions amongst individuals, and yet its boundary is open. As there are endless possibilities to one's own contexts, a certain boundary is required for a meaningful shared context to emerge. Yet *ba* is still an open place where participants with their own contexts can come and go, and the shared context (*ba*) can continuously evolve. By providing a shared context in motion, *ba* sets

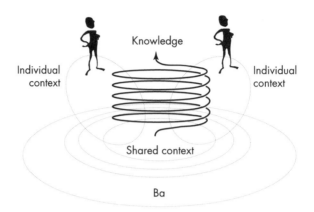

Knowledge

Individual context

Individual context

Shared context

Ba

FIGURE 3.5 Ba *as shared context in motion*

binding conditions for the participants by limiting the way in which the participants view the world. And yet it provides participants with higher viewpoints than their own.

Ba lets participants share time and space, and yet it transcends time and space. In knowledge creation, especially in socialization and externalization, it is important for participants to share time and space. A close physical interaction is important in sharing the context and forming a common language among participants. Also, since knowledge is intangible, unbounded and dynamic and cannot be stocked, *ba* works as the platform of knowledge creation by collecting the applied knowledge of the area into a certain time and space and integrating it. However, as *ba* can be a mental or virtual place as well as a physical place, it does not have to be bound to a certain space and time.

The concept of *ba* seemingly has some similarities to the concept of 'communities of practice'.[23] Based on the apprenticeship model, the concept of communities of practice argues that members of a community learn through participating in the community of practice and gradually memorizing jobs. However, there are important differences between the concepts of communities of practice and *ba*. While a community of practice is a living place where the members learn knowledge that is embedded in the community, *ba* is a living place where new knowledge is created. While learning occurs in any community of practice, *ba* needs energy to become an active *ba* where knowledge is created. The boundary of a community of practice is *firmly* set by the task, culture and history of the community. Consistency and continuity are important for a community of practice, as it needs an identity. In contrast, the boundary of *ba* is fluid and can be changed quickly as it is set by the participants. Instead of being constrained by history, *ba* has a 'here and now' quality. It is constantly moving; it is created, functions and disappears according to need. *Ba* constantly changes, as the contexts of participants or the membership of *ba* change. In a community of practice, changes mainly take

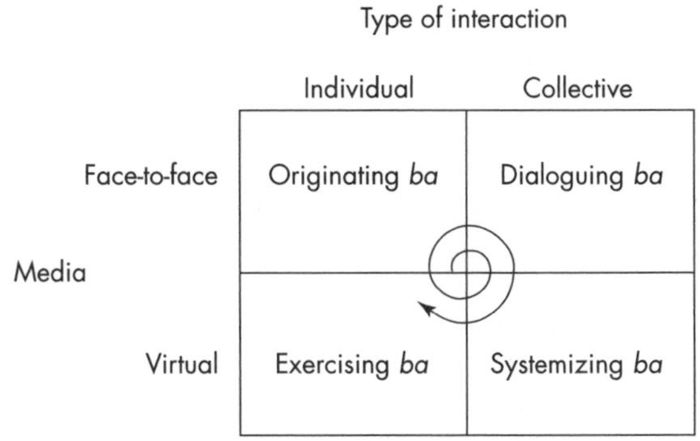

Type of interaction

	Individual	Collective
Face-to-face	Originating *ba*	Dialoguing *ba*
Virtual	Exercising *ba*	Systemizing *ba*

Media

FIGURE 3.6 *Four types of* ba

place at the micro (individual) level, as new participants learn to be full participants. In *ba*, changes take place at both the micro and the macro level, as participants change both themselves and *ba* itself. While the membership of a community of practice is fairly stable, and it takes time for a new participant to learn about the community to become a full participant, the membership of *ba* is not fixed; participants come and go. Whereas members of a community of practice belong to the community, participants of *ba* relate to the *ba*.

There are four types of *ba*: that is, originating *ba*, dialoguing *ba*, systemizing *ba* and exercising *ba*, which are defined by two dimensions of interactions (see Figure 3.6). One dimension is the type of interaction, that is, whether the interaction takes place individually or collectively. The other dimension is the media used in such interactions, that is, whether the interaction is through face-to-face contact or virtual media such as books, manuals, memos, emails or teleconferences. Each *ba* offers a context for a specific step in the knowledge-creating process, though the respective relationships between each single *ba* and conversion modes are by no means exclusive. Building, maintaining and utilizing *ba* is important to facilitate organizational knowledge creation. Hence, one has to understand the different characteristics of *ba* and how they interact with each other. The following sections describe the characteristics of each *ba*.

Originating ba Originating *ba* is defined by individual and face-to-face interactions. It is a place where individuals share experiences, feelings, emotions and mental models. It mainly offers a context for socialization, since an individual face-to-face interaction is the only way to capture the full range of physical senses and psycho-emotional reactions, such as ease or discomfort, which are important elements in sharing tacit knowledge. Originating *ba* is an existential place in the sense that it is the world where an individual transcends the boundary between self and others, by sympathizing or empathizing with others. From originating *ba* emerge care, love, trust and commitment, which form the basis for knowledge conversion among individuals.

Dialoguing ba Dialoguing *ba* is defined by collective and face-to-face interactions. It is the place where individuals' mental models and skills are shared, converted into common terms, and articulated as concepts. Hence, dialoguing *ba* mainly offers a context for externalization. Individuals' tacit knowledge is shared and articulated through dialogues amongst participants. The articulated knowledge is also brought back into each individual, and further articulation occurs through self-reflection. Dialoguing *ba* is more consciously constructed than originating *ba*. Selecting individuals with the right mix of specific knowledge and capabilities is the key to managing knowledge creation in dialoguing *ba*.

Systemizing ba Systemizing *ba* is defined by collective and virtual interactions. Systemizing *ba* mainly offers a context for the combination of existing explicit knowledge, as explicit knowledge can be relatively easily transmitted to a large number of people in written form. Information technology, through such things as on-line networks, groupware, documentation and databanks, offers a virtual collaborative environment for the creation of systemizing *ba*. Today, many organizations use such things as electronic mailing lists and news groups through which participants can exchange necessary information or answer each other's questions to collect and disseminate knowledge and information effectively and efficiently.

Exercising ba Exercising *ba* is defined by individual and virtual interactions. It mainly offers a context for internalization. Here, individuals embody explicit knowledge that is communicated through virtual media, such as written manuals or simulation programs. Exercising *ba* synthesizes the transcendence and reflection through action, while dialoguing *ba* achieves this through thought.

Let us illustrate how a firm utilizes various *ba* with the example of Seven-Eleven Japan, the most profitable convenience store franchiser in Japan. The success of Seven-Eleven Japan stems from its management of knowledge creation through creating and managing various *ba*.

Seven-Eleven Japan uses the shop floors of the 7,000 stores around Japan as originating *ba*, where store employees accumulate tacit knowledge about customers' needs through face-to-face interactions with customers. Long-term experiences in dealing with customers give store employees unique knowledge of and insight into the local market and customers. They often say that they can just 'see' or 'feel' how well certain items will sell in their stores, although they cannot explain why.

To promote the use of its stores as originating *ba*, Seven-Eleven Japan gives its employees extensive on-the-job training (OJT) on the shop floor. Every new recruit is required to work at Seven-Eleven stores in various functions for about two years to accumulate experiences in dealing directly with customers, and in actually managing Seven-Eleven stores. Another instrument to create originating *ba* is 'Burabura Shain' (Walking Around Employee), who has the task of wandering around and socializing with customers in stores to discover new knowledge in the field.

The tacit knowledge about the customers is then converted into explicit knowledge in the form of 'hypotheses' about market needs. Since local employees are the ones who hold tacit knowledge about their local markets, Seven-Eleven Japan let them build their own hypotheses about the sales of particular items by giving store employees the responsibility to order items. For example, a local worker can order more beer, based on the knowledge that the local community is having a festival.

To facilitate hypothesis building, Seven-Eleven Japan actively builds and utilizes dialoguing *ba*, where the tacit knowledge of local employees is externalized into explicit knowledge in the form of hypotheses through dialogue with others. Several employees are responsible for ordering merchandise instead of just one manager. Each employee is responsible for certain merchandise categories, and through dialogues with others who are responsible for other categories they can build hypotheses that better fit changing market needs.

Another instrument to facilitate hypothesis building is the use of field counsellors, who visit the stores regularly to engage in dialogues with the owners and employees of local stores, and give them advice in placing orders and managing stores so that owners and employees can articulate their tacit knowledge well. If a field counsellor notices a unique hypothesis, such as a new way to display merchandises at one store, s/he takes note and shares that hypothesis with other stores.

The hypotheses built at shop floor level are shared throughout the company through various dialoguing *ba*. Field counsellors report on the knowledge built at the stores they are responsible for to their zone managers, who then disseminate knowledge acquired from one field counsellor to other field counsellors. Zone managers from across Japan meet at the headquarters in Tokyo every week, where success stories and problems at local stores are shared with Seven-Eleven's top management and other zone managers. Field counsellors also have meetings every week, where field counsellors and staff members from the headquarters, including the top management, share knowledge.

The cost of maintaining such *ba* is not small. To hold such meetings in Tokyo every week, it has been estimated that Seven-Eleven Japan spends about $18 million per year on travelling, lodging, and so on. However, Seven-Eleven Japan emphasizes the importance of face-to-face interaction.

The hypotheses built at dialoguing *ba* are tested by the actual sales data that are collected, analysed and utilized through a state-of-the-art information system. The information system works as systemizing *ba*, where explicit knowledge in the form of sales data is compiled, shared and utilized by the headquarters and local stores.

The explicit knowledge compiled at systemizing *ba* is immediately fed back to stores through the information system so that they can build new hypotheses that suit the reality of the market better. Utilizing point-of-sales data and its analysis, store employees test their hypotheses about the market everyday at their local store, which works as exercising *ba*. In exercising *ba*, knowledge created and compiled in systemizing *ba* is justified by being compared with the reality of the world, and the gap between the knowledge and the reality then triggers a new cycle of knowledge creation.

The plurality of ba   *Ba* exists at many ontological levels and these levels may be connected to form a greater *ba*. Individuals form the *ba* of teams, which in turn form the *ba* of organization. Then, the market environment becomes the *ba* for the organization. As stated above, *ba* is a concept that transcends the boundary between micro and macro. The organic interactions amongst these different levels of *ba* can amplify the knowledge-creating process.

As *ba* often acts as an autonomous, self-sufficient unit that can be connected with other *ba* to expand knowledge, it seems to work in a similar way to a modular system or organization, in which independently designed modules are assembled and integrated together to work as a whole system. However, there are important differences between a modular organization and *ba*. Knowledge, especially tacit knowledge, cannot be assembled in the way in which various modular parts are assembled into a product. In a modular system, information is partitioned into visible design rules in a precise, unambiguous and complete way. 'Fully specified and standardized component interfaces' make the later integration of modules possible.[24] However, relationships amongst *ba* are not necessarily known a priori. Unlike the interfaces between modules, the relationships amongst *ba* are not predetermined and clear.

The coherence amongst *ba* is achieved through organic interactions amongst *ba* based on the knowledge vision, rather than through a mechanistic concentration in which the centre dominates. In organizational knowledge creation, neither micro nor macro dominates. Rather, both interact with each other to evolve into a higher self. The 'interfaces' amongst *ba* also evolve along with *ba* themselves. And the interactive organic coherence of various *ba* and individuals that participate in *ba* has to be supported by trustful sharing of knowledge and continuous exchanges between all the units involved to create and strengthen the relationships.

For example, Maekawa Seisakusho, a Japanese industrial freezer manufacturer, consists of 80 'independent companies' that operate as autonomous and self-sufficient *ba*. These companies interact with each other organically to form Maekawa as a coherent organization. Some of the independent companies share office space and work closely together. Individual employees of the different independent companies often spend time together and form informal relationships, out of which a new project or even a new independent company can be created. When they encounter problems too large to deal with alone, several independent companies form a group to work on the problem together. Such interactions amongst independent companies are voluntarily created and managed, not by a plan or order from the headquarters.

Knowledge assets

At the base of knowledge-creating processes are knowledge assets. We define assets as 'firm-specific resources that are indispensable to create values for the firm'. Knowledge assets are the inputs, outputs and moderating factors of the knowledge-creating process. For example, trust amongst organizational members is created as an output of the knowledge-creating process, and at the same time it moderates how *ba* functions as a platform for the knowledge-creating process.

Although knowledge is considered to be one of the most important assets for a firm to create a sustainable competitive advantage today, we do not yet have an effective system and tools for evaluating and managing knowledge assets. Although a variety of measures have been proposed,[25] existing accounting systems are inadequate for capturing the value of knowledge assets, due to the tacit nature of knowledge. Knowledge assets must be built and used internally in order for their full value to be realized, as they cannot be readily bought and sold. We need to build a system to evaluate and manage the knowledge assets of a firm more effectively. Another difficulty in measuring knowledge assets is that they are dynamic. Knowledge assets are both inputs and outputs of the organization's knowledge-creating activities, and hence they are constantly evolving. Taking a snapshot of the knowledge assets that the organization owns at one point in time is never enough to evaluate and manage the knowledge assets properly.

To understand how knowledge assets are created, acquired and exploited, we propose to categorize knowledge assets into four types: experiential knowledge assets, conceptual knowledge assets, systemic knowledge assets and routine knowledge assets (see Figure 3.7).

Experiential knowledge assets Experiential knowledge assets consist of the shared tacit knowledge that is built through shared hands-on experience

Experiential knowledge assets	Conceptual knowledge assets
Tacit knowledge shared through common experiences	Explicit knowledge articulated through images, symbols, and language
• Skills and know-how of individuals • Care, love, trust and security • Energy, passion and tension	• Product concepts • Design • Brand equity
Routine knowledge assets	**Systemic knowledge assets**
Tacit knowledge routinized and embedded in actions and practices	Systemized and packaged explicit knowledge
• Know-how in daily operations • Organizational routines • Organizational culture	• Documents, specifications, manuals • Database • Patents and licences

FIGURE 3.7 *Four categories of knowledge asset*

amongst the members of the organization, and between the members of the organization and its customers, suppliers and affiliated firms. Skills and know-how that are acquired and accumulated by individuals through experiences at work are examples of experiential knowledge assets. Other examples of such knowledge assets include emotional knowledge, such as care, love and trust, physical knowledge such as facial expressions and gestures, energetic knowledge such as senses of existence, enthusiasm and tension, and rhythmic knowledge such as improvisation and entrainment.

Because they are tacit, experiential knowledge assets are difficult to grasp, evaluate or trade. Firms have to build their own knowledge assets through their own experiences. Their tacit nature is what makes experiential knowledge assets the firm-specific, difficult-to-imitate resources that give a sustainable competitive advantage to a firm.

Conceptual knowledge assets Conceptual knowledge assets consist of explicit knowledge articulated through images, symbols and language. They are the assets based on the concepts held by customers and members of the organization. Brand equity, which is perceived by customers, and concepts or designs, which are perceived by the members of the organization, are examples of conceptual knowledge assets. Since they have tangible forms, conceptual knowledge assets are easier to grasp than experiential knowledge assets, though it is still difficult to grasp what customers and organizational members perceive.

Systemic knowledge assets Systemic knowledge assets consist of systematized and packaged explicit knowledge, such as explicitly stated technologies, product specifications, manuals, and documented and packaged information about customers and suppliers. Legally protected intellectual properties such as licences and patents also fall into this category. A characteristic of systemic knowledge assets is that they can be transferred relatively easily. This is the most 'visible' type of knowledge asset, and current knowledge management focuses primarily on managing systemic knowledge assets, such as intellectual property rights.

Routine knowledge assets Routine knowledge assets consist of the tacit knowledge that is routinized and embedded in the actions and practices of the organization. Know-how, organizational culture and organizational routines for carrying out the day-to-day business of the organization are examples of routine knowledge assets. Through continuous exercises, certain patterns of thinking and action are reinforced and shared amongst organizational members. Sharing the background to and 'stories' about the company also helps members to form routine knowledge. A characteristic of routine knowledge assets is that they are practical.

Mapping knowledge assets These four types of knowledge asset form the basis of the knowledge-creating process. To manage knowledge creation and exploitation effectively, a company has to 'map' its stocks of knowledge assets. However, cataloguing the existing knowledge is not enough. As stated above, knowledge assets are dynamic, and new knowledge assets can be created from existing knowledge assets.

LEADING THE KNOWLEDGE-CREATING PROCESS

In the previous section, we presented a model of the organizational knowledge-creating process consisting of three elements: SECI, *ba* and knowledge assets. Using its existing knowledge assets, an organization creates new knowledge through the SECI process that takes place in *ba*. The knowledge created then becomes part of the knowledge assets of the organization, which become the basis for a new spiral of knowledge creation. We now turn our attention to how such a knowledge-creating process can be managed.

The knowledge-creating process cannot be managed in the traditional sense of 'management', which centres on controlling the flow of information.[26] Managers can, however, lead the organization to actively and dynamically create knowledge by providing certain conditions. In this section, we discuss the roles of top and middle managers in leading a dynamic knowledge-creating process. Especially crucial to this process is the role of knowledge producers, that is, middle managers who are at the intersection of the vertical and horizontal flows of information in the company and actively interact with others to create knowledge by participating in and leading *ba*. In knowledge creation, 'distributed leadership' as seen in 'middle-up-down' management[27] is the key, as it cannot be 'managed' with traditional top-down leadership.

Top and middle management take a leadership role by 'reading' the situation, as well as leading it, in working on all three elements of the knowledge-creating process. Leaders provide the knowledge vision, develop and promote sharing of knowledge assets, create and energize *ba*, and enable and promote the continuous spiral of knowledge creation (see Figure 3.8). Especially important is the knowledge vision, which affects all three layers of the knowledge-creating process.

Providing the knowledge vision

To create knowledge dynamically and continuously, an organization needs a vision that synchronizes the entire organization. It is top management's role to articulate the knowledge vision and communicate it throughout (and outside) the company. The knowledge vision defines what kind of knowledge the company should create in what domain. The knowledge vision gives a direction to the knowledge-creating process, and the knowledge created by it, by asking such fundamental questions as 'What are we?', 'What should we create?', 'How can we do it?', 'Why are we doing this?' and 'Where are we going?' In short, it determines how the organization and its knowledge base evolve over the long term. Since knowledge is unbounded, any form of

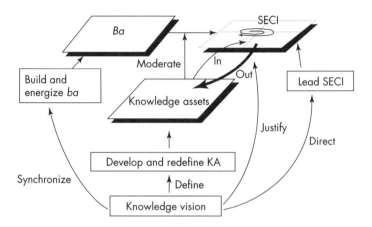

FIGURE 3.8 *Leading the knowledge-creating process*

new knowledge can be created regardless of the existing business structure of the company. Therefore, it is important for top management to articulate a knowledge vision that transcends the boundaries of existing products, divisions, organizations and markets.

The knowledge vision also defines the value system that evaluates, justifies and determines the quality of the knowledge the company creates. The aesthetic value of higher aspiration sets a boundary to the expansion of knowledge creation. Together with organizational norms, routines and skills, value system determines what kinds of knowledge are to be needed, created and retained.[28] It also fosters the spontaneous commitment of those who are involved in knowledge creation. To create knowledge, organizations should foster their members' commitment by formulating an organizational intention, as commitment underlies the human knowledge-creating activity.[29]

Serving as a bridge between the visionary ideals of those at the top and the chaotic reality of the front line, the middle then has to break down the values and visions created by the top into concepts and images that guide the knowledge-creating process with vitality and direction. Middle managers work as knowledge producers to remake reality, or 'produce new knowledge', according to the company's vision.

Developing and promoting the sharing of knowledge assets

Based on the knowledge vision of the company, top management has to facilitate dynamic knowledge creation by taking a leading role in managing the three elements of the knowledge-creating process. First, top management has to develop and manage the knowledge assets of the company, which form the basis of its knowledge-creating process. Recently, many companies have created the position of chief knowledge officer (CKO) to perform this function.[30] However, the role of these CKOs has so far been mostly limited to managing knowledge assets as a static resource to be exploited. Top management has to play a more active role in facilitating the dynamic process of building knowledge assets from knowledge.

Since knowledge is unbounded, top management has to redefine the organization on the basis of the knowledge it owns, rather than by using existing definitions such as technologies, products and markets. Top management and knowledge producers have to read the situation, in terms of what kind of knowledge assets are available to them. It is perhaps even more important to read the situation in terms of what kind of knowledge they are *lacking*, according to the knowledge vision that answers the question 'Where are we going?'

To do so, they can take an inventory of the knowledge assets and on that create a strategy to build, maintain and utilize the firm's knowledge assets effectively and efficiently. For example, after studying a hybrid power system that uses both a conventional engine and an electric motor, Toyota realized that it did not have the technology to make the main components of the hybrid system, such as the battery, motor, converter and inverter. Realizing that it lacked knowledge assets that could determine the future of the firm, the top management of Toyota took a major initiative to research, develop and produce the hybrid system internally.

It is also important to have knowledge producers who know where they can find the knowledge or personnel that will enable the firm to create and exploit its knowledge. It is often difficult for a large organization to know exactly what it knows. Top management has to foster and utilize knowledge producers who can keep track of the firm's knowledge assets, and utilize them when they are needed.

It should be noted that knowledge assets, especially routine knowledge assets, can hinder as well as foster knowledge creation. Organizations are subject to inertia and it is difficult for them to diverge from the course set by their previous experiences. Successful experience leads to excessive exploitation of the existing knowledge, and in turn hinders the exploration of new knowledge.[31] Therefore, current capabilities may both impel and constrain future learning and actions taken by a firm.[32] Core capabilities may turn into 'core rigidities'[33] or a 'competence trap'[34] which hinders innovation rather than promotes it. To avoid rigidities and traps, a firm can use an R & D project which requires different knowledge from the existing knowledge assets as an occasion for challenging current knowledge, and for creating new assets.

Building, connecting and energizing *ba*

Ba can be built intentionally, or created spontaneously. Top management and knowledge producers can build *ba* by providing physical space such as meeting rooms, virtual space such as a computer network, or mental space such as common goals. Forming a task force is a typical example of the intentional building of *ba*. To build *ba*, leaders also have to choose the right mix of people to participate, and promote their interaction. It is also important for managers to 'find' and utilize spontaneously formed *ba*, which changes or disappears very quickly. Hence, leaders have to read the situation in terms of how members of the organization are interacting with each other and with outside environments in order to quickly capture the naturally emerging *ba*, as well as to form *ba* effectively.

Further, various *ba* are connected with each other to form a greater *ba*. For that, leaders have to facilitate the interactions amongst various *ba*, and among the participants, based on the knowledge vision. In many cases, the relationships amongst *ba* are not predetermined. Which *ba* should be connected in which way is often unclear. Therefore, leaders have to read the situation to connect various *ba* as the relationships amongst them unfold.

However, building, finding and connecting *ba* is not enough for a firm to manage the dynamic knowledge-creating process. *Ba* should be 'energized' to give energy and quality to the SECI process. For that, knowledge producers have to supply the necessary conditions, such as autonomy, creative chaos, redundancy, requisite variety, and love, care, trust and commitment.

Autonomy Autonomy increases the chances of finding valuable information and motivating organization members to create new knowledge. Not only does self-organization increase the commitment of individuals, but it can also be a source of unexpected knowledge. By allowing the members of the organization to act autonomously, the organization may increase the chances of accessing and utilizing the knowledge held by its members.[35]

A knowledge-creating organization with autonomy can be depicted as an 'autopoietic system'.[36] Living organic systems are composed of various organs, which are made up of numerous cells. The relationship between system and organs, and between organ and cells, is neither dominant–subordinate nor whole–part. Each unit, like an autonomous cell, controls all of the changes occurring continuously within itself, and each unit determines its boundary through self-reproduction. Similarly, autonomous individuals and groups in knowledge-creating organizations set their task boundaries for themselves in pursuit of the ultimate goal expressed by the organization.

In the business organization, a powerful tool for creating autonomy is provided by the self-organizing team. An autonomous team can perform many functions, thereby amplifying and sublimating individual perspectives to higher levels. Researchers have found that the use of cross-functional teams that involve members from a broad cross-section of different organizational activities is very effective in the innovation process.[37] NEC has used autonomous teams to foster the expansion of its technology programme. Sharp uses its 'Urgent Project System' to develop strategically important products. The team leader is endowed by the president with responsibility for the project and the power to select his or her team members from any unit in Sharp.

Creative chaos Creative chaos stimulates the interaction between the organization and the external environment. Creative chaos is different from complete disorder; it is intentional chaos introduced to the organization by its leaders to evoke a sense of crisis amongst its members by proposing challenging goals or ambiguous visions. Creative chaos helps to focus members' attention and encourages them to transcend existing boundaries to define a problem and resolve it. Facing chaos, organization members experience a breakdown of routines, habits and cognitive frameworks. Periodic breakdowns or 'unlearning' provide important opportunities for them to reconsider their fundamental thinking and perspectives.[38] The continuous process of questioning and re-evaluating existing premises energizes *ba*, and hence fosters organizational knowledge creation. Some have called this phenomenon creating 'order out of noise' or 'order out of chaos'.[39] It is important for leaders to read the situation in order to introduce creative chaos into *ba* in the right place at the right time, and to lead the creation of order out of chaos so that the organization does not fall into complete disorder.

For example, when the development team of the Toyota Prius came up with a plan to improve fuel efficiency by 50%, which was ambitious enough, the top management rejected the plan and set a new goal to increase it by 100% instead. This threw the team into turmoil; it eventually discarded its original plan to use the direct injection engine, and developed the world's first commercially available hybrid car.

Redundancy 'Redundancy' refers to the intentional overlapping of information about business activities, management responsibilities and the company as a whole. Redundancy of information speeds up the knowledge-creating process in two ways. Firstly, sharing redundant information promotes the sharing of tacit knowledge, because individuals can sense what others are trying to articulate. Redundant information enables individuals to transcend functional boundaries to offer advice or provide new information from different perspectives. Secondly, redundancy of information helps organizational members understand their role in the organization, which in turn functions to control their direction of thinking and action. Thus it provides the organization with a self-control mechanism for achieving a certain direction and consistency.

Redundancy of information is also necessary to realize the 'principle of redundancy of potential command' – that is, the principle whereby each part of an entire system carries the same degree of importance and has the potential to become its leader.[40] At Maekawa Seisakusho, different people take leadership in turn during the course of a project, from research and prototype building to implementation. The person whose abilities can best address the issues or problems at hand takes the leadership role to drive the project forward, guaranteeing 'the right man in the right place' in each phase of the project. Redundancy of information makes such a style of management possible, and allows team members to recognize the strengths of their colleagues. By the rotation of specialists in different positions and roles within the team, such as leader, support and so on, specialists gain additional knowledge in related fields as well as management skills and knowledge. In short, redundancy facilitates transcendence between leaders and subordinates, generalists and specialists, and creators and users of knowledge.

Redundancy of information, however, does increase the amount of information to be processed and can lead to information overload. It also increases the cost of knowledge creation, at least in the short run. Leaders have to read the situation to deal with the possible downside of redundancy by making it clear where information can be located and where knowledge is stored within the organization.

Requisite variety Creation lies at the edge between order and chaos. Requisite variety helps a knowledge-creating organization to maintain the balance between order and chaos. An organization's internal diversity has to match the variety and complexity of the environment in order to deal with challenges posed by that environment.[41] To cope with many contingencies, an organization has to possess requisite variety, which should be at a minimum for organizational integration and a maximum for effective adaptation to environmental changes.

Requisite variety can be enhanced by combining information differently, flexibly and quickly, and by providing equal access to information throughout the organization. When an information differential exists within the organization, organization members cannot interact on equal terms, which hinders the search for different interpretations of new information. An organization's members should know where information is located, where knowledge is accumulated, and how information and knowledge can be accessed at the highest speed. Kao Corporation, Japan's leading manufacturer of household products, utilizes a computerized information network to give every employee equal access to corporate information as the basis for opinion exchanges amongst various organizational units with different viewpoints.

There are two ways to realize requisite variety. One is to develop a flat and flexible organizational structure in which the different units are interlinked with an information network, thereby giving organization members fast and equal access to the broadest variety of information. Another approach is to change organizational structure frequently or rotate personnel frequently, thereby enabling employees to acquire interdisciplinary knowledge to deal with the complexity of the environment.

Love, care, trust and commitment Fostering love, care, trust and commitment amongst organizational members is important as it forms the foundation of knowledge creation.[42] For knowledge (especially tacit knowledge) to be shared and for the self-transcending process of knowledge creation to occur, there should be strong love, caring and trust amongst organization members. As information creates power, an individual might be motivated to monopolize it, hiding it even from his or her colleagues. However, as knowledge needs to be shared to be created and exploited, it is important for leaders to create an atmosphere in which organization members feel safe sharing their knowledge. It is also important for leaders to cultivate commitment amongst organization members to motivate the sharing and creation of knowledge, based on the knowledge vision.

To foster love, care, trust and commitment, knowledge producers need to be highly inspired and committed to their goal. They also need to be selfless and altruistic. They should not try to monopolize the knowledge created by the organization, or take credit for other members' achievements. Also, knowledge producers need to be positive thinkers. They should try to avoid having or expressing negative thoughts and feelings. Instead, they should have creative and positive thoughts, imagination, and the drive to act.

Promoting the SECI process

The leadership should also promote the SECI process. Following the direction given by the knowledge vision, knowledge producers promote organizational knowledge creation by facilitating all four modes of knowledge conversion, although their most significant contribution is made in externalization. They synthesize the tacit knowledge of front-line employees, top management and outside constituents such as customers and suppliers, to make it explicit and incorporate it into new concepts, technologies, products or systems. To do so, knowledge producers should be able to reflect upon their actions. As Schon states, when one reflects while in action, one becomes independent of established theory and technique, and is able to construct a new theory of the unique case.[43]

Another important task for knowledge producers is to facilitate the knowledge spiral across the different conversion modes, and on different organizational levels. To facilitate the knowledge-creating process effectively, knowledge producers need to read the situation, in terms of where the spiral is heading and what kind of knowledge is available to be converted, both inside and outside the organization. With this reading, knowledge producers need to improvise to incorporate necessary changes in the knowledge-creating process. Improvisation is an important factor in dynamic knowledge creation, especially when dealing with tacit knowledge.[44] Knowledge producers should be able to improvise and facilitate improvisation by the participants in the knowledge-creating process.

Knowledge producers need to be able to create their own concepts and express them in their own words and thus should be able to use language effectively. Language here includes tropes (such as metaphor, metonymy, synecdoche), 'grammar' and 'context' for knowledge, and non-verbal visual language such as design. Each mode of knowledge conversion requires different kinds of language for knowledge to be created and shared effectively. For example, non-verbal language such as body language is essential in the socialization process, as tacit knowledge cannot be expressed in articulated language. In contrast, clear, articulated language is essential in the combination process, as knowledge has to be disseminated and understood by many people. In externalization, tropes such as metaphor, metonymy and synecdoche are effective in creating concepts out of vast amounts of tacit knowledge. Therefore, knowledge producers should carefully choose and design language according to the process of knowledge creation.

CONCLUSION

In this chapter we have discussed how organizations manage the dynamic process of knowledge creation, which is characterized by dynamic interactions amongst organizational members, and between organizational members and the environment. We have proposed a new model of the knowledge-creating process to understand the dynamic nature of knowledge creation and to manage such a process effectively. Three elements, the SECI process, *ba* and knowledge assets, have to interact with each other organically and dynamically. The knowledge assets of a firm are mobilized and shared in *ba*, where tacit knowledge held by individuals is converted and amplified by the spiral of knowledge through socialization, externalization, combination and internalization.

We have also discussed the role of leadership in facilitating the knowledge-creating process. Creating and understanding the knowledge vision of the company, understanding the knowledge assets of the company, facilitating and utilizing *ba* effectively, and managing the knowledge spiral are the important roles that managers have to play. Especially important is the role of knowledge producers, the middle managers who are at the centre of the dynamic knowledge-creating process.

All three elements of the knowledge-creating process should be integrated under clear leadership so that a firm can create knowledge continuously and dynamically. The knowledge-creating process should become a *discipline* for organization members, in terms of how they think and act in finding, defining and solving problems.

In this chapter we have focused primarily on the organizational knowledge-creating process that takes place within a company. We have described the knowledge-creating process as the dynamic interaction between organizational members, and between organizational members and the environment. However, the knowledge-creating process is not confined within the boundaries of a single company. The market, where the knowledge held by companies interacts with that held by customers, is also a place for knowledge creation. It is also possible for groups of companies to create knowledge. If we further raise the level of analysis, we arrive at a discussion of how so-called national systems of innovation can be built. For the immediate future, it will be important to examine how companies, governments and universities can work together to make knowledge creation possible.

NOTES

1. A. Toffler, *Powershift: Knowledge, Wealth and Violence at the Edge of the 21st Century*, Bantam Books, New York, 1990.
2. R. M. Cyert, P. K. Kumar and J. R. Williams, 'Information, market imperfections and strategy', *Strategic Management Journal*, Winter Special Issue, 14: 47–58 (1993); P. Drucker, *Post-Capitalist Society*, Butterworth Heinemann, London, 1993; R. M.

Grant, 'Prospering in dynamically competitive environments: organizational capability as knowledge integration', *Organization Science*, 7: 375–387 (1996); R. Henderson and I. Cockburn, 'Measuring competence: exploring firm effects in pharmaceutical research', *Strategic Management Journal*, 15 (Winter Special Issue): 63–84 (1994); D. Leonard-Barton, 'Core capabilities and core rigidities: a paradox in managing new product development', *Strategic Management Journal*, 13 (5): 363–380 (1992); D. Leonard-Barton, *Wellsprings of Knowledge*, Harvard Business School Press, Boston, MA, 1995; R. R. Nelson, 'Why do firms differ, and how does it matter?', *Strategic Management Journal*, 12 (Winter Special Issue): 61–74 (1991); I. Nonaka, *Chishiki-Souzou no Keiei* (A Theory of Organizational Knowledge Creation), Nihon Keizai Shimbun-sha (in Japanese), 1990; I. Nonaka, 'The knowledge-creating company', *Harvard Business Review*, Nov.–Dec.: 96–104 (1991); I. Nonaka, 'A dynamic theory of organizational knowledge creation', *Organization Science*, 5(1): 14–37 (1994); I. Nonaka and H. Takeuchi, *The Knowledge-Creating Company*, Oxford University Press, New York, 1995; J. B. Quinn, *Intelligent Enterprise: A Knowledge and Service Based Paradigm for Industry*, The Free Press, New York, 1992; K. Sveiby, *The New Organizational Wealth*, Berret-Koehler, San Francisco, 1997; S. G. Winter, 'Knowledge and competence as strategic assets', in D. J. Teece (ed.), *The Competitive Challenge: Strategies for Industrial Innovation and Renewal*, pp. 159–184, Ballinger, Cambridge, MA, 1987.

3. J. C. Spender and R. M. Grant, 'Knowledge and the firm: overview', *Strategic Management Journal*, 17 (Winter Special Issue): 5–9 (1996).

4. R. M. Cyert and J. G. March, *A Behavioral Theory of the Firm*, Prentice-Hall, Englewood Cliffs, NJ, 1963; D. Levinthal and J. Myatt, 'Co-evolution of capabilities and industry: the evolution of mutual fund processing', *Strategic Management Journal*, 15 (Winter Special Issue): 45–62 (1994).

5. J. B. Barney, 'Firm resources and sustained competitive advantage', *Journal of Management*, 17(1): 99–120 (1991); D. Lei, M. A. Hitt and R. Bettis, 'Dynamic core competences through meta-learning and strategic context', *Journal of Management*, 22(4): 549–569(1996); Nelson (1991), op. cit.; D. J. Teece, G. Pisano and A. Shuen, *Firm Capabilities, Resources, and the Concept of Strategy: Four Paradigms of Strategic Management*, CCC Working Paper No. 90–8 (1990); M. Wilkins, *The History of Foreign Investment in the United States to 1914*, Harvard University Press, Cambridge, MA, 1989.

6. F. A. Hayek, 'The use of knowledge in society', *American Economic Review*, 35: 519–530 (1945).

7. A. N. Whitehead, as recorded by L. Price, *Dialogues of Alfred North Whitehead*, Little, Brown, Boston, MA, 1954.

8. Nonaka and Takeuchi, 1995, op. cit.

9. D. A. Schon, *The Reflective Practitioner*, Basic Books, New York, 1983.

10. M. Polanyi, *The Tacit Dimension*, Routledge and Kegan Paul, London, 1966.

11. L. Vygotsky, *Thought and Language*, Massachusetts Institute of Technology, Boston, MA, 1986.

12. I. Prigogine, *From Being to Becoming: Time and Complexity in the Physical Sciences*, W. H. Freeman, San Francisco, 1980.

13. Nonaka, 1990, 1991, 1994; Nonaka and Takeuchi, 1995, all op. cit. (See n. 2 above.)

14. Adapted from I. Nonaka, P. Byosiere, C. C. Borucki and N. Konno, 'Organisational knowledge creation theory: a first comprehensive test', *International Business Review*, 3(4): 337–351 (1994).

15. J. L. Badaracco Jr., *The Knowledge Link: How Firms Compete through Strategic Alliances*,

Harvard Business School Press, Boston, MA, 1991; A. C. Inkpen, 'Creating knowledge through collaboration', *California Management Review*, 39(1): 123–140 (1996); Nonaka, 1990, 1991,1994; Nonaka and Takeuchi, 1995 op. cit. (see n. 2 above); S. Wikstrom and R. Normann, *Knowledge and Value: A New Perspective on Corporate Transformation*, Routledge, London, 1994.

16. E. Jantsch, *The Self-organising Universe*, Pergamon Press, Oxford, 1980.
17. K. Nishida, *An Inquiry into the Good* (1921), trans. M. Abe and C. Ives, Yale University, New Haven, CT, 1990.
18. E. S. Casey, *The Fate of Place: A Philosophical History*, University of California Press, Berkeley, CA, 1997.
19. Nishida, 1921, op. cit.; K. Nishida, *Fundamental Problems of Philosophy: the World of Action and the Dialectical World*, Sophia University, Tokyo, 1970.
20. H. Shimizu, '*Ba*-principle: new logic for the real-time emergence of information', *Holonics*, 5(1): 67–79 (1995). However, the concept of place has also been talked about by philosophers such as Plato, Kant, Husserl and Whitehead.
21. I. Nonaka and N. Konno, 'The concept of "*ba*": building a foundation for knowledge creation', *California Management Review*, 40(3): 1–15 (1998); I. Nonaka, N. Konno and R. Toyama, 'Leading knowledge creation: a new framework for dynamic knowledge management', 2nd Annual Knowledge Management Conference, Haas School of Business, University of California, Berkeley, 22–24 September 1998.
22. H. A. Simon, *Reason in Human Affairs*, Stanford University Press, Stanford, CA, 1983; R. M. Grant, 'Toward a knowledge-based theory of the firm', *Strategic Management Journal*, 17 (Winter Special Issue): 109–122 (1996).
23. J. Lave and E. Wenger, *Situated Learning–Legitimate Peripheral Participation*, Cambridge University Press, Cambridge, 1991; E. Wenger, *Communities of Practice: Learning, Meaning, and Identity*, Cambridge University Press, Cambridge, 1998.
24. R. Sanchez and J. T. Mahoney, 'Modularity, flexibility and knowledge management in product and organisation design,' *Strategic Management Journal*, 17(10): 63–67 (1996).
25. L. Edivinsson and M. S. Malone, *Intellectual Capital*, Harper Business, New York, 1997; T. Stewart, *Intellectual Capital: The New Wealth of Organization*, Doubleday, New York, 1997.
26. G. von Krogh, I. Nonaka and K. Ichijo, 'Develop knowledge activists!', *European Management Journal*, 15(5): 475–483 (1997).
27. Nonaka and Takeuchi, 1995, op. cit.; I. Nonaka, 'Toward middle-up-down management: accelerating information creation', *Sloan Management Review*, 29(3): 9–18 (1988).
28. Leonard-Barton, 1992, op. cit.
29. M. Polanyi, *Personal Knowledge*, University of Chicago Press, Chicago, 1958.
30. T. H. Davenport and L. Prusak, *Working Knowledge*, Harvard Business School Press, Boston, MA, 1998.
31. J. March, 'Exploration and exploitation in organizational learning', *Organization Science*, 2(1): 101–123 (1991); J. March, *The Pursuit of Organizational Intelligence*, Blackwell Publishers, Maiden, MA, 1999.
32. C. K. Prahalad and G. Hamel, 'The core competence of the corporation', *Harvard Business Review*, 68(3): 79–91 (1990).
33. Leonard-Barton, 1992, op. cit.
34. B. Levitt and J. G. March, 'Organisational learning', *Annual Review of Sociology*, 14: 319–340 (1988).

35. Grant, 1996, op. cit. (n. 2 above); 1996 (n. 22 above); K. H. Wruck and M. C. Jensen, 'Science, specific knowledge, and total quality management', *Journal of Accounting and Economics*, 18: 247–287 (1994).
36. G. von Krogh, *Organizational Epistemology*, St Martin's Press, New York, 1995; H. R. Maturana and E. J. Varela, *Autopoiesis and Cognition: The Realization of the Living*, Reidel, Dordrecht, 1980.
37. K. B. Clark and T. Fujimoto, *Product Development Performance: Strategy, Organization and Management in the World Auto Industry*, Harvard Business School Press, Boston, MA, 1991; W. Imai, I. Nonaka and H. Takeuchi, 'Managing the new product development process: how Japanese companies learn and unlearn', in K. B. Clark, R. H. Hayes and C. Lorenz (eds), *The Uneasy Alliance: Managing the Productivity–Technology Dilemma*, pp. 337–381, Harvard Business School Press, Boston, MA, 1985.
38. T. Winograd and F. Flores, *Understanding Computers and Cognition: A New Foundation for Design*, Addison-Wesley, Reading, MA, 1986.
39. H. von Foerster, 'Principles of self-organization in a socio-managerial context', in H. Ulrich and G. J. B. Probst (eds), *Self-Organization and Management of Social Systems*, pp. 2–24, Springer-Verlag, Berlin, 1984; T. J. Peters, *Thriving on Chaos*, Alfred A. Knopf, New York, 1987; I. Prigogine and I. Stengers, *Order Out of Chaos: Man's New Dialogue with Nature*, Bantam Books, New York, 1984.
40. W. McCulloch, *Embodiments of Mind*, MIT Press, Cambridge, MA, 1965.
41. W. R. Ashby, *An Introduction to Cybernetics*, Chapman & Hall, London, 1956.
42. G. von Krogh, 'Care in knowledge creation', *California Management Review*, 40(3): 133–153 (1998); G. von Krogh, I. Nonaka and K. Ichijo, 'Enabling knowledge creation', in G. von Krogh, J. Roos and D. Kleine (eds), *Knowledge and Organization*, Sage, London (forthcoming).
43. Schon, 1983, op. cit. (see n. 9 above).
44. K. E. Weick, 'The non-traditional quality of organizational learning', *Organizational Science*, 2(1): 116–124 (1991).

4

Bridging Epistemologies: the Generative Dance between Organizational Knowledge and Organizational Knowing

S. D. N. Cook and J. S. Brown*

It's funny what's happened to this word *knowing*. . . . The actual *act* of apprehending, of making sense, of putting together, from what you have, the significance of where you are – this [now] oddly lacks any really reliable, commonly used verb in our language . . . [one] meaning the *activity* of knowing. . . . [Yet], every culture has not only its own set *body* of knowledge, but its own *ways* of [knowing]. Sir Geoffrey Vickers, 1976

In recent years, knowledge has become a prominent theme in the organizational literature. However, in such discussions, as in informal contexts, knowledge is typically spoken of as though it were all of a piece, as though essentially it comes in only one kind. It is our contention that there are, in fact, a number of distinct forms of knowledge, and that their differences are relevant, both theoretically and practically, to an effective understanding of organizations.

There is now much discussion of organizational knowledge, knowledge-based organizations, knowledge-creating organizations, knowledge work, etc. There are numerous related themes such as organizational learning, the collective mind (Weick and Roberts, 1993), and the organizational brain. It has become common to talk of knowledge in the context of both individuals and groups, and even to consider knowledge in explicit and tacit senses (where, for example, explicit knowledge is treated as knowledge that can be spelled out or formalized, and tacit knowledge as that associated with skills or 'know-how'). Accordingly, there are discussions about: how explicit knowledge acquired by individuals in an organization is associated with 'learning' at the level of the organization (March and Olsen, 1976; Argyris and Schon, 1978; Sims and Gioia, 1986; Simon, 1991; Sitkin, 1992); how a group's mastering of

* Reprinted by permission of the Institute for Operations Research and the Management Sciences (INFORMS) from S. D. Noam Cook and John Seely Brown, 'Bridging Epistemologies: The Generative Dance Between Organizational Knowledge and Organizational Knowing' © *Organization Science*, 1999.

explicit routines can be an aspect of organizational memory (Cohen and Bacdayan, 1994); how the tacit skills of an individual can and cannot be tapped for the benefit of the organization (Nonaka, 1994; Nonaka and Takeuchi, 1995; Spender, 1996); and how the activities of groups can constitute organizational learning (Weick, 1991; Weick and Westley, 1996). Meanwhile, such concepts are clearly vital to such concerns as the management of intellectual capital (Stewart, 1997), core competencies (Hamel and Prahalad, 1994), and innovation (Leonard-Barton, 1995). Increasingly, such work has pushed provocatively and insightfully at the boundaries of the theoretical frames used in understanding knowledge and organizations – as in Weick and Roberts's (1993) application of 'taking heed' and 'mindfulness' to operations of teams; in Cohen and Bacdayan's (1994) use of notions of procedural memory from psychology as a way of understanding organizational routines; in what Hutchins (1991: 2) sees as the 'pattern of communication' within the 'cognitive system' of a group; in Nonaka and Takeuchi's spiral of knowledge creation; and in Kogut and Zander's (1996) considerations of the interplay between individuals' social knowledge and the organizing principles of work in explaining what organizations know how to do.

Yet, even in this growing body of literature that explores epistemologically significant themes, there typically remains an expressed or implied tendency to treat knowledge as being essentially of one kind. That is, the epistemology assumed in the literature tends to privilege the individual over the group, and the explicit over the tacit (as if, for example, explicit and tacit knowledge were two variations of one kind of knowledge, not separate, distinct forms of knowledge). The former tendency is reflected in the insistence that organizational learning is really about individual learning since 'All learning takes place inside individual human heads' (Simon, 1991: 125). The latter, meanwhile, can be seen in Nonaka's argument that 'While tacit knowledge held by individuals may lie at the heart of the knowledge creating process, realizing the practical benefits of that knowledge centers on its externalization', where 'externalization' for Nonaka entails a process of 'converting' tacit knowledge into explicit knowledge (1994: 20). Cohen and Bacdayan, meanwhile, contend that organizational routines arise when 'individuals store components of a routine as a procedural memory' (1994: 554). And even Weick and Roberts have made the epistemologically provocative move of describing 'collective mind' in terms of 'a distinct higher-order pattern of interrelated activities' grounded in and emerging from 'individual actions' (1993: 374). Meanwhile Hutchins (1991: 284) speaks of investigating the 'ways in which the cognitive properties of human groups may depend on the social organization of individual cognitive capabilities'.

As we will detail below, we believe that the tendency to treat all knowledge as being essentially the same severely limits the current work on epistemologically relevant organizational themes, both theoretically and operationally. Theoretically, these tendencies fail to honor aspects of the distinction between explicit and tacit, and individual and group knowledge that we see as germane to understanding the acquisition, maintenance, and exercise of competencies by individuals and groups. Practically, it limits our ability to assess and support these competencies in their own right.

The first contention of this chapter is that each of the four categories of knowledge inherent in the explicit/tacit and individual/group distinctions is a distinct form of knowledge on equal standing with the other three (i.e. none is subordinate to or made up out of any other). Also, this distinct character is reflected in the fact that each form of knowledge does work that the others cannot. We view these four forms of knowledge as constituting the appropriate focus of what we call *the epistemology of possession*, since these forms of 'what is known' are typically treated as something people *possess*.[1] To say, for example, 'Robert knows auto mechanics' points to Robert *possessing* knowledge of auto mechanics.

The second contention is that not all of what is known is captured by this understanding of knowledge. Put another way, there is more epistemic work being done in what we know how to do than can be accounted for solely in terms of the knowledge we possess.[2] So, in addition to talking about the four distinct forms of knowledge we *also* want to be able to speak about the epistemic work done by human action itself – that is, about what is *part of practice* as well as what is *possessed in the head*. To say, for example, 'Robert is fixing cars' points not only to knowledge he possesses but also to things he is doing. To give an account of what Robert knows, we claim, calls for an understanding of the epistemic work done, which needs to include both the knowledge he possesses and the actions he carries out.

Borrowing from the epistemological perspective of the American Pragmatist philosophers, we call what is possessed 'knowledge' and what is part of action 'knowing'. Individuals and groups clearly make use of knowledge, both explicit and tacit, in what they do; but not everything they know how to do, we argue, is explicable solely in terms of the knowledge they possess. We believe that understanding of the epistemological dimension of individual and group action requires us to speak about both knowledge *used in* action and knowing *as part of* action. Therefore, in addition to the traditional epistemology of possession, there needs to be, in our view, a parallel *epistemology of practice*, which takes ways of knowing as its focus. By this, we do not mean that practice needs to be brought under the umbrella of traditional epistemology (nor do we mean that all of human action needs to be accounted for epistemologically). Rather, we contend that there needs to be a radical expansion of what is considered epistemic in its own right, which includes knowledge and knowing.

Furthermore, we do not see knowledge and knowing as competing, but as complementary and mutually enabling (see Figure 4.1).[3] Indeed, as we will spell out in detail in what follows, understanding what is entailed in bridging the two epistemologies provides a more robust account of such matters as: how individuals and groups can draw on tacit and explicit knowledge simultaneously; how what individuals know tacitly can be made useful to groups; and how explicit instructions can be made more useful aids for the development of tacit skills. Also (and quite importantly) we see the interplay

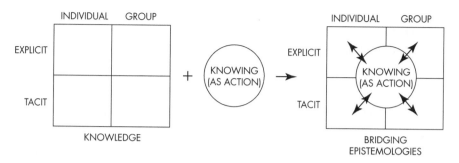

FIGURE 4.1 *Knowledge and knowing*

of knowledge and knowing as a potentially generative phenomenon. That is, for human groups, the source of *new* knowledge and knowing lies in the use of knowledge as a tool of knowing within situated interaction with the social and physical world. It is this that we call the *generative dance*. Understanding the generative dance (how to recognize, support, and harness it) is essential, we believe, to understanding the types of learning, innovation, and effectiveness that are prime concerns for all epistemologically oriented organizational theories.

In what follows, we explore the epistemologies of possession and practice and some implications of our perspective. We first sketch out our interpretation of the epistemology of possession, along with what we see as its strengths and limitations. Then we offer what in our view are some essential elements of an epistemology of practice – in particular, we define what we mean by (1) the term *practice*, (2) the distinction between *knowledge* and *knowing*, (3) the Pragmatist philosopher John Dewey's concept of *productive inquiry*, (4) the notion of *interaction with the world*, and (5) the idea of *dynamic affordance*. Following this, we look at how seeing knowledge as a tool of knowing can help explain how individuals and groups draw on all four forms of knowledge and, importantly, how the interplay of knowledge and knowing can generate new knowledge and new ways of knowing. In the final section, we explore these ideas in the context of three cases, and consider some broader implications of them for a more robust understanding of the epistemological dimension of organized human activity.

THE EPISTEMOLOGY OF POSSESSION

Each of the four categories that come from the explicit/tacit and individual/group distinctions identifies a unique and irreducible form of knowledge. We see each of the four as on equal footing with the other three, and hold that no one of them can be derived from or changed into one of the others. We believe that each needs to be understood *conceptually* as distinct, in no small part because *in practice* each does work that the others cannot. In arguing for this position, we first address the conventional inclination to treat knowledge either as if it were all of a piece or, if different forms are considered, to privilege explicit over tacit and individual over group knowledge.

Privileging the explicit and the individual is not unique to organizational studies. It reflects the dominant epistemology of Western culture for the last three centuries, at least. This view is often referred to as the Cartesian view, given its substantial grounding in the work of the seventeenth-century French philosopher René Descartes. For Cartesians past and present, the individual, indeed the individual analytic thinker, is taken as primary. All knowledge, accordingly, is believed to be best acquired through reason and the use of concepts and methods that are freed as much as possible from the fallibilities of our senses or the exigencies of given situations.

Descartes's famous 'Cogito ergo sum' (I think therefore I am) is both a beginning and a conclusion for the traditional epistemology. It is the conclusion that the thinking self is the one thing we cannot doubt – everything else, from the impressions of our senses to 'objective' claims about the world, is subject to one or another degree of uncertainty. It is through analytic reasoning, Cartesians maintain, that we can best minimize or 'control for' the clouding influences of our senses and subjective impressions, and thus acquire our most reliable knowledge about the world. It is a beginning in that the thinking (or reasoning or doubting) self becomes the one fundamental, irreducible starting point for any search for knowledge about the world, and the repository for that knowledge once acquired. All this should have a familiar ring to anyone who received a traditional introduction to 'the scientific method' and 'the scientific worldview'.

What follows from all this has become part of the conventional understanding of knowledge in our culture: the idea that knowledge, particularly anything that might pass as rigorous knowledge, is something that is held in the head of an individual and is acquired, modeled, and expressed most accurately in the most objective and explicit terms possible. It is this Cartesian tradition, as well, that we see underlying such statements quoted above as 'All learning takes place inside individual human heads' (Simon, 1991) and 'realizing the practical benefits of [tacit] knowledge centers on its externalization' (Nonaka, 1994).

Our aim here, it should be noted, is not to reject the Cartesian epistemology wholesale. Rather, we wish to critique some of its elements that we believe have made difficult the development of a productive understanding of the forms of knowledge suggested by categories other than individual/explicit. We believe Cartesian epistemology needs to be broadened into an 'epistemology of possession' that can incorporate a conceptually sound and useful understanding of knowledge possessed tacitly and knowledge possessed by groups.

Explicit/tacit

The grip that the Cartesian tradition has had on the exploration of explicit and tacit knowledge has been particularly strong. When the idea of tacit knowledge is addressed, for example, it is most often treated as an informal, inchoate, or obscure kind of knowledge, whose very nature calls for it to be made explicit in order to be truly understood or useful in practice. Indeed, the very term 'tacit' suggests to many people (quite understandably) the sense that any such knowledge must be 'hidden' from our understanding or 'inaccessible' for practical purposes. We believe that this predilection of the traditional epistemology has held back the development of an understanding of the explicit/tacit distinction that is called for and increasingly needed, given the growth of significant work on epistemological themes in the literatures concerned with organized human action. Indeed, we base our claim that the explicit/tacit distinction is one between two separate forms of knowledge on practical utility: we argue that the distinction needs to be *conceptually* clear because, in practice, each form of knowledge does work the other cannot. A sounder, more robust conceptual understanding of the distinction should help make it possible to recognize, support, and harness the different forms of work that each, in fact, makes possible in practice.[4]

We base our understanding of the tacit/explicit distinction on the work of the scientist and philosopher Michael Polanyi (1983). Polanyi's distinction is exemplified very compellingly in the simple but rich example of riding a bicycle. Many people who say they can ride a bicycle will claim, when asked, that they do not know which way to turn the handlebars to prevent a fall to the left or right. However, since staying upright is part of knowing how to ride a bicycle, anyone who can ride must, by definition, know which way to turn the handlebars to avoid a fall. What they can't do is *say* which way to turn. So there's something known by everyone who can ride that most cannot say. What they can say is an example of what Polanyi called the explicit dimension of knowledge, while what is known by everyone who can keep upright on a bike is what he called the tacit dimension of knowledge.

Building on Polanyi, we argue that explicit and tacit are two distinct forms of knowledge (i.e. neither is a variant of the other); that each does work the other cannot; and that one form cannot be made out of or changed into the other. We explore these and other aspects of the distinction below, again beginning with the example of bicycle riding.

To be able to ride a bicycle, one needs to have the (tacit) knowledge of how to stay upright. This is knowledge one possesses; it is *not* the activity of riding itself but knowledge used in riding (you still possess the tacit knowledge even when you are not riding). Possessing this tacit knowledge makes it possible to keep upright, which is something that the explicit knowledge of which way to turn cannot do. We can't put a novice on a bicycle saying 'OK, take off – and if you start to fall like so, turn this way' and expect the person to be able to ride successfully. The novice would have the explicit knowledge but not the necessary tacit knowledge. Whatever epistemic work that explicit bit of knowledge can make possible, it cannot do *all* of the work that is necessary for someone to know how to ride. In order to acquire the tacit knowledge, a novice has to spend a certain amount of time on a bicycle. Indeed, it would even be possible for someone to be able to say in great technical detail what must be done to keep a bicycle upright, yet still be unable to ride one. No amount of explicit knowledge alone can enable someone to ride; it simply cannot enable all the necessary epistemic work.

At the same time, we argue that each form of knowledge can often be used as an *aid* in acquiring the other. If you know how to ride, for example, you might use your tacit knowledge to ride around in a way that helps you discover which way you turn when you begin to fall. Likewise, if a novice is told how to turn to avoid a fall, that explicit knowledge could be used while learning to ride as an aid in getting a feel for staying upright. However, neither tacit nor explicit knowledge can be used by itself to acquire the other: one must also, at the very least, get on a bicycle (an important point, to which we will return shortly).

We can now see that each form of knowledge does its own work. Explicit knowledge can be used as an aid to help acquire the tacit knowledge, but cannot by itself enable one to ride. The tacit knowledge is necessary in being able to ride, but it does not by itself enable a rider to say which way to turn.

Furthermore, it is important not to mistake using one form of knowledge as an aid in acquiring the other with one form being 'converted' into the other. Tacit knowledge cannot be turned into explicit, nor can explicit knowledge be turned into tacit. If you ride around using your tacit knowledge as an aid to discovering which way you turn, when you ultimately acquire the explicit knowledge you still possess the tacit knowledge, and you still use it in keeping upright. When we ride around with the aim of acquiring the explicit knowledge, we are not performing an operation on our tacit knowledge that turns it into explicit knowledge; we are using the tacit, within the activity of riding, to generate the explicit knowledge. The explicit knowledge was not lying inside the tacit knowledge in a dormant, inchoate, or hidden form; it was generated in the context of riding with the aid of what we knew tacitly. Likewise, if you know explicitly which way to turn but cannot ride, there is no operation you can perform on that explicit knowledge that will turn it into the tacit knowledge necessary to riding. That tacit knowledge is acquired on its own: it is not made out of explicit knowledge. Prior to being generated, one form of knowledge does not lie hidden in the other.

Also, there is no guarantee that one form will always be a useful aid to acquiring the other. In fact, in some cases using one can be a hindrance to acquiring the other. In learning how to drive, for example, you may be told (explicitly) to accelerate when coming out of a turn, only to be told later that you are using this knowledge mechanically 'as a crutch' rather than 'getting a feel for it'. Similarly, in learning a skill like dancing or tennis many people experience a period when explicit knowledge about how to move one's feet or hold one's shoulders can actually impair one's ability to acquire the tacit knowledge necessary to performing the skill in a fluid or masterful way. Even experts in a given skill can find their ability to use their tacit knowledge 'thrown off' when they are asked to describe explicitly what they are doing.

Individual/group

We have also inherited a cultural predilection for privileging the individual over the group. Whether stated emphatically or presented implicitly, a sense that whatever can be said about groups actually 'boils down' to things about individuals is taken almost as though it were self-evident, and particularly so when the concern at hand is an epistemological one (Cook, 1994). As the Cartesian view would have it, it is the *individual* thinker who is the primary (if not exclusive) wielder and repository of what is known. This predilection is reflected, for example, in Simon's insistence (noted above) that all learning takes place inside the heads of individuals. For many who are not as orthodox as Simon, such topics as 'organizational learning', 'organizational knowledge', or 'organizational routines' are still spoken of in ways that often leave it unclear as to whether groups are being treated on an equal footing with individuals or as a derivative of them. (This is often so, it should be noted, even in cases where it is not authors' intention either to address or to dodge the issue.)

In recent years, however, there has been a growing volume of research and publication that has begun to treat groups and organizations in their own right. This has been an implicit concern in our own work as well as that of a number of our colleagues at Xerox PARC and the Institute for Research on Learning. This trend is also strongly suggested in the literature treating such concepts as 'communities of practice' (Wenger, 1997; Brown and Duguid, 1991), 'core competencies' (Hamel and Prahalad, 1994), 'situated cognition', 'legitimate peripheral participation' (Lave and Wenger, 1991), and the 'spiral of organizational knowledge creation' (Nonaka and Takeuchi, 1995). Discussions of communities of practice look at how individuals establish themselves and function as a group by engaging in practices that are unique to or characteristic of that group. Within the growing body of work on core competencies one can see serious attention being given to how teams, as well as individuals, do 'real work' and how that work can be supported, enriched, and directed. The concept of legitimate peripheral participation, originally used to explore apprenticeship learning, takes as its central concern the role of participation by seemingly peripheral individuals in the innovative and very *central* capacities of the group itself. In more and more instances, authors are addressing such epistemological issues at the level of the group, including recent direct explorations of such terms as 'organizational knowledge' and 'organizational epistemology' (Krogh and Roos, 1995). By taking the group as a primary unit of analysis, such approaches, implicitly at least, treat groups as something to be investigated in their own right with respect to epistemological concerns.

As with the explicit/tacit distinction, we propose that individuals and groups each do epistemic work that the other cannot. So, for example, while only individual physicians know how to diagnose nephritis using palpation (groups do not have hands), the knowledge of what constitutes acceptable and unacceptable practice in nephrology is possessed by nephrologists as a group. Likewise, while individual copier technicians have a sense of how a particular copier ought to sound when operating properly (groups do not have ears), it is a group of technicians that possess 'war stories' about what odd noises can mean. Indeed, an individual technician's account only becomes a 'war story' when it is held in common and can be used by the group in its discussions about machines (Orr, 1996). In both cases, part of what is known about a given domain is possessed by individuals, part by groups. Individual technicians and nephrologists possess various bits of knowledge in their respective fields, but the 'body of knowledge' of copier repair or nephrology is possessed by groups, not by individuals. Put another way, the body of knowledge of a group is 'held in common' by the group. We do not expect every individual in a group (discipline, profession, craft, etc.) to possess everything that is in the 'body of knowledge' of that group (in fact, this is likely to be impossible, unnecessary, and perhaps even undesirable). The body of knowledge is possessed by the group as a whole and is drawn on in its actions, just as knowledge possessed by an individual is drawn on in his or her actions. The work done by a group, as informed by the body of knowledge it possesses, is work that is epistemically distinct from work done by an individual in it, as informed by the knowledge he or she possesses.[5]

With respect to both distinctions, the lesson we wish to draw here is *not* that we ought now to reverse tradition and privilege the group and the tacit over the individual and the explicit. Indeed, our aim has been to argue for an expanded epistemology of possession that includes each of four types of knowledge and treats each as distinct from (not superior to) the other three, both conceptually and in the sense of each doing work that the others cannot.

TOWARD AN EPISTEMOLOGY OF PRACTICE

We are now able to focus on an important aspect of what people know that is *not* captured by the four forms of knowledge considered above. In the bicycle example we argued that tacit and explicit knowledge alone are insufficient in acquiring the ability to ride; what has to be added is the actual act of riding (or trying to). This leads us now to make a specific claim: *the act of riding a bicycle does distinct epistemic work of its own*. Indeed, we hold that this type of epistemic work is an inextricable facet of human action itself, not something people possess. We mark this distinction by referring to it as 'knowing' rather than 'knowledge'. Furthermore, we believe that knowing does not belong to an epistemology of possession, but rather that it calls for an epistemology of practice. Following Vickers's (1976: 2) assertion that every human group 'has not only its own set *body* of knowledge, but its own *ways* of [knowing]', we now turn to outlining some of what we believe 'knowing' and an 'epistemology of practice' entail. In particular, we propose specific understandings of (1) the term *practice*, (2) the distinction, drawn from the Pragmatists, between *knowledge* and *knowing*, (3) John Dewey's concept of *productive inquiry*, (4) the notion of *interaction with the world*, and (5) the idea of *dynamic affordance*.

Practice

Practice implies doing. Intuitively, it refers to things we do as individuals and as groups. Conceptually, practice has received a growing amount of careful theoretical attention in recent years (see, for example, Bourdieu, 1977; Turner, 1994). In common usage, 'practice' can mean either to develop a competency through drill or rote actions as in 'to practice the piano' or to exercise a competency as in 'to practice medicine'. The former suggests drill in preparation for doing the 'real work', while the latter suggests the 'real work' itself. In our use of the term, we mean doing real work: the practice of engineers, managers, physicians, woodworkers, etc. (in which, meanwhile, drill and other rotelike activities can play an important part).

For our purposes, then, we intend the term 'practice' to refer to *the co-ordinated activities of individuals and groups in doing their 'real work' as it is informed by a particular organizational or group context*. In this sense, we wish to distinguish practice from both behavior and action. Doing of any sort we call 'behavior', while 'action' we see as behavior imbued with meaning. By 'practice', then, we refer to action informed by meaning drawn from a particular group context. In the simplest case, if Vance's knee jerks, that is behavior. When Vance raps his knee with a physician's hammer to check his reflexes, it is behavior that has meaning, and thus is what we call action. If his physician raps his knee as part of an exam, it is practice. This is because the meaning of her action comes from the organized contexts of her training and ongoing work in medicine (where it can draw on, contribute to, and be evaluated in the work of others in her field).

Knowledge and knowing

Drawing a distinction between knowledge and knowing may seem at first pass an unduly subtle point. We believe it is at root quite a substantial one, both epistemologically and in its implications for understanding organized human activity. Above, we have expanded our understanding of knowledge to include the forms suggested by the explicit/tacit and individual/group distinctions. With respect to all four forms, however, we have maintained the sense of knowledge as something that is possessed. When we say 'Miriam has knowledge of physics', the knowledge is something that Miriam possesses (as concepts, rules, procedures, etc.). Furthermore, her knowledge (whether explicit or tacit) is abstract since it is something that is *about* but not *in* the tangible world. And it is static, in that possessing it does not require that it be always in use: when Miriam is playing tennis or sleeping she still has knowledge of physics. Finally, while knowledge itself is static, it is common to see it as necessary to action: 'Miriam can solve the problem because she has knowledge of physics' or 'Miriam cannot solve the problem until she acquires knowledge of the conservation of angular momentum.' That is, knowledge is commonly thought of as something we *use* in action but it is not understood to *be* action.

Accordingly, we use the term 'knowing' to refer to the epistemological dimension of action itself. By 'knowing' we do not mean something that is *used in* action or something *necessary to* action, but rather something that is a *part of* action (both individual and group action). 'Knowing' refers to the epistemic work that is done as part of action or practice, like that done in the actual riding of a bicycle or the actual making of a medical diagnosis. Knowing is dynamic, concrete, and relational. If we talk about André reflecting 'knowing' in physics, our focus is on what he is actually doing; it is on the ways he deploys the knowledge he possesses in his interactions with the materials of a specific concrete task in physics (such as testing an experimental laser design).

In developing an understanding of the knowledge/knowing distinction, we have found it useful to draw on the work of the American philosophical school of Pragmatism, in particular the work of John Dewey, as an alternative to the dominant Cartesian perspective. Those interested in organizations have generally seen the work of the Pragmatists as limited essentially to educational settings. We believe that a new look at the Pragmatist perspective can yield very important and timely implications for organizations of all sorts. The resurgence of interest in American Pragmatism, which has centered on Dewey (see, for example, Rorty, 1982; Hickman, 1990), makes the re-examination of this perspective even more timely for organizational concerns.

A basic conviction of the Pragmatist perspective in both theory and practice is that our primary focus should *not* be (solely) on the likes of abstract concepts and principles (as has been common more broadly in philosophy and the social sciences) but on concrete action. Pragmatists have been centrally concerned with doing, particularly forms of doing that entail making or producing something (from technologies to ideas). Accordingly, when it comes to questions of what we know and how we know, the Pragmatist perspective takes a primary concern not with 'knowledge', which is seen as abstract and static, but with 'knowing', which is understood as part of concrete, dynamic human action. Following the Pragmatist perspective, for us 'knowing something' refers to an *aspect of* action, not to something assumed to underlie, enable, or be used in action.[6] By 'knowing' we mean that aspect of action or practice that does epistemic work.

'Knowing', Dewey maintained, 'is literally something which we do', not something that we possess. For Dewey, to talk about activity in terms of knowledge is to mistake an abstract, static concept for a concrete, dynamic activity. It is to make a kind of category error. To be accomplished in a profession, discipline, or craft, for example, is necessarily tied up with practicing it. This does not mean that its body of knowledge is useless to practice, only that it is not the same as the epistemic dimension of practice. An accomplished engineer may possess a great deal of sophisticated knowledge; but there are plenty of people who possess such knowledge yet do not excel as engineers (as is often observed in many fields). This means that if you want to understand the essentials of what accomplished engineers know, you need to look at what they do as well as at what they possess. It also means that our fundamental understanding of the relationship between a body of knowledge and activities of a practice must change: we must see knowledge as *a tool at the service of knowing* not as something that, once possessed, is all that is needed to enable action or practice. (Improved practice may not always be the product of acquiring more knowledge; at times it may be the result of developing innovative ways of using knowledge already possessed.)

This Pragmatist focus on action has broad implications for those areas where organizational and epistemological concerns intersect. And the value of these implications can be carried further, we believe, by drawing on the key Deweyan concept of 'productive inquiry'.

Productive inquiry

One of the most important things that knowing can do in using knowledge as a tool is what Dewey called 'productive inquiry'. To engage in productive inquiry is to be actively pursuing a problem, puzzle, point of fascination, object of wonder, or the like; it is to seek an answer, solution, or resolution. It is *inquiry* because what motivates us to action is in some sense a query: a problem, a question, a provocative insight, or a troublesome situation. It is *productive* because it aims to produce (to make) an answer, solution, or resolution. Productive inquiry includes a broad range of actions from the problem solving of mathematics to computer programming to fixing a photocopier to finding the proper placement of the voice in singing. *Productive inquiry is that aspect of any activity where we are deliberately (though not always consciously) seeking what we need, in order to do what we want to do.*

Productive inquiry is not a haphazard, random search; it is informed or 'disciplined' by the use of theories, rules of thumb, concepts, and the like. These tools of productive inquiry are prime examples of what Dewey understands the term 'knowledge' to mean. Conversely, using knowledge in this way is an example of that particular form of knowing that Dewey called 'productive inquiry'. So, using knowledge in productive inquiry gives inquiry a systematic or disciplined character: just as knowledge is a tool of knowing, so must knowing respect the demands and constraints of knowledge. (To wield any tool skillfully, we must respect the constraints it places on our actions in using it, as the haphazard use of a hammer can all too painfully demonstrate.)

Significantly, Dewey also saw knowledge as one of the possible outcomes of productive inquiry: one end result of engaging in the (situated, dynamic) activity of productive inquiry is the production of (abstract, static) knowledge, which then can be used as a tool of further knowing, including knowing in the mode of productive inquiry.

Building on these key points from Dewey, we make a number of further arguments about the distinction between knowledge and knowing. Knowledge by itself cannot enable knowing. As a tool, knowledge disciplines knowing, but does not enable it any more than possession of a hammer enables its skillful use. Likewise, the principles of engineering alone cannot enable an accomplished engineer to engage in the productive inquiry of resolving a difficult design problem. However, it is precisely such things as the principles of engineering that an accomplished engineer uses *in practice* as tools in addressing a problem at hand, in interacting with it through the use of those tools, in seeking to resolve a design problem.

Furthermore knowing should not be confused with 'tacit knowledge'. As we have defined tacit knowledge, it is a tool or an aid to action, not part of action itself. Everyone who can ride a bike can be said to know tacitly which way to turn to avoid a fall, whether or not they are at that moment actually riding. Knowing requires present activity. Tacit knowledge does not. Knowing makes use of tacit knowledge as a tool for action – as when we ride around on a bike using our tacit knowledge to stay upright (acquiring the tacit knowledge of how to stay upright, meanwhile, is acquiring know-how useful to bike riding). Finally, tacit knowledge alone does not enable us to ride; there is more epistemic work that needs to be done. Being able to ride requires interaction between the (tacit) knowledge we possess and the present activity of being in motion on a bike. The activity of riding, itself, is a form of knowing; it does distinct epistemic work. *Knowing is that aspect of action (or practice) that does epistemic work* – including doing things we know how to do, and (through productive inquiry) producing what we need, in order to do something we want to do, which can include producing new knowledge. We will explore this notion further in the next two sections.

Interaction with the world

We act within the social and physical world, and since knowing is an aspect of action, it is about interaction with that world. When we act, we either give shape to the physical world or we affect the social world or both. Thus, 'knowing' does not focus on what we possess in our heads: it focuses on our interactions with the things of the social and physical world.

'Knowledge' is about possession; it is a term of predication. In all its forms we use it to indicate something an individual or group possesses, can possess, or needs to possess. 'Knowing' is about relation: it is about interaction between the knower(s) and the world.

To interact with the world effectively we need to honor it. One cannot make reliable objects through the haphazard use of clay or steel: it is possible to make the walls of a pot too thin or the span of a bridge too long: objects give way when design pushes them beyond the constraints of their materials. To make use of the power of materials, their inherent constraints must be honored. The master of a craft – whether potter or materials engineer – is constantly engrossed in a kind of conversation with the materials of his or her craft. The master puts out ideas by giving shape to the material, and 'hears back' from it as he or she discovers and explores what the material can and cannot make possible. Part of what it means to master any craft is to learn how to turn the constraints of its materials into opportunities for design.

Similarly, in the social world, one must honor the strengths, limitations, and character of individuals and groups to engender co-ordinated and directed action or practice – as all good managers, football coaches, and orchestra conductors know, at least intuitively (as do the members of such groups).

Knowledge also helps us 'honor' the world in our interactions with it. As noted above, knowing as an aspect of action can make use of bits of knowledge (in any of its forms) as tools. In doing so, the knowledge about the social and physical world 'disciplines' our interaction with the world, just as the use of a pair of pliers gives particular form to how we interact with a bolt.

Within the relational and interactive character of knowing, the world shapes our actions by requiring that we honor it, just as we shape the world by interacting with it in a disciplined way. *Knowing is to interact with and honor the world using knowledge as a tool.* We will look more precisely at how this works in the next section.

Dynamic affordance

We now wish to focus on some specific characteristics of 'interaction with the world' that are at the center of our understanding of 'knowing'. In doing so, we first borrow two general points from the work of the Spanish philosopher José Ortega y Gasset that frame 'interaction with the world' in a way that further develops an alternative to the Cartesian frame of the 'thinking self'. Then we explore the idea of 'affordance', as introduced in the work on perception by J. J. Gibson (1979) and as significantly developed in the design work of W. W. Gaver (1991, 1996). Finally we argue for our sense of what we call 'dynamic affordance'.

Interaction with the social and physical worlds is a central concern in the work of Ortega. Very much in keeping with the American Pragmatists, Ortega abandoned the frame of the abstracted, analytic thinking self and throughout his work approached questions of epistemology, action, etc. from the perspective of 'myself within this context'. For Ortega, what we can know and what we can do are not discovered through an abstract Cartesian thought experiment, but are products of ongoing concrete interaction between 'myself' (or 'ourselves') and the specifics of the social and physical 'context' or 'circumstances' we are in at any given time. 'I invent projects of being and of doing,' Ortega insisted, 'in light of circumstance' (1961a: 202).

In keeping with this, Ortega argues that in interacting with the world we encounter both 'facilities' and 'frustrations' (1961b). It is important to note that facilities and frustrations are *not* properties of the world, but properties that lie solely in our interaction with the world. The tensile strength of clay is a property of the world, but it becomes a facility or a frustration only when we are interacting with it (e.g. when we are making pots). Likewise, the bits of knowledge that members of a team may possess are a property of that social world. They can only become facilities or frustrations, however, when we are interacting with the group within the context of a specific piece of work (or when the members of the group interact with each other in such a context).

The phenomenon of certain properties arising solely in the context of interaction with the world can also be seen in connection with the idea of 'affordance'. There is a common meaning of 'affordance' that is a progenitor of the sense we have in mind, but it is one we need to go beyond, because it suggests a static (i.e. not 'interactive') character. This is the elemental sense of how a material, design, or situation 'affords' doing something: metal affords making buckets; buckets afford carrying water; bucket brigades afford fire fighting.

This sense of affordance is reflected in everyday objects in ways that can attract a great deal of conscious attention or none at all. This is particularly true of objects that are the product of human design. What they afford can give rise to shape and fluidity or incoherence and clumsiness in our activities. This can be seen, for example, even in the simple case of an ordinary book. The design of a book, as distinct from a newspaper or a scroll, affords such things as skimming or random access by using a thumb index or flipping from one part of the text to another and back again.

A doorknob, to take another example, affords opening and closing a door. The particular design of a doorknob can afford fluid or clumsy action. In Figure 4.2 we show the design of a doorknob that affords pushing or pulling the door from the appropriate side. On the side where the door needs to be pushed, the knob is a flattened hemisphere flush with the door; it is a knob that would, in fact, be difficult to pull. On the opposite side the same shape is raised from the surface of the door and one's fingers can fold easily around the edge so one's hand is almost invited to pull (particularly when paired with resistance from the door, if one should try pushing from that side). Although the design elements of common objects like books and doorknobs are often at the border of our attention, they nonetheless can constitute important resources in our interactions with them (Brown and Duguid, 1994).

How characteristics of the world give clues to our perceptions as to what we can and can't do with them is the sense of 'affordance' that is explored in depth in the work of Gibson (1979). Gaver has carried this notion further

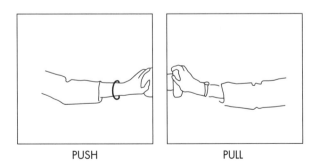

PUSH   PULL

FIGURE 4.2 *Affordance*

by arguing for an understanding of affordance that is not primarily about perception but about relationships between characteristics of the world and issues of inherent concern to people. For Gaver (1991, 1996), questions of affordance with respect to elevation in architecture, for example, emerge as issues of 'accessibility', which come from the relationship between elevation and the necessity of expending energy climbing to higher surfaces of support.

As we have indicated, there is a sense of affordance that lies beyond these inherently static senses, which deserves to be understood in its own right. We call this additional sense 'dynamic affordance' and mean by it forms of affordance that emerge as part of the (dynamic) interaction with the world. In talking about design elements of ordinary objects, for example, we said that they 'can give rise to shape and fluidity or incoherence and clumsiness in our activities'. We would note now that 'shape, fluidity, incoherence, and clumsiness' are not properties of the objects (i.e. of the world). Rather, like Ortega's facilities and frustrations, they are properties of our interactions with those objects.[7] The emergence of these properties raises the question as to how we might deal with them: what use might we make of shape and fluidity, and how might we address incoherence and clumsiness are questions about what those properties of interaction afford. They are questions about dynamic affordance.

What we mean by 'dynamic affordance' has both an *intuitive* sense and a very particular *conceptual* sense. Both senses can be seen in the bicycle riding example. Intuitively, most of us understand that learning to ride requires 'getting a feel' for what it is like to stay in balance, and we recognize that we need to get on a bike to acquire that knowledge. So, the activity of riding around *dynamically affords* the acquisition of the needed knowledge.

Conceptually, we see 'dynamic affordance' as lying in the real and subtle interaction between the rider and the bike in motion. When bicycle wheels turn, they become gyroscopes – and like all gyroscopes their tendency is to remain in the plane of rotation: to get spinning bicycle wheels to tip to one side or the other requires that a force be applied to them that will overcome this gyroscopic tendency. A rider uses his or her body weight as that force: shifting one's weight pushes against the gyroscopic force of the moving wheels. This is what we do (or part of it) when we are riding or learning to ride. In the activity of riding, shifting our weight against the gyroscopic force of the wheels 'dynamically affords' learning to stay upright; it also 'dynamically affords' the enactment of that skill once acquired. These are things we can learn and do *only* when we are in dynamic interaction with bicycle wheels in motion. Without the dynamic affordance of that interaction there is no learning and no enactment of what is learned. Both are always inextricably tied to riding itself: without the activity of riding there is no gyroscopic force to be used or pushed against. This dynamic character is an essential element of our conceptual sense of 'dynamic affordance'.

Finally, because interaction between rider and bicycle dynamically affords *both* the acquisition of knowledge *and* the use of knowledge once acquired, we see it as doing epistemic work that the knowledge alone cannot. Indeed, we argue that dynamic affordance is intimately connected to the distinct epistemological form we have called 'knowing'. Dynamic interaction with the world opens the unique realm in which knowing takes place: the activity of addressing facilities and frustrations dynamically affords knowing.

We hold that dynamic affordance and knowing play an essential role in how knowledge – explicit and tacit, individual and group – is generated, transferred, and used in organizations. We also hold that these activities acquire particular shape and meaning from their organizational contexts – that is, they are not only actions; they are also practices. Consequently, understanding how what is known functions in organizations requires understanding the interplay of the epistemology of possession and the epistemology of practice. It is to these matters that we now turn our attention.

BRIDGING EPISTEMOLOGIES

The four distinct forms of knowledge of the epistemology of possession as discussed above are displayed in Figure 4.3.

The cells of the figure array knowledge among the categories of individual/group and explicit/tacit. The upper left cell contains things an individual can know, learn, and express explicitly. Examples of things that would fit this cell would include (but certainly not be limited to) concepts, rules, and equations that typically are presented explicitly and are typically known and used by individuals. In the upper right are things that are also expressed explicitly yet typically are used, expressed, or transferred in a group. This includes, for example, stories about how work is done or about famous successes or failures (Orr, 1990, 1996), as well as the use of metaphors or phrases that have useful meaning within a specific group. In the lower left are examples of tacit knowledge possessed by individuals, such as a skill in making use of concepts, rules, and equations or a 'feel' for the proper use of a tool or for keeping upright

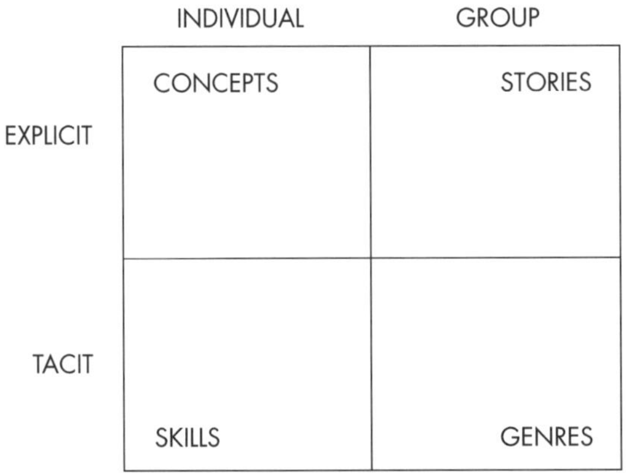

	INDIVIDUAL	GROUP
EXPLICIT	CONCEPTS	STORIES
TACIT	SKILLS	GENRES

FIGURE 4.3 *Four forms of knowledge*

on a bike. Finally, in the lower right is tacit knowledge possessed by groups. Although everyone has daily experience with this form of knowledge, it is perhaps the most difficult of the four to define. A working definition of it, however, is crucial to understanding the relationships among the four forms of knowledge and to appreciating the distinction between knowledge and knowing. We wish to label this form of knowledge with an expanded definition of the term 'genre'.

Conventionally, 'genre' is most familiar as a literary term, where it refers to types of literature – e.g., 'novel' and 'biography' are two distinct literary genres. Such genres do more than constitute a tidy scheme of classification: they also provide frames for understanding and interpreting what we read, without which a text could be utterly baffling or dangerously misleading. We read or 'take in' a text one way if we understand it to be a novel, quite another if we think it is a biography. Importantly, it is the meaning of the term 'novel' or 'biography' that constitutes the genre, not the actual text or the meaning the text acquires when it is understood to belong to a given genre. As literary historians would remind us, this meaning is constantly evolving and under-going a kind of implicit negotiation among writers, readers, and publishers as they read and discuss texts.

The power of genres to enable us to make sense of and use a text is so common in experience that we often are unconscious of it (Brown and Duguid, 1994). The characteristics of the genre 'newspaper' (folds, pulp paper, narrow columns of text, headlines, bylines, etc.) have meanings that we pay little, if any, conscious attention to; however, our ability to make sense of what newspapers say is highly dependent upon them. Without having been taught it or even reflecting on it consciously, most of us 'read' the importance of front-page stories that appear above a newspaper's fold as greater than those that appear below it.

Genres are no less important to the organizational world than they are to the literary world (Orlikowski and Yates, 1994). A message from a co-worker can signal one thing if it arrives as a handwritten note, but quite another if it is a printed memo or a formal letter. The genre (note, memo, or letter) provides a frame for interpreting a given text. Each of these forms of communication has a meaning understood and used by members of the organization. Indeed, employing genres is one way people in organizations communicate. As such, organizational genres acquire their very distinct (and quite effective) meanings not by deliberate design but (like that of 'novel' and 'biography') in the course of their being used (or misused) in the context of work practices.

The power of organizational genres is reflected, for example, in the case of the manager who reads email only as printed-out hard copy. After reading one such message, he phoned its author to tell him in no uncertain terms that such subjects 'should never be circulated in a memo'. The author replied that he had 'never written a memo like that', and that he had discussed the subject with people 'only through email'. In their organization, memos and email had in practice become two distinct genres; they had acquired two distinct meanings (with which the manager was perhaps not yet familiar). What was appropriate to communicate in one genre was inappropriate in the other. The boss misread the author's message (not necessarily his words) because he took what was intended as one genre (one form of communication) to be another.

We wish to generalize this sense of 'organizational genre' in defining what we mean by tacit group knowledge. For our purposes, 'organizational genre' applies not only to the distinctive and useful meanings a given group attaches to its various literary artefacts. It also applies to its various physical and social artefacts – that is, to different types of things (technologies or products, for example) and to different types of activities (such as ways of doing a task or types of meetings). These genres are not explicitly learned or known (although they can, for example, have explicit counterparts such as a label or a name). Their meanings emerge and undergo constant confirmation and/or modification through a kind of 'negotiation in practice' as they are used in the context of the group's ongoing 'real work'. What an organizational genre means at any one time is, in a sense, the accretion or product of the history of its use: it is meaning laid down in past use, and tapped into or 're-evoked' each time the members of the group use it in subsequent work. Accordingly, organizational genres have useful meaning solely in the context of a given group's practices – in this sense, they are possessed or 'held in common' by that group and are unique to it.

Two organizations, for example, could have *ad hoc* workgroup meetings, in each case called 'gatherings', that to an outsider could appear to be a single kind of semiformal update. However, the meaning that 'gathering' has within each organization could be immensely different from its meaning in the other. In one, a 'gathering' could be understood by that organization's members to be where 'the real decisions' are made. In the other, it could be seen as a time to make subtle political moves. The events are alike. The names are the same. The genres are different. In each case, what 'gathering' means is known by the members of that organization; it is group knowledge. And that knowledge can be used effectively or ineffectively (as were 'email' and 'memo' in the above example) without any explicit discussion ever occurring. Accordingly, it is also tacit knowledge. For our purposes, then, this expanded sense of genre defines what we mean by group/tacit knowledge.

As group/tacit knowledge, genres do epistemically distinct work. This is reflected in a corporate executive's remarks on how a group of senior managers has made use of their organization's mission statement. 'The senior staff developed the statement', he reported, 'and the group has a sense of what it means, and we make use of that meaning in our discussions.' The group's 'sense' of what the mission statement means does not refer to its text but to the mission statement itself. Like 'novel' or 'memo' or 'gathering', it has become a genre within that group; it has acquired, in practice, tacit meaning that is known by the group. It can be used appropriately or inappropriately, effectively or ineffectively, but only in the context of group practice: as tacit/group knowledge (as an organizational genre), 'mission statement' does the epistemically distinct work of giving shape and direction to the group's discussions. This is underscored by the executive's next remark. 'But when I think about the statement on my own,' he reflected, 'it can . . . lead my thinking in directions I wouldn't go if I were working on the same issues along with members of the group.' How the genre functions within group practice is distinct from its role in the executive's thinking on his own. The group's 'sense' of what the mission statement means exemplifies what we have in mind by tacit knowledge possessed (or held in common) by a group.

Adding knowing to knowledge

Individuals and groups make use of knowledge in interaction with the things and activities of the social and physical world. Knowledge, as we have said, gives particular shape, meaning, and discipline to our interactions with the world. At the same time, it has been our contention that not all of what we know in interacting with the world lies in our knowledge: some also lies in our actions themselves. Riding a bicycle requires that we use tacit knowledge in interaction with a bicycle in motion: some of what we know in being able to ride is in that interaction itself. For the manager mentioned above, being able to have effective communication with his colleagues required using the right genre ('email' rather than 'memo') in his interactions with messages (the action of interpreting them) and their authors (the action of conversing with them): some of what he knows in fostering successful communication in his organization is in those interactions themselves. In the example of the workgroup, a productive meeting is the product of the group using the genre 'the gathering' to help give the 'right' shape and meaning to the interactions that take place in their weekly sessions: some of what they know in conducting productive meetings is in their interactions with one another.

Each of these is an example of dynamic affordance – of what becomes possible when knowledge is used as a tool in the context of situated activity. Each is also an example of the importance of both knowledge and knowing in understanding the role played by what we know in organized human activity. It is by adding knowing to knowledge that we can begin to account for the relationship between what we know and what we do. And it is also how we can begin to see how new knowledge and knowing are generated.

Figure 4.4 shows the four forms of knowledge from Figure 4.3, the focus of the epistemology of possession, with a circle superimposed that represents knowing, the focus of the epistemology of practice. The arrows suggest active use of knowledge in our interaction with the social and physical world. Within this interaction lies what we have called the generative dance.

Knowing does not sit statically on top of knowledge. Quite the contrary: since knowing is an aspect of our interaction with the world, its relationship with knowledge is dynamic. Each of the forms of knowledge is brought into play by knowing when knowledge is used as a tool in interaction with the world. Knowledge, meanwhile, gives shape and discipline to knowing.[8] It is this reciprocal interplay of knowledge and knowing that we call 'bridging epistemologies'.

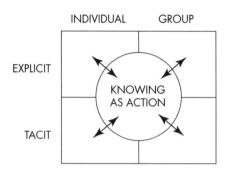

FIGURE 4.4 *Adding knowing to knowledge*

It is by bridging epistemologies that it is possible to draw among the four forms of knowledge within the same activity. Individual and group knowledge are both used, for example, in activities that dynamically afford both the practice of a given skill by an individual and 'trying it out' by a group learning it – as when a choreographer teaches through demonstrations while a dance troupe follows. The group acquires tacit knowledge in practice as they develop a useful understanding, for example, of the moves employed in the piece through interacting with the demonstrations of the instructor (Cook, 1982; Lave and Wenger, 1991). It is within this interaction, moreover, that the troupe's new knowledge (genres) and new forms of knowing (performing the dance) are generated (a generative dance – literally).

What we are proposing here is more than a shift in language; it is a shift in focus from performing operations on existing knowledge to making something new. It is a shift in perspective that is meant to provoke different ways of assessing the role of what is known (both as knowledge and knowing) in an organization's ability to learn, to maintain quality, to develop competencies, to innovate, etc. Organizations not only create knowledge, they also – and usually primarily – create goods and services. In doing so, they need to be increasingly innovative. And this requires, we believe, attention not only to what they possess, but also to how they practice. This calls for a broadening of focus from one epistemology to two, including the generative potential of interplay between them.

In this sense, the generative dance entails productive inquiry in a substantial and robust sense: it is not only productive as a team is productive when it meets a preset quota; it is truly *generative*. By this we mean that it is a source of innovation, of productive change – as when a team invents new ways of working more effectively. In a very basic sense, for example, the activity that conversation affords is not limited to a merely additive back and forth exchange of information. When Emma says to Andrew 'I've been doing it this way', Andrew not only adds that knowledge to his own, but he also takes it into the context of his own experiences, skills, sensitivities, and the like (and vice versa when Andrew makes his reply). By placing Emma's knowledge into Andrew's contexts, the conversation can evoke novel associations, connections, and hunches – it can generate new insights and new meaning. As everyone has experienced, a conversation's back-and-forth not only dynamically affords the exchange of knowledge, it can also afford the generation of new knowledge, since each remark can yield new meaning as it is resituated in the evolving context of the conversation. Through conversation, Emma and Andrew can negotiate a joint understanding of what 'doing it this way' means. This shared meaning, then, constitutes for them the genre 'Emma's way', which, in turn, can become an innovative and more effective means to read, understand, and carry out their work together. In this way, conversation affords more than an exchange in which the net sum of knowledge remains the same; it dynamically affords a *generative dance* within which the creation of new knowledge and new ways of using knowledge is possible.

Engaging in such conversation is a practice that does epistemic work; it is a form of knowing. Knowing entails the use of knowledge as a tool in the interaction with the world. This interaction, in turn, is a bridging, a linking, of knowledge and knowing. And bridging epistemologies makes possible the generative dance, which is the source of innovation. The generative dance, within the doing of work, constitutes the ability to generate new knowledge and new ways of using knowledge – which knowledge alone cannot do. And which the organizations of the future cannot afford to neglect.

IMPLICATIONS

We have found the perspective outlined above to have far-reaching implications for our work, in theory and in practice, and in assessing the work of others. Seeing each of the four forms of knowledge as unique, finding knowledge and knowing to be distinct, seeing how different epistemic work is done by different forms of knowledge and knowing, and understanding the notions of dynamic affordance and the generative dance – all this has not left our sense of how groups can and do work undisturbed. Below we briefly sketch out three cases that help make clearer some of the actionable and theoretically significant implications of this perspective.

The first case is drawn from Nonaka and Takeuchi's work on the 'knowledge-creating company' (1995). Among their insightful explorations of 'knowledge creating' is a case of a company's development of a breadmaking machine. We build on their case, and argue that the perspective we have put forth here expands and makes more robust their notion of 'knowledge creation'. The second case deals with three Boston-area workshops that make world-class flutes. What the flutemakers know that enables them to make instruments of the highest quality, we argue, is found both in the knowledge they possess and in the ways they interact with the instruments and each other. The third case is a brief look at how a group of mechanical engineers in Xerox have created innovative *new* technologies in part through generative interactions with *old* mechanisms.

Machine design

In their study of 'the knowledge-creating company' Nonaka and Takeuchi (1995) illustrate what they call the 'conversion' of tacit knowledge into explicit knowledge with the example of a company's development of a breadmaking machine. A good breadmaking machine must be able to knead dough properly. Yet, Nonaka and Takeuchi note, this is something 'which is essentially tacit knowledge possessed by master bakers' (p. 63). So one of the company's software developers became an apprentice to a prominent hotel's head baker. She was then able, according to Nonaka and Takeuchi's interpretation, to 'transfer' the tacit knowledge she acquired in working with the master baker to the engineers who were designing the machine's kneading mechanism by 'converting' it into explicit knowledge 'by using the phrase "twisting stretch"' (p. 104). The engineers used this knowledge in their work on the mechanism, and the software developer evaluated the results in a 'trial-and-error process [that] continued for several months' (p. 104). Ultimately a good mechanism was produced. Nonaka and Takeuchi's argument, then, is that the tacit knowledge the software developer acquired by 'observing and imitating the head baker' was converted into explicit knowledge through the use of the phrase 'twisting stretch' (p. 105), which, along with the engineers' technological knowledge, enabled the group to produce a prototype of the machine (p. 106). In this way, they argue, the group was engaged in 'knowledge creation'.

We interpret this example somewhat differently. Yet, we believe an interpretation from the perspective of the generative dance serves to strengthen Nonaka and Takeuchi's central claims about 'knowledge creation'.

We see in the case the same distinct epistemological forms we saw in the bike-riding example, but now also at the organizational level. For us. the case is also an instance of bridging epistemologies, where the practices of the group (its ways of knowing) enabled it to draw simultaneously on different forms of knowledge possessed by different people. In this way, the individual tacit knowledge of the software developer and the explicit group knowledge of the engineers were both used by the team as a whole as tools within a productive inquiry (the trial-and-error process) that enabled them to design a successful kneading mechanism: various interactions by the group using specific tacit and explicit knowledge afforded the generation of both knowledge and new ways of knowing.

Following our interpretation, the example entails both 'bridging epistemologies' and the 'generative dance'. In making the machine, the design team drew on all four types of knowledge (by bridging epistemologies). There was the explicit technical knowledge each member of the team possessed. We imagine that there were also explicit group stories or metaphors, since such are all but universally found in groups. Individual tacit knowledge comes into play in both the master baker's skill and in what the apprenticed developer acquired. And there was group tacit knowledge, we claim, in the form of the useful meaning that 'twisting stretch' (as a genre) came to have for them (more on this in a moment).

In addition to the use of the different forms of knowledge, there was also knowing – that is, epistemic work that was part of the team's interaction with machine parts, bread dough, and each other. This interaction (this way of knowing) entailed use of the team's various bits of knowledge as tools. The interaction also involved dynamic affordance within which (alone) the team was able to recognize and make use of the knowledge associated with the term 'twisting stretch' (just as being able to ride a bicycle requires the dynamic affordance of being on a bicycle in motion in order to make use of the knowledge associated with 'turn this way'). In particular, the term 'twisting stretch' referred to both the individual tacit knowledge of the developer and the tacit knowledge of the group. Using the term in the trial-and-error process provided a way of going back and forth between the two. In essence, the term functioned as a kind of 'boundary object' (Star and Griesemer, 1989) that straddled breadmaking and machine making. Through the successive iterations of mechanism design, the engineers negotiated with the developer the proper meaning and use of the term in application to the motion from breadmaking that they were aiming to capture in a machine operation. In this way, the meaning of the term 'twisting stretch' became a genre for the team as a whole (i.e. group tacit knowledge): it was the way they identified and understood the 'right' movement in both breadmaking and machine making. By bridging knowledge and knowing in actual interaction with the machine and each other (that is, by treating knowledge as a tool of knowing), the team was able to use the term 'twisting stretch' to draw on both individual and group tacit knowledge simultaneously in practice.

The generative dance can also be seen in the 'twisting stretch' example. 'Twisting stretch' as a genre (the shared meaning of the term), and the ability to use it in designing the prototype, were *new* things – a *new* bit of knowledge and a *new* way of knowing. They were not variant expressions of knowledge that already existed. They were created, we maintain, through the generative dance. That is, the design team used explicit and tacit knowledge as tools in interaction with machine parts and one another in an instance of productive inquiry that ultimately generated new knowledge and knowing. One of the team's aims was for the engineers to acquire a sense of the proper kneading motion. This entailed interaction between the engineers' machine making (a way of knowing) and the software developer's tacit knowledge (associated with her breadmaking). This resulted in the *generation* of the genre 'twisting stretch' (the group knowledge of what the term means). It was *not* tacit knowledge converted into explicit knowledge, it was *new* knowledge generated by the team. As a bit of knowledge, 'twisting stretch' became a meaningfully useful tool in two forms of knowing: the software developer's breadmaking and the engineers' machine making.

It is our focus on new knowledge and new knowing that leads us to prefer the concept of 'generating' to that of 'converting' (as used by Nonaka and Takeuchi). 'Conversion' tends to suggest an operation that is *applied to* knowledge rather than a concrete interaction with the world that generates knowledge. In converting feet to meters, an equation is applied to the measurement in feet and yields a measurement in meters, *without going back to the object at hand* to remeasure it. In our view, given one kind of knowledge, the only way to get the other is precisely *by going back to the object at hand* and *interacting* with it. For us, the 'trial-and-error process' Nonaka and Takeuchi identify is an example of just this sort of interaction with the world. What the design team did was not a conversion process applied to the software developer's tacit knowledge; it was an exercise in productive inquiry carried out by the group in interaction with bread dough, machine parts, and each other. This interaction dynamically afforded the use of both explicit and tacit knowledge, and ultimately generated new knowledge and a new way of knowing.

Flutemakers

The case of the three flute companies that manufacture world-class instruments allows us to take these notions further. They are particularly illustrative of the notion of dynamic affordance and its role in the generative dance.

The Boston workshops produce flutes that are embraced by the flute world as instruments of the finest quality. And the flutes of each workshop have a distinctive character recognizable by knowledgeable flutists as the flute's 'feel' (generally, how the instrument feels when it is being played – not, incidentally, how it sounds). Both the high standard of quality and the unique character of each brand of flute are highly valued by the flute world.[9]

For most of their history, each workshop has had between 20 and 40 flutemakers (including those who are owners and managers) plus one or two office staff. The flutemakers work in teams, each flute being the product of a number of flutemakers, with each flutemaker working only on part of the instrument. (It is rare that a single person has the ability at any one time to make an entire flute, although some work on numerous aspects of flutemaking over the course of their careers.) A flutemaker, meanwhile, might work with a particular set of colleagues on one batch of flutes and with a different set on a later one. Over their history, the workshops have gone through generations of flutemakers (the oldest of the workshops dates from around 1900, the newest was established in 1977).

Because flutes are physical objects, the quality and character of each flute is inextricably tied to very fine degrees of dimension and tolerance in how their pieces work and fit together. Many of these dimensions and tolerances, however, are not known or used explicitly by the flutemakers. Rather, they are set by judgments of hand or eye. Typically, each flutemaker works on his or her part of the flute until it meets his or her standard of appearance and/or feel. Then it is handed on to the next flutemaker, who judges the work of the first by his or her own standards. If the work is not 'right', it goes back to the previous flutemaker to be reworked until both are satisfied. Some measurement tools are used, such as calipers and feeler gauges; but even when a part is measured, it is also checked out by feel or by eye, which are the final courts of appeal.

When an apprentice joins a workshop there are many things he or she must learn (apprenticeships have taken up to five years). Elements of what needs to be learned reflect all four forms of knowledge. There are concepts and rules about the types of parts, how they are connected, which tools are used for which functions, and so on. There are the skills needed to make flutes with the 'right feel'. These bits of explicit and tacit knowledge are learned and used by the individual apprentices just as they are used daily by master flutemakers.

At the group level, there are stories and metaphors used explicitly among flutemakers that help guide and co-ordinate their work. At one of the workshops flutemakers would argue that a piece of work or a new company policy ought to be 'the way the old man would want it', referring to the founder of the company (this continued long after 'the old man' had retired and died). There are also genres that constitute the shared meaning of the 'right way' to use certain equipment (feeler gauges, for example) or how to identify and understand what is wrong with a piece of work. When a part is handed back to a previous worker, for example, it can come with a comment such as 'this is a clunky one'. The flutemakers then hand the piece back and forth discussing its 'clunkiness'. This interaction with the piece and with each other dynamically affords a negotiation in practice as to what exactly 'clunky' means in reference to the piece at hand and concerning what work needs to be done to it. When the meaning associated with 'clunky' becomes commonly used by the flutemakers in recognizing, discussing and, working on subsequent problems, it functions as a genre in that workshop.

The examples above reflect different forms of knowledge that fit the four categories of the traditional epistemology. But having such knowledge is only part of what is needed to make world-class flutes. Knowing is also required. Accordingly, it is typical for an apprentice to work on flutes starting on his or her first day in the shop: he or she engages in the practice of flutemaking, and begins to acquire not only knowledge but also ways of knowing. An apprentice may be told explicitly that 'these keys need to work more solidly'. But it is only through practice, through actual working jointly with other flutemakers on the piece, that he or she will 'get a feel' for what 'solidly' actually means in that shop ('solidly' could mean quite a different thing at one of the other workshops). When a master flutemaker says something such as 'this is what we call clunky', an apprentice can only know what that means by learning what it feels like – and a master flutemaker can only agree that an apprentice's work ultimately feels right by feeling the piece.

This is also true of accomplished flutemakers: part of what they know is in the daily handing of pieces back and forth and negotiating that a piece of work looks or feels right. Interaction with the instruments and other flute-makers dynamically affords the use, in practice, of the different forms of knowledge possessed by the flutemakers, individually and as a group. Another part of what the flutemakers know, another part of their epistemic work, is in their interactions themselves. The genre 'clunky' is a tool flute-makers use in their interactions with each other; it does the epistemic work of group tacit knowledge. Being able to recognize when 'clunky' gives way to the 'right feel' and being able to negotiate that with fellow flutemakers are also part of what flutemakers know, they are instances of epistemic work done as part of the practice of world-class flutemaking. And they are instances of knowing. The interaction with the instruments and among flutemakers also entails the generative dance; it is here that new knowledge and new ways of knowing are created. The back and forth between an apprentice and a master flutemaker, for example, dynamically affords two things at once: (1) the use, in practice, of existing tacit knowledge possessed by the master in judging the feel of the apprentice's work; and (2) the *generation* of new tacit knowledge and new ways of knowing for the apprentice. This is an instance of the generative dance.

An apprentice acquires new tacit knowledge in his or her interaction with the instrument and with a master flutemaker, and those interactions also dynamically afford the master using his or her tacit knowledge as a part of the practice of flutemaking. That is, the apprentice's *new* knowledge is *generated* in an interaction that has been given particular shape and form by the master's use of his or her *existing* knowledge. While on the surface this can appear to be a *transfer* of knowledge from the master to the apprentice, we see it as an interaction with the social and physical world (flutemakers and instrument parts) in which the master's knowledge is used and the apprentice's knowledge is *generated*.

The importance of tacit knowledge and its dissemination in organizations are also topics emphasized by Nonaka and Takeuchi (1995). For them this dissemination, including its role in the creation of new knowledge, occurs in a process they call 'socialization'. They hold that 'the sharing of tacit knowledge . . . is a limited form of knowledge creation' because unless tacit knowledge 'becomes explicit, it cannot be easily leveraged by the organization as a whole'. They then contend that 'Organizational knowledge creation is a continuous and dynamic interaction between tacit and explicit knowledge' (p. 70).

We propose three shifts that we believe build on and strengthen Nonaka and Takeuchi's general insight. First, as we have noted in detail above, we contend that it is not possible, under any circumstances, for tacit knowledge to become explicit (or vice versa). We do hold, however, that one can be a useful tool in the generation of the other through productive inquiry.

Second, since we hold that explicit and tacit knowledge are generated and disseminated each in its own right, whether either can 'be easily leveraged by the organization as a whole' depends, in our view, on the specific needs and resources that an organization has at hand in a given situation. The generation of explicit knowledge can, at times, be necessary to the dissemination of tacit knowledge (or even to making tacit knowledge more 'easily leveraged by the organization as a whole'). However, this is determined by its usefulness as a tool in productive inquiry in a given situation, not by general characteristics of explicit and tacit knowledge, as Nonaka and Takeuchi suggest. If explicit knowledge is needed, then it is explicit knowledge that needs to be generated and made sharable; if tacit knowledge is needed, then it must be generated and made sharable (as we see in the flute case). Or both (as is found in the case of the breadmaking machine).

Finally, for us, the production of new knowledge does not lie in 'a continuous interaction between tacit and explicit knowledge' but rather in our interaction with the world. Specifically, it lies in the use of knowledge (explicit and/or tacit) as tools of productive inquiry (of the sort we have called 'knowing') as part of our dynamic interaction with the things of the social and physical world.

Paper handling

The significance of interaction with the *physical* world to dynamic affordance and the generation of knowledge and knowing found particular meaning for us in a recent research project in Xerox. In this research, it was discovered that, for a group of design teams, interacting with *old* artefacts is often a source of insights that are valuable in designing *new* technologies.

As part of a broader research project, what is known in Xerox about the design of 'paper paths' was examined.[10] These are the various electro-mechanical devices that move blank paper from a paper tray through a copier, printer, fax machine, etc. as it is 'marked' and then out of the machine as a printed page. These are surprisingly sophisticated devices, and there are often significant challenges in designing them as product cycles and technological innovations call for their evolution and change. This work is typically done by small teams composed mainly of mechanical engineers.

This expertise in paper path design is one of Xerox's traditional core competencies. Yet, through the course of the recent research, we came to recognize how some very valuable aspects of this competency are also embodied in the paper path mechanisms themselves. With time, engineers can forget, retire, move on, and the like – including, over enough time, entire cohorts or generations of engineers. By one way of thinking, then, some features of a given paper path's design and functioning, particularly subtle or sophisticated features, would no longer be available to Xerox. But the research revealed that when design teams sense that there is something in an old paper path that could be of use in designing new ones, they pull out the old one and begin to work with it. It is clear in this 'working with' old mechanisms that the teams are after tacit knowledge, not explicit knowledge (they have the technical drawings for that). In fact, they refer to being interested in how the mechanisms 'sound, feel, and work together' when in operation and when being assembled and disassembled.

This case complements Nonaka and Takeuchi's breadmaking machine example. In that example, what the engineers needed was *explicit* knowledge about the 'twisting stretch' movement so they could design a mechanism that would replicate it. While in the paper path example, the engineers needed *tacit* knowledge about the feel, sound, and operation of older mechanisms, which they could use in designing new ones. Moreover, in the Xerox engineers' interactions with the older mechanisms, tacit knowledge was leveraged by the organization as a whole without requiring the use of explicit knowledge.

This research has led us to believe that we need radically to rethink what is needed to create and support 'core competencies'. Since part of Xerox's paper path competency is embodied in old artefacts, design teams need to have the kind of 'hands on' interaction with those artefacts that affords the recapture or (to follow our terminology) the regeneration of those particular bits of knowledge associated with that part of the competency. For the design team, this regeneration occurs as part of group practice: their dynamic interaction with the old paper path apparatus affords the acquisition by the team of (tacit) knowledge about significant aspects of how the mechanism looks, feels, and sounds when it is operating well. It can also afford the identification of significant dimensions, tolerances, and functions (explicit knowledge) associated with the look, sound, and feel of proper operation.[11]

We also believe there is a need to rethink how competency is distributed – in particular, how it can be found both in what individuals and groups know and in their practices. Part of Xerox's competency in paper handling is embodied in existing artefacts, part in knowledge people possess. Part also lies in the ability of design teams to interact with old artefacts in ways that afford the regeneration, for the team, of the knowledge associated with those mechanisms. That is, the ability of these groups to do this is also part of Xerox's paper handling competency.

A design team's practices also include the generation of knowledge new to the group. This can be seen, for example, in the case of genres. In the context of their interaction with old mechanisms, a team will identify (through negotiation in practice) which aspects of how a mechanism sounds, feels, and works are significant and which not. That is, bits of machine design and behavior will take on particular meaning (they will become genres), and those meanings will play a role in how the team frames, understands, or reads both their further interactions with the old mechanisms and their design work on the new one.

Finally, we would note that putting the knowledge associated with the older mechanisms in the context of new product design efforts results in more than adding old knowledge to new projects. It is a dynamic practice that can also afford the generation of new ideas and new ways of working – something that is not in the knowledge alone. Given this, we argue that understanding such things as the retrieval of 'intellectual capital' solely as a matter of tapping into a knowledge base (that is, as solely concerned with knowledge) leaves untapped (as well as unsupported, unrecognized, and underutilized) the generative power of the practices associated with recapturing old knowledge.

CONCLUSION

This chapter aims to broaden the existing understanding of what and how people know, as that relates to the epistemological dimension of organized human activity. We have offered the notions of distinct kinds of knowledge, productive inquiry, dynamic affordance, and the generative character of knowing to enrich such related themes as organization knowledge, knowledge creation, knowledge-based organizations, the management of intellectual capital, knowledge work, etc. Clearly, the perspective we have proposed both suggests and would benefit from further theoretical and empirical work. Among the numerous areas where further work could be done are the following.

How might issues of core competency be broadened if we were to ask not only what knowledge is entailed, but also what forms of knowing (i.e. how particular groups use the knowledge they have or acquire)? We see the core competencies of the flute workshops, for example, to include, along with the four forms of knowledge distributed among individuals and groups, ways of knowing reflected in the interactions flutemakers have with each other and the instruments. Such knowledge and knowing are essential to the organizations' world-class status, yet they are also unique to each workshop, and therefore cannot be transferred from one company to another. (In fact, when accomplished flutemakers have moved from one workshop to another, they have had to undergo 'retraining' in order to do work consistent with the new company's style and standards.) Thus, there is a need for a better understanding and better models of how this essentially nontransferable or 'situated' dimension of knowledge and knowing, as elements of an organization's core competency, can be 'generated in' (rather than 'transferred to') other groups or organizations.

There is a need for more case studies of knowledge-creating organizations, knowledge work, and knowledge management that focus not only on the body of knowledge that an organization acquires, stores, and transfers. Equally important are the ways organizations can dynamically afford, within the situated practices of ordinary daily work, the productive inquiry essential to ongoing innovation.

There is also the very practical question of how training and educational programs can be redesigned. Such programs need to take as their aim both passing on knowledge to individuals *and* creating situations that help groups develop practices (ways of knowing) that make use of knowledge in new, innovative, and more productive ways.[12]

We hope that an expanded understanding of what and how people know can help provide an enriched, more robust way of assessing, supporting, and honoring the epistemological dimension of all 'real work', which alone gives life and power to such concepts as core competency, knowledge creation, knowledge work, and intellectual capital.

ACKNOWLEDGMENTS

For their careful reading of and valuable comments on earlier drafts of this work the authors are indebted to Johan de Kleer, Daniel Denison, Paul Duguid, Larry

Hickman, Kristian Kreiner, Charles F. Sabel, Edgar Schein, Sim Sitkin, Susan Stucky, Jeanne Vickers, Hendrik Wagenaar, Jay Zimmerman, and Betty Zucker. They are also indebted to the anonymous reviewers of this chapter and, in particular, to Paul Adler for their exceptionally provocative and useful comments. Portions of the research that contributed to the writing of this chapter were supported by a grant from the National Science Foundation (#9320927).

NOTES

1. The term 'epistemology' refers properly to the study of knowledge, including questions concerning what counts as knowledge and how bodies of knowledge can be systematically organized. More casually, it can also refer to knowledge and bodies of knowledge themselves (rather the way 'ecology' can refer both to the study of environmental systems and to those systems themselves). We make use of both senses of the term (depending on the context).

2. By 'epistemic work' we refer to the work people must do to acquire, confirm, deploy, or modify what needs to be known in order for them to do what they do.

3. We are indebted to Susan Stucky of the Institute for Research on Learning and to J.-C. Spender for the initial idea of this 2 x 2 table.

4. Discussion of explicit and tacit knowledge has a long history and has not by any means come to consensus. The terms used, how they are related, and the realities they point to vary considerably. Ryle (1949), for example, cast the discussion in terms of what it means to 'know *how*', and to 'know *that*'. For some (including us) the two types of knowledge are seen as quite distinct, while others may see them as two ends of a continuum.

5. The ontological status of groups has long been an unresolved issue. For our purposes, we take the view that not every action by a human collective can be meaningfully or usefully reduced to an account of actions taken by the individuals in them (as the practices of coaches, orchestra conductors, and organizational managers would suggest). To this extent, we believe collectives can be coherently and usefully considered in their own right with respect to actions they perform and with regard to the possession of any knowledge used in those actions.

6. Schon (1983), whose work also draws strongly on Dewey, makes a similar distinction in discussing what he sees as the need to shift from pure technical rationality to what he calls 'reflection-in-action' in professional practice.

7. This sense of significant properties arising in the interaction between the self (or group) and the world is also a central theme in the work of the twentieth-century Japanese philosopher Watsuji (1961).

8. Our language here (and at other points) suggests a resonance with structuration theory, especially with Giddens (see, for example, Giddens, 1979, especially Chapter 2; and Cohen, 1989, especially Chapter 1). Structuration theory's treatment of praxis as constitutive of social structure, while social structure informs praxis, parallels our characterization of knowledge as brought into play by knowing, while knowing is disciplined by knowledge. Some might reject any such parallel, given that our focus is essentially epistemological, while structuration theory (particularly Giddens himself) deliberately eschews epistemological concerns in favor of ontological ones. Others may see our treatment of the interaction of knowledge and knowing as an instance of structuration. For our part, we find the

parallel a provocative one, both epistemologically and ontologically. Although a systematic consideration of this similarity is not within the scope of this chapter, we would make the following observations. We do not take the relationship between knowledge and knowing to be nothing more than a straightforward example of the more general relationship between structure and agency found in structuration theory (if for no other reason than that we believe neither structuration theory nor pragmatism makes the other epistemologically and/or ontologically redundant). At the same time, we believe that a fuller investigation of pragmatist epistemology and structuration ontology could find in the practice of productive inquiry a way to help the epistemological more fully rejoin the ontological within the purview of structuration theory.

9. A fuller presentation of this case focusing on organizational learning can be found in Cook and Yanow, 1993. An extensive presentation and analysis of the case, focusing on tacit skills, judgment, and apprenticeship within the cultural context of groups can be found in Cook, 1982.

10. This research was conducted as part of a project headed by Robert S. Bauer of Xerox Corporation and Estee Solomon Gray of Congruity. We are indebted to them for this example and for the project's influence on our thinking in general.

11. In addition to innovation, the use of older artefacts can also be seen in the case of training. Clark and Wheelwright (1992) have observed that Braun maintains a collection of their old products for use in training new product designers.

12. The theories and practices of 'progressive education' might offer some provocative points of reference in this regard.

REFERENCES

Anderson, R. and W. Sharrock (1993) *Can Organizations Afford Knowledge?* Xerox Technical Report EPC-92-104.

Argyris, C. and D. A. Schon (1978) *Organizational Learning*, Addison-Wesley, Reading, MA.

Bourdieu, P. (1977) *Outline of a Theory of Practice*, Cambridge University Press, Cambridge.

Brown, J. S., A. Collins and P. Duguid (1989) 'Situated cognition and the culture of learning', *Educational Researcher*, 18(1): 32–41.

—— and P. Duguid (1991) 'Organizational learning and communities-of-practice: toward a unified view of working, learning, and innovation', *Organ. Sci.*, 2: 40–57.

——, —— (1994) 'Borderline issues: social and material aspects of design', *Human-Computer Interaction*, 9(1): 3–36.

Clark, K. B. and S. C. Wheelwright (1992) *Managing New Project and Process Development*, Free Press, New York.

Cohen, I. J. (1989) *Structuration Theory: Anthony Giddens and the Constitution of Social Life*, St Martin's Press, New York.

Cohen, M. D. and P. Bacdayan (1994) 'Organizational routines are stored as procedural memory: evidence from a laboratory study', *Organ. Sci.*, 5(4): 554–568.

Cook, S. D. N. (1982) 'Part of what a judgment is'. Ph.D. dissertation. Massachusetts Institute of Technology (available from the author or from University Microfilms).

—— (1994) 'Autonomy, interdependence and moral governance: pluralism in a rocking boat', *Amer. Behavioral Sci.*, 38(1).

—— and D. Yanow (1993) 'Culture and organizational learning', *J. Management Inquiry*, 2(4): 373–90.

Gaver, W. W. (1991) 'Technology affordances', *Proceedings of CHI '91*. ACM Press, New Orleans: 79–84.

—— (1996) 'Affordances for interaction: the social is material for design', *Ecological Psych.*, 8(2): 111–129.

Gibson, J. (1979) *The Ecological Approach to Visual Perception*, Houghton Mifflin, New York.

Giddens, A. (1979) *Central Problems in Social Theory: Action, Structure and Contradiction in Social Analysis*, University of California Press, Berkeley and Los Angeles.

Hamel, G. and C. K. Prahalad (1994) *Competing for the Future*, Harvard Business School Press, Boston.

Hickman, L. (1990) *John Dewey's Pragmatic Technology*, Indiana University Press, Bloomington.

Hutchins, E. (1991) 'The social organization of distributed cognition', in L. B. Resnick, J. M. Levine and S. D. Teasley (eds) *Perspectives on Socially Shared Cognition*, American Psychological Association, Washington, DC.

Kogut, B. and U. Zander (1996) 'What firms do? – Coordination, identity, and learning', *Organ. Sci.*, 7(5): 502–519.

Krogh, G. von and J. Roos (1995) *Organizational Epistemology*, St. Martin's Press, New York.

Lave, J. and E. Wenger (1991) *Situated Learning: Legitimate Peripheral Participation*, Cambridge University Press, Cambridge.

Leonard-Barton, D. (1995) *Wellsprings of Knowledge: Building and Sustaining the Sources of Innovation*, Harvard Business School Press, Boston.

March, J. G. and J. P. Olsen (1976) 'Organizational learning and the ambiguity of the past', *Ambiguity and Choice in Organizations*, Universitetsfortaget, Oslo, Norway.

Nonaka, I. (1994) 'A dynamic theory of organizational knowledge creation', *Organ. Sci.*, 5(1): 14–37.

—— and H. Takeuchi (1995) *The Knowledge Creating Company*, Oxford University Press, New York.

Orlikowski, W. J. and J. Yates (1994) 'Genre repertoire: the structuring of communicative practices in organization', *Admin. Sci. Quart.*, 39: 541–574.

Orr, J. E. (1990) 'Sharing knowledge, celebrating identity: war stories and community memory in a service culture', in D. S. Middleton and D. Edwards (eds) *Collective Remembering: Memory in Society*, Sage, London.

—— (1996) *Talking About Machines: An Ethnography of a Modern Job*, Cornell University Press, Ithaca, NY.

Ortega y Gasset, Jose (1961a) [orig. 1941] 'History as a system', in *History as a System*, W. W. Norton, New York.

—— (1961b) [orig. 1941] 'Man the technician', in *History as a System*, W. W. Norton, New York.

Polanyi, M. (1983) [orig. 1966] *The Tacit Dimension*, Peter Smith, Magnolia, MA.

Rorty, R. (1982) *Consequences of Pragmatism*, University of Minnesota Press, Minneapolis.

Ryle, G. (1949) *The Concept of Mind*, Hutchinson, London.

Schon, D. A. (1983) *The Reflective Practitioner: How Professionals Think in Action*, Basic Books, New York.

Simon, H. A. (1991) 'Bounded rationality and organizational learning', *Organ. Sci.*, 2(1): 125–134.

Sims, H. P., Jr., D. A. Gioia, and associates (1986) *The Thinking Organization; Dynamics of Organizational Social Cognition*, Jossey-Bass, San Francisco.

Sitkin, S. B. (1992) 'Learning through failure: the strategy of small losses', *Res. Organ. Behavior*, 14: 231–261.

Spender, J-C. (1996) 'Competitive advantage from tacit knowledge? Unpacking the concept and its strategic implications', in B. Moingeon and A. Edmondson (eds) *Organisational Learning and Competitive Advantage*, Sage, London.

Star, S. L. and J. R. Griesemer (1989) 'Institutional ecology, "translations" and boundary objects: amateurs and professionals in Berkeley's Museum of Vertebrate Zoology, 1907–39', *Soc. Stud. Sci.*, 19: 387–420.

Stewart, T. A. (1997) *Intellectual Capital: the New Wealth of Organizations*, Doubleday/Currency, New York.

Turner, S. (1994) *The Social Theory of Practices: Tradition, Tacit Knowledge, and Presuppositions*, University of Chicago Press, Chicago.

Vickers, G. (1976) 'Technology and culture'. Invited paper given at the Division for Study and Research in Education, Massachusetts Institute of Technology, Cambridge, MA.

Watsuji, T. (1961) *Climate and Culture*, Monbusho, Tokyo.

Weick, K. E. (1991) 'The nontraditional quality of organizational learning', *Organ. Sci.*, 2(1): 116–124.

—— and Roberts, K. H. (1993) 'Collective mind in organizations: heedful interrelating on flight decks', *Admin. Sci. Quart.*, 38: 357–381.

—— and F. Westley (1996) 'Organizational learning: affirming an oxymoron', *Handbook of Organization Studies*, Sage, Thousand Oaks, CA.

Wenger, E. (1997) *Communities of Practice: Learning, Meaning and Identity*, Cambridge University Press, Cambridge.

5

Managing Japanese Organizational Knowledge Creation: the Difference

*Tim Ray**

In 1950, MacArthur's economic experts advised that the Japanese economy's best course in the post-war era would be to make 'knickknacks' – their word – for underdeveloped countries (Fingleton, 1997: 2)

Patronized but undaunted, Japan has become the world's second largest economy with a seat next to the United States at the high table of economically significant nations. It has moved from competing mainly as a low-wage, low-cost supplier of goods that imitated Western designs to a country that epitomizes high-quality, high-reliability products. In the process, leading Japanese manufacturing firms have emerged as the custodians of world-beating knowledge about the virtues of continuous incremental innovation. Unlike Anglo-American market-rational entrepreneurship and Schumpeter's process of 'creative destruction' (Schumpeter, 1976: 83), Japan's post-war economic recovery has exploited what might be called *steady state* organizational knowledge creation. New technologies typically emerge from existing organizations as employees re-use and adapt individual skills and collective competencies to generate new knowledge – as illustrated by the transition from cameras to photocopiers.

Japan's stable organizations nest within a stable economic structure and organizational boundaries define a space for knowledge creation that exploits mutual understanding amongst individuals who spend their careers working together. This nested stability and the lack of labour mobility means that organizations are effective 'social containers' for accumulated individual and collective tacit knowledge. Shared know-how or 'sticky knowledge' (see Brown and Duguid, Chapter 2 of the present book) emerges readily within Japanese organizations, where close relationships amongst colleagues help meaningful information to flow easily. At the same time, insider values tend to exclude outsider-perspectives and Western-style personal networking; self-organizing communities of practice, for example, lack legitimacy (Ray,

* The Open University Business School

1998).[1] Expectations of lifelong loyalty mean that Japanese employees can only serve one master (head-hunting and job-hopping are considered unethical) and the organization's interaction with the wider knowledge-creating ecology centres on 'appropriate connections', such as links with suppliers or customers.

Relationships amongst permanent employees inside Japan's company-as-family organizations have automatic priority over other knowledge-creating relationships. The implicit obligations and sense of belonging that underpin the Japanese notion of 'our company' are not commensurate with Western expectations about explicit terms and conditions of employment and the possibility of moving to another employer if things do not go well. Japan's regular employees are committed to a long-term relationship with their employer and place organizational affiliation before personal expertise. There is an unwavering distinction between organizational insiders (*us*) and outsiders (*them*). From the point of view of interpreting Japanese knowledge creation, the organization rather than the individual is the more appropriate unit of analysis.

While there are significant differences amongst knowledge-creating processes in leading Western nations, Japan is the only advanced industrial country whose traditional culture owes almost nothing to Mediterranean origins (Dore, 1973: 419). After reflecting on why Japan does not fit easily with Western assumptions about knowledge creation, this chapter considers the evolution of Japan's economic structure and the role of Japanese organizational knowledge creation within that structure.

THE JAPAN PROBLEM

Many of the Westerners who flocked to Japan in the 1980s to discover the secret of miracle growth might have been bewildered by a group-oriented culture that does not conform to Western expectations about individual accountability and explicit reasoning. Japan's social etiquette stresses the subtle art of indirect communication, ritualized understatement about one's own achievements, and the significance of what is not said. It eschews hubris or open disagreement and dictates that guests be treated with respect. Hard-hitting questions from visitors – and especially the desire to know 'why?' – are politely countered by a search for more neutral topics of conversation.

Solace for the new army of confused Japan watchers started to emerge in the early 1990s – when the country's miracle growth faltered, just as the United States started to recover. It no longer seemed to matter that Japan's differences remained largely incomprehensible. As Western confidence improved, Anglo-American triumphalists proclaimed that Japan's recovery would depend on becoming 'more like us'. Progress in information and communication technologies, together with 'friction-free' data flows across cyberspace, encouraged the idea that international business culture would gravitate towards Anglo-American individualism and explicit knowledge transactions conducted in English. But, notwithstanding outward appearances that might resemble those of its Western counterparts, Japan's façade masks a fundamentally different approach to knowledge creation.

Although Japan has an American-style constitution (introduced by the occupation forces) and a legal framework that appears to guarantee individual rights (including equal employment opportunities for women), Japan's informal sanctions, taboos, customs, traditions, and implicit expectations emphasize an obligation to the group. Complying with these implicit conventions is an act of faith in a country where – as the famous saying warns – the nail that sticks out gets hammered down. Japan does not have a tradition of settling disputes by resorting to the law and – as if to underline the point – the chances of becoming a qualified lawyer are limited. In 1991, Japan had 14,400 licensed lawyers, rising to 16,800 by 1999, whereas the corresponding US figures were 700,000 and 900,000 respectively. Japan's institutions tend to link the past with the present and future in a way that emphasizes *change with continuity*. While the cumulative effects of incremental advance can be spectacular, the engine of progress is mainly concerned with producing more of the same. Substantial shifts in direction are comparatively rare and tend to be intertwined with foreign pressure.

Anglo-American market-rational entrepreneurship incorporates taken-for-granted expectations that individuals might seize opportunities to initiate change and seek recognition for being 'the nail that sticks out'. While experience at work generates sticky knowledge that gives organizations a sense of joint enterprise, this often vies with employee interest in communities of practice and knowledge-creating networks that criss-cross organizational boundaries. For Wenger (2000), communities of practice are the basic building blocks that make up a social learning system. They act as the 'social containers' for communal resources – such as language, routines, sensibilities, artefacts, tools, stories, styles, or whatever – that bind the community together and support the development of its collective competencies. Nevertheless, Schumpeterian 'creative destruction' associated with entrepreneurial economic development can undermine the relevance of established communities and foster the development of new communities, as practitioners regroup to pursue activities that are more congruent with their emerging interests.

Amid the upheaval of Anglo-American business systems, employers know that employees, who are recruited as agents to act on behalf of the organization, have underlying self-interests that might pull them in different directions – giving rise to the agency problem. Managing organizational knowledge creation is a matter of encouraging individual agents (who tend to align themselves with a multiplicity of communities of practice and social learning systems) to co-operate with the evolution of organizational objectives. In Japanese organizations, close community relationships within the organization enable members to act as a group to ostracize and retaliate against agents who violate their code.[2] The lack of a labour market for specialists coupled with a social prohibition on job-hopping mean that there is no alternative but to comply with the code. Lifetime loyalty is a taken-for-granted aspect of Japanese culture and Japan's work institutions have effectively redefined the agency problem.

Japan's company-as-family work organizations have been instrumental in the evolution of a different type of university system. The ranking of Japanese universities does not depend directly on research activities nor the quality of teaching, but on the extent to which graduates are able to secure permanent positions with a prestigious employer. Higher-ranking universities have harder entrance examinations and thereby select the country's elite. Graduation is virtually assured and many students view their undergraduate years as respite from a career shaped by on-the-job training. Salaries depend on time served with the employer. Compared to its Western counterparts, Japan produces few PhDs. Employers prefer bachelor or master level graduates who can more easily assimilate organizational culture. Attending graduate school can seriously damage the chance of securing a permanent position with a prestigious employer. Despite having less than half the population of Japan, the UK produces about eight times as many science doctorates per year. In social science, which is by far the largest single category of British doctorates, Japan's output is negligible.[3]

JAPAN: A DIFFERENT INDUSTRIAL HISTORY

The precursor to Japan's rapid industrialization was more than two centuries of self-imposed international isolation. Fearing that foreign religious influences would undermine its authority, the Tokugawa Shogunate secluded Japan from the outside world in 1639. At a time when entrepreneurial forces propelled the West into an industrial era, the Tokugawa Shogunate's system of stable government operated without serious opposition for more than 250 years. Feudal lords presided over domains where the ethical code of the warrior (bushidô), food production, and making things, all took precedence over trading for money. The lives of the lord and his retainers were linked by a sense of joint enterprise. Indigenous culture flourished and there was a steady stream of technological developments, along with notable progress in mathematics and the provision of elementary education (Odagiri and Goto, 1993, 1996).

The events that led to the birth of modern Japan were triggered by the arrival of Commodore Matthew Perry in 1853. American interest in using Japanese ports for provisioning and sheltering ships engaged in trade with China had prompted the US government to dispatch Perry with a letter demanding trade relations with Japan. The military superiority represented by Perry's 'black ships' forced Japan to acquiesce and precipitated events that caused the Tokugawa Shogunate to return sovereignty to the emperor. But the 1868 Meiji Restoration was neither a Norman Conquest nor a French Revolution – dominant groups in the old regime weakened, but subordinate or similar elements moved into their place (Mason and Caiger, 1972: 217).

Under the slogan *fukoku kyôhei* (rich nation, strong army) the Meiji government sought to establish a prosperous country that remained free from colonization by a Western power. The Meiji government took the initiative in almost every major industry – either by putting up capital or encouraging private investors – and government control over the economy became automatic (van Wolferen, 1990: 492–493). According to Chalmers Johnson (1995), Japan contrasts with market-rational Anglo-American capitalism – where government simply sets the rules of play – by being a 'plan-rational state' in which the government actively nurtures particular avenues of industrial development. More prosaically, it might be argued that Anglo-American concerns about government intervention resemble the hesitance of someone trying to get into a bath that is slightly too hot – with much concern about what part of the body to insert first, how far and for how long – whereas the Japanese state effectively created the industrial bathtub and is intimately bound up with the processes that control its water temperature. Mutual adhesion (*yuchaku*) binds the government to industry.

The Meiji government orchestrated the acquisition of a pick-and-mix selection of Western technology for exploitation according to Japanese precepts. Along with overseas missions, Japan employed some 2,400 foreigners from 23 different countries (Westney, 1987: 19). Its approach to comprehending and exploiting the desirable features of Western technology focused on re-inventing ideas within a Japanese context; thereby mimicking the technology's outward appearance and performance characteristics through intrinsically different development processes. Similarly the re-invention of Western institutions produced results that were more Japanese than many outsiders realized. When the National Diet (parliament) opened in 1890, Meiji rulers created a weak parliament and sought to counterbalance it with a strong bureaucracy, staffed by their own supporters (Johnson, 1992: 37). Parliament became concerned with ratifying rather than initiating policy.

GOVERNMENT CO-ORDINATION ACROSS A STABLE ECONOMIC STRUCTURE

By the First World War, Japan's version of co-ordinated capitalism was well established. In the early twentieth century *zaibatsu* (groups of companies owned and operated by a single family) became increasingly prominent and during the First World War entered a golden age as Japan supplied the Allies with munitions and other goods. War in Europe also reduced the supply of goods imported to Japan, allowing Japanese manufacturers to sell more at home and exploit access to international markets. But this trajectory of development became more difficult to sustain as Western competitors recovered after the war. Meanwhile, Japan's industrialization became increasingly connected with military expansionism.[4] In 1943, the Ministry of Commerce and Industry became the Ministry of Munitions, but reverted to its original title for the period 1945–49 before emerging as the Ministry of International Trade and Industry (MITI).

Japan's war machine pushed small and medium sized enterprises towards particular *zaibatsu*, thereby curtailing much of their freedom to negotiate business arrangements (Miyashita and Russell, 1996: 117) and reinforced the trend towards relatively fixed trading patterns. In the aftermath of the Second World War, Allied reformers unwittingly strengthened Japan's ability to operate as a plan-rational state by removing its military interests, thereby freeing the civilian bureaucracy from its greatest rival (Johnson, 1995: 29). Moreover, the limited impact of Allied attempts to dismantle the *zaibatsu* allowed scope for MITI to offer companies 'administrative guidance'. With the end of occupation in 1952, MITI exploited its links with industry to bring about horizontal *keiretsu* groupings based on banks (as opposed to a *zaibatsu*-style family holding companies), with the four largest *zaibatsu* re-emerging amongst the 'big six' *keiretsu*.

Horizontal *keiretsu* feature cross-share holdings, interlocking directorates (created when the *keiretsu* bank or leading group firms assign representatives to the boards of member companies), inter-group trade, and meetings amongst the presidents of member companies. Almost all the upper-level companies are simultaneously heads of their own vertical supply-chain *keiretsu* stacked, wedding-cake style, below the big names (Miyashita and Russell, 1996: 11). There are also distribution *keiretsu*, involving chains of dependent wholesalers and retailers that stretch from the top firm. Although the unthinkable is beginning to happen, it is being thought about in a distinctly Japanese manner. In 1999, the Dai-ichi Kangyo Bank, Fuji Bank and the Industrial Bank of Japan announced plans to integrate their businesses by forming a holding company, while the merger between Sumitomo and Sakura banks marked the apparent integration of two major *zaibatsu*-cum-*keiretsu* groupings – but the 'revolutionary' nature of these shifts in direction has been brokered according to give-and-take incrementalism.

Compared to Western market-style transactions with independent suppliers, Japan's production *keiretsu* are able to lean heavily on subcontractors and develop 'sticky knowledge' about just how far they can push them. Upper-level firms reduce costs by subcontracting to lower-level firms that have correspondingly lower status and labour costs. Firms at the top can avoid the discomfort of economic downturns by forcing lower-level firms to supply at lower prices. In the short term, these firms might be able to sustain periods of 'bicycle business' (*jitensha-sôgyô*) when they run at a loss as, by analogy with riding a bicycle, stopping means falling over. In circumstances where Western firms might simply go out of business and produce nothing (like fallen bicycles), Japan's stable economic structure tends to remain intact and is poised for rapid recovery when the upturn comes.

LIFETIME EMPLOYMENT?

Many in the West are apt to dismiss Japan's lifetime employment system as a luxury for ineffective workers or a threat to managerial efficiency that can no longer be afforded – but this misrepresents a system of obligations that do not translate into the logic of hire-and-fire market rational economies. Fingleton makes the point succinctly:

> No aspect of Japan's remarkable economy has been so consistently underestimated as its employment system. Because the system's three main principles – lifetime employment, company unions, and seniority pay – flout free-market ideals, Westerners consider it self-evidently incapable in the long run of withstanding global competition of 'more efficient' hire-and-fire labor system of the US and Europe. (Fingleton, 1995: 79)

To be sure, not everybody in Japan *works for life*. Most of Japan's female employees remain peripheral to organizational knowledge-creating processes; less than 1 per cent occupy managerial posts, compared to 35 per cent in the US (Lorriman and Kenjo, 1996: 74). Japanese employers anticipate that female employees will leave to have a family. The system also relies on various categories of temporary employees who might, for example, work full-time alongside regular employers on a *de facto* permanent basis, but with less status and pay. Nevertheless, lifetime employment does apply to regular employees who would only be dismissed in extreme circumstances. During the first few years of employment, it might be possible to 'start again' on the bottom rung of another firm's career ladder, but social pressure and lack of opportunity discourage this. After a few years, even those with specialist skills find it difficult to negotiate comparable employment with another Japanese organization.

Age-based promotion means that Japanese managers are able to help their subordinates without fear of being overtaken and can draw on years of experience in deciding who should work where. Employers and permanent employees have a mutual interest in organizational success; and enterprise unionism is mainly concerned with advancing common goals. Japanese employees generally welcome innovation as a useful addition to the workplace; for example, 1996 figures indicate that, for every 10,000 workers in Japan, there were 338 robots, compared to 21 for the UK (Barker, 1996: 9). New technology is a family asset that can be exploited for the benefit of the family – it is not a substitute for family members.

JAPAN'S COMPANY-AS-FAMILY ORGANIZATIONS

In tandem with Japan's post-war recovery, the metaphor of company-as-household became popular as an expression of filial piety – representing a space where foreign technology and hard-edged Anglo-American capitalism could be domesticated. Chie Nakane's influential book *Japanese Society* (1970) explained that – in the early days of Japan's industrialization – there was a high rate of labour mobility amongst factory workers. But the uncertainty of contractual arrangements ran against Japanese expectations of trust. Employers started to strengthen links with employees by providing various welfare benefits, such as company houses at nominal rent, and other payments in kind.

By the end of the First World War, large companies had established a practice of taking on boys leaving school each spring. As new types of machinery were introduced from Germany and the United States, employers found that these recruits were better able to meet technical and moral expectations. The cherished qualities of loyalty and willingness to undergo social integration were suspect in people who had worked elsewhere. In the 1920s and 1930s, uniforms for workers appeared along with badges and insignia denoting rank. The war machine responsible for military expansionism accentuated the trend.

Nakane argues that, while the Japanese word *kaisha* roughly translates as 'company' or 'enterprise', it also symbolizes the expression of group consciousness and the community to which one belongs primarily.

> In an extreme case, a company may have a common grave for its employees, similar to the household grave. With group consciousness so highly developed there is almost no social life outside the particular group on which an individual's major economic life depends. The individual's every problem must be solved within the frame. Thus group participation is simple and unitary. It follows then that each group or institution develops a high degree of independence and closeness, with its own internal law which is totally binding on members. (Nakane, 1970: 10)

For Nakane, 'frame' equates to the Japanese notion of *ba* – which may be a locality, an institution or a particular relationship that binds a set of individuals into one group: 'in all cases it indicates a criterion which sets a boundary and gives a common basis to a set of individuals who are located or involved in it' (Nakane, 1970: 1). Frame contrasts with 'attribute', which is a personal characteristic that may be a result of birth or endeavour.

Whereas communities of practice provide a frame of reference – or *ba* – that relates individual attributes to a collective body of practitioners who possess similar attributes, Japan's company-as-family metaphor presents the organization as the frame of reference for colleagues who spend their lives working together to solve whatever problems come along. The Western antithesis between the need to organize and learning's tendency to increase variety – as explored in Weick and Westley's (1996) perceptive review entitled 'Organizational learning: affirming an oxymoron' – is less applicable to a Japanese organization. Unlike a Western community of practice, sticky knowledge that evolves within Japanese organizations does not dissipate easily. The greater challenge for Japanese management is to guard against the danger of organizational ossification.

JAPANESE MANAGEMENT

Nonaka, Toyama and Konno argue that the frame of reference or *ba* for knowledge creation has to be 'energized' – for example, by paying attention to 'autonomy, creative chaos, redundancy, requisite variety, and love, care, trust and commitment' (Chapter 3 of the present book). Japanese management processes include every part of the organization, and strategy emerges from a process of creative churning that takes account of many points of view. If everyone has a hand in the planning process, they are generally more willing to commit themselves to putting the plan into practice. Nonaka and Takeuchi's (1995) landmark account of Japanese knowledge creation emphasized the importance of mutual understanding and shared experience in facilitating middle-up-down management that is neither 'top down' nor 'bottom up', but a synthesis of the two.

Japan's middle managers marry top-level visions to something that is achievable by front-line workers, whose dreams have long since passed. By Western standards, these top-level visions might be vague, ambiguous or even meaningless. What matters is the underlying mutual understanding of those in the leadership role and their coterie of understudies, who have evolved an instinctive knowledge of what their superior expects. By presenting the leader with a host of options, subordinates can sense what finds favour and act accordingly – hence the leader's 'instruction' is effectively issued without anyone being told to do anything. Vague visions indicate that the leader trusts them to implement the preferred option. In return for this support, the leader is expected to look after the interests of subordinates.

An astute interpretation of Japanese management in practice is evident in Sir John Harvey-Jones's recollection of building a chemical plant in competition with a Japanese firm. Each organization was building an identical plant and started at the same time, but the Japanese team finished first. Sir John reflected on the process and concluded that there were three reasons for the difference.

> the most important was that the Japanese plant was built by a team which shared a single large office and lived, worked and dreamt together, twelve hours or more a day, during the whole time of the development and planning of the plant. They were each in each other's minds and did not have to send a memo, or make a telephone call, to check the effects of, for example, locating a valve somewhere else. Any one of them could cover for anybody else . . .

> . . . The second reason was that exactly the same team which had done the designing were also involved in the construction. There was no hand over, no communication problems – the thing just flowed. (Harvey-Jones, 1993: 178)

He goes on to note that the third apparent reason for the Japanese achievement was that they had the forethought to erect a Shinto shrine in front of their plant. However, when Sir John put a similar structure up, it did not compensate for his side's lapses in management.

Japanese firms long ago discovered that the sources of information used in innovation come from many parts of the firm and not just those parts with a specific responsibility to be creative (Macdonald, 1995). Employees move with projects as they progress from research and development through production and sales departments. Huge amounts of apparently redundant information are stored within the collective memory and – while the whole process hardly squares with Western notions of efficiency – it provides enormous scope for flexibility. Colleagues who 'work and dream' together can implement a host of changes on a here and now basis without recourse to endless streams of memos and emails that, perforce, involve events that have already passed.

Japanese employees derive their identity from the status of their employer and in the course of a career they will do many jobs. Personal skills at any particular point are inconsequential; what matters is the sense of belonging to the organization and earning the respect of colleagues as a good team player – everyone is on the same side, irrespective of inevitable shifts in the nature of the game. As Michael Porter noted: 'Japanese knowledge creation has taken place in companies much more than in any other institution. . . . University research is limited, and interchange between companies and universities is modest compared to a number of other nations' (Porter, 1990: 397). Japan leads the world in per capita R&D expenditure, but this takes place mainly in private companies.[5] Whereas the older European universities have histories and academic traditions that pre-date industrialization, Japan's universities have emerged within the context of its government co-ordinated industrialization.

JAPANESE UNIVERSITIES

Japan established its first university – the University of Tokyo – in 1877. While this initially reflected a European influence, with a Faculty of Science – but no separate Faculty of Engineering – by the early 1890s, it had a strong base in the practical subjects of engineering and agriculture. The formation of Japan's Imperial Universities (which are the leading institutions in today's national university sector) replicated Tokyo's emphasis on applied technology and agriculture rather than science. Thus from an early point in their history Japanese universities appeared to place an emphasis on applied research. But, in reality, these universities were not properly equipped for research and were essentially agencies for training bureaucrats (Itakura and Yagi, 1974: 166).

After the Second World War, the number of universities in Japan increased dramatically, rising from 50 in 1950 to well over 500 today. But there has not been a commensurate strengthening of university research. According to the *Economist*:

Japan's universities are not places conducive to doing profound basic research. Most have rigid, hierarchical structures. Elderly faculty heads dominate the research programmes and publishing process. Intellectual dissent is discouraged. And in addition to having their ideas stifled, younger researchers often find themselves carrying out the grunt work that is done in America or Europe by technicians. Lack of money for support staff means that many people who would be better employed doing experiments are doing the washing up instead. (*Economist*, 1996: 102)

In Japan's university-research-group-as-family model, the relationship between leaders and subordinates resembles the pattern found in other work organizations. While the senior figure is always the senior figure (subordinates cannot outperform their mentor), an important part of effective leadership depends upon an ability to maintain the group's emotional stability and elicit a collective sense of purpose. And, if the research agenda is relatively straightforward, progress can be spectacular. But the leaps of creativity associated with basic research conducted by individual heroes can be difficult to replicate in a Japanese context. Whereas an insightful individual might jump onto the shoulders of an intellectual giant, it is more difficult for a team to organize a co-ordinated effort to leap and, in the meantime, the giant might move. Exploring dramatically new possibilities can jeopardize the sticky knowledge that underpins team spirit.

Writing after a decade of faltering economic growth, Michael Porter – together with Japanese co-authors Hirotaka Takeuchi and Mariko Sakakibara – posed the question 'Can Japan compete?' Part of the book's agenda for reform addressed problems in Japan's university system.

Japan's advanced education system has long left much to be desired. Not only is university- and graduate-level training uneven in quality, but Japanese universities also fail to produce enough students in important disciplines, such as computer software and biotechnology. The number of Japanese college graduates who majored in biology-related subjects was 1,875 in 1996, versus 62,081 in the United States. The number of graduate students per 1,000 population was 1.3 students for Japan in 1996 compared with 7.7 in the United States (1994) and 3.5 in France (1995). The percentage of graduate students relative to undergraduate students in the same year was 6.9% in Japan, 16.4% in the United States, 21.3% in the United Kingdom, and 17.7% in France. (Porter et al., 2000: 144)

The authors argue that a vibrant university research system is fundamental to a nation's research, and comment that some signs of change are just beginning to appear. But Japanese university research and scientific achievement – of the type reflected in Nobel prizes – remains limited.

While changing the deeply embedded custom and practice found in Japanese universities is problematic, there is a more promising strand to Japanese research. This centres on activities conducted through the Institute of Physical and Chemical Research, which – after a chequered history – has emerged at the vanguard of Japan's efforts to make a greater contribution to international progress in basic research.

THE INSTITUTE OF PHYSICAL AND CHEMICAL RESEARCH (RIKEN)

In the early twentieth century, Japanese scientists who had studied abroad became increasingly concerned about the lack of research opportunities in Japan. Progress in American electrical technology and the German chemical industry focused attention on the need for Japan to develop its own research capability and proposals were submitted to the Diet in 1915 for an Institute of Physical and Chemical Research. As the excerpt below suggests, Japan's current concerns with fostering creative research have a long history:

> We have equipped ourselves more or less adequately with the material aspects of civilisation, but in the realm of scientific research and its technical applications, we are still doing little more than following or imitating others. It is most unfortunate that when scientists here undertake creative research or seek to develop new inventions they often find necessary facilities and supporting services to be lacking. (Itakura and Yagi, 1974: 186)

Japan's first research institute was officially established on 20 March 1917. The Institute of Physical and Chemical Research or RIKEN (an abbreviation of its Japanese title Rikagaku Kenkyû-jo) was a conscious attempt to encourage creative research that would support economic development and make Japan less dependent on Western science. In 1922, RIKEN introduced a system whereby chief scientists – who could hold concurrent appointments as university professors – were given considerable freedom to determine the research programmes of their respective laboratories.

By 1941, RIKEN had 63 affiliated companies operating 121 factories. It was the largest research institute in Japan and the place where some of Japan's most distinguished scientists did their best work – including the establishment of nuclear physics. As one member of the Allied Occupation observed: 'No similar institution in the United States attained the status that RIKEN achieved during the nearly thirty years previous to the end of World War II, although comparable American institutions have existed for decades' (Dees, 1997: 119). Nevertheless, RIKEN's industrial interests had become heavily oriented towards Japan's militarism and the occupation separated the institute from its affiliated companies.

After the Second World War, RIKEN had a difficult time, but in 1958 it was reorganized as a semi-public corporation (*tokushu-hôjin*). The powerful, but conservative, education ministry that presides over Japan's university system rejected involvement with RIKEN, which instead fell under the wing of the recently formed Science and Technology Agency (STA). In 1992, *Nature* (1992: 578) described RIKEN as 'Japan's Leading Light' and a 'remarkably dynamic research organization that is fast becoming a truly international centre of excellence'. RIKEN has expanded its original base in physics and chemistry to include engineering, biology, medical sciences and, from 1997, a Brain Science Institute.

Japan's 1995 Science and Technology Act committed the nation to bringing public sector research spending into line with allocations in the United States and leading European countries. Since the Act was passed, government expenditure on research has doubled and now stands at about 1 per cent of GDP. RIKEN's budget has mirrored this spectacular growth. It simultaneously straddles Japan's university research system and interacts with research organizations across the world.[6]

KNOWLEDGE CREATION IN JAPAN AND THE WEST

For the last three centuries, the West has placed the positivist model of science on a pedestal. The traditions of scientific research were established before the industrial revolution, although it was a long time before science emerged as a significant tool in the development of new trajectories of technological development. Nevertheless, the importance of technologies that exploited knowledge of physics and chemistry was evident by the First World War – and the establishment of RIKEN reflected Japan's eagerness to develop an indigenous capability in these areas. After the Second World War, a host of science-related technologies (such as nuclear power, radar, rockets, antibiotics and plastics) appeared to confirm the West's faith in a linear model in which science provided the basis for applied technology.

On the other hand, Japan's spectacular economic growth – despite a relatively low expenditure on basic research – suggested that other forms of knowledge creation are important. This chapter has explored Japan's *steady state* knowledge creation in which stable organizations nesting in a stable economic structure have aligned the country's group-oriented culture to the overarching objective of post-war recovery. The company-as-family approach to organizational knowledge creation proved to be an important element in the continuous improvement that sustained the country's economic miracle. Although the catch-up model that once bedazzled the West has been looking increasingly beleaguered during a decade of faltering economic growth, Japan has been rapidly increasing its expenditure on basic research.

Japan's approach to change with continuity is mediated by the accumulated wisdom situated in work organizations. The Western idea that science should determine its own agenda according to peer-group judgements of what constitutes scientific excellence (i.e. science for its own sake) has not held similar sway in Japan. Throughout Japan's industrial history, science has been a tool for use in knowledge creation directed towards practical goals. Recognition that physics and chemistry were important tools of knowing in the First World War was instrumental in the establishment of RIKEN. And current concerns continue to give an application-oriented flavour to Japan's 'basic' research. The increasing average age of the Japanese population, for example, places greater emphasis on need to better understand the mental processes of older people and RIKEN's establishment of a Brain Science Institute is relevant in this context.

In many ways, the research-group-as-family model found in Japanese universities militates against the creativity associated with Western individualism and labour mobility. However, the insights of an individual genius can be lost if nobody pays attention to the message. Thus, the apparently redundant knowledge that emerges in group-based projects, in which researchers 'work and dream' together, helps them to appreciate each other's problems and the type of information that might be useful. Notwithstanding the *inside–outside* split that delineates organizational boundaries, the organization as an entity is interconnected with the wider environment. Furthermore, this interconnectedness can facilitate impressive levels of coherence that acts against the well-known British lament that others exploit many of its best inventions.

CONCLUSION

Japan is the first non-Western nation for half a millennium to become a great power. It leads the world in manufacturing and the supply of credit. Even so, a decade of mediocre economic performance has encouraged a Western tendency to belittle Japan's achievements and portray it as a laggard in global convergence towards Anglo-American business systems. Arguably, the more significant point is that Japan's approach to knowledge creation is grounded in non-Western traditions (Nonaka et al., 1998) that are not commensurate with the tendency to privilege individualism and explicit knowledge. In the West, knowledge management has emerged as a fashionable weapon in the uneven struggle with information. But Japan remains less vulnerable to the vicissitudes of Western management theory.

Japanese typically abstain from overt individualism in favour of actions that demonstrate support for the group. Knowledge-creating activities have more to do with moving in appropriate directions than arriving at conclusions. In this respect, the whole system is geared up to continuous improvement and – in the absence of end-points – the process of improvement is never finished. In Japan's steady state knowledge creation, work organizations mediate the application of objective knowledge with the wisdom embodied in accumulated individual and collective tacit knowledge. Meanwhile, the success of RIKEN in developing an agenda for basic research suggests that Japan is more than capable of moving towards tomorrow's technologies, albeit in a distinctly Japanese way. This emphasizes sustained effort in areas that are consistent with Japan's overall objectives for economic and social development. A distribution of power across the high peaks of Japan's industrial, bureaucratic and political sectors makes it difficult for any one interest group to establish a clear advantage, but the endless process of negotiation and brokering compromises allows many viewpoints to shape the emerging consensus.

NOTES

1 Contrary to popular Western images of Japan's government-sponsored, pre-competitive collaborative research projects, *ad hoc* inter-firm collaboration is problematic.
2 Douglass North (1991) notes that eleventh-century Jewish traders in the Mediterranean 'solved' the agency problem in just this way.
3 Based on data supplied by Japan's Monbusho and the US National Science Foundation for the period 1990–95.
4 A special feature on Japan in the September 1936 issue of *Fortune* (Vol. 14, no 3, p. 120) reported that 46 per cent of Japan's national expenditure was devoted to the armed services, more than 2.5 times that of the US.
5 In 1997, Japan's private sector R&D expenditure was 12,494 billion yen, accounting for 79.4 per cent of the total.
6 RIKEN has constructed major research facilities in the UK and US. It has concluded research collaboration agreements with institutes across the world and in 1999 was host to some 600 overseas scientists who spent an average of one year at the institute.

REFERENCES

Barker, B. (1996) *Japan: a Science Profile*, London: The British Council.
Dees, B. (1997) *The Allied Occupation and Japan's Economic Miracle: Building the Foundations of Japanese Science and Technology 1945–52*, Richmond: Curzon Press/Japan Library.
Dore, R. (1973) *British Factory – Japanese Factory: the Origins of National Diversity in Industrial Relations*, London: George Allen and Unwin.
Economist (1996) 'Science and technology: back to basics in Japan', 25 May: 102.
Fingleton, E. (1995) 'Jobs for life: why Japan won't give them up', *Fortune*, 20 March: 79–84.
Fingleton, E. (1997) *Blindside: Why Japan is Still on Track to Overtake the US by Year 2000*, Tokyo: Kodansha International.
Harvey-Jones, J. (1993) *Managing to Survive*, Reading: Mandarin.
Itakura, Kiyonobu and Yagi, Eri (1974) 'The Japanese research system and the establishment of the Institute of Physical and Chemical Research', in S. Nakayama, D. Swain and E. Yagi (eds), *Science and Society in Modern Japan*, MIT and University of Tokyo Press.
Johnson, C. (1992) *MITI and the Japanese Miracle: the Growth of Industrial Policy, 1925–1975*, Tokyo: Charles E. Tuttle (1st edn 1982).
Johnson, C. (1995) *Japan: Who Governs? The Rise of the Developmental State*, New York: W. W. Norton.
Lorriman, J. and Kenjo, T. (1996) *Japan's Winning Margins*, Oxford: Oxford University Press.
Macdonald, S. (1995) 'Learning to change: an information perspective on learning in the organization', *Organization Science*, 6 (2): 557–568.
Mason, R. and Caiger, J. (1972) *A History of Japan: Tokyo*, Rutland: Charles E. Tuttle.
Miyashita, Kenichi and Russell, David (1996) *Keiretsu: Inside the Hidden Japanese Conglomerates*, New York: MacGraw-Hill.

Nakane, C. (1970) *Japanese Society*, Berkeley, CA: University of California Press.

Nature (1992) 'RIKEN – Japan's leading light', 359, 15 October.

Nonaka, I. and Takeuchi, H. (1995) *The Knowledge Creating Company: How Japanese Companies Create the Dynamics of Innovation*, New York: Oxford University Press.

Nonaka, I., Ray, T. and Umemoto, K. (1998) 'Organizational knowledge creation in Anglo-American environments', *Prometheus: The Journal for Issues in Technology Change, Innovation, Information, Economics, Communications and Science Policy*, 16 (4), December: 421–439.

North, D. (1991) 'Institutions', *Journal of Economic Perspectives*, 5 (1): 97–112.

Odagiri, H. and Goto, A. (1993) 'The Japanese system of innovation', in R. Nelson (ed.), *National Innovation Systems*, New York: Oxford University Press. pp. 76–114.

Odagiri, H. and Goto, A. (1996) *Technological and Industrial Development in Japan*, Oxford: Clarendon Press.

Porter, M. (1990) *The Competitive Advantage of Nations*, New York: The Free Press.

Porter, M., Takeuchi, H. and Sakakibara, M. (2000) *Can Japan Compete?* Houndmills: Macmillan.

Ray, T. (1998) 'Collaborative research in Japan and the West: a case study of Britain's response to MITI's fifth generation computer initiative', in M. Hemmert and C. Oberländer (eds), *Technology and Innovation in Japan*, London: Routledge. pp. 151–169.

Schumpeter, J. (1976) *Capitalism, Socialism and Democracy*, London: George Allen & Unwin (1st edn 1943).

Van Wolferen, K. (1990) *The Enigma of Japanese Power: People and Politics in a Stateless Nation*, London: Macmillan/PAPERMAC.

Weick, K. and Westley, F. (1996) 'Organizational learning: affirming an oxymoron', in S. Clegg, C. Hardy and W. Nord (eds), *Handbook of Organization Studies*, London: Sage. pp. 440–458.

Wenger, E. (2000) 'Communities of practice and social learning systems', *Organization*, 7 (2): 225–246.

Westney, D. (1987) *Imitation and Innovation: the Transfer of Western Organizational Patterns to Meiji Japan*, Cambridge: Harvard University Press.

Part II Resources and Capabilities

Alfred Marshall in the late nineteenth century, Edith Penrose in the 1950s and Peter Drucker in the 1960s were among those seminal contributors who recognized the key significance of knowledge as an economic resource, a realization numerous current latecomers have claimed as their own. To Drucker, by the late 1960s knowledge had become *the* crucial resource of the economy (Drucker, 1969: ix).

Within the current knowledge management paradigm the dominant focus on knowledge resources (or assets) leads to preoccupation with the knowledge that already exists within organizations, such as the knowledge 'in people's heads' and challengingly unavailable to the wider organization, or in the form of intangible assets such as brands. However, organizations cannot secure advantage by identifying the knowledge that already exists, assuming this is possible, or simply owning an intangible asset. Attention must also be paid to the processes that surround knowledge or intangible assets – the capabilities to utilize, share and create new knowledge, to name but three key areas.

The importance of organizational capabilities to do things has a practical resonance that we may readily appreciate: the mere possession of a resource is unlikely to lead to profit if that resource is ignored or poorly managed. The conceptual basis of the capabilities focus is also soundly rooted in the theory of the firm. Before knowledge emerged centre stage in the late 1990s as a key focus for managers, strategic management thinkers seeking to explain the superior performance of some organizations above others focused on organizational resources and capabilities. Whereas previous economics-derived thinking emphasized resources as static bundles of assets, the notion of capabilities (or core competencies) introduces a dynamic aspect to thinking about resources and their management (Scarborough, 1998).

The four contributions in this part explore different and complementary aspects of knowledge resources and capabilities. The first chapter, by Ysanne Carlisle, presents a 'view from strategy' of knowledge management, locating knowledge within the resources and capabilities strategic framework. Indeed she argues that this strategic perspective is the precursor to the emergence of the current knowledge management perspective.

For Carlisle, consideration of knowledge leads to a critique of conventional approaches to organizational strategy, focused on three key aspects: an inappropriate *information processing* model of strategic decision making; an incomplete view of human nature and the basis upon which effective communities of practice are built; and a neglect of the internal organizational dynamics of change.

Carlisle argues that all other resources depend on knowledge in order to create value, and knowledge can provide advantage by enabling organizations to use other resources more effectively. Ultimately, she argues, firms exist to facilitate the acquisition, creation, transfer and exploitation of knowledge, with advantage being gained by those with superior capabilities for managing these processes. A key difference between traditional strategic thinking and a knowledge-centred view is that the former seeks advantage through cost efficiencies and differentiation in the marketplace, the latter through the creation and use of knowledge. Whereas organizational economics stresses rationality in human behaviour, knowledge management leads to a central concern with human interactions and the social processes that surround knowledge creation and use, such as communication, learning and innovation.

Carlisle also raises a key issue that is explored in Chapter 7 by Wendy Faulkner. This concerns the relationship between knowledge and innovation, which Carlisle explores in the context of biotechnology. The popular view is that innovation results from scientific knowledge (how often do we hear that 'scientists' are responsible for one or another technological development, rather than engineers, technologists or indeed entrepreneurs?). The knowledge outputs from scientific research are among the most rigorously codified of all forms of knowledge (the peer review process depending on codification, published papers, etc.), and codified scientific knowledge may be regarded a resource. Carlisle emphasizes the need also to pay attention to the key capabilities for managing and exploiting scientific knowledge – capabilities that may be tacit, and that are often ignored as components of innovation.

Faulkner provides a detailed exploration of the types of knowledge that result in innovation. The chapter draws on a wide range of perspectives and literatures, resulting in a composite typology of knowledge used in innovation. She begins with an analysis of the distinction between science and technology, dispelling any preconceptions that technology is simply applied science. Again the importance of tacit knowledge emerges, particularly in the context of experiential learning. Here Faulkner emphasizes the generation of new knowledge within the innovation process itself, and the complex social processes through which it is created and applied. Key processes include iterative learning and the integration of knowledge of different types. The process of innovation cuts across social groupings and communities of practice, unlike much scientific research, and therefore presents inherent challenges for management. Though not directly explored in the chapter, the importance of organizational capabilities to manage these complex processes is implicit.

Chapter 8 by Paul Feldwick takes us further into the area of intangible resources or assets, dealing with the topic of brands. Organizations that own an internationally recognized brand are likely to possess a resource of great value; indeed brands are sometimes regarded as having greater value than an organization's physical assets. But how are we to identify the source of that value, and begin to measure it; i.e. to measure brand equity? Brands may be considered as powerful means of communicating subtle and complex ideas about values, identity, aspirations, reputation, quality, and so on, and the customer's perception of these things is dependent on the brand owner's ability to manage and maintain the relationship with the customer through the brand.

The chapter provides insights into the factors that make up a brand and its value, as well as exploring different methods of measuring brand equity. In doing this, these measurement techniques provide indications of how well the brand owner is doing in terms of capability to manage the brand and maintain or enhance its value. The discussion of brand equity therefore enables us to develop our understanding of intangible resources, and the capabilities required to manage these.

When we think of an *individual*'s knowledge resources these are generally presumed to exist in the person's memory. The concept of memory has also been applied at the level of the organization, where by analogy 'organizational memory' represents the knowledge resources of the firm. While organizational memory is an attractive and simple idea, the notion of memory as a repository or store has its limitations. The fourth chapter in this part, by Liam Bannon and Kari Kuutti, explores the notion of organizational memory from a critical perspective. The authors question the notion of memory as a passive repository, and instead emphasize the active processes involved. Here we can see parallels with the resources and capabilities argument.

Bannon and Kuutti show that human memories, rather than being retrieved from a passive store according to a database model, are *reconstructed* in the context of recall. When we look at how human memory actually works, the cognitive sciences show that 'memory as active reconstruction' is a much better model than the passive store. The implications of this perspective for organizational memory highlights the need to focus on the social processes through which knowledge is remembered and shared. The key capabilities for effective organizational memory recall focus on the communication and the reconstruction of learning and meaning. Experiential learning is often shared through storytelling, one of the most ancient means by which memory is socially reconstructed. The chapter also explores the role of information systems in supporting organizational memory. The emphasis on memory as active reconstruction has significant implications for the kinds of computer 'support' that may be appropriate for these organizational memory processes.

REFERENCES

Drucker, P. F. (1969) *The Age of Discontinuity: Guidelines to our Changing Society*, London: Heinemann.
Scarborough, H. (1998) 'Path(ological) dependency? Core competencies from an organizational perspective', *British Journal of Management*, 9: 219–232.

6

Strategic Thinking and Knowledge Management

*Ysanne Carlisle**

It has long been acknowledged that knowledge is central to wealth creation and organized competitive performance (e.g. Hayek, 1945; Penrose, 1959; Teece, 1977). Some authors, like Marshall, writing in 1920, have been explicit in stating that 'knowledge is our most powerful engine of production; it enables us to subdue nature and force her to satisfy our wants. Organization aids knowledge' (Marshall, 1969: 115). Until recently, however, the full implications of such observations were still ignored. The terms 'information' and 'knowledge' were often used synonymously, and knowledge acquisition, creation, exploitation and transfer in organizations were infrequently researched topics.

From the mid-1980s onwards it became apparent that established understandings of strategy had serious limitations in the increasingly competitive and changing global environment. These understandings were mostly derived from organizational economics. Organizational economics underpinned conventional strategic prescriptions for creating and sustaining a competitive performance, but during the 1980s these were found to be wanting. A number of well-established large organizations which had been cited as 'excellent' in accordance with accepted strategic wisdom actually suffered performance decline. IBM and Microsoft are examples. Their decline occurred in the face of competition from smaller firms which conventional theory suggested should not have triumphed. In one sense, knowledge management is a practical response to this problem. For example, the efforts of organizations like Skandia and CICB to measure and manage their knowledge bases are practically oriented towards sustaining and improving performance. In another sense, the emergence of a new strand of knowledge-based organizational theory can be viewed as an academic response to the need to provide better theoretical perspectives to inform management practice. This need was highlighted by the decline of companies like IBM and it took on a sense of urgency in the strategy literature of the late 1980s and 1990s. What is emerging is an understanding of organization focused on the role of knowledge. It underpins a very different approach to strategy from that which was, until recently, the received wisdom.

* The Open University Business School

Knowledge management is not simply a modern term for information management. It requires the pursuit of different types of objectives and the development of different types of resource strengths, process capabilities and organizational structures. Researching the new knowledge-based understanding requires a focus upon the development of new 'organizational advantages' (Moran and Ghoshal, 1996) to create and sustain a competitive performance in the modern global economy (Gee, 1996). These advantages are derived from superior capabilities in the management of the organizational knowledge process. The development of organizational advantages requires a focus upon issues of internal organizational dynamics. This represents a move away from traditional emphases upon market imperfections and positioning which are to be found in the established literature. This chapter contrasts the understandings of organization found in the conventional and the knowledge-based literatures. Some fundamental differences which affect the role of information and knowledge are summarized in Table 6.1.

The next sections explore these key differences in understanding and outline their implications for strategists. The chapter moves on to describe how competitive advantage is created and sustained in both frameworks. Finally, the limitations of the older understandings and approaches are considered along with the contexts in which they came to be questioned. The key questions are: can knowledge management address these limitations and, if so, how radical a shift in strategic thinking is required? Is knowledge management complementary to the older strategic approaches or does it require a more complete paradigm shift?

TABLE 6.1 *Conventional and knowledge-based understandings of organization*

Key issues	Conventional understandings	Knowledge-based understandings
Why do organizations exist?	To process environmental information To deal with problems arising from informational imperfections To reduce uncertainty To meet shareholder needs	To create and exploit knowledge
How do we understand human nature?	People are rational, calculating and self-interested individuals	People are creative, visionary and collectively ambitious
What is the basis for human relationships in and between organizations?	Explicitly or implicitly contractual	Commitment based upon shared visions, meanings and identities

THE NEED FOR ORGANIZATIONS

Traditionally, economists have devoted attention to answering the question 'why do organizations exist?' Strategists, building upon their answers, have devised strategies to develop the ways and means by which organizations can fulfil their functions better. Clearly, how we answer this basic question about organizations has implications for the way we conceptualize strategic requirements for performance success. Knowledge may only recently have surfaced as a major focus in the economics and strategy literatures, but several conventional economic theories of the firm have accorded a central place to information in explaining organization as a means of achieving the effective and efficient deployment of scarce resources. Some of the best-established perspectives are premised, explicitly or otherwise, upon assumptions about information. Information about the competitive environment which organizations process is seen as a major determinant of organizational strategy; imperfect information leads to informational 'asymmetries' and this is why organizations can fail.

For example, Alchian and Demetz (1972) suggest that asymmetries in the information held by people co-operating in a task make it impossible to match their contributions to their remuneration. If efficiency losses are to be avoided, they believe, it is necessary to incur the costs of controlling and monitoring their activities and output. Jensen and Meckling (1976) suggest that informational asymmetries between principals and agents in contractual relationships create the need to incur monitoring costs to ensure that agents act in the interests of principals. Williamson (1975, 1985), whose transaction costs understanding is one of the best-established and most influential economic understandings of the firm, does not accord informational asymmetries a direct role in competitive success, but he sees them indirectly as crucial. In Williamson's understanding, informational asymmetries make it possible for individuals to engage in opportunistic behaviour which gives rise to the need for governance structures. For Williamson, market imperfections in the acquisition and utilization of resources, including informational resources, provide some organizations with opportunities to deploy resources more effectively and efficiently than their rivals.

The 'knowledge-based view of the firm' is a theoretical perspective on organizations which has emerged in the strategy literature to propose an alternative primary reason for organizing. From this perspective firms exist to facilitate the acquisition, creation, exploitation and transfer of useful knowledge. This alternative response to the question 'why organize?' is reflected in Kogut and Zander's definition of the firm as 'a social community specializing in the speed and efficiency of the creation and transfer of knowledge' (Kogut and Zander, 1996: 503).

The knowledge-based view explicitly recognizes that information and knowledge are distinctly different phenomena. Information can be understood to consist of facts and data pertaining to natural or social states of affairs, natural or social events and the consequences of such events under given circumstances, or states of affairs. The total stock of information available, or potentially available, to organizations is vast but, as Fransman (1998) points out, it is also theoretically finite. At any given point in time there is a finite number of natural and social states of affairs in the world. The events that might occur as a result may be numerous and may not all be anticipated by an organization. They are nevertheless finite in number, and the number of potential consequences is also finite. In contrast, knowledge is potentially limitless.

Leonard highlights the fact that knowledge is a potentially limitless 'wellspring' which is 'constantly replenished with streams of new ideas' (Leonard, 1995: 3). Following Nonaka (1991, 1994) and Nonaka and Takeuchi (1995), knowledge is often defined in the knowledge-based literature as 'justified' belief. Information can be an input into the decision-making process, and it can be interpreted to justify belief, but it also depends upon knowledge for that interpretation. Information is seen to be important and relevant in the light of knowledge which may be added to, amended or changed in the light of new information.

Knowledge is a critical resource. Virtually all other resources depend upon some degree of knowledge exploitation for their value – including natural resources. Gas, for example, would have no value if we did not know what to do with it and possess the know-how to extract it and exploit it. At the abstract level of theoretical knowledge, depending upon the nature of the business, organizations may require a wide range of specialist inputs – from business specialisms, such as accountancy and business law, to scientific and technical specialisms, such as chemistry, computer science and engineering. At the concrete level, organizations require practical know-how in a wide range of areas and an ability to exploit these disparate contributions effectively. Some kinds of abstract knowledge can be codified. Such knowledge can be commodified and distributed in the manner of information, but the tacit knowledge embodied in practical know-how cannot.

Within the context of the simple model *input–process–output*, knowledge is a more dynamic resource than many other inputs which may be used up or otherwise deployed time and again in relatively unchanged forms. In the process of exploiting knowledge, knowledge is changed. The input–process–output model can be applied to the process of exploiting knowledge itself. An engineer, for example, may be recruited with theoretical knowledge gained from a university. As this theoretical knowledge is deployed in the performance of tasks at work the new engineer gains work experience. With work experience practical know-how is acquired to complement the original theoretical knowledge. As a result, the knowledge contribution which the new engineer can make to the firm changes.

The 'knowledge-based view of the firm' is a theoretical perspective which has grown out of the 'resource-based view' in the strategy literature. The inspiration for the development of the resource-based view is generally attributed to Selznick (1957) and Penrose (1959). Neither of these writers placed the knowledge resource at centre stage, although Penrose pointed to the possibility that knowledge could be a resource with special properties in that the effective utilization of all other resources depended upon it. She suggested that the need to deploy the under-utilized productive services of other resources, 'shape(s) the direction of the search for knowledge' (Penrose, 1959: 77). The idea that diversification can bring economies of scope to an organization if its diversification strategy enables it to use large indivisible assets more efficiently is well established. How can we reconcile this idea with the equally well known strategic prescription for companies to 'stick to the knitting'? One of the implications of Penrose (1959) is that the acquisition of new knowledge is an essential ingredient in the success of such strategies. It is knowledge that creates a cost advantage in enabling the organization to deploy its productive resources more efficiently. Resource-based theorists have stressed that over time organizations can develop particular strengths in the form of 'capabilities' and 'competencies'. Capabilities enable organizations to manage particular types of resource-utilizing process especially well, for example manufacturing processes. Competencies are strengths in doing particular things especially well, such as manufacturing engines. Organizations exploit knowledge by building capabilities and competencies.

HUMAN NATURE AND THE BASIS OF HUMAN RELATIONSHIPS

Conventional understandings of human nature in organizational economics are based upon a (sometimes jaundiced) view of humanity as inherently rational, calculative and instrumental. For example, we have noted that Alchian and Demetz (1972) see organization as a means of minimizing efficiency loss in the context of co-operative production. Informational asymmetries make it difficult for co-operating team members to assess relative contributions. The presupposition is that human beings are by nature instrumental reasoners who will adopt courses of action from which they can derive maximum benefit for minimum effort. Under such a utilitarian presumption, individuals in co-operative production have an 'incentive to shirk'. Jensen and Meckling (1976) focus upon the nature of the relationship between principals and agents. They see human beings as 'utility maximizers' individually pursuing maximum personal utility. From this perspective agents may not always be motivated to pursue the best possible interests of principals. Hence the need to incur agency costs and to provide agents with appropriate incentives.

Williamson's transaction costs understanding 'characterizes human nature as we know it by reference to bounded rationality and opportunism' (Williamson, 1985: 44). Bounded rationality arises to avoid information overload. Information overload leads to selective perception of and attention to information. Information which is attended to is then processed in accordance with accepted 'procedural rationality', which stems from the decision-maker's ideological environment (Walford, 1979). According to March and Simon, the concept of bounded rationality 'incorporates two fundamental characteristics: 1) choice is always exercised with respect to a limited, approximate simplified model of the real situation. . . . 2) The elements of the definition of the situation are not "given" . . . but are themselves the outcome of psychological and sociological processes, including the chooser's own activities and the activities of those in his environment' (March and Simon, 1958: 12).

The scope for opportunism, defined by Williamson as behaviour which is 'self-interest seeking with guile' (Williamson, 1975, 1985), arises because of informational asymmetries between organizations and between individuals within them. The scope for exercising opportunistic behaviour in organizations may be tempered by the decision-maker's ideological environment. Nonetheless, the basic view of human nature which transaction costs theory adopts is one of a rational, instrumentally oriented, self-seeking individual of the type originally characterized by Adam Smith's 1776 *An Inquiry into the Nature and Causes of the Wealth of Nations*.

Organizational economists have adopted a contractual view of human relationships. Jensen and Meckling explicitly define the firm in contractual terms as 'the nexus of a set of contracting relationships between individuals' (Jensen and Meckling, 1976: 315). Relationships between, for example, principals and agents, employers and employees, organizations and customers, organizations and shareholders and other stakeholders can all be analysed from a contractual standpoint. Some contracts are understood to be more implicit than explicit, and the costs of making and monitoring transactions are of central concern in relation to efficiency issues.

Where organizational economics stresses the importance of March and Simon's first characteristic of bounded rationality, knowledge-based theorists stress the second. Writers like Williamson emphasize the rationality in human reasoning and information processing. In contrast the knowledge-based view of the firm emphasizes creativity, vision and ambition as essential human traits. Selznick (1957) pointed the way in writing about 'the creative leader' who matches 'aspiration' to the nature of the organization in guiding it along a path between long-term 'utopianism' and short-term 'opportunism'. For organizational economists, the environment is a source of incomplete information to be processed as rationally as possible in reaching decisions. For Penrose, it is 'an "image" in the entrepreneur's mind of the possibilities and restrictions with which he is confronted, for it is, after all, such an image which in fact determines a man's behaviour' (Penrose, 1959: 5). The 'productive opportunity' of the organization is therefore shaped as much by subjective judgement and creativity as it is by the rational processing of environmental information.

More modern writings in the knowledge-based mould have adopted a social constructivist approach to the understanding of human relationships. Writers seeking to advance knowledge management as a practical endeavour are therefore crucially concerned with internal organizational dynamics. The social processes which operate in the course of human interaction are central rather than peripheral considerations. Knowledge management attention has been directed towards a diverse range of topics of direct relevance to how people interact with each other in organizational contexts to maintain and change their socially constructed worlds. It would be possible to compile a lengthy list of such topics including, for example, contexts and conditions for information and knowledge sharing, mechanisms for communications and control, organizational structures, language and conservation in organizational and interorganizational contexts, the nature of learning and learning organizations, formal and informal networks, self-managing teams and communities of practice. The point is that human interaction and how it takes place is central to knowledge creation and transfer. It is also formative in shaping organizational routines (Nelson and Winter, 1982) within which useful knowledge can be exploited as an organizational rather than an individual resource.

IMPLICATIONS FOR STRATEGISTS

The conventional and knowledge-based approaches to strategy carry different implications for strategists, as is shown in Table 6.2. Differences in goals and strategic focus are considered in this section and their different implications for creating and sustaining competitive advantage are discussed in the next.

The traditional theoretical underpinnings for strategy derived from organizational economics have encouraged strategy scholars to explore the causes and consequences of market failures. Managers have been encouraged to focus on developing strategies which achieve the best possible fit between the organization and its environment to secure a favourable and sustainable market position.

Following the conventional understanding of transaction costs and market imperfections identified in the organization's environment by means of information processing, strategic management must strive to take advantage of the opportunities they present. At the same time it must guard against the

TABLE 6.2 *The conventional and knowledge-based approaches to strategy*

Key differences	Conventional approach	Knowledge-based approach
Goal for strategists	Achieve a good strategic fit	Achieve an ambitious strategic intent
Strategic focus	Value appropriation	Value creation
Sources of competitive advantage	Market imperfections providing opportunities for cost and differentiation advantages enabling firms to achieve favourable market positions	Unique competencies and capabilities which cannot be substituted, imitated, replicated or transferred, and are 'causally ambiguous'
How competitive advantage is sustained	By maintaining a favourable market position	Through capabilities in knowledge processes which can deliver new competencies for the future

adverse effects of the opportunistic behaviour of those individuals and organizations with which it has business relationships or 'contracts' and those organizations with which it competes.

Andrews (1971) has formulated a classic statement of the approach to strategic analysis that such understandings support. In this statement, strategy formulation and implementation are separated for purposes of analysis, and internal organizational dynamics are considered to be an implementation issue. Strategy formulation is approached as a rational top-down endeavour involving the processing of environmental information to identify opportunities and threats. Alternative courses of action are identified and an assessment of their risks is undertaken. In the light of this analysis and an appraisal of internal organizational strengths and weaknesses, a choice is made. The emphasis is upon rational planning.

The knowledge-based view encourages scholars to explore the structural, social and relational aspects of organizations within which knowledge creation, exploitation and transfer take place. Hamel and Prahalad (1989) argued that many corporations which rise to positions of global market dominance begin with an ambitious vision or 'strategic intent'. Targets are set which demand a great deal of effort and commitment, and involve stretching resources and capabilities beyond their limits. This means that organizations must tap into the creativity and inventiveness of their members to achieve their goals. In the process, unplanned strategies for the exploitation of knowledge created may emerge. Strategy is not viewed as an exclusively top-down process in which formulation and implementation issues are distinct and separate. Good ideas can arise almost anywhere in the organization and putting them into practice may require an input at the planning stage from almost anywhere. Developing shared meanings and purposes in accordance with an ambitious mission requires more than a directive process, and the importance of emergent strategy is explicitly recognized (Clegg, 1990).

In practical terms, Moran and Ghoshal (1996) and more recently Nahapiet and Ghoshal (1998) have pointed out that transaction costs theory, as an underpinning for strategy, leads strategists to emphasize processes of *value appropriation*. The knowledge-based view leads them to stress processes of *value creation*. This implies a shift in the focus for strategic thinking away from traditional market concerns to issues of internal organizational dynamics. The conventional focus on value appropriation calls for strategies which will ensure the development and maintenance of effective and efficient means of appropriating value from available scarce resources which will add value to organizational outputs. If the organization can thereby maintain a favourable market position it will sustain its competitive performance. The more recent focus calls for strategies which will create value in knowledge and lead to its effective exploitation to produce outputs based upon unique competencies and capabilities which cannot readily be rivalled. The conventional and knowledge-based approaches therefore seek to create and sustain competitive advantage in different ways: the one by searching out cost efficiencies and differentiation advantages which can lead to unassailable market positions; the other by investing in the creation and exploitation of useful new knowledge which cannot be readily appropriated by competitors irrespective of their market position.

CREATING AND SUSTAINING COMPETITIVE ADVANTAGE

Porter is one of the most influential strategists to have proposed the type of conventional approach which is described above. For reasons which will be outlined later in this chapter, disenchantment with conventional strategic prescriptions from the mid-1980s onwards fuelled a resurrection of the older 'resource-based view' of the firm. The resource-based view is important because it provides the basic theoretical springboard from which knowledge-based theory has taken off. Resource-based theorists argue that capabilities and competencies are intangible assets which provide unique sources of competitive advantage to the firm. Knowledge-based theorists argue that firms which further develop unique capabilities in the management of knowledge processes can build distinctive competencies based upon exploiting the growing knowledge these processes generate.

Selznick (1957) and Penrose (1959) may have provided inspiration for resource- and knowledge-based theory, but it has been left to more modern writers to spell out in greater detail how competitive advantage derived from resources like knowledge can be further created and sustained (e.g. Rumelt, 1984; Wernerfelt, 1984; Dierickx and Cool, 1989; Barney, 1991; Hall, 1993; Peteraf, 1993). These writers have argued that resources can create competitive advantages because each organization accumulates unique bundles of resources that can potentially sustain a competitive advantage if they are difficult to substitute, replicate, imitate or transfer to other companies. If the precise form of a particular resource is difficult to specify and its precise effect on performance difficult to isolate, it is said to be 'causally ambiguous'. Causal ambiguity is an attribute of some resources which makes it more likely that they can sustain a competitive advantage.

It can be argued that knowledge is a resource which meets these resource-based criteria for sustaining competitive success. Explicit knowledge can be codified, which makes replication and transfer easier to achieve. Indeed, one of the reasons for codifying knowledge is to enable it to be more readily communicated to others, but applications of explicit knowledge may still be causally ambiguous. Tacit knowledge is by definition unarticulated and therefore less amenable to transfer. It is a human resource and manifest only in human use. The resource-based view suggests that organizations exploit their human resources by developing organizational capabilities to deploy them in uniquely advantageous ways. Over time this can lead to the development of core competencies. Core competencies based on knowledge may be sustainable for a time in resource-based terms until or unless they are superseded by developments elsewhere. As Porter (1991) notes, the value of any useful resource can be eroded by innovations elsewhere. All knowledge of course is vulnerable to this process, but tacit knowledge is not so readily appropriated as information.

This means that additional organizational capabilities for managing knowledge processes are required. Grant (1996) suggests that the capability for integrating knowledge from a wide range of disparate sources is an example of a key capability of this type.

Organizational knowledge-based capabilities draw upon tacit knowledge (Polanyi, 1958, 1966) as well as explicit knowledge. They are culturally bounded (Nonaka, 1991; Hall, 1993; Lave, 1993; Blackler, 1995) and context dependent. They develop in organizational cultures which are the unique and path-dependent result of human action, rather than human design (Barney, 1986; Camerer and Vespalainen, 1988; Fiol, 1991). The path-dependency concept is used to refer to the fact that decisions and actions taken in the early days shape the parameters within which future developments can take place. For these reasons, cost and/or differentiation advantages stemming from knowledge-based capabilities cannot normally be installed overnight by would-be competitors. Furthermore, even when knowledge itself can be made fully explicit and transferable, its effective application in one cultural setting does not ensure that it can be exploited to the same effect in another if the capability that enables it to be effectively exploited cannot also be readily transferred.

We have said that, given time, advantages derived from knowledge-based core competencies in doing particular things may be eroded, for example by technological change. Organizations which have developed strong organizational capabilities for managing knowledge creation and exploiting the value in knowledge created are better able to adapt to such change by developing new sustainable core competencies for the future. The importance of both types of capability in managing knowledge for competitive success is illustrated in the biotechnology context in Box 6.1.

Box 6.1 Knowledge and knowledge-based capabilities in biotechnology

In biotechnology, scientists bring highly specialized skills and knowledge to research teams. Although they bring specialized explicit knowledge, it is knowledge which could not be acquired overnight by a novice. They also bring tacit knowledge which is by definition difficult to transfer. In the processes of team interaction new knowledge is created and developed as participants pool their knowledge and skills.

Developments with commercial potential are patented and are difficult to substitute, replicate or imitate. But with or without patent protection, which

continued . . .

does not in any event last indefinitely, most advances are years in the making and could not be repeated independently outside the kinds of scientific culture which are characteristic of many biotechnology firms. These firms may develop a core competency in particular types of process technologies and/ or potential new knowledge applications. But if these technologies and/or applications fail at the development stage, these firms may still survive because of their ability to create new knowledge with the potential to lead to future successful developments.

CONVENTIONAL VERSUS KNOWLEDGE-BASED STRATEGY

Three key limitations to conventional understandings of and approaches to strategy can at this point be highlighted. The first is an over-reliance upon an information-processing model to understand and explain strategic decision-making. The second is a partial and incomplete view of human nature and the basis upon which effective human relationships are built. The third is a neglect of internal organizational dynamics of change.

Conventional understandings and approaches to strategy adopt an explicit or implicit information-processing view of the strategy formulation process. It is suggested that this emphasis upon information and information-processing issues neglects other important factors upon which the success of information processing depends. In the mid-1980s, Miller and Porter (1985) pointed out that 'the information revolution' was a key factor affecting relations between organizations and innovation. They suggested that information technologies can affect international organizations in three major ways. First, by changing the industry structure they can alter the rules of competition in some industries. Second, by creating new ways in which companies can outperform one another to gain competitive advantage, they can create new ways of competing. Third, they can spawn new business, often from within a company's existing operations. Miller and Porter (1985) argued that information technology could transform the linkages between value-creating activities in organizations and the way in which those activities were performed. They argued that every value-creating activity has both a physical and an information-processing component. New information flows enabled companies to exploit the linkages between value-creating activities more effectively, both within the firm and in networks and alliances with other firms. For example, information technologies have made it easier for buyers and suppliers to co-ordinate their activities. Miller and Porter suggested that many industries were moving towards a higher information content in both products and processes and that 'the information revolution' was creating interrelationships between industries that would otherwise have been separate. The fact that information technology had both strategic and structural implications was recognized, and the literature placed a new emphasis upon the strategic significance of information flows.

By stressing the value of information *flows*, Miller and Porter highlighted the fact that communications are as important as information-processing capability in explaining the human thinking which underpins decisions. From the mid-1980s onwards, however, it became increasingly apparent that this was only part of the story and that even this refinement to the information-processing model of organizations could not on its own explain the changes that were occurring. In some industries, established firms with dominant market positions, many of which had invested heavily in new information and communication technologies, were proving vulnerable to technological challenges from smaller firms, many of which were also industry outsiders. These companies, despite their seeming disadvantages in terms of size, resources, information-processing capabilities, market position and access to industry-specific information, were able to successfully pioneer radical technological changes which transformed the industry. For example in the computer industry, companies like Apple, Compaq and Dell pioneered and promoted the PC, which challenged IBM's supremacy in the computer market.

This phenomenon has been dubbed 'the attackers' advantage' (Foster, 1986). It does not appear to be readily explicable in terms of the conventional transaction costs paradigm and contradicts established strategic thinking about the importance of market position. It is possible to argue that there are asymmetries involved in such situations. Market leaders have their positions of dominance to lose by championing radical new technologies, whereas outside attackers have only the opportunity to benefit, but 'the attackers' advantage' does not apply to all cases of the radical technological change which transforms an industry. Some established companies have successfully pioneered changes which have eroded their existing technological competencies. Dupont, for example, developed and promoted synthetic fibres, even though synthetics were a challenge to rayon in which Dupont was the market leader (Hounshell and Smith, 1988).

What, therefore, is 'the attackers' advantage'? Did established firms like Dupont also possess it? The point is that information-processing capability is not on its own sufficient to create a competitive advantage in a firm of any size, irrespective of its original market position. The smaller 'attackers' which triumphed in the computer industry with the PC did so in competition with a world-beater in information processing. Some writers (e.g. Remenyi et al., 1995) have commented upon the numerous documented cases in which the large investments in information technology made by comparatively resource-rich firms have failed to deliver expected returns. During the 1980s, recognizing the sorts of potential for IT which were highlighted by Miller and Porter above, many organizations invested heavily in IT and in IT training. Some of them later engaged in downsizing exercises in the face of an intensification of competition and subsequently found that, in doing so, they had lost important *knowledge*. Information is only one of the inputs required to create and exploit knowledge.

Knowledge management is about more than the management of hardware and software and solving problems of user friendliness. It is also concerned with making the best possible use of the creativity and expertise of people and the effective management of dynamic social processes which generate and exploit a wide range of differing types of knowledge. It does not matter how sophisticated the information and communication technology is in a firm. If the employees are not inclined and trained to use it to its best advantage it is not the investment that it might be.

The second limitation noted earlier was the unrealistic perspective on the nature of human beings and the basis for effective human relationships which has been adopted by some of the conventional approaches to strategy. The rational understanding of human nature and its associated contractual understanding of human relationships in the firm overlooks a range of 'non-rational' behaviours and 'non-contractual' relationships both within and without the organization that are just as vital to considerations of performance.

Taking transaction costs theory as one of the most important influences on the traditional approach, we may ask a number of questions which are directly relevant to the creation and exploitation of knowledge. For example, if we focus upon the contractual aspect of transaction costs theory, can we arrive at an adequate appreciation of the nature of group knowledge? Is trust in an organization really part of an implicit contract? If in some ways it is, how far would this implicit contract of trust extend? If knowledge is a source of power in organizational contexts, is sharing knowledge part of an implicit contract of trust? What is contractual about the development of practical know-how based on experience? Does the idea of a contract account for individual differences in personal motivation and development over time?

Human beings clearly are capable of rational instrumental thinking. Rational problem-solving is integral to the decision-making process, but human beings have other qualities which are recognized in the knowledge-based literature and these qualities are also important. These are the qualities of vision, ambition, creativity and inventiveness which the knowledge management approach endeavours to tap. Human beings can be 'self-seeking' at times, but to regard them as self-seeking all the time is surely to adopt a jaundiced view. They can also be loyal and altruistic. Human nature is much more complex than the picture of boundedly rational man suggests. Similarly, productive human relationships depend upon more than explicit, implicit or psychological contracts. Common visions, shared ambitions, meanings, and group identities are important in groups and teams. Human beings operate in a world that is socially constructed (Berger and Luckmann, 1967), and organizational worlds are a long way from being rationally planned and constructed.

Most strategies, formally planned or emergent, originate with groups and teams. Group decision-making involves rational problem-solving and decision-making processes of the type Andrews (1971) describes in connection with strategy formulation. It also involves communications and reflective processes of the type described by Schon (1983) as 'reflection in action'.

These are the processes stressed in connection with knowledge management. A realistic view of human relationships is one in which *both* types of process are seen to be operative in reaching effective decisions. They are not alternative approaches. Both are integral to effectiveness (Carlisle and Dean, 1999).

Mary Douglas, an anthropologist, had this to say about Williamson's transaction costs theory: 'He believes firms vary, but not individuals. He has the same representative rational individual marching into one kind of contract or refusing to renew it and entering into another kind for the same set of reasons, namely the cost of transactions in a given economic environment' (Douglas, 1990: 102). At this point, it is worth stating that the transaction costs understanding, while adopting the notion of bounded rationality, has tended to stress the rational aspects of decision-making at the expense of equally important sociological and psychological ones. These processes are crucial to considerations of internal organizational dynamics and change. We may recall the fact that in March and Simon's original formulation of the bounded rationality concept, these two types of process were seen to be equally important.

The sociological and psychological processes which help to shape 'images' of the competitive environment and through which processes of knowledge creation, exploitation, transfer and change take place are not accorded a high profile in conventional approaches to strategy. Informal networks and communities of practice (Brown and Duguid, 1991), for example, are not discussed in the mainstream literature. It has already been said that conventional strategic approaches regard internal organizational dynamics as a strategy implementation concern. We may also be reminded at this point of Kogut and Zander's (1996) definition of organization as a 'social community', a definition which directs the attention of knowledge-based theorists towards those very processes as a mainstream strategy concern. In commenting on the charge that the transaction costs understanding neglects the dynamics of organization development and change, Williamson himself has repeatedly pointed out that his approach to understanding organizations is based on comparative statics. In simple terms this means that one organization is compared with another and found to have lower transaction costs. Strategists are encouraged to focus upon cost-minimizing efficiency at the expense of the dynamic efficiencies of knowledge creation and exploitation, innovation and technological change. Williamson appreciates that his understanding is partial in suggesting that 'much more study of the relations between organizations and innovation is needed' (Williamson, 1985: 144). In the knowledge-based view of the firm these neglected dynamics have a central place.

CONCLUSIONS

This chapter has argued that conventional approaches to strategy are based upon a partial understanding of information and knowledge, human nature, human relationships and the dynamics of change. However, partial understandings are not necessarily wrong. Circumstances may arise which highlight their deficiencies, which is what this chapter suggests happened in the context of the performance declines of companies like IBM. The tendency which was apparent throughout most of the 1980s to equate knowledge with information can now be seen more clearly to have been a mistake. Knowledge cannot be codified and subsequently commodified in the way that information can, but this is not to say that information and information processing are unimportant. It is simply to say that on their own they are not sufficient to create and sustain a competitive performance. Conventional approaches to strategy highlight rational rather than reflective decision processes, whereas rational *and* reflective communicative processes are equally important. Some aspects of human relationships are contractual, but once again this is only part of the picture and not all change can be understood in directive top-down terms.

This chapter has suggested that knowledge-based understandings and approaches to strategy can remedy this kind of shortcoming. Knowledge-based approaches to strategy raise the profile of human interactive processes and the dynamics of organizational change. These are precisely the kinds of process which the conceptualization of rational people engaging in contractual relationships has a tendency to under-rate.

A knowledge management approach to strategy clearly has the potential to provide a useful antidote. Earlier I raised the key question: how radical a shift in strategic thinking is required to move to a knowledge management approach? Does knowledge management require a paradigm shift? Is it incompatible with conventional approaches to strategy? Obviously not, in the opinion of this author. Conventional understandings can still offer useful insights into *what* an organization needs to achieve in order to sustain a successful performance. Conventional strategy approaches on the other hand might be considered to be somewhat naïve in respect of *how* to do it. The knowledge-based understanding offers a more realistic process perspective. It offers a better understanding of human nature, human relationships and internal organizational dynamics, and it is founded upon a better grasp of the differences between information and knowledge. It may be suggested that the two understandings of strategy are not incompatible and that there are obvious complementarities.

REFERENCES

Alchian, A. and Demetz, H. (1972) 'Production information costs and economic organization', *American Economic Review*, 62: 777–795.

Andrews, K. (1971) *The Concept of Corporate Strategy*, Homewood, IL, Dow Jones Irwin.

Barney, J.B. (1986) 'Organizational culture: can it be changed?', *Academy of Management Review*, 11: 656–665.

Barney, J.B. (1991) 'Firm resources and sustained competitive advantage', *Journal of Management*, 17: 99–120.

Berger, P. and Luckmann, T. (1967) *The Social Construction of Reality*, New York, Doubleday.

Blackler, F. (1995) 'Knowledge, knowledge work and organizations: an overview and interpretation', *Organization Studies*, 16: 1021–1046.

Brown, J.S. and Duguid, P. (1991) 'Organizational learning and communities of practice: towards a unified view of working, learning and innovation', *Organization Science*, 2: 40–57.

Camerer, C. and Vespalainen, A. (1988) 'The economic efficiency of corporate culture', *Strategic Management Journal*, Vol. 9: 115–126.

Carlisle, Y.M. and Dean, A. (1999) 'Design as knowledge integration capability', *Creativity and Innovation Management*, 8 (2): 112–121.

Clegg, S.R. (1990) *Modern Organizations: Organization Studies in the Post-Modern World*, London, Sage.

Dierickx, I. and Cool, K. (1989) 'Asset stock accumulation and sustainability of competitive advantage', *Management Science*, 35: 1504–1511.

Douglas, M. (1990) 'Converging on autonomy: anthropology and institutional economics', in O. E. Williamson (ed.) *Organization Theory: from Chester Barnard to the Present and Beyond*, Oxford, Oxford University Press, pp. 98–115.

Fiol, C.M. (1991) 'Managing culture as a competitive resource: an identity-based view of sustainable competitive advantage', *Journal of Management*, 17: 191–211.

Foster, R.N. (1986) *Innovation: The Attackers' Advantage*, New York, Summit Books.

Fransman, M. (1998) 'Information, knowledge, vision and theories of the firm', in G. Dosi, D.J. Teece and J. Chytry (eds) *Technology, Organization and Competitiveness*, Oxford, Oxford University Press, pp. 147–192.

Gee, P. (1996) 'On mobots and classrooms, the converging languages of the new capitalism and schooling', *Organization*, 3: 147–192.

Grant, R. (1996) 'Prospecting in dynamically competitive environments: organizational capability as knowledge integration', *Organization Science*, 7: 375–387.

Hall, R. (1993) 'A framework linking intangible resources and capabilities to sustainable competitive advantage', *Strategic Management Journal*, 14: 607–618.

Hamel, G. and Prahalad, C.K. (1989) 'Strategic intent', *Harvard Business Review*, 67, May/June: 63–76.

Hayek, F. (1945) 'The use of knowledge in society', *American Economic Review*, 35 (4): 519–530.

Hounshell, D.A. and Smith, J.K. (1988) *Science and Corporate Strategy: DuPont R&D, 1902–1980*, Cambridge, Cambridge University Press.

Jensen, M. and Meckling, W. (1976) 'Theory of the firm, managerial behaviour, agency costs and ownership structure', *Journal of Financial Economics*, 3: 305–360.

Kogut, B. and Zander, U. (1996) 'What do firms do? Co-ordination, identity and learning', *Organization Science*, 7: 503–518.

Lave, J. (1993) 'The practice of learning', in S. Chaiklin and J. Lave (eds) *Understanding Practice: Perspectives on Activity and Context*, Cambridge, Cambridge University Press, pp. 3–32.

Leonard, D. (1995) *Wellsprings of Knowledge: Building and Sustaining the Sources of Innovation*, Boston, MA, Harvard Business School Press.

March, J.G. and Simon, H.A. (1958) *Organizations*, New York, Wiley.

Marshall, A. (1969) *Principles of Economics* (first published 1920), London, Macmillan.

Miller, V.E. and Porter, M.E. (1985) 'How information gives you competitive advantage', *Harvard Business Review*, 63, July/Aug.: 149–160.

Moran, P. and Ghoshal, S. (1996) 'Value creation by firms', in J.P. Keys and L.N. Dosier (eds) *Academy of Management, Best Paper Proceedings*, Georgia Southern University, pp. 41–45.

Nahapiet, J. and Ghoshal, S. (1998) 'Social capital, intellectual capital and the organizational advantage', *Academy of Management Review*, 23: 242–266.

Nelson, R.R. and Winter, S.G. (1982) *An Evolutionary Theory of Economic Change*, Cambridge, MA, Harvard University Press.

Nonaka, I. (1991) 'The knowledge creating company', *Harvard Business Review*, 69, Nov./Dec.: 96–104.

Nonaka, I. (1994) 'A dynamic theory of organisational knowlege creation', *Organisation Science*, 5 (1) February: 14–37.

Nonaka, I. and Takeuchi, H. (1995) *The Knowledge Creating Company*, Oxford, Oxford University Press.

Penrose, E. (1959) *The Theory of the Growth of the Firm*, Oxford, Basil Blackwell.

Peteraf, M.A. (1993) 'The cornerstones of competitive advantage: a resource-based view', *Strategic Management Journal*, 14: 179–191.

Polanyi, M. (1958) *Personal Knowledge: Towards a Post Critical Philosophy*, London, Routledge and Kegan Paul.

Polanyi, M. (1966) *The Tacit Dimension*, London, Routledge and Kegan Paul.

Porter, M.E. (1991) 'Towards a dynamic theory of strategy', *Strategic Management Journal*, 12: 95–117.

Remenyi, D., Money, A. and Twite, A. (1995) *Effective Measurement and Management of IT Costs and Benefits*, Oxford, Butterworth-Heinemann.

Rumelt, R.P. (1984) 'Towards a strategic theory of the firm', in R.B. Lamb (ed.) *Competitive Strategic Management*, Englewood-Cliffs, NJ, Prentice-Hall, pp. 556–570.

Schon, D.A. (1983) *The Reflective Practitioner*, New York, Collins.

Selznick, P. (1957) *Leadership in Administration: A Sociological Perspective*, New York, Harper.

Teece, D.J. (1977) 'Technology transfer by multinational firms: the resource cost of transferring technical know-how', *The Economic Journal*, 87: 242–261.

Walford, G. (1979) *The Function of Ideology*, London, George Walford, Villiers Publications.

Wernerfelt, B. (1984) 'A resource-based view of the firm', *Strategic Management Journal*, 5: 171–180.

Williamson, O.E. (1975) *Markets and Hierarchies: Analysis and Anti-Trust Implications*, New York, Free Press.

Williamson, O.E. (1985) *The Economic Institutions of Capitalism: Firms, Markets, Relational Contracting*, London, Macmillan.

7

Conceptualizing Knowledge Used in Innovation: a Second Look at the Science–Technology Distinction and Industrial Innovation

*Wendy Faulkner**

This chapter reviews empirical and conceptual material from two distinct research traditions: on the science–technology relation and on industrial innovation. It aims both to shed new light on an old debate – the distinction between scientific and technological knowledge – and to refine our conceptualization of the knowledge used by companies in the course of research and development leading to innovation. On the basis of three empirical studies, a composite categorization of different types of knowledge used in innovation is proposed as part of a broader framework encompassing two further taxonomic dimensions. It is hoped that this typology and framework might provide useful research tools in furthering our understanding of the knowledge transfers and transformations that occur in the course of innovation. It could also prove useful for organizations and groups facing difficult strategic choices about technology.

This chapter joins other recent attempts to conceptualize technological knowledge and expertise[1] used in the course of research and development (R&D)[2] and design activities leading to innovation. It draws together conceptual and empirical threads from two distinct research traditions in science and technology studies: on the science–technology distinction and on industrial innovation. My primary objective is to propose a composite categorization of different *types* of knowledge used in innovation which, it is hoped, will prove useful as a research tool. As a secondary aim, I also consider whether we can distinguish between scientific and technological types of knowledge, and to what extent each is used in the course of industrial innovation.

The term *knowledge* is used here in its broadest sense to encompass what we call knowledge, expertise, skills, and information. Of course, the processes by

* Reprinted from *Science, Technology and Human Values*, Vol. 19, No. 4, pp. 425–458.
Copyright © 1994 Sage Publications, Inc. Reprinted by permission of Sage Publications, Inc.

which scientific and technological knowledge is created and deemed legitimate are very political in nature – witness the institutional authority associated
with medical knowledge, for example. My main concern here is more narrowly
focused, on the cognitive or epistemological features of the knowledge used
in innovation. These features are never simply 'internal', however. They are
intimately related to questions of who possesses particular knowledge and
how easy it is for particular groups to access and make use of this knowledge.
Indeed, my hope is that a more sophisticated characterization of technical
knowledge – one that identifies specific and substantive differences of type –
will further our understanding of what happens to knowledge as it moves
between, and is developed by, different groups in the course of innovation.

My interest in this project arose out of a particular concern with the flows
of knowledge between public sector research (PSR) organizations and
industry, which was the subject of a recent study I conducted with Jacqueline
Senker and Léa Velho.[3] This study sought to identify the particular types of
knowledge obtained from academic and government laboratories by firms
in three different technological fields, in order to understand variations in
the extent and nature of industry–PSR research linkage in different fields. The
findings of this study are reported fully elsewhere (Senker and Faulkner, 1992;
Faulkner et al., 1994). However, I present some of our findings here, together
with some findings from a similar study by Gibbons and Johnston (1974), to
examine the range of knowledge types used in the course of innovation, and
to illustrate the general applicability of a research approach that utilizes
detailed categorizations of knowledge.

The first section reviews literature on the science–technology relation,
including work in the history of technology that highlights a number of important cognitive and epistemological features of technological knowledge.
The second section reviews literature on knowledge used in industrial
innovation, focusing on the contribution of internal and external sources
of knowledge used in innovation, and on broad differences in the types of
knowledge obtained. The following section compares various attempts
to categorize technological knowledge and proposes a composite typology of
knowledge types. Possible research and policy uses of this typology are
outlined in the conclusions.

THE SCIENCE–TECHNOLOGY DISTINCTION

The science–technology relation was the subject of recurring debate in the field
of science studies, more or less from its inception until the early 1980s. During
the 1970s interest in the science–technology relation was largely superseded
by a concern with technology *per se*, in particular a concern to characterize
more adequately the nature of technological knowledge (Staudenmaier,
1985). Ironically, whereas the early literature tended to stress the increasing
proximity and overlap of science and technology, the latter work has tended
to highlight the distinctiveness of technology.

THE EARLY DEBATE: BLURRING THE BOUNDARIES

The early literature challenged the prevalent linear model of the science–technology relation. Within this model, science is the 'springhead' of innovation, as if scientific discovery necessarily implies technological invention, whereas technology involved the rather humdrum, responsive activity of applying science (see Barnes and Edge, 1982 for a review). Critics of this model pointed to the numerous occasions – not least, the advent of the steam engine – when technology 'led' science (e.g. Layton, 1988). Even where the reverse appeared to hold, detailed case studies revealed that the linearity was illusory. For instance, although the scientific quantum theory of semiconduction was a necessary precondition for the invention of the transistor, the theory itself did not suggest the technology: rather, the transistor arose primarily out of the development of rectifier technology within the fields of radar and radio (Gibbons and Johnson, 1982). The linear model was thus shown to be fundamentally flawed in its perception of both science and technology.

The alternative, 'two stream' model, championed by Derek de Solla Price, accords better with the historical evidence. On the basis of extensive citation analysis of science and technology publications, de Solla Price (1965) concluded that science tends to build on old science and technology on old technology, but there is a weak and reciprocal interaction between the two. He argued that maximum interaction occurs during the period of training when budding scientists and technologists read the archival literature of their respective endeavors, 'packed down' in textbooks. Accordingly, the education cycle accounts for a *time lag* (of approximately ten years) in the translation of new science into new technology, and vice versa (de Solla Price, 1965).

Later, de Solla Price revised his views somewhat. He argued that 'basic and applied research are linked inseparably to technology by the crafts and techniques of the experimentalist and inventor', and proposed the term *instrumentalities* 'to carry a general connotation of a laboratory method for doing something to nature or to the data in hand' (de Solla Price, 1984). A pertinent example is Rosalind Franklin's ability to make good X-ray diffraction pictures from very small samples of poorly crystallizable material: without this instrumentality, Watson and Crick would not have been able to 'see' the double helix. De Solla Price cited numerous instances when the advent of such instrumentalities has simultaneously opened up major new opportunities for scientific investigation and technological innovation.[4] At such times at least, he conceded, any time lag in the interaction between science and technology may be very short indeed.

More recent bibliometric analyses reveal just how short the time lag can be. In some technological fields (for example, biotechnology) the citation behavior of patent applicants (and examiners), in terms of the frequency of references to basic research publications and the time distribution of these citations, is very similar to that of researchers in neighboring scientific fields (Carpenter et al., 1980, 1981; Narin and Noma, 1985). Thus some technologies are strongly science related. Far from relying on archival literature, technologists keep up with the 'research front' literature in science.[5] In a study of solid-state technology publications between 1955 and 1975, Marvin Lieberman found that the frequency and age of scientific citations followed a pattern of 'overlapping waves' that, he concluded, were associated with 'the continual birth of new science-related technologies within the solid state field' (Lieberman, 1978).

Although this pattern explains the generally high level of coupling between science and technology evident in many advanced fields, it also suggests that such coupling is greatest during the early stages of development of a technological field. This theme is evident in economic theories of technological development, even though these theories do not explicitly model the science–technology relation (Granberg and Stankiewicz, 1978; Dosi, 1982). Empirical evidence that industrial innovation and growth tend to be 'knowledge-led' during the early development of an industry is provided by Vivien Walsh's (1984) detailed examination of time trends in scientific publication, patenting, and output in the chemical industry.

The emergence of the research-based chemical and electronics industries (Freeman, 1982: chs 1–3), and of the more science-related technologies identified above, indicates that science and technology have become increasingly intimate endeavors during this century. This trend has its historical roots in the establishment of R&D laboratories in industry and of specialist science and engineering departments in universities. Ironically, these developments involved an institutional separation of science and technology. Hendrick Bode (1965) argued that science was able to overlap with, and contribute to, technology in the areas of theory, experimental technique, and specialized knowledge precisely because it had earlier achieved its own momentum. At a cognitive level, the institutional changes signaled 'a more profound and subtle sort of science . . . it meant that by digging deeply enough we could expect to turn up new phenomena and new relationships not readily predictable from ordinary experience' (Bode, 1965: pt. 2). So, modern scientific inquiry demands not only lengthy training in the relevant specialisms but also the use of sophisticated equipment and instrumentation (Bud and Cozzens, 1992).

Taken together, the case studies and bibliometric evidence lead to two conclusions about the science–technology relation. First, it is a strongly interactive relationship between two semiautonomous activities, with instrumentalities as an important area of overlap. Second, science and technology are now particularly intimate activities, at least in some new fields and at times of major change. This latter conclusion obliges us to accept a blurring of the boundaries between science and technology as these terms are conventionally understood. Otto Mayr sums up the issue:

> [although] a practically usable criterion for making sharp and neat distinctions between science and technology simply does not exist . . . the two words 'science' and 'technology' are useful precisely because they serve as vague umbrella terms that roughly and impressionistically suggest areas of meaning without precisely defining their limits. (Mayr, 1982: 159)

We are left, it seems, with only nuances of meaning to distinguish science and technology. Indeed, for some, these boundaries are all but obliterated – witness Bruno Latour's use of the term *technoscience* (Latour, 1987). It seems pertinent, therefore, to review what others have to say about what makes technological knowledge distinct.

HISTORICAL STUDIES OF TECHNOLOGICAL KNOWLEDGE

The demise of the science–technology debate coincided with the shift of attention within the field of science studies toward the subject of technology. 'Revisionism' in the understanding of the science–technology distinction has come from scholars of technology, in particular, historians of technology. They have provided a strong empirical basis for the critique of the linear model, and much evidence about the nineteenth-century changes through which technology is held to have become more closely science related.

Edwin Layton's (1974) article 'Technology as knowledge' effectively launched a project to elucidate the nature of technological knowledge. This project has focused largely on the emergence of engineering as a distinct academic discipline (e.g. Layton, 1976; Channell, 1982; Constant, 1984a), and we should be careful not to conflate engineering and technology. Walter Vincenti (1991: 6) argues that, whereas technology properly includes drafts-people, shopfloor workers, and so on, engineers have a special relationship to technology. In line with the commonly accepted definitions of engineering, he identifies engineers as those who organize, design, construct, and operate artefacts that transform the physical world to meet a recognized need.

Studies of engineering have examined various aspects of the development of engineering curricula in universities, including the adoption of scientific methods and principles, and the balance of theoretical and practical training in different countries. David Channell (1982) concluded that 'engineering science' occupies an intermediate position between 'pure' engineering and science, by *translating* knowledge and techniques from one to the other. He thus rejects the assumption (made, for example, by Musson and Robinson, 1969) that engineering simply 'lifted' the scientific methodology. Layton (1976) and Channell (1982) both stressed that the closer organization and interplay of science and engineering were ideological as well as practical expedi-ents; engineers were keen also to acquire some of the image and status that nineteenth-century science enjoyed. Indeed, in a pertinent but rather facetious critique of Layton's and Channell's work, Fores (1988) argued that the transformation associated with the emergence of modern engineering has been grossly overstated, precisely because of the 'totemic' qualities of the label 'science'.[6]

Layton's project has been considerably furthered by the engineer-turned-historian Walter Vincenti. In *What Engineers Know and How They Know It*, Vincenti starts from the now traditional view within the history of technology that engineering is not a derivative of science but an autonomous body of knowledge that interacts with it (Vincenti, 1991: 1). He seeks to develop an epistemology of engineering based on a series of detailed empirical studies of the growth and maturation of aeronautical engineering between 1900 and 1950. At the beginning of this period, aircraft design was largely 'cut and try'; by the end, there existed a substantial body of underpinning theory, experimental techniques, and data. As a result of these developments, Vincenti argues, the level of uncertainty surrounding design declined dramatically because 'acts of [communicable] skill' increasingly reduced reliance on 'acts of insight', and aeronautical engineering is now a more or less systematic and cumulative body of knowledge (Vincenti, 1991: 168).

A number of important conclusions emerge from Vincenti's work. First, an extended *learning* process is often necessary if the requirements of the user are to be understood and integrated into design specifications. For example, it took twenty-five years of close interaction between engineers and pilots before flying quality specifications could be drawn up. The 'hands-on' experience of pilots had to be translated into codified design parameters. Second, much of the practical experience and knowledge required was *local* and *tacit* in character: shopfloor experience with different flush riveting techniques, for example, could not be easily codified or communicated between firms. Third, the generation of *data* was vital to improved analytical capability and this required the emergence of *vicarious testing techniques* to reduce reliance on the always costly and sometimes disastrous field trials. A key aeronautical example here is the use of wind tunnels for simulation tests. Fourth, certain *theoretical tools* and ways of thinking (for example, experimental parametric variation) were crucial to this development.

THE DISTINCTIVENESS OF TECHNOLOGICAL KNOWLEDGE

Historical work on engineering has highlighted rather than blurred the distinctions between science and technology. This cannot be entirely due to historians having a retrospective orientation, because scholars of modern technology reach similar conclusions (e.g. Sørenson and Levold, 1992). Drawing on both the historical and contemporary literatures, we can point to three closely related areas in which technology is distinguished from science: (1) in its purpose or orientation, (2) in its sociotechnical organization, and (3) in its cognitive and epistemological features.

With respect to orientation, there are familiar nuances of difference: technology is about *controlling* nature through the production of *artefacts* and science is about *understanding* nature through the production of *knowledge*. Mayr (1982: 159) argued that, although this distinction does indeed separate science and technology, 'it is valid only on the level of semantics. If we analyse actual historical events, we find that the motives behind actions are usually mixed and complex.' Vincenti nevertheless privileged the distinction:

'However phrased, the essential difference is one between intellectual understanding and practical utility' (Vincenti, 1991: 254). In a similar vein, Layton (1988) described engineering, medicine, and agriculture as 'techno-logical science' because they involve the 'science of the artificial' in contrast to the 'basic sciences' of the natural.

The practical–artefactual orientation of technology has important consequences for its organization, both as a body of knowledge and as a social activity. With respect to the latter, Edward Constant (1984b) and others have stressed the *hierarchical* features of the development of complex technological systems. Once a project specification has been drawn up and an overall concept design selected, the task of detailed design is 'decomposed' into major components of the system, specific problems and subproblems, and specialist disciplines. The technological project is thus highly structured, but in a way that allows maximum interaction and co-ordination between specific groups. Development of the design is co-ordinated and iterative, and the end product succeeds in *integrating* all of the necessary knowledge.

Scholars of modern technology, working in a constructivist framework also stress the socio-institutional complexity of technology, but they argue that this extends far beyond the laboratory or individual company. The recent article of Sørensen and Levold (1992: 19) is particularly helpful here. They synthesize John Law's concept of heterogeneous technology with Constant's hierarchy, arguing that the heterogeneity of technology is evident both in the terrain of the technoscientific – that is, the decomposition into problems requiring expertise from various groups – and in the sociotechnical – that is, 'how they [problems] are analysed and integrated' (Sørensen and Levold, 1992: 19). Sørensen and Levold conclude that technology is far more complicated than science on both counts: 'technology is usually surrounded by a larger number of powerful political and economic actors than is science . . . [thus] . . . science involves less of the social, and the social terrain on which scientists manoeuvre is much simpler than that of engineers' (Sørensen and Levold, 1992: 16).[7]

Science can be distinguished from engineering in terms of five distinct cognitive and epistemological features. First, because of its practical–artefactual orientation, the central activity in technology is *design*. In practice, design only sometimes demands the generation of new knowledge. Although design always enters into R&D, much of it is quite distinct from R&D both institutionally and cognitively (Walsh et al., 1992). According to Sørensen and Levold:

> Technology . . . is far more than what can reasonably be subsumed under the concept of engineering science. Development of technology still involves activities better described by the metaphor of art than of science. Practical intuition and a developed 'engineering gaze' are frequently more important than calculation and analysis. (1992: 19–22)

A second and related distinction is Sørensen and Levold's point that problem solving in technology is a more heterogeneous activity than it is in science.[8] Most science is also more homogeneous than technology in terms of disciplinarity, expertise, and social groupings, with the result that knowledge claims in science are generally far less heterogeneous than are innovations in technology.

A third distinction, which has been widely recognized since Polanyi's (1966) book on the subject, is the vital importance of local and tacit knowledge in technological innovation (Senker, 1993; Winter, 1987). This is demonstrated, for example, in Vincenti's (1991: ch. 5) study of flush riveting. James Fleck (1988) showed that the development of complex information technology (IT) systems demands extensive knowledge of the *contingencies* operating in user organizations. The picture that emerges is in stark contrast to the presumed universality of scientific knowledge. Of course, the work of Harry Collins (1974) shows that tacit knowledge is also important in scientific experiments. Sørensen and Levold argue, nevertheless, that its significance is far greater in technology because replication of reported experiments is not widespread in practice,[9] and because failure to replicate in science merely raises questions about a knowledge claim, whereas failure of an artefact can have disastrous social and economic consequences.

The final two areas of distinction are more problematic. They are the role of theory and the character of methodology in technology. Another of the nuances of meaning commonly attached to science and technology is that the former is more theory based and the latter more empirical. As the debate between Fores and Layton and Channell indicates, this assumption is highly contestable. In any case, it would be wrong to assume that all theory is necessarily scientific. Vincenti argues that the theoretical tools in engineering lie on a science–engineering spectrum. At the 'essentially scientific' end are the purely mathematical tools, followed by mathematically structured theoretical knowledge about the physical world. Such theories generally originate in science and attract scientific interest for their explanatory powers. However, they generally need to be reformulated or 'recast' in order to make them applicable to technological problems. The 'essentially engineering' end includes theory 'based on scientific principles but motivated by and limited to a technologically important class of phenomena or even a specific device' (Vincenti, 1991: 214). Interest in such theory depends entirely on the utility of the artefact to which it relates. At the far end of the spectrum, Vincenti identifies phenomenological theory, based primarily on *ad hoc* assumptions (presumably derived from trial and error practice) and only marginally on scientific principles. The explanatory power of such theory is limited, although its practical utility is high.

In the area of methodology, most scholars see little to distinguish science and technology. Sørensen and Levold (1992), for example, noted that there is much methodological variety within both science and technology. Constant nonetheless argues that modern technology may be distinguished from both craft technology and science by the application of a methodology based on 'bold total-system conjecture and rigorous testing to large-scale, complex, multi-level systems' (Constant, 1984a). Vincenti similarly identifies what he calls 'characteristically engineering methodology' suggestive of something akin to scientific methodology (1991: ch. 5). He cites the use of experimental parametric variation and scale models to test aircraft propellers – activities that took place independently of physical theory and that provided vital data for design and analysis where no useful theory existed to predict performance.[10] Like Channell (1988), Vincenti (1991: 168) concluded that although elements of engineering methodology appear scientific, engineering methodology as a whole did not emerge within science.

We should remember that there are important respects in which science and technology are still generally held to be similar. Both conform to the same natural 'laws'.[11] Both are cumulative and diffuse largely through the same mechanisms: education, publications, and informal communication. And both are organized around professional communities with marked disciplinary autonomy. Nonetheless, the studies cited here point to some quite significant distinctions between these two activities and associated bodies of knowledge – distinctions that hinge on the practical and artefactual orientation of technology, and include a number of socio-institutional and epistemological differences that flow from this orientation. I would argue that this work does indeed oblige us to rethink earlier conclusions about the apparently vanishing boundaries between science and technology. Further support for this position comes from scholarship on knowledge used in industrial innovation, to which we now turn.

KNOWLEDGE USED IN INDUSTRIAL INNOVATION

Our concern here is with knowledge actually used in the process of innovation. To the extent that innovation relates to artefacts and not understanding *per se*, it is decidedly technological. However, I am not assuming that the knowledge used in innovation is exclusively technological, hence the formulation adopted here. Indeed, it is clear that scientific knowledge also contributes to innovation. This section summarizes literature that seeks to calibrate and explain the relative contribution of internal and external sources to the knowledge used in innovation. The studies reported here are based on quite different research questions and methodologies from those described above. They are contemporary rather than historical studies, with a specific focus on the innovating firm rather than on science or technology more broadly. In spite of this, both literatures point to similar conclusions about the types of knowledge used in innovation.

KNOWLEDGE FROM INTERNAL AND EXTERNAL SOURCES: THE EVIDENCE

The early concern in science studies with the science–technology relation was paralleled in the new field of science policy by a concern to assess the contribution of public 'science' to technological innovation. This concern underpinned the celebrated but now widely discredited retrospective studies such as TRACES (Illinois Institute of Technology Research Institute, 1968; Batelle Columbus Laboratory, 1973) and Project Hindsight (Sherwin and Isenson, 1967).[12] It also informed many of the early innovation studies of the 1970s. In contrast to the retrospective studies, this research focused on the knowledge actually used in the course of innovation, rather than knowledge that in some abstract and convoluted way might have contributed to it. The innovation studies sought to identify the main institutional source of the original idea for the innovation under investigation and of the major technical inputs to subsequent problem solving (see Rothwell, 1977 for a review).

Averaging across industries, there is remarkable convergence in the results of these studies. Around two-thirds of the knowledge used by companies in the course of innovation derives from their own in-house R&D effort and expertise; the remaining third comes from external sources. The largest single external source of scientific and technological contributions to innovation is other industrial companies, especially users or suppliers but also competitors. The contribution of academic and government laboratories varies across sectors from 5 percent to 20 percent (Rothwell, 1977).

The early innovation studies revealed that the translation of new knowledge into new artefacts is an extremely complex process; that the relationship between academic and industrial research is neither obvious nor direct; and that innovation demands knowledge from a range of internal and external sources. Most significantly, success in industrial innovation rests on the effective organizational 'coupling' of technical and market opportunities and intelligence (Rothwell et al., 1974; Freeman, 1982: ch. 5). Thus management capability is required in a range of areas, not simply in research. The challenge posed by innovation now tends to be seen more as one of organization than of intellect, and this has become the central preoccupation of the innovation literature. Perhaps as a result, there has been little concern to examine further the cognitive features of industrial innovation.

An important exception was the study by Gibbons and Johnston (1974) of 30 award-winning innovations. It sought to assess the particular contribution of 'public science' to innovation by asking industrial R&D staff to identify all of the scientific and technological 'information' used by them in the course of new product development. This yielded 887 units of information that were then analysed in terms of the content of the information, the sources from which that information was obtained, and its impact on problem-solving activity. Table 7.1 summarizes their data on the content of information obtained from different sources.[13]

The results in Table 7.1 can be compared with those in Table 7.2, which analyse the 'impact' of knowledge from different sources on different areas of companies' innovative activities, grouped under six broad headings.[14] These data were generated in our recent study based on 44 interviews with R&D staff in 23 firms, covering three fields of technology. This study investigated

TABLE 7.1 *Content of scientific and technological input (STI) to innovation by source**

Content of knowledge	Info units		Source		
			Internal	Other companies[a]	PSR[b]**
Theories, laws, and general principles	8%	(69)	52% (36)	16% (11)	32% (22)
Properties of materials and components	32%	(270)	74% (200)	16% (42)	10% (28)
Design-based information, operating principles	24%	(205)	81% (165)	15% (30)	5% (10)
Test procedures and techniques	10%	(78)	80% (62)	12% (9)	9% (7)
Knowledge of knowledge	26%	(217)	57% (124)	30% (66)	12% (27)
Total	100%	(839)	70% (587)	19% (158)	12% (94)

[a] 'Other companies' includes here the trade and technical literature, plus contacts with organizations such as British Standards and Research Associations.

[b] PSR = public sector research, which is described by Gibbons and Johnston as 'public science' and defined as scientific journals, books, and so on, as well as personal contacts in government and academic laboratories.

* Percentage of information units; numbers in parentheses.

** PSR is referred to as 'public science' by Gibbons and Johnston, and defined as Public Sector Research.

Source: Gibbons and Johnston, 1974

the knowledge flows or scientific and technological inputs (STI) associated with industry–PSR linkage activity. Following a similar approach to that of Gibbons and Johnston, it examined the type, source, and impact of STI on innovation.[15] The major difference is that we did not attempt to quantify the types of knowledge used in innovation.

The two studies have a crucial common feature: both start from an analysis of firms' total knowledge requirements (or use) as the most appropriate basis for assessing the particular contribution of PSR. This makes the findings in Tables 7.1 and 7.2 interesting for two reasons. First, they reveal that companies obtain different types of knowledge from different sources. Second, they provide a quite detailed picture of the full range of knowledge types utilized in the course of R&D leading to innovation.

The dominant contribution of internal sources to knowledge used in innovation is confirmed by the data in both tables.[16] Researchers we interviewed reported almost unanimously that what they called tacit skills, acquired largely on the job, make a greater overall contribution to innovation than does formal knowledge, acquired from literature and education. Further questioning revealed that tacit knowledge is also obtained from other companies and from PSR (Senker and Faulkner, 1993). Significantly, though, industrial R&D activities demand a synthesis of these diverse contributions from both internal and external sources.

Table 7.1 shows that internal sources make a particularly high contribution to design and to test procedures and techniques, and contribute substantially to properties of materials and components. Similarly, in Table 7.2, internal

TABLE 7.2 *Impact of scientific and technological input (STI) on innovative activities by source**

Activity	Source			
	Internal	Other companies	PSR[a]**	NR[b]
Future innovations	57% (52.0)	33% (30.0)	10% (9.0)	(5)
Search activity				
Scouting for new applications	45% (13.5)	27% (8.0)	28% (8.5)	(2)
Scanning research frontier	30% (8.5)	18% (5.0)	52% (14.5)	(4)
Subtotal	37% (22.0)	22% (13.0)	40% (23.0)	(6)
Ongoing R&D[c]				
Underpinning knowledge	40% (12.5)	2% (0.5)	58% (18.0)	(1)
Routine problem solving	88% (28.0)	9% (3.0)	3% (1.0)	(0)
Subtotal	65% (40.5)	6% (3.5)	30% (19.0)	(1)
Instrumentalities				
Research equipment	18% (5.5)	52% (15.5)	30% (9.0)	(2)
R&D[c] procedures	47% (14.5)	24% (7.5)	29% (9.0)	(1)
Skills in experimentation and				
testing	55% (16.5)	17% (5.0)	28% (8.5)	(2)
Subtotal	40% (36.5)	31% (28.0)	29% (26.5)	(5)
Production	51% (23.5)	46% (21.0)	3% (1.5)	(18)
Technical backup	73% (14.5)	10% (2.0)	18% (3.5)	(12)
Overall total	51% (189.0)	27% (97.5)	22% (82.5)	(47)

a   PSR Public Sector Research
b   NR = non-responses; this includes a small number of responses that gave equal weight to all
    three sources.
c   R&D = research and development.
*   Percentage of responses; numbers in parenthesis.
** PSR is referred to as 'public science' by Gibbons and Johnston (1974), and defined as Public
    Sector Research.
Source: Faulkner et al., 1994

sources dominate in routine problem solving (as well as technical backup) and contribute substantially to skills in experimentation and testing. Thus the type of knowledge obtained from internal sources is primarily associated with the core activities of R&D and design. Gibbons and Johnston found that half of all knowledge from internal sources is collectively generated, as a result of in-house activities (mostly experimentation and analysis), and half is personal in the sense that it is already known to the individual researcher, as a result of previous education and work experience.[17]

Instrumentalities are an important aspect of R&D. Table 7.2 shows that the impact of internal sources in this area is slightly less than average. This, in part, reflects the fact that other companies make a major contribution to research equipment (and a relatively high contribution to production and knowledge of knowledge). A second factor is the slightly greater than average contribution of PSR to the procedures and skills used in R&D (although this is not particularly evident in Table 7.1). Other evidence from our study highlights the practical help with experimentation provided by contacts in

PSR, which supports de Solla Price's contention that instrumentalities are an important area of overlap between academic and industrial research.

Table 7.1 indicates that internal sources contribute less to theory than to any other category of knowledge, although still more than external sources. Conversely, theory is the only category in which PSR makes a greater than average contribution: one-third of all theory-related knowledge comes from this source. This is consistent with our finding that PSR contributes most significantly in two areas: scanning the research frontier and underpinning knowledge.[18] In Table 7.1, design is the category to which PSR contributes least, whereas Table 7.2 indicates that PSR can contribute materially to product design and development (at least in the more design-based fields) and to scouting for new applications. Nonetheless, our finding that PSR has a very minor impact on future innovation supports the conclusion of Gibbons and Johnston that 'public science' is generally 'not the springhead of innovative ideas' (1974).

It is not possible to separate scientific and technological knowledge within the various categories used in these two studies. However, the data presented here do shed light on the relative contribution of each to innovation, which is relevant to the science–technology debate outlined earlier. First, it is clear that scientific knowledge (as defined earlier) is a part of the theory, knowledge of properties, and methodology used in the R&D that leads to innovation. Second, at least some of this scientific knowledge comes from internal sources (and, sometimes, other companies): there is a considerable in-house contribution in the areas of theory, underpinning knowledge, scanning the research frontier, and instrumentalities. Third, PSR also contributes some technological knowledge through its input to research equipment and, in some fields, to engineering research and design.

Biotechnology is an interesting case in point because the boundaries between science and technology appear particularly indistinct in this field. Yet our study and my own earlier research (Faulkner, 1986, 1989) reveal that even here the nuances of distinction between scientific and technological knowledge still have some meaning. Significantly, industrial researchers in this field – unlike those in advanced ceramics and parallel computing – unambivalently call themselves scientists.

The various threads of evidence presented here lead to three broad conclusions. First, with regard to the overall knowledge used in innovation, the dominant contribution of internal sources is confirmed; this knowledge is primarily associated with design and R&D activities. Second, the more significant contribution identified as coming from PSR is in research rather than in design and development; PSR contributes new knowledge, theoretical knowledge, and knowledge related to research techniques, which is consistent with the idea that the balance of frontier research occurs within PSR. Third, these studies clearly show that industrial research is by no means exclusively concerned with technological knowledge, any more than public sector research solely constitutes 'public science'.

WHY COMPANIES USE INTERNAL AND EXTERNAL SOURCES OF KNOWLEDGE

Keith Pavitt (1984) noted that by privately funding R&D activities, companies add to the total stock of knowledge as well as drawing on knowledge that is publicly available. Three factors explain the dominant role of internal knowledge. First, firms need to appropriate technology related to specific artefacts, normally by patenting or trade secrecy, in order to extract a reasonable rent from them. When a product is a radical improvement on the existing ones, obtaining proprietary advantage may even secure the innovator monopoly profits for a while. Appropriating external technology is often necessary but problematic. The experience of technology transfer reveals that ownership of intellectual property alone is inadequate, because additional tacit knowledge and skills are generally needed in order to effect the transfer.[19] And in this, as in other forms of external knowledge acquisition, an under-stated but significant irony is that companies must have some related in-house expertise if they are to make sense of and to fully exploit external knowledge (Gambardella, 1992).

This relates to the second reason for the dominant role of internal sources of knowledge in innovation, namely the cumulative nature of technological development. This is a recurring theme in economic histories of technology, and one I would stress.[20] At the level of technological fields, the cumulative nature of development is reflected in 'path dependence' whereby one development appears to suggest the next. Path dependence is captured in the now common use of the terms *technological trajectories* and *paradigms* (Dosi, 1982).[21] Knowledge acquisition and generation are also strongly cumulative at the level of the firm. It is easier for companies to build on existing capability than to start afresh, and organizational learning is necessary to build up capability. Learning is particularly crucial in relation to difficult-to-acquire tacit and skill-based knowledge, which may explain why tacit knowledge is often identified as being derived primarily from in-house capability and efforts.

The third reason for the dominance of internal sources of knowledge is the role of specific, as opposed to general, knowledge in innovation. Pavitt (1984), for example, explains the overriding importance of internally generated knowledge by the specificity of the knowledge inputs necessary for product differentiation in the marketplace and for appropriability. Giovanni Dosi (1988) relates the concept to the breadth of in-house R&D, arguing that low product specificity in R&D enables companies to achieve synergy across product areas, whereas high firm specificity is more likely to secure appropriability. These comments on specific knowledge in product innovation resonate with Fleck's (1988) concern with contingent knowledge in complex process innovation.

Specificity pertains primarily to design and development work, some three quarters of industrial R&D expenditure. By contrast, industrial research is likely to have a broader remit; it may be characterized as a *search activity*, undertaken to identify new opportunities and to resolve attendance problems. Nathan Rosenberg (1992) stressed that companies are simply unable to know fully in advance what they should be searching for, or to pursue all possible alternatives in their search efforts. Richard Nelson (1982) conceptualizes knowledge as 'capability for efficient search' and argues that corporate expenditure on basic research 'enhances the productivity of applied research and development' by helping companies to establish where they should be looking. This is likely to be crucial at times of technological discontinuity or paradigm shift. Nevertheless, companies tend to underinvest in basic research because of the uncertainty surrounding its outcome and the difficulty of appropriating any benefits (Nelson, 1959).

Both the knowledge contribution of PSR to innovation and the 'division of labor' between industrial R&D and PSR are broadly explicable within this framework (Rosenberg, 1990; Pavitt, 1991). In effect, government funding of basic research underwrites the long-term interests of industry by conducting an open-ended and speculative search operation on its behalf.

The contribution of other companies is most easily explained in terms of the importance to innovation of knowledge flow among companies in the supply chain. Innovations of all types may demand knowledge from suppliers of materials or components incorporated into the final product (von Hippel, 1988). Moreover, success in innovation depends crucially on the quality of knowledge flow about user needs (Rothwell, 1977). The relationship is of course particularly strong with specialist users of complex technologies (Fleck, 1988, 1993). Such considerations should not blind us to the importance of knowledge flow between competitors, however. Nelson (1982) argued that, in addition to companies' interests in securing proprietary advantage by keeping certain knowledge private, companies have a collective interest in keeping much technological knowledge in the public domain. Without this knowledge, no companies on their own would be innovative. Of course, the patent system and other publications are formal mechanisms by which technological knowledge is shared. Our field experience suggests that although industrial staff are careful not to disclose commercially sensitive information, some types of technological knowledge (for example, knowledge of instrumentalities) are quite extensively shared through informal interaction.[22]

The question why some knowledge is generated internally and other knowledge is obtained from external sources is very significant for economists of technology. A useful conceptual framework for addressing such issues has come from the field of evolutionary economics, in particular from the work of Stanley Metcalfe and Michael Gibbons (1989) who write about the organizational knowledge base that companies must 'articulate' in order to produce a given set of artefacts. This framework seeks to explain the dual occurrence of continuity and change in technological innovation. Path dependence and cumulative knowledge acquisition within the firm explain why companies articulate knowledge most effectively in fields that are familiar to them, and why they find it difficult to extend their existing knowledge base into new areas of innovative activity. Metcalfe and Gibbons suggest that external

sources of knowledge will be especially important in cases of radical innovation because movement into new fields is strongly constrained, not only by
the existing capability of a firm but also by technological paradigms. According
to Dosi (1982: 155), technological paradigms have a 'powerful exclusion effect'
and so limit the ability of firms to 'see' knowledge (including technological
options) that is available outside. Firms' external search activity and research
linkages are important means to overcome these constraints.

CATEGORIZATIONS OF KNOWLEDGE USED IN INNOVATION

Given that companies use a range of knowledge types in the course of R&D
leading to innovation, how should we best conceptualize this epistemological
variety? Five different attempts to categorize knowledge used in innovation
are summarized in Tables 7.3 and 7.4. As indicated, these categorizations differ
in terms of the disciplinary perspective of their authors and the purposes for
which they were devised. They also fall into two distinct groups in terms of
the level of conceptualization attempted. The contributions in Table 7.3
concern what we might call broad distinctions in the character of knowledge
used in innovation, whereas those in Table 7.4 represent more specific
categories of knowledge. The latter categorizations provide the basis of the
typology proposed here, and the broader distinctions provide a useful context
for this typology.

BROAD DISTINCTIONS IN THE CHARACTER OF KNOWLEDGE USED IN INNOVATION

Table 7.3 presents a synthesis of the contributions of Sidney Winter (1987)
and Giovanni Dosi (1988), both of whom attempt to understand knowledge
used in innovation from within the framework of evolutionary economics.

TABLE 7.3 *Broad categorizations of knowledge used in innovation*

Authors	Fleck and Tierney (1991)	Winter (1987); also Dosi (1988)
Perspective	Social shaping of technology	Evolutionary economics
Aim	To conceptualize knowledge in terms of sociocognitive structures that relate the content of knowledge to how it is distributed among individuals and organizations	To distinguish features of technological knowledge that impinge on the ease of technology transfer between firms
Categories	Metaknowledge	Tacit–articulated
	Milieu	(Teachable–nonteachable)
	Contingent knowledge	(Articulate–nonarticulate)
	Tacit knowledge	Nonobservable–observable
	Informal knowledge	Complex–simple
	Formal knowledge	Elements of a system–independent
	Instrumentalities	Specific–general

Although not directly empirically derived, both contributions build on earlier case studies. The contribution of James Fleck and Margaret Tierney (1991) is based on a detailed study of the development and management of expertise in the course of strategic innovations in financial services that they analyse from a 'social shaping of technology' perspective.

Elsewhere, Fleck (1992) proposed a useful framework in which he characterizes technological expertise as involving a tripartite relationship along the three axes of knowledge, power, and tradability, addressed respectively by the disciplines of epistemology, politics, and economics. He concluded that, although some work successfully addresses two of these three axes (one or the other side of the triad), no existing approach integrates all three. The categorization proposed by Fleck and Tierney (1991: 12) is an attempt to move in this direction. It explicitly links the social context within which expertise is generated and utilized with its cognitive character: 'Viewing knowledge in terms of components of socio-cognitive structures provides a means for relating the content of knowledge to its specific embodiment' (Fleck and Tierney, 1991).

Fleck and Tierney's sociocognitive structures have two major dimensions: (1) the components of knowledge (identified in Table 7.3), and (2) the distribution of knowledge among different carrier groups or individuals. Issues of power and tradability clearly enter the latter dimension, because these issues determine the monetary value and status attributed to particular competence or knowledge. Labor process factors, for example, shape both the construction of skills and expertise, and internal and external labor markets for specific expertise. Similarly, the extent to which knowledge can be appropriated impinges crucially on the success of the innovating organization and on the wider diffusion of this knowledge.

As noted earlier, the tradability and ease of transfer of knowledge between companies are central concerns for economists of technology. Winter (1987) and Dosi (1988) separately suggested continua that characterize technological knowledge and together have a strong bearing on cross-sector variety in appropriability regimes and technology transfer. These have been amalgamated in Table 7.3. (The features listed on the right-hand side are likely to be associated with ease of transfer.)

These continua echo a number of elements in the Fleck and Tierney categorization. The concepts of specific and contingent knowledge refer to the important role of local knowledge discussed earlier, and they may be contrasted with Fleck and Tierney's category of the more taken-for-granted metalevel knowledge that is universal.[23] In addition, their distinction between formal and informal knowledge appears to be subsumed in Winter's distinction between tacit and articulated knowledge. He elaborates on this aspect by distinguishing between what is nonarticulated and nonarticulable, and between what is teachable and nonteachable. These distinctions usefully focus on skills that may be taught (by example) although they are not articulable, and on articulable knowledge that sometimes gets 'lost' because it is never articulated.[24] The category 'observability in use' describes how easily the underlying knowledge embodied in a product is revealed in practice. This is likely to depend both on the capability of the observer and on the willingness of the producer to co-operate and share relevant tacit knowledge. Finally, Winter suggests that the more complex and system dependent the particular technological artefact and knowledge, the less accessible it will be. This resonates with Fleck's (1988, 1993) earlier work on configurational technologies in which he classifies technologies in relation to the complexity of the knowledge associated with them.

In principle, it should be possible to combine the elements of the two categorizations in Table 7.3. The broad character of knowledge could be related to the wider social and economic factors that influence where knowledge is located and what knowledge gets transferred between individuals and groups. My purpose here is not to attempt the synthesis Fleck envisions but to elaborate primarily on the more narrowly cognitive or epistemological aspects of his triad. However, it should be borne in mind that the two other axes of expertise identified by Fleck – power and tradability – cut across the more detailed categorizations of knowledge that we explore below.

DETAILED CATEGORIES OF KNOWLEDGE USED IN INNOVATION

Table 7.4 lists sets of categorizations constructed on the basis of the studies by Vincenti, Gibbons and Johnston, and ourselves. Differences in emphasis among these categorizations largely reflect differences in the empirical studies from which they were derived. Vincenti's study was based on case studies of 'normal' design in one field of engineering over an extended period ending in 1950; Gibbons and Johnston's categorization was based on individual successful innovations from a range of sectors in the 1970s; and our own categorization was based on R&D into promising new technologies in the 1980s and 1990s that have not yet yielded significant innovations. Although they all address technological processes, these studies highlight different aspects and different periods of recent history. The historical research methods of Vincenti are distinct from Gibbons and Johnston's and our interview-based methodology. Nevertheless, all three categorizations have been derived from open-ended and detailed empirical inquiries into the totality of technical knowledge utilized in the course of innovation. The categories have then been imposed on these data by the researchers.[25] Both Vincenti and I have striven to use labels and categories identifiable to, if not identified by, practitioners (and so meaningful to them) – except for the term 'instrumentalities'.

Table 7.5 draws together what I see as the main elements identified in Table 7.4. It presents a composite typology that groups 15 different types of knowledge used in industrial innovation, under five headings. These categories should be fairly self-explanatory, but their main features are briefly outlined below with reference, where appropriate, to the three studies from which they were derived.

TABLE 7.4 *Detailed categorizations of knowledge used in innovation*

Authors	Vincenti (1991)	Gibbons and Johnston (1974)	Faulkner et al. (1994)
Perspective	History of technology	Innovation studies	
Aim	To develop an epistemology of engineering, in particular to relate categories of knowledge to knowledge-generating activities	To establish the extent and character of knowledge flows from public sector research into industrial innovation by investigating the full range of knowledge inputs to innovation	
Categories	*Categories of knowledge* Fundamental design concepts Criteria and specifications Theoretical tools Quantitative data Practical considerations Design instrumentalities	*Content of information* Theories, laws, general principles Properties, composition, characteristics of materials and components Operating principles or rules Required specifications, technical limitations	*Broad knowledge types* Knowledge of particular fields Technical information Skills Knowledge related to artefacts
	Knowledge-generating activities Transfer from science Invention Theoretical engineering research Experimental engineering research Design practice Production Direct trials	Design-based information Test procedures and techniques Existence of equipment or materials with particular properties Existence of specialist facilities or services Location of information	*Impact on company activities* New product ideas Articulation of user needs Feedback on existing products Scouting for new applications Scanning the research frontier Underpinning knowledge Routine problem solving New research equipment New R&D procedures Skills in experimentation and testing New process technology New production methods Technical backup

Knowledge related to the natural world. This includes theories and knowledge of the properties of materials, two categories that are generally easy to identify. The domains of science and technology are both present. Theory, in the sense described by Vincenti, includes the theoretical tools (such as parametric variation) used in engineering experimentation, whereas the category 'properties' encompasses properties of artefacts and of nature.

Knowledge related to design practice. Design-related knowledge, most evident in Vincenti's categories and least in ours,[26] constitutes a vital aspect of technological innovation. Typically, design and development activities follow four stages (Walsh et al., 1992: ch. 70). First, *design criteria* are drawn up on the

TABLE 7.5 *Composite typology of knowledge used in innovation*

Related to natural world
    Scientific and engineering theory
        'laws' of nature; theoretical tools
    Properties of materials
        Natural and artificial materials
Related to design practice
    Design criteria and specifications
        Understanding of user requirements
        Demands of company and technology
        Specifications of components
    Design concepts
        Fundamental operating principles
        Normal configurations
        Creative ideas
    Design instrumentalities[a]
    Design competence[a]
        General design competence
        Competence in specific product area
    Practical experience
Related to experimental R&D
    Experimental and test procedures
    Research instrumentalities[a]
        Ability to utilize experimental techniques and equipment
        Ability to interpret test and experimental results
    Research competence
        General research competence
        Competence in particular specialism
    Experimental and test data
Related to final product
    New product ideas
    Operating performance
        Performance of components or materials
        Pilot production, field trials, and so on
        User experience
    Production competence[a]
        Design requirements for manufacture
        Competence in pilot production/scale-up
Related to knowledge
    Knowledge of knowledge
        Location of particular knowledge
        Availability of equipment, materials, specialist facilities, or services

[a] Indicates knowledge that is heavily skill based.

basis of the dual requirements of the companies and the potential users. Second, more detailed *specifications* are then produced on the basis of technical considerations (feasibility, etc.). Third, alternative concept designs are considered and one is eventually selected. Finally, the detailed design of the product is elaborated.

The various types of *design concepts* listed in Table 7.5 come from Vincenti. 'Fundamental operating principles' are the principles that make a particular artefact work: for example, the fixed-wing aircraft that flies because of Cayley's principle that one can 'make a surface support a given weight by the application of power to the resistance of air' (cited in Vincenti, 1991: ch. 7). 'Normal configurations' are the arrangements and shapes commonly taken to be the best embodiments of operating principles; they represent the framework of 'normal' design. Such knowledge is intrinsically technological rather than scientific and is often taken for granted, having been absorbed from earlier engineering. The role of creative ideas in both concept design and detailed design is everywhere acknowledged, even if 'creative ideas' are a little awkward as a category of knowledge. Good ideas rarely emerge in a vacuum.

The category *design instrumentalities* adopted by Vincenti encompasses structured procedures (such as decomposing a problem into subproblems), ways of doing things and thinking (for example, the use of analogy and 'what would happen if?' approaches), and judgmental skills (for example, the ability to balance conflicting design requirements) (Vincenti, 1991: ch. 7). The role of skills or *competence* in all aspects of design – general and specific – is self-evident (although there is arguably considerable overlap between design skills and design instrumentalities). *Practical considerations*, in Vincenti's use, imply knowledge drawing more on experience than skill (1991: ch. 7). They include the vital elements of user experience of operation, shopfloor experience of construction or production, and the 'rules of thumb' from previous design experience.[27]

Knowledge related to experimental R&D. Experimental and test procedures are accepted ways of setting up experiments and tests.[28] *Research instrumentalities*, following de Solla Price (1984), are knowledge and skills related to the techniques and artefacts used in the course of experimental R&D. As with the example of Rosalind Franklin's skill at X-ray crystallography, instrumentalities include the ability to use research instruments effectively. Senker's work on advanced engineering ceramics demonstrates that the ability to interpret test results obtained from sophisticated equipment is also crucial (Senker and Faulkner, 1992).

The nature of general and specific *research competence* is self-evident, as is the category of *experimental and test data*. The latter is perhaps the most tangible knowledge output of R&D. Vincenti's work stressed the importance of data to engineering capability and showed that quantitative data may be either theoretically or empirically derived and may be either descriptive or prescriptive (Vincenti, 1991: ch. 7). Our study and Gibbons and Johnston's reveal that data often relate to both properties of materials and to operating performance (see below).

Knowledge related to the final product. We have found that *new product ideas* rarely emerge in a single step from a single source but rather 'coalesce' over a period of time. Knowledge about the *operating performance* of the product is clearly vital and is obtained variously through pilot production, direct trials, and user experience. Knowledge about the *performance of components or materials* is obtained from suppliers and users, and from experience. *Production competence* contributes to early concept design (ideally), as well as to later detailed design through pilot production.

Knowledge related to knowledge. The category *knowledge of knowledge* comes from Gibbons and Johnston's study. It captures the facility to find out things that are necessary to new product development but that are not known to those immediately involved. Our study confirmed that, in the course of search activity and problem solving, external contacts are widely used to locate facilities, literature, and other contacts in particular specialisms.

SOME COMMENTS ON THE COMPOSITE TYPOLOGY

Because of the quantitative methodology employed by Gibbons and Johnston, their data (in Table 7.2) give some indication of the relative importance of different knowledge types. Thus information relating to *design* accounts for one quarter of knowledge used in innovation, as does *knowledge of knowledge*. Knowledge of the *properties of materials and components* together accounts for one third (unfortunately, we do not know the distribution between materials and components). And knowledge of *test procedures* and *theories* together account for nearly one-fifth.

There is a fair degree of overlap and fluidity between the 15 categories in the typology. This is in the nature of the beast: knowledge used in innovation does not come in watertight boxes but is mutable and multidimensional, precisely because of the complex social processes by which it is generated and utilized. In an attempt to 'get a handle' on some of this complexity, I would tentatively suggest that at least two taxonomic axes cut across the specific categories of knowledge listed in Table 7.5. The first axis concerns the *object* of the knowledge in question, which may be the knowledge of:

1   the natural world
2   design practice
3   experimental R&D
4   the final product
5   knowledge itself

These headings provide a convenient and relatively straightforward way of grouping specific knowledge types, as indicated in Table 7.5.

The second axis cutting across these categories refers to the more slippery but nonetheless significant distinctions concerning the broad character of knowledge. To these I would add the frequently cited distinction between knowing and doing, and a distinction that, in my view, is still not sufficiently grasped in this 'Information Age', namely, that between knowledge and infor-mation (Wildavsky, 1983). This suggests a three-way distinction between knowing as understanding, knowing as holding information, and knowing as holding skills, alongside the main dualistic distinctions identified in Table 7.3:

1   understanding–information–skill
2   tacit–articulated
3   complex–simple
4   local–universal
5   specific/contingent–general/metalevel

The importance of these broad distinctions is likely to vary with different specific categories of knowledge. Thus, for example, skill-based knowledge appears in my typology under Design, R&D, and Production. Specific and local knowledge is likely to be particularly significant in Design, Production, and Operating performance (see Vincenti, 1991: ch. 6), as is tacit knowledge, which is also likely to be dominant in Practical experience.

In summary, we may usefully conceive of the knowledge used in innovation in terms of three taxonomic dimensions, namely:

1   specific types of knowledge (the typology);
2   the object or activities with which they are associated (product, R&D, etc.);
3   broad distinctions in the character of knowledge (tacit, specific, etc.).

Although elements in the last two dimensions relate closely to the social and economic issues of power and tradability noted by Fleck, these dimensions do not in themselves account adequately for the more external aspects of knowledge. They do, however, provide a reasonably rich and rounded framework for conceptualizing the cognitive and epistemological aspects of knowledge used in innovation.

On this basis, I suggest we need a conceptualization that integrates the three dimensions of type, object, and character. The approach developed by us to investigate knowledge flows between industry and public sector research begins to achieve such an integration empirically. As indicated in Table 7.4, we asked three sets of questions about the knowledge inputs to innovation. First, we asked interviewees to specify the types of knowledge they use, under four headings: knowledge of particular fields, technical information, skills, and knowledge related to artefacts.[29] We then asked them to characterize these types of knowledge in terms of whether they were predominantly tacit or formal in nature. Finally, we asked them to indicate the 'impact' or contribution of knowledge from various sources in terms of different company activities (also indicated in Table 7.4). It is not difficult to see how each of these steps could be refined or extended by application of the composite typology proposed here, together with further questioning on the broad distinctions of character suggested above.

CONCLUSIONS

To further our conceptualization of the types of knowledge used in innovation, I have reviewed the literature on the science–technology distinction and on industrial innovation. This review led to the conclusion that there is a strongly interactive relationship between science and technology, instrumentalities being an important area of overlap. In some new fields, such as biotechnology, the relationship between science and technology is so intimate that the boundaries between them appear blurred, if not obliterated. Nonetheless, technology can be distinguished from science because of its practical, artefactual orientation. This has implications for both its sociotechnical organization and its cognitive epistemological character.

Empirical findings confirm that what we commonly take to be scientific knowledge is used in the course of R&D leading to innovation, and that industrial organizations and PSR institutions both contribute to this knowledge. Such conclusions must be placed in context, however, because the contribution of science is relatively small. Other more strictly technological knowledge plays a greater role in innovation. Moreover, technology also contributes to science – at least to the extent that instrumentalities relate to artefacts – and may thus be considered to encompass both scientific and technological knowledge. With respect to the institutional distinction between industry and PSR, in-house R&D and expertise generally make a greater contribution to knowledge used in innovation than PSR, which is often less important than knowledge originating from other companies. The dominance of knowledge from internal sources is explained by the need to appropriate knowledge, by the cumulative nature of innovation, and by the importance of specific knowledge. Significantly, though, industrial R&D activities demand a synthesis of tacit and formal knowledge from internal and external sources.

This chapter has compared various attempts to capture the heterogeneity of technological knowledge. The categories proposed by Winter, Dosi, and Fleck and Tierney identify broad distinctions in the character of technological knowledge (tacit–articulated, specific–general, etc.). To a degree, these categories relate to the wider economic and power-related factors shaping the distribution of knowledge among individuals and organizations, although they do not account for them. The categories developed by Vincenti, Gibbons and Johnston, and my colleagues focus in greater detail on the content of knowledge utilized in innovation. The composite typology proposed here draws together the main features identified in these latter categorizations. It identifies 15 different types of knowledge, grouped under five headings that reflect the different activities or objects to which each knowledge type relates: the natural world, design, R&D, the final product, and knowledge itself. It is argued that the broad distinctions in the character of knowledge identified by Winter, Dosi, and Fleck and Tierney also cut across the more specific categories in the proposed typology. Thus a more complete conceptualization of technological knowledge should incorporate three taxonomic dimensions: the specific knowledge types (viz., our typology), the object or activities to which they relate, and the broad differences of character.

This conceptualization is a refinement of the categories used in our empirical study. I believe that this refinement strengthens and extends the applicability of a research approach that seeks to characterize in detail the range of knowledge used in the course of R&D leading to innovation. The studies by Gibbons and Johnston and ourselves have utilized this approach to good effect as a means of examining the particular knowledge contribution of PSR to innovation. But there is a real need, and considerable scope, to improve and refine our conceptualization of the knowledge flows associated with all aspects of industrial innovation, not solely public–private research linkage. For example, collaborations between user and supplier companies may also be addressed in terms of science and technology flows. Indeed, work being conducted at Edinburgh specifically focuses on different types of expertise utilized in the development and modification of complex IT systems (Fleck, 1992). There is also a connection with recent work at Manchester that investigates technology strategy in terms of the relationship between companies' knowledge base and corporate strategies (Coombs and Richards, 1991).

These developments appear to signal a more 'holistic' approach to the study of industrial innovation that genuinely spans sociological and economic approaches to the subject. Moreover, the kind of work I have in mind offers the possibility to explore how knowledge itself changes during the innovation process. For example, it is already widely recognized that technology transfer involves a *transformation* of knowledge (Gold, 1980; Peláez, 1991). Perhaps our most exciting challenge is to 'get inside' the process of knowledge transformation, using research tools like the typology proposed here.

Substantial policy and management benefits could result from such work. For example, the typology could be used by companies to investigate the extent and nature of their knowledge base and knowledge requirements in specific areas – perhaps in areas that are new to them – or to assess whether they are making the best use of available sources of knowledge to meet their requirements. Similarly, government organizations might use this approach to assess the strengths and weaknesses of the R&D system in a particular field – perhaps one of strategic interest – or to assess the effectiveness of policy measures geared to enhancing the R&D system and flows of knowledge around it. Discussions of these important issues are often lamentably superficial and policy interventions are not sufficiently targeted.

Perhaps the greatest need for more sophisticated tools for understanding the knowledge required in innovation lies in those countries and firms least advantaged in terms of scientific and technological infrastructure. In such cases, technology strategy demands a means to address questions such as: what types of knowledge about available technologies do we need and how do we gain access to them? What types of knowledge do we need if we are to acquire an external technology, or to develop our own internally? In principle at least, the conceptualization I have proposed here could act as a checklist and enable organizations to make informed decisions that avoid wasting limited scientific and technological resources.

NOTES

An earlier version of this chapter was presented and discussed at the University of Edinburgh Programme on Information and Communication Technologies (PICT) workshop 'Exploring Expertise' held in November 1992, and I am grateful to colleagues who provided feedback on that occasion. I would also like to thank David Edge, Keith Pavitt, Jacqueline Senker and Andrew Webster for their time and effort in reading and commenting on earlier drafts of the article.

1. The workshop entitled 'Exploring Expertise' sought to draw together different conceptualizations. See especially Fleck, 1992 and Winter, 1987.
2. I am using the conventional shorthand of research and development (R&D) to include design, but I would stress that design and development are often more important to innovation than R&D.
3. The study was entitled 'Public–Private Research Linkage in Advanced Technologies'. It was funded by the UK Economic and Social Research Council under the Science Policy Support Group Initiative on Public Science and Commercial Enterprise. Dr Jacqueline Senker of the Science Policy Research Unit, University of Sussex, and Dr Léa Velho, now of the University of Campinas, conducted most of the fieldwork for this study. I am grateful to them both for permission to use some of the findings here.
4. Utterback (1971) and Rosenberg (1992) make a similar point about innovation in scientific instruments.
5. They also, contrary to de Solla Price's assumptions, contribute to this literature (Hicks et al., 1993).
6. Fores may be justified in stressing the primarily empirical character of engineering, but it is hard to refute the case that the transition from craft to modern technology represents two 'epochs' (Constant, 1984b) in the history of technology, even though elements of the former inevitably remain an important part of what we today call technology. See Layton (1988) and Channell (1988) for their responses to Fores.
7. The greater number and importance of 'relevant social groups' was, of course, also recognized in Pinch and Bijker's seminal call for a sociology of technology built on conceptual frameworks from the sociology of science. As David Edge (1992) notes, the greater social complexity of technology makes it more difficult to study than science. More forcefully, Sørensen and Levold (1992) argue that scholars who transfer conceptual frameworks from the study of science to the study of technology are likely to have 'blind spots' concerning technology. Indeed, sociologists of technology have been strongly criticized for failing to grasp macrolevel forces shaping technology (e.g. Russell and Williams, 1988).
8. This view is explored empirically in Edge (1992, see p. 158).
9. Collins (1974) himself does problematize what constitutes replication in science.
10. These techniques involve some theory (e.g. laws of similitude and dimensional analysis), but such theory is more engineering than scientific in character, in the sense outlined above.
11. Although, as Vincenti (1991: ch. 4) noted, it may involve an act of considerable reduction to reveal this in the case of engineering theory.
12. These studies attempted to identify the key cognitive or research 'events' that contributed to specific innovations (in industry and defense, respectively) and then to analyse what proportion of these events took place in publicly funded laboratories. The studies were criticized because the time frame adopted had a

crucial bearing on the results produced, because the method of retrospective reporting was highly selective and assumed that the *origin* of an idea or '*piece*' of knowledge could be sensibly identified, and because of the inadequacies of the linear model on which the approach was based (Barnes and Edge, 1982).

13. Their data have been reworked in two ways. First, their content categories have been grouped under five headings, to reflect more closely the composite categorization developed below. Second, their external sources have been broken down as far as the data allow to reveal the respective contributions of public sector research (PSR) and other companies. A small proportion of their data could not be easily categorized in this way, and so only 254 of the total 300 units of information for external sources are represented in this table, and only 94 of the total 107 obtained from 'public science'.

14. Originally, 13 subheadings were used under these six main headings, but there was little variation between sources for the subheadings under Future Innovations, Production, and Technical Backup, so these have been aggregated. The numbers of responses sometimes include halves because many of our respondents were unable to identify a single source as having the major impact on an activity and so gave dual responses; these numbers have been allocated equally between each source involved.

15. A full account of the methodology developed can be found in Faulkner (1992).

16. It should be stressed that the unit of analysis in Table 7.2 is numbers of responses and not units of information as in Table 7.1. Also, the responses are to categories that are in no way equally weighted. As a result, the absolute values are not significant although the relative ones are – at least within each 'impact' category.

17. Our study revealed some variation in the relative importance of collectively derived and individually held knowledge, but we did not examine this systematically.

18. PSR accounts for 53 percent of the reported impact on scanning the research frontier and 43 percent of that on underpinning knowledge.

19. This explains the importance of 'on the hoof' or 'person embodied' mechanisms of transfer.

20. See, for a review, Rosenberg (1982: ch. 1); also his early work on the nineteenth-century machine tool industry (1976).

21. These terms have perhaps been adopted too easily: Fleck, et al. (1990) demonstrate that trajectories of technological development do not always follow the path anticipated for them and that alternative trajectories can exist side by side.

22. We have found that industrial R&D workers and designers communicate quite frequently with their opposite numbers in competitor companies (Senker and Faulkner, 1993). Barden and Good (1989) found such discussions, although not frequent, to be highly influential in terms of the direction of projects.

23. They give as an example assumptions of technocratic rationality.

24. A common example is the failure to document fully programming code.

25. Although in the case of our categories, this took place at the pilot stage of the research.

26. This largely reflects our initial decision to subsume design into R&D, and the fact that our categories derived primarily from a study of biotechnology, where design is relatively unimportant compared with research. The gap became particularly evident in our study of parallel computing and represents an obvious area of improvement for future work.

27. Vincenti (1991: ch. 7) gives as an example the knowledge that successful jets require a ratio of engine thrust to loaded aircraft weight of between 0.2 and 0.3.
28. Note that this category might be subsumed under research instrumentalities. Although this would parallel Vincenti's use of instrumentalities in relation to design, it would create a rather large category and so potentially lead to a loss of 'resolution'.
29. *Knowledge of particular field* includes scientific theory, engineering principles, and knowledge of knowledge (after Gibbons and Johnston, 1974); *technical information* includes specifications and operating performance of products or components, plus experimental or test procedures and results; *skills* includes specific skills, such as programming, and more general research or production competence; *artefacts* includes knowledge relevant to process or research instrumentation (overwhelmingly the latter), and other intermediates used in R&D.

REFERENCES

Barden, P. and Good, B. (1989) *Information Flows into Industrial Research*, London, Centre for the Exploitation of Science and Technology.

Barnes, B. and Edge, D. (1982) 'The interaction of science and technology', in Barnes, B. and Edge, D. (eds) *Science in Context: Readings in the Sociology of Science*, Milton Keynes, Open University Press, pp. 147–154.

Batelle Columbus Laboratory (1973) *Interactions of Science and Technology in the Innovative Process: Some Case Studies. Final Report to the National Science Foundation* (NSF–C667), Ohio, Batelle Columbus Laboratory.

Bode, H. W. (1965) 'Reflections on the relation between science and technology', in National Academy of Science, *Basic Research and National Goals: A Report to the Committee on Science and Astronautics, US House of Representatives*, Washington, DC, Government Printing Office.

Bud, R. and Cozzens, S. (eds) (1992) *Invisible Connections: Instruments, Institutions and Sciences*, Bellingham, WA, SPIE Optical Engineering Press.

Carpenter, M. P., Cooper, M. and Narin, F. (1980) 'Linkage between basic research and patents', *Research Management*, 23 (2): 30.

Carpenter, M. P., Narin, F. and Woolfe, P. (1981) 'Citation rates to technologically important patents', *World Patent Information*, 3 (4): 160–163.

Channell, D. F. (1982) 'The harmony of theory and practice: the engineering science of W.J.M. Rankine', *Technology and Culture*, 23(1): 39–52.

Channell, D. F. (1988) 'Engineering science as theory and practice', *Technology and Culture*, 29 (1): 98–103.

Collins, H. (1974) 'The TEA set: tacit knowledge and scientific networks', *Science Studies*, 4: 165–186.

Constant, E. (1984a) 'Scientific theory and technological testability: science, dynamometers, and water turbines in the 19th century', *Technology and Culture*, 24 (2): 183–198.

Constant, E. (1984b) 'Communities in hierarchies: structures in the practice of science and technology', in Laudan, R. (ed.) *The Nature of Technological Knowledge: Are Models of Scientific Change Relevant?*, Dordrecht, Reidel.

Coombs, R. and Richards, A. (1991) 'Technologies, products and firm strategies: part II – Analysis of three cases', *Technology Analysis and Strategic Management*, 3 (2): 157–175.

de Solla Price, D. J. (1965) 'Is technology historically independent of science? A study of statistical historiography', *Technology and Culture*, 6 (4): 553–568.

de Solla Price, D. J. (1982) *Inside the Black Box. Technology and Economics*, Cambridge, Cambridge University Press.

de Solla Price, D. J. (1984) 'The science/technology relationship, the craft of experimental science, and policy for the improvement of high technology innovation', *Research Policy*, 13 (1): 3–20.

de Solla Price, D. J. (1990) 'Why companies do basic research (with their own money)', *Research Policy*, 19: 165–174.

de Solla Price, D. J. (1992) 'Scientific instrumentation and university research', *Research Policy*, 21: 381–390.

Dosi, G. (1982) 'Technological paradigms and technological trajectories: a suggested interpretation of the determinants and direction of technical change', *Research Policy*, 11: 147–162.

Dosi, G. (1988) 'The nature of the innovative process', in Dosi, G., Freeman, C., Nelson, R., Soete, L. and Silverberg, G. (eds) *Technical Change and Economic Theory*, London, Pinter.

Edge, D. (1992) 'Mosaic arrays in infrared astronomy', in Bud, R. and Cozzens, S. (eds) *Invisible Connections: Instruments, Institutions and Science*, Bellingham, WA, SPIE Optical Engineering Press.

Faulkner, W. (1986) 'Linkage between industrial and academic research: the case of biotechnological research in the pharmaceutical industry', D. Phil. thesis, Science Policy Research Unit, University of Sussex, Brighton.

Faulkner, W. (1989) 'Industry–academic linkages in the case of biotechnology in the UK: practice and policy', paper presented at ECPR workshop in Technology Transfer and Techno-Industrial Innovation, 12–14 June, Como, Italy.

Faulkner, W. (1992) *Understanding Industry–Academic Research Linkage: towards an Appropriate Conceptualisation and Methodology*, Edinburgh PICT Working Paper, No. 35, Edinburgh, Research Centre for Social Science, University of Edinburgh.

Faulkner, W., Senker, J. and Velho, L. (1994) *Knowledge Frontiers: Industrial Innovation and Public Sector Research in Biotechnology, Engineering Ceramics and Parallel Computing*, Oxford, Clarendon Press.

Fleck, J. (1988) *The Development of Information Integration: beyond CIM?* Edinburgh PICT Working Paper, No. 9, Edinburgh, Research Centre for Social Science, University of Edinburgh.

Fleck, J. (1992) 'Expertise: knowledge, tradability and power', paper presented at PICT Workshop on Exploring Expertise, November, Edinburgh.

Fleck, J. (1993) 'Configuration: crystallising contingency', *International Journal of Human Factors in Manufacturing*, 3 (1): 15–36.

Fleck, J. and Tierney, M. (1991) *The Management of Expertise: Knowledge, Power and the Economics of Expert Labour*, Edinburgh PICT Working Paper, No. 29, Edinburgh, Research Centre for Social Science, University of Edinburgh.

Fleck, J., Webster, J. and Williams, R. (1990) 'The dynamics of IT implementation: a reassessment of paradigms and trajectories of development', *Futures*, 22 (6): 618–640.

Fores, M. (1988) 'Transformations and the myth of "engineering science": magic in a white coat', *Technology and Culture*, 29 (1): 62–81.

Freeman, C. (1982) *The Economics of Industrial Innovation*, 2nd edn, London, Pinter.

Gambardella, A. (1992) 'Competitive advantages from in-house scientific research: the US pharmaceutical industry in the 1980s', *Research Policy*, 21: 391–407.

Gibbons, M. and Johnson, C. (1982) 'Science, technology and the development of the transistor', in Barnes, B. and Edge, D. (eds) *Science in Context: Readings in the Sociology of Science*, Milton Keynes, Open University Press, pp. 177–185.

Gibbons, M. and Johnston, R. (1974) 'The roles of science in technological innovation', *Research Policy*, 3 (3): 220–242.

Gold, B. (1980) 'On the adoption of technological innovations in industry: superficial models and complex decision processes', *Omega*, 8 (5): 505–516.

Granberg, A. and Stankiewicz, R. (1978) *The Production of Knowledge in Technological Fields*, Research Policy Studies Discussion Paper, No. 122, Lund, Research Policy Institute.

Hicks, D., Isard, P. and Martin, B. (1993) 'An analytical comparison of research in European and Japanese corporations', in *Proceedings of the Kyoto Meeting of the R&D Dynamics Network*, May, Kyoto, Japan.

Illinois Institute of Technology Research Institute (1968) *Technology in Retrospect and Critical Events in Science: Final Report to the National Science Foundation*, NSF–C535, Illinois, Illinois Institute of Technology Research Institute.

Latour, B. (1987) *Science in Action: How to Follow Scientists and Engineers through Society*, Milton Keynes, Open University Press.

Layton, E. T. (1974) 'Technology as knowledge', *Technology and Culture*, 15 (1): 31–41.

Layton, E. T. (1976) 'American ideologies of science and engineering', *Technology and Culture*, 17 (October): 688–700.

Layton, E. T. (1988) 'Science as a form of action: the role of the engineering sciences', *Technology and Culture*, 29 (1): 82–97.

Lieberman, M. B. (1978) 'A literature citation study of science–technology coupling in electronics', *Proceedings of the IEEE*, 6 (1): 5–13.

Mayr, O. (1982) 'The science–technology relationship', in Barnes, B. and Edge, D. (eds) *Science in Context: Readings in the Sociology of Science*, Milton Keynes, Open University Press, pp. 155–163.

Metcalfe, J. S. and Gibbons, M. (1989) 'Technology, variety and organization: a systematic perspective on the competitive process', in Rosenbloom, R. S. and Bergelman, R. (eds) *Research on Technological Innovation, Management and Policy*, Greenwich, CT: JAI Press.

Musson, A. E. and Robinson, E. (1969) *Science and Technology in the Industrial Revolution*, Manchester, Manchester University Press.

Narin, F. and Noma, E. (1985) 'Is technology becoming science?', *Scientometrics*, 7 (3–6): 369–381.

Nelson, R. (1959) 'The simple economics of basic scientific research', *Journal of Political Economy*, June: 297–306.

Nelson, R. (1982) 'The role of knowledge in R and D efficiency', *Quarterly Journal of Economics*, 388: 453–70.

Pavitt, K. (1984) 'Sectoral patterns of technical change: towards a taxonomy and a theory', *Research Policy*, 13 (6): 343–374.

Pavitt, K. (1991) 'Key characteristics of the large innovative firm', *British Journal of Management*, 2: 41–50.

Peláez, E. (1991) *From Symbolic to Numerical Computing: the Story of Thinking Machines*, Edinburgh PICT Working Paper, No. 23, Edinburgh, Research Centre for Social Science, University of Edinburgh.

Polanyi, M. (1966) *The Tacit Dimension*, London, Routledge and Kegan Paul.

Rosenberg, N. (1976) *Perspectives on Technology*, Cambridge, Cambridge University Press.

Rosenberg, N. (1982) *Inside the Black Box: Technology and Economics*, Cambridge, Cambridge University Press.

Rosenberg, N. (1990) 'Why do firms do basic research (with their own money)?', *Research Policy*, 19 (2): 165–174.

Rosenberg, N. (1992) 'Scientific instrumentation and university research', *Research Policy*, 21 (4): 381–390.

Rothwell, R. (1977) 'The characteristics of successful innovators and technically progressive firms', *R&D Management*, 7 (3): 191–206.

Rothwell, R., Freeman, C., Horsley, A., Jervis, V. T. P., Robertson, A. B. and Townsend, J. (1974) 'SAPPHO updated – project SAPPHO, phase II', *Research Policy*, 3 (3): 258.

Russell, S. and Williams, R. (1988) *Opening the Black Box and Closing it behind you: on Micro-sociology in the Social Analysis of Technology*, Edinburgh PICT Working Paper, No. 3, Edinburgh, Research Centre for Social Science, University of Edinburgh.

Senker, J. (1993) 'The contribution of tacit knowledge to innovation', *AI and Society*, 7: 208–224.

Senker, J. and Faulkner, W. (1992) 'Industrial use of public sector research in advanced technologies: a comparison of biotechnology and ceramics', *R&D Management*, 22 (2): 157–175.

Senker, J. and Faulkner, W. (1993) 'Networks, tacit knowledge and innovation', paper presented at ASEAT Conference on Technology Collaboration: Networks, Institutions and States, Manchester, University of Manchester Institute for Science and Technology (UMIST) and Manchester University.

Sherwin, C. W. and Isenson, R. S. (1967) 'Project hindsight', *Science*, 156: 571–577.

Sørensen, K. and Levold, N. (1992) 'Tacit networks, heterogeneous engineers, and embodied technology', *Science, Technology and Human Values*, 17 (1): 13–35.

Staudenmaier, J. M. (1985) *Technology's Storytellers: Reweaving the Human Fabric*, Cambridge, MA, MIT Press.

Utterback, J. M. (1971) 'The process of innovation: a study of the origination and development of ideas from new scientific instruments', *IEEE, Transactions on Engineering Management*, 18: 124.

Vincenti, W. (1991) *What Engineers Know and How They Know It: Analytical Studies from Aeronautical History*, Baltimore, Johns Hopkins University Press.

von Hippel, E. (1988) *The Sources of Innovation*, Oxford, Oxford University Press.

Walsh, V. (1984) 'Invention and innovation in the chemical industry: demand–pull on discovery–push', *Research Policy*, 13 (4): 211–234.

Walsh, V., Roy, R., Bruce, M. and Potter, S. (1992) *Winning by Design: Technology, Product Design and International Competitiveness*, Oxford, Blackwell.

Wildavsky, A. (1983) 'Information as an organizational problem', *Journal of Management Studies*, 20 (1): 29–40.

Winter, S. (1987) 'Knowledge and competence as strategic assets', in Teece, D. (ed.) *The Competitive Challenge: Strategies for Industrial Innovation and Renewal*, Cambridge, MA, Ballinger.

8

What is Brand Equity Anyway, and How Do You Measure It?

*Paul Feldwick**

> What is the answer to the question being asked in cocktail lounges, all the time, all over America – 'What is brand equity anyway, and how do you measure it?' (Thornton C. Lockwood, Communications Research Manager, AT&T)

INTRODUCTION: FROM BRAND IMAGE TO BRAND EQUITY

Brands have been a major aspect of marketing reality now for over a hundred years. The *theory* of branding came some time later. David Ogilvy was talking about the importance of brand image as early as 1951 (quoted in Biel, 1993). It was first fully articulated, as far as I know, by Burleigh Gardner and Sidney Levy in their classic *Harvard Business Review* paper of 1955. But despite such distinguished origins, the concept of 'brand image' remained – until recently – peripheral to the mainstream of advertising theory and evaluation. Although it was endorsed from the 1960s onward by the British Account Planning movement (e.g. King, 1970; Cowley, 1989), it was also seen by many advertisers and researchers (especially in the United States) as a rather woolly theory – the sort of thing advertising agency people talked airily about when they failed to 'get a hard product message across' or to 'convert prospects' or 'to make sales', as they were supposed to be doing. 'Brand image' was associated with expressions like the 'soft sell' (Reeves, 1961: 77–86) and the 'weak theory of advertising' (Jones, 1991), which gave it, for many, the air of a whimsical luxury that a businesslike advertiser could hardly afford.

Then, in the 1980s, the hardnosed business people began to notice that brands appeared to be changing hands for huge sums of money! As takeover fever spread, the difference between balance sheet valuations and the prices paid by predators was substantially attributed to 'the value of brands'. Suddenly, the brand stopped being an obscure metaphysical concept of dubious relevance. It was something that was worth money.

* Reprinted from the *Journal of the Market Research Society*, Vol. 38, No. 2, April 1996, The Market Research Society.

This shift of perception was reflected in the way that the traditional expression 'brand *image*' (with its suggestion of a ghostly illusion) was increasingly displaced by its solid financial equivalent, 'brand equity'. It is not clear who invented the expression, but few uses of it have been traced before the mid-1980s (Ambler and Styles, 1995). It achieved respectability when it was taken up by the prestigious Marketing Science Institute, which held a major seminar on the subject in 1988, and has been going strong ever since.

In fact, the last few years have seen brand equity become one of the hottest topics in business. In America, there is now an influential body called the Coalition for Brand Equity (founded 1991), which evangelizes for the importance of building brand relationships and brand loyalty. Excellent (and very different) books have been published on the subject (Aaker, 1991; Kapferer, 1992). It has spawned numerous conferences and seminars. It has attracted a lot of interest from academic researchers, although the greatest part of their work has been connected with brand equity as applied to brand extensions (Barwise, 1993). Meanwhile commercial researchers have been busily designing and selling methods for measuring, tracking, and optimizing brand equity.

All of this, in my view, is fundamentally a good thing. It represents a long overdue shift in business and advertising thinking: from focus on making a sale, to creating and keeping a customer; from a purely short-term perspective to one that includes the longer-term profitability of the business; away from volume alone to recognize the importance of price and loyalty. (The brand equity movement, especially in the States, comes as a necessary reaction to a decade of ever greater dependence on sales promotion.) It has legitimized the idea that the consumer's perceptions are more important than objective reality. And it raises serious questions about the adequacy of ways of evaluating advertising that focuses purely on message communication, conversion, or short-term incremental sales response.

But while I joined the cheering crowds lining the great brand equity parade, I was still bothered by two questions which it did not seem to me had clear enough answers. I have written this chapter as an attempt to answer them to myself, and perhaps for anyone else who has ever wondered about them.

These are the questions:

- What exactly do we mean by the term brand equity – and do we all mean the same thing?
- How far can we expect to measure brand equity in an objective way?

WHAT IS BRAND EQUITY ANYWAY?

Karl Popper warned against a common mistake made by philosophers which he called 'nominalism'. The mistake is supposing that you will find the truth by starting with a word and arguing about what it 'really' means. But words, as Humpty Dumpty suggested, mean just what their users want them to mean. They can have various different meanings, and it is pointless to argue about which is 'right' or 'wrong'. When a common expression does have distinct meanings, however, it is as well to be aware of the fact so as to avoid unnecessary confusion. This is true of the expression 'brand equity', which seems to be used in three quite distinct senses (and each of these three has several further nuances of meaning). These are:

a = the total value of a brand as a separable asset – when it is sold, or included on a balance sheet;
b = a measure of the strength of consumers' attachment to a brand;
c = a description of the associations and beliefs the consumer has about the brand.

Of these three concepts, the first could less ambiguously be called 'brand valuation' (and often is). For the present argument I shall refer to it as 'brand value'.

The concept of measuring the consumer's level of attachment to a brand can be called 'brand loyalty' – although this phrase is almost as ambiguous as 'brand equity' itself. I prefer 'brand strength' for this sense, and although I am aware that this is also potentially confusing, that is what I shall call it in this chapter.

The third could be called by the traditional name of 'brand image', but for clarity I shall here call it 'brand description'. This reflects its fundamental difference from the other two senses of 'brand equity'; it is unlike them because we would not expect it to be represented by a single number.

Brand value could also be seen as the odd one out in another way, as it refers to an actual or notional business transaction while the other two focus on the consumer. In fact, brand strength and brand description are sometimes referred to as 'consumer brand equity' to distinguish them from the asset valuation meaning.

We would not expect these three concepts to be completely independent of each other. Brand strength should be one of the factors affecting the overall brand value; brand description might be expected to affect, or at least to explain, some of the brand strength. Underlying much of the talk about brand equity, and some of the more elaborate proposals for measuring it, such as the Yankelovich methodology (Taylor, 1992), seems to be the assumption of a causal chain along the following lines:

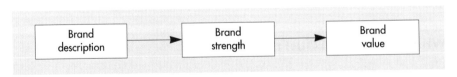

It may become apparent why I consider both the links in this chain are weak, or at best, obscure. I worry about the dangers of using the same name for all three (or even any two) of these concepts – it gives the impression (deliberately or through carelessness) that they are all aspects of the same thing. Like the arrows in the above diagram, it is an easy way to create the illusion that an operational relationship exists which, in reality, cannot be demonstrated.

So I intend to treat these three meanings of 'brand equity' as distinct concepts which require separate discussion. For each one, the questions of definition and measurement are closely linked; an 'operational definition', after all, means just knowing (or at least agreeing) on how something is to be measured. Brand strength will be the one I examine at the greatest length, because it is the most relevant to my current interest in advertising evaluation, and, for what it is worth, because it seems to me the central meaning of 'brand equity'. The issue of brand valuation has been written about at great length by people better qualified to do so than myself (Barwise et al., 1989; Kapferer, 1992), while a full discussion of brand description would raise other questions beyond the scope of what this chapter should attempt.

SENSE 1. BRAND EQUITY = BRAND VALUE

The need to put a value on a brand arises for two main reasons:

- to set a price when the brand is sold;
- to include it as an intangible asset on a balance sheet, a practice which is now possible in the UK but not everywhere.

It has been suggested, following from this, that the balance sheet valuation of a brand should become one of the measures by which the management of the brand (and various inputs such as advertising) can be evaluated.

Consultants have devised formulae which are now widely used for creating brand valuations, foremost among these being Interbrand and management consultancies such as Arthur Andersen (Murphy, 1990; Barrett and Bertolotti, 1992). However, there remain a number of difficulties of which we should be aware, particularly if using these formulae as indications of a brand's overall strength or health, or as a basis for evaluating performance.

First of all there is the significant difference between an 'objective' valuation created for balance sheet purposes, and the actual price that a brand might fetch in a real sale.

If we think of brands like houses, it seems reasonable to us that an expert should be able to say, within quite narrow limits, what a particular one might fetch – its market value. However, estate agents and surveyors are able to do this for property (not always, but most of the time) because they have many points of comparison. They have seen similar houses sold and with a little experience can form a sound idea of a 'market price'. But brands are both more different and less frequently sold than houses, so the norms needed to estimate a market price do not usually exist.

More importantly, a brand is likely to have a much higher value to one purchaser than another. If a company already owns factories, manufacturing skills, means of distribution, or indeed other brands (Barwise and Robertson, 1992), there may be synergies that make it worth paying a great deal for a particular brand. To a company without the same assets, the same name could be worth relatively little. For acquisition purposes, the value of a brand to a particular purchaser is best estimated by scenario planning – what future cash flows could this company achieve if it owned and exploited that brand? Takeover prices can be higher than current valuations because these incremental cash flows might be far greater than the brand could ever deliver to the existing user.

We can think of brands in this sense as being like properties on the Monopoly board. The face value of Coventry Street is £280: but if you own the other two streets in the yellow set, and have plenty of cash to develop the set when complete, its value to you will be far more. Another player, even paying face value, would never be able to recoup his or her investment.

There is therefore no such thing as an absolute value for a brand. What it might actually realize, if sold, depends a great deal on who might be interested in buying it at the time, and why. If two companies both want it, this might inflate the price considerably more as, in addition to the cash one could generate from the brand is added the strategic advantage of keeping it out of the hands of a competitor. The battle between Nestlé and Jacob Suchard to own Rowntree (perhaps the most often quoted example of 'the value of brands') is a good example of this.

Another unresolved difficulty surrounding brand valuation is the issue of *separability*. John Stuart, when Chairman of Quaker Oats Ltd., was famously quoted: 'If this business were to be split up, I would be glad to take the brands, trademarks, and goodwill, and you could have all the bricks and mortar – and I would fare better than you.' He may, in his particular case, have been right, but the claim would not always apply. And a successful business has other assets besides trademarks and bricks and mortar. Many brand names, removed from the management, the skills, the culture, the support that they normally enjoy, would rapidly lose their customer base. Again, this makes the point that a brand – essentially, the right to a particular name or identity – has a value that fluctuates according to who uses it.

Balance sheet valuations can only concern themselves with the current user and on this basis they try to estimate the future profit stream derived from the brand and within this how much can be attributed to the brand name itself. The main motives for having balance sheet valuations at all are financial, with which I shall not concern myself here. But it has also been argued that the act of valuing brands formally is a good discipline for a company, which will shift its attention away from a concentration on the immediate profit and loss account to a consideration of the longer term.

This sounds as if it should be the case, but how far it really works depends on the formula used to create the brand's value. The preferred methods commonly in use start by considering the brand's current profitability. They then apply probabilities to the current situation growing or continuing, based on various measures of 'brand strength', which in this sense may include consumer research and also other factors such as competitive position (Murphy, 1990). The in-depth analysis of all aspects of the brand which is involved is likely to be a valuable exercise. What is questionable is whether such approaches are looking at 'brand value' in a purer sense, or at the business unit as a whole. As sales and, particularly, profitability can be manipulated faster and more easily than the underlying measures of brand strength (which are in any case necessarily subjective), the simple way to increase a brand's valuation on this basis could [be] by continuing a short-term focus on profits; which is exactly what many advocates of brand equity are keen to get away from.

This raises another crucial issue which we shall return to again – that of separating 'brand *strength*' from 'brand *size*'. Coca-Cola will appear a stronger brand than Pepsi, on most usual measures, because it is a *bigger* brand than Pepsi. One of the key issues in the whole field of brand equity measurement is finding an indication of brand strength which is not simply a tautology for brand size. One extreme view is that the two are, in fact, the same (Ehrenberg, 1993). While I disagree with this, it is certainly true that large brands, particularly market leaders, derive a great deal of competitive strength from their relative size, and that many measures of 'brand strength' are strongly affected by brand size.

In summary then, a valuation for balance sheet purposes is not the same as a valuation made on behalf of a particular purchaser. Neither of these is objective and, while the valuation process may have usefulness, it is questionable whether it is practical or desirable to treat such figures as the ultimate criterion of marketing success.

SENSE 2. BRAND EQUITY = BRAND STRENGTH: A MEASURE OF RELATIVE CONSUMER DEMAND FOR THE BRAND

David Aaker (1991) describes brand equity as having five components:

- Brand loyalty
- Awareness
- Perceived quality
- Other associations
- Other brand assets

This is a pragmatic recognition of the different concepts that have been associated with brand strength, and which can be measured. It can be criticized for lacking an underlying theory that links these five ideas (McWilliam, 1993), but by the same token we may have to be prepared for the fact that no such underlying theory really exists – in which case the concept of brand equity can hardly be said to be a scientific one.

The many different methods that have been published can, for the most part, be described as using one or a combination of the following basic types of measure:

- Price/demand measures (including modelling approaches);
- Behavioural measures of loyalty (buying behaviour);
- Attitudinal measures of loyalty;
- Awareness/salience measures.

Of these, the second is similar to Aaker's *loyalty* component, the third to his *awareness* component, while the last is related to – but not the same as – his concept of 'perceived quality'.

Aaker's 'brand associations' broadly describes the area I have chosen to separate out as the third principal sense of brand equity, i.e. brand description. Aaker is quite right to include it as one of the dimensions on which a brand should be appraised; I have dealt with it separately because it seems to me essentially descriptive, rather than evaluative.

He is also right, I think, not to include price premium as a core dimension of 'brand equity', though he discusses it briefly (1991: 22–23). I would agree that this is best seen as a measurable *output* of brand equity, rather than a part of brand equity itself (which raises another possible debate about what the phrase actually means). I start with it because it has nevertheless formed one of the most popular approaches to *measuring* brand equity.

PRICE/DEMAND MEASURES (INCLUDING MODELLING APPROACHES)

One of the frequent benefits of a strong brand is its ability to command a higher price and/or less sensitivity to price increases than its competitors. It follows from this that two dimensions on which the strength of a brand can be measured are its price premium and its price elasticity.

In other words, a brand is strong if people are prepared to pay more for it.

Each of these can be measured in one of two ways: using market data and using experimental data.

Price 1. Using market data

Suppose we consider that an improvement in price premium, while sustaining share (or in share while sustaining price), is an improvement in brand equity. This has the merit of simplicity and needs no special research beyond reliable data on relative price and share, such as can be had from a good retail audit. The simplest way to imagine this is by plotting brand share and relative price on two axes of a graph. For each brand, we expect to see a relationship between price and share, popularly referred to as the 'demand curve'. 'Changing the shape of the demand curve' or 'moving the demand curve to the right' have

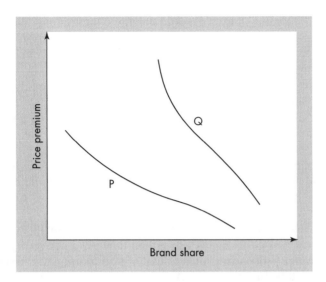

FIGURE 8.1

long been recognized as possible desired outcomes of advertising (Jones, 1986: 95–96). This increase in demand could also be seen as an increase in the brand's equity (Figure 8.1).

In this figure the Brand Q has a higher share than P when they both charge the same price premium over the market average, or can charge a higher price when they both have the same share. Also, Q loses less share than P when the price goes up; the slope of the line is steeper. These could be seen as two measures of Q's greater brand strength. If P and Q represent the same brand at different time periods, Q later than P, this could be taken as evidence of improved brand equity, caused, for instance, by advertising.

Price elasticity can also be estimated using econometric modelling; in the PG Tips case history (Grand Prix winner in the 1990 IPA Advertising Effectiveness Awards) there is an example of relative price elasticity quoted as evidence of brand strength/advertising effect (Feldwick, 1991).

A refinement of the price premium approach is offered by Longman Moran Analytics in the US (Moran, 1994). Here the definition of brand equity is market share, times price premium, times a 'durability' factor. This last is an estimate of price elasticity based on market data. Crucial to this method (which is not as easy as it sounds) is the importance of correctly defining the competitive set on which to base share and price differences, so that an apparently small brand may really need to be considered as a dominant niche player in a smaller category.

A further development of this approach is also to take distribution into account. Distribution and price are thus regarded as two 'contaminating' factors which disguise the 'real' underlying demand for competing brands. Simon Broadbent has developed a measure of consumer brand equity which he defines as: 'The sales share we would get, if we were at average price and had average distribution – and average price and distribution elasticities applied. Equity is, in effect, the residual after price and distribution effects have been allowed for.'

It is conceptually a short step from this to identifying equity with the underlying 'base' or constant in an econometric model of sales or share. Broadbent has also been very active in exploring the idea that the constant in such equations can, and does, move over time, reflecting the underlying strength of a brand when all short-term factors – price, distribution, advertising, competitive activity or whatever – have been allowed for. This is referred to as the 'floating base' (Broadbent, 1992, 1993). A similar concept can be found in the modelling approach to brand equity measurement offered by the Consumer Affinity Company in the US (Eubank, 1993).

The idea of searching for brand equity (brand strength) by factoring out all influences on market performance other than the brand name itself can lead into some complex procedures, such as that of Kamakura and Russell (1993). However, it is interesting that these American academic researchers validate their highly sophisticated approach by comparing results against a simple plotting of price premium versus brand share. In fact, this scatter plot approach remains one of the simplest and most practical ways to consider a brand's strength in the marketplace; for most purposes the use of multinomial logit models to estimate something similar may be using a complicated sledge-hammer to crack a fairly simple nut.

Price 2. Experimental approaches

Other approaches based on price take a different route. Instead of using market data, they use various forms of pricing research to estimate what share the brand would have at various different relative price levels. The equity measure is basically a calculation of the relative price at which each brand would have an equal share. (This is recognizable as the inversion of Broadbent's definition, given above.)

Joel Axelrod (1992) defines brand equity as 'the incremental amount your customer will pay to obtain your brand rather than a physically comparable product without your brand name'. In order to measure this, customers are divided into different cells and shown different combinations of the test brand and competitors at different price levels, and express preference using a constant sum technique.

Jim Crimmins (1992) of DDB Needham has a somewhat similar approach to measuring 'the amount of value added by a brand name' (to his credit, he avoids the dreaded E word!) The interviewing approach sounds similar to Axelrod's. The output is an estimation of the price at which the test brand and each competitor are equally likely to be chosen. Notice that this measure of 'brand value added' is not absolute, but varies according to which competitor is taken as the comparison. Crimmins reports that the value added by the number one brand in a market averages at 40% compared with store brands, but only averages 10% compared with the number two brand; in both cases there is a wide variation around this median figure.

Steve Roth (1991) describes the use of Brand Price Trade-Off analysis to estimate brand equity. In this approach respondents choose their preferred brand at various different sets of price levels. By pooling all the respondents' individual decision processes the computer can simulate market outcomes at any set of prices. From a brand equity viewpoint, this micro modelling approach shows that a brand can have different 'equity' for different respondents.

As we shall see in looking at behavioural or attitudinal loyalty measures, any serious investigation into quantifying consumers' degree of 'attachment' to a brand is likely to discover this unsurprising truth – that some customers will be far more attached to the brand than others. It follows from this that figures which average all customers to provide a total brand score may be misleading. Conversely, the process of decomposing a brand's user base into more or less loyal users may be valuable in itself in planning marketing strategy. It may be that one of the main benefits of some 'brand equity research' lies in this area, rather than in the quest for a single yardstick for measuring brand strength.

Trade-off or conjoint approaches make it appear quite easy to separate brand name effects from other factors, which may make us forget that in real life separability is not always so clear cut. Can one really separate the Mercedes Benz name, for example, from the reality of the Mercedes Benz car?

PRICE: SOME GENERAL OBSERVATIONS

The merits of using price as an indication of brand strength are that it relates closely to one of the main business benefits of branding. It is valuable in that it takes the focus off volume and adds the dimension of commanding a fair price for a trusted product. Certainly it is a dangerous error to look for evidence of brand strength or advertising effect by considering volumes alone.

However, there is more to brand equity than price premiums. There are strong brands which do not command a premium price, either because they are examples of 'scale economy branding' or because there is no directly substitutable product in the market. Mars Bars would be an example of both. It is possible that relatively low price elasticity would still be an indication of brand strength, but if the policy of the manufacturer were to keep prices low – e.g. to keep competitors out of the market – this would be a somewhat hypothetical measure.

Another danger is a possible lag effect between price rises and share loss. It is a dangerous game to suppose that a brand can be made 'stronger' by increasing its price premium, but this could be one logical outcome of a system which measures brand equity in this way. The story of Marlboro in the period leading up to Marlboro Friday illustrates the risks (Feldwick and Bonnal, 1995).

This raises another question fundamental to defining what we mean by brand equity. Is it enough to consider a 'snapshot' of the brand's relative position at one point in time? Or are we really interested in its future potential for growth, its future resilience against attack? If we want to predict the likelihood of future profit streams, price premiums may be a legacy of past strength (or present greed), more than a guarantee of future performance. Many brands in the UK grocery market might be seen as illustrating this uncertainty.

BEHAVIOURAL MEASURES OF BRAND LOYALTY

'Brand loyalty' is another expression whose meaning can vary. It is sometimes used, for instance, to describe the consumer's attitudinal orientation towards the brand. Its narrower sense, however, is based on records of actual purchasing behaviour as gathered in consumer panels.

One common method of using panel data to generate a measure of loyalty has been the concept of 'Share of Category Requirements', often abbreviated as Share of Requirements (SOR or SCR). The SOR for Nescafé is all Nescafé volume expressed as a share of all instant coffee bought by respondents who bought Nescafé during the analysis period. This overall figure disguises a wide variation between individual buyers, some of whom will have bought no other coffee in the period (SOR = 100%), to those who only bought it once out of n coffee purchases (SOR – $1/n*100\%$).

On this basis the more loyal customer is the one for whom the brand represents a higher share of category requirements; for instance, someone who buys seven jars of Nescafé on ten coffee purchasing occasions is more 'loyal' than someone who buys only three.

A good deal of attention has been paid to this behavioural definition of loyalty as an indicator of brand equity, especially in America. This idea is that the buyer with a higher share of category requirements is, obviously, far more important to the business (overall weight of purchase being equal) – also, implicitly, more emotionally attached to the brand and less willing to accept a substitute. (It does not, in fact, follow that this should always be the case and I am not sure what evidence exists for this assumption.) Therefore, if a brand's buyers show, overall, a higher average SOR, this could be seen as a sign of brand strength. (More usually nowadays the criterion is a higher proportion of buyers with an SOR above a certain level, rather than the average. Crimmins (1992) suggests the proportion of buyers with an SOR over 60%; Christiani (1993) argues for considering the whole distribution.)

Larry Light (1994), a distinguished American researcher and Chairman of the Coalition for Brand Equity, uses the following example to demonstrate that brands with the same market shares can differ in loyalty as measured by SOR. He posits three imaginary brands: Brand A, which 100% of the user population buy 15% of the time; Brand B, which 15% buy 100% of the time; and Brand C, which half of the population buy 30% of the time. It will be seen that

TABLE 8.1

US instant coffee (annual)	Market share %	Share of category requirements %
Maxwell House	19	39
Sanka	16	36
Taster's Choice	14	32
High Point	13	31
All other brands	12	32
Folgers	11	29
Nescafé	8	29
Brim	4	21
Maxim	3	23

Source: Ehrenberg and Scriven, 1995

each of these brands has an identical 15% market share; but in terms of profitability, Brand B is claimed to be the most profitable (and the most secure?), and Brand A the least.

The problem with this (admittedly hypothetical) example is that brands like A, B and C are not known to exist in normal markets. We have already observed that every brand shows a distribution of different loyalty levels ranging from 100% loyalists to those who only bought the brand once. Andrew Ehrenberg and his colleagues have shown repeatedly that, over any time period, this distribution follows a standard pattern, which can be predicted within fairly narrow limits from three parameters. Two of these are market specific and can be estimated from knowing the category rate of purchase and the number of brands in the market; the third is simply the brand's market share. Hence any brand's average 'share of category requirements' can also be predicted, within narrow limits, from the same three parameters. Ehrenberg also shows that average share of requirements actually varies little between brands in a market, though it is normally higher for brands with a larger share, an instance of the so-called 'Double Jeopardy' (Ehrenberg, 1988; Ehrenberg et al., 1990; Ehrenberg and Scriven, 1995). Table 8.1 illustrates a typical finding.

There is an apparent conflict between Ehrenberg's findings (which have never been seriously disputed, though often ignored) and much American research based on SOR. The logic following from Ehrenberg's data is that brand equity measures based on share of category requirements are, once again, mere tautologies for brand share; share of category requirements will only go up if brand share goes up.

An alternative to SOR as a way of defining loyalty is to look at patterns of purchasing over time, and use this to estimate the probability of each panel member buying the brand on the next purchase occasion. Alain Pioche of Nielsen describes such a system, and illustrates how it can be more sensitive than SOR by the following three purchasing sequences, where 1 = a purchase of the brand and 0 = purchase of another brand:

1,1,1,1,1,0,0,0,0,0
1,0,1,0,1,0,1,0,1,0
0,0,0,0,0,1,1,1,1,1

The SOR here is identical for all three at 50%. On the basis that past buying is the best single predictor of future buying behaviour, Pioche estimates the probability of each respondent buying the brand next time as A= 0.21, B = 0.43 and C = 0.79. The results must be aggregated to create an overall measure for loyalty to a brand. This would then have the potential to vary continuously in time (Pioche, 1992).

This idea has an intuitive appeal – it is like reading the form at a horse race. We might think, however, that at the aggregate level it will be unlikely to tell us anything new about the brand's health – if more people are buying the brand more often, this should be reflected in its overall brand share!

What both SOR and this 'stochastic' approach show us is that any brand is bought by different groups of people, some very loyal (in behavioural terms), some not at all so. This mode of analysis is valuable in that it recognizes that some customers are far more important to the brand than others, and that if these can be identified and targeted there can be significant improvements in marketing efficiency. This is the reverse of traditional 'conversion' models of marketing where the target was essentially conceived of as a non-user; it reflects a new and proper emphasis on the importance of the existing customer base.

Once the attempt is made to decompose the customer base in this way, a number of interlocking segmentations become possible which can make the process a complex one. Three common divisions are as follows:

- Weight of category purchase. Here we should expect a wide distribution from heavy to very light users, where (at least) the 80: 20 rule generally applies – a minority of buyers account for a majority of total category consumption.
- Share of category requirements (SOR) cuts across this, so that some of a brand's more loyal users will be heavy category users, and some very light. (Ehrenberg (e.g. 1988: 174) pointed out that customers whose share of category requirements is 100% are likely to include a lot of very light users, as the easiest way to be classified as 100% loyal is to have only bought the category on a single occasion in the analysis period. This will also apply to others with a high SOR. Nevertheless there will be some heavy category users who are 80%–100% loyal and these will account for a disproportionate volume of the business.)
- In America, where deep price discounting has become a major force in packaged goods markets, there have been attempts to find general consumer segmentations that hold true across categories – so that some individuals are more brand loyal, some buy across a wide repertoire, and some are particularly likely to buy on deal (McQueen et al., 1993). Discussion then arises as to whether an occasional buyer of your brand is a more or less attractive prospect if he/she is a loyal buyer of a competing brand or a 'deal selective'.

All this may seem to be straying far away from our particular inquiry, and so in a way it is. However, the relevance of this to an overall measurement of brand equity is that a buyer whose 50% SOR is based on preference would constitute a greater asset than a buyer whose same SOR was based on deal buying. This suggests that analysis of buying patterns alone can be misleading unless it also includes some information about price.

Behavioural loyalty measures attempt to use consistency of behaviour as a proxy for attitude, or what we might call commitment. Given the influence of other factors such as inertia, availability and price it is not obvious that this is entirely sound. Another way of looking at brand equity is to get a fix attitudinally on the number of buyers who are strongly committed to your brand, compared with the number who simply buy it because of price, because of habit or inertia, or just because it is the only one there.

ATTITUDINAL MEASURES OF BRAND LOYALTY

In this section we concern ourselves with general evaluative measures (affective or 'liking') more than with specific associations and beliefs about the brand (cognitive or 'thinking'), which belong more properly under our third main definition of brand equity as brand description.

These can take various forms, which we need not describe in detail: scales ranging from 'the only one I would ever consider' to 'I would never consider'; constant sum preference scales; brand 'for me' – 'not for me'. Any form of experimental price testing (such as that of Axelrod or Crimmins, above) can be seen as a form of attitudinal research which takes claimed willingness to pay a price as its scale (hence it has been whimsically called 'dollarmetric scaling'). General measures of 'esteem' or 'quality' are intended to be sufficiently vague to cover all types of product or service, so we can include them under general affective measures.

In a way such attitudinal measures take the most direct approach to the underlying concept which we suppose we want to measure – the relative preference, 'wantability', or attachment the consumer has for the brand, separated from 'external' factors such as price or distribution. Brand strength defined in this way is essentially attitudinal, following Gordon Allport's classic definition:

> Attitude: A mental and neural state of readiness, organized through experience, exerting a directive or dynamic influence upon the individual's response to all objects and situations with which it is related.

If brand attitudes are handled crudely on the 'eight out of ten cats prefer' basis or, worse still, as a single averaged figure, we need to be careful – again: we may be confounding *numbers* of a brand's devotees with the *degree* of their individual devotion to it. If we do this, then larger brands will tend to get the higher scores, and once again, we will learn nothing other than the fact they are big (Barwise and Ehrenberg, 1985). In fact, the use of preference and other measures to stand for 'brand equity' has led to renewed interest in trying to understand how they represent different parts of the customer base by disaggregating them into groups (as in the analysis of loyalty, with which some researchers have tried to combine it).

One method of attitudinal segmentation is the conceptually very simple one proposed by Cramphorn (1992). This segments buyers of a brand into two groups, the discriminating and the undiscriminating, on the basis of a validated series of attitudinal statements. The percentage of discriminating buyers, plotted against brand share on the other axis, positions a brand as relatively stronger or weaker than others the same size.

A more complex attitudinal segmentation is Market Facts Inc.'s Conversion Model (Ceurvost, 1994). This segments buyers and non-buyers into four groups each: users are entrenched, average, shallow or convertible, while non-users can be available, ambivalent, weakly unavailable or strongly unavailable. It is claimed that trends in movements between these groups anticipate and predict market share movements; in particular, that as early as April 1991 the model predicted the decline in Marlboro share which led to Marlboro Friday.

If this is true, it means that the questions are a major advance on the traditional 'intention to buy' question which was used for many years as a predictor of behaviour. In fact, as Bird and Ehrenberg found, claimed intention to buy reflects past behaviour much more than future behaviour (Bird and Ehrenberg, 1966, 1967; Barnard, 1990). So a brand with a higher intention to buy than its present brand share would imply is generally not, as you might expect, a brand that is about to grow, but a brand that is probably in decline. The number of respondents expecting to buy it is merely a reflection of past glories.

The proponents of the Conversion Model argue that behavioural loyalty alone can misrepresent consumers' level of emotional attachment to a brand, quoting evidence that many buyers with a high SOR have low emotional commitment. They also point out that in infrequent purchase choices, such as banks, cars, or credit cards, SOR is not a practically useful concept (Ceurvost, 1994).

AWARENESS/SALIENCY MEASURES

Brand awareness is one of Aaker's five dimensions of brand equity. He defines it as 'the ability to identify a brand as associated with a product category' – an important qualification. There is a difference between 'mere' awareness of a name, and associating it with a particular product. Being the first name to come to mind when thinking of coffee, hand drills or mouthwash is one indication that a brand 'owns' that particular category. Such associations can persist for a long time.

Brand awareness has a long pedigree as a desired outcome of marketing activity, deriving from the very earliest models of advertising effectiveness such as St Elmo Lewis's AIDA in 1907. In most markets, recognition or a sense of familiarity with a brand name is considered a step towards improving acceptability and preference, other things being equal.

Awareness can be measured as recognition (prompted by the brand name), or spontaneous (prompted by some definition of the product field), with a further refinement in collecting the first name mentioned.

One of the best known general measures of brand equity, the Landor Image Power study, consists of two measures: one is a simple measure of brand awareness, the other a more complex factor called 'esteem' (a general quality rating) (Owen, 1993). The findings of this survey indicate that these two measures are substantially independent of each other, showing that brands that are well known or easily called to mind are not always highly thought of or likely to be preferred (although more so in America than in Europe!).

Another major cross-category survey of relative brand strength, the Young and Rubicam Brand Asset Valuator (1994), includes 'familiarity' as one of four key dimensions of brand strength (the others being esteem, relevance and differentiation). Even here they are careful to point out that their definition of 'familiarity' embraces more than mere name awareness.

In fact it is arguable that high levels of awareness are created by a brand's size, ubiquity, and/or scale of promotional activity, while they tell us relatively little about the brand's 'strength' in the sense of the consumer's attachment to it or preference for it. Such measures tend to favour brands that are relatively or absolutely large, so that once more we are in danger of confounding size with strength.

SENSE 3. BRAND EQUITY = BRAND DESCRIPTION: DESCRIPTIVE ASSOCIATIONS/ATTRIBUTES OF THE BRAND

Some researchers talk about the collection of brand image data, positioning mapping and the like as if this is 'brand equity'. David Aaker includes this as one of his dimensions of brand equity. It is widely assumed that the associations or attributes which a brand acquires are the main creators of the brand's strength, as when Alex Biel (1992) argues that 'Brand image drives brand equity'.

A wide variety of techniques, qualitative and quantitative, exist for eliciting consumers' associations with and perceptions of a brand, by inviting the respondent to link each brand with words or pictures, or in multidimensional scaling, to position them relative to each other.

More relevant to the brand equity debate are attempts to relate this kind of data, which are essentially descriptive, to dimensions of attitudinal or behavioural loyalty, i.e. brand strength, as described above. It is through this linkage that what we might call brand image data have attached themselves to the brand equity concept, in procedures which are often known in America as 'brand equity modelling'.

Attempts to model general affective attitudes to brands in this way can follow two main approaches, which I shall call cross-sectional or time series. Cross-sectional is to look for correlations between the individuals in the sample – so that if the strongest preferrers show a strong tendency to rate the brand on attribute Y, the inference is that associating the brand with attribute Y creates preference. This procedure is not new; it goes back to the St James Model of the 1960s, and the objection made to it at the time – that it is impossible to distinguish cause and effect in such correlations – is still a matter for debate. Time series analysis requires a set of such data over time from a tracking study; if a sudden decline in one particular attribute happens at the same time as a decline in general favourability scores, that attribute is assumed to be an important 'driver'. Both approaches can be and often are combined with the loyalty segmentations described, so that the 'drivers' for each brand's loyalists or rejectors (including competitive brands) can be computed. All these procedures are controversial, but undeniably attractive for many reasons that go beyond the measurement aspect of brand equity; they offer guidance for advertising and marketing strategy, and an appearance, at least, of controlling complexity – 'If we can improve *this* image dimension for *these* people, our brand equity – and profit – will go up *this* much'. In their favour it must be said that they grapple with the complexity of a real user base, where individuals vary. Not everyone will be convinced they deliver all they promise.

SO WHAT IS BRAND EQUITY?

All the research methodologies described above have been linked with the attempt to measure 'brand equity'. I will not attempt to pontificate on their relative 'validity' or usefulness. But what is clear is that they are far from measuring the same thing. For example:

- a brand's ability to command a price premium is different from its SOR. (The brand leader may have 40% more 'equity' than the store brand measured as price premium, but the same SOR among its buyers, or less.)
- 'loyalty' as shown by probability models is different from attitudinal measures (Pioche, 1992: 37–39); also, as mentioned, different from SOR.
- different price measures give quite different results. (Crimmins is explicit (1992: 18) in pointing out that his measure of brand value is not the same as the price premium in the market.)
- Ceurvost points out that the Conversion Model's measure of 'commitment' is not related to SOR.

And no doubt others.

What we have, in fact, is an array of dimensions. Any of these *might* be considered a relevant measure of a brand's health, strength (or even 'equity'), depending on the brand's individual circumstances – and depending, importantly, on the use to which the findings will be put. Some measures, such as the basic combination of share and price difference, are obviously useful as a general retrospective indication of the brand's competitive performance (and add something to other standard measures such as brand shares). Others, for instance the attempts to measure levels of consumer 'commitment' to the brand, can act as early warning systems to detect future defections – and the same research can often add diagnostic information suggesting the necessary action to avoid this. Brand awareness may be relevant when considering extending a brand into a new category. Price premium may be important to some brands, not at all to others.

But as Barwise (1993) points out, none of these short-term measures of brand loyalty has yet been shown to have any long-term predictive power; so there is an element of judgement involved in their use. And there is no reason to suppose that any of these measures – or even a cocktail of different ones – represent an objective and absolute measure of something called 'brand equity', still less that this is equivalent to the value which a brand should be sold or accounted for.

When we look for an operational definition of brand equity, we are asking the wrong question. Brand equity is necessarily a vague concept, like 'personal health and fitness', or 'a sound economy'. These concepts imply general questions: how well are we doing now? how well can we expect to do in the future? Such questions are not answered fully by any one measure. At certain points in time, one or more measures may be of crucial importance – such as cholesterol level or inflation. But there is also a danger that continuing to concentrate on one measure to the exclusion of others creates its own problems (low inflation leads to unemployment; low cholesterol diets cause depression). Brand equity needs to be approached in the same spirit.

REFERENCES

Aaker, D. (1991). *Managing Brand Equity: Capitalizing on the Value of a Brand Name*. New York: The Free Press.

Aaker, D. and Biel, A. (1993). *Brand Equity and Advertising*. Hillsdale, NJ: Lawrence Erlbaum Associates.

Ambler, T. and Styles, C. (1995). *Brand Equity: towards Measures That Matter*. Pan'agra Working Paper No. 95–902, London Business School.

Axelrod, J. N. (1992). 'The use of experimental design in monitoring brand equity'. *Proceedings of the ESOMAR Seminar: the Challenge of Branding Today and in the Future*. Brussels, October, pp. 13–26.

Barnard, N. (1990). 'What can you do with tracking studies and what are their limitations?' *Admap*, 295 (April): 23.

Barrett, H. and Bertolotti, N. P. (1992). 'Brand evaluation'. *Proceedings of the ESOMAR Seminar: the Challenge of Branding Today and in the Future*. Brussels, October, pp. 1–12.

Barwise, P. (1993). 'Brand equity: snark or boojum'. *International Journal of Research in Marketing*, 10 (1) March: 93–104.

Barwise, P. and Ehrenberg, A.S.C. (1985). 'Consumer beliefs and brand usage'. *Journal of the Market Research Society*, 27 (2) April: 81–93.

Barwise, P. and Robertson, T. (1992). 'Brand portfolios'. *European Management Journal,*
10 (3) September: 277–285.

Barwise, P., Higson, C., Likierman, A. and Marsh, P. (1989). *Accounting for Brands.*
London Business School and the Institute of Chartered Accountants.

Biel, A. L. (1992). 'How brand image drives brand equity'. ARF Workshop, New York,
February, in *Exploring Brand Equity.* New York: ARF, 1995.

Biel, A. L. (1993). 'Converting image into equity'. In Aaker and Biel, p. 67.

Bird, M. and Ehrenberg, A.S.C. (1966, 1967). 'Intentions to buy and claimed brand
usage'. *Operational Research Quarterly,* 17: 27–46 and 18: 65–66.

Brand Asset Valuator Prospectus (1994). Young and Rubicam Ltd.

Broadbent, S. (1992). 'Using data better – a new approach to sales analysis'. *Admap,*
January: 48–54.

Broadbent, S. (1993). 'Advertising effects: more than short term'. *Journal of the Market
Research Society,* 35 (1) January: 37–49.

Ceurvost, R. W. (1994). 'A brand equity measure based on consumer commitment to
brands'. ARF Brand Equity Workshop, New York, February, in *Exploring Brand
Equity.* New York: ARF, 1995.

Christiani, A. (1993). 'Measuring and monitoring brand loyalty and its role in
managing brand equity', ARF Research Day, New York, October, in *Exploring
Brand Equity.* New York: ARF, 1995.

Cowley, D. (ed.) (1989). *Understanding Brands.* London: Kogan Page with the Account
Planning Group.

Cramphorn, M. F. (1992). 'Are there bounds on brand equity?' *Proceedings of the
ESOMAR Seminar: the Challenge of Branding Today and in the Future,* Brussels,
October, pp. 41–54.

Crimmins, J. C. (1992). 'Better measurement and management of brand value'. *Journal
of Advertising Research,* 32 (4) July–August: 11–19.

Ehrenberg, A.S.C. (1988). *Repeat Buying.* London: Charles Griffin and Co.; New York:
Oxford University Press.

Ehrenberg, A.S.C. (1993). 'If you're so strong, why aren't you bigger? Making the case
against brand equity'. *Admap,* October: 13–14. (See also *Admap,* December 1993 for
comments by Ambler and Feldwick and Ehrenberg's reply.)

Ehrenberg, A.S.C. and Scriven, J. (1995). *Joab Report 1 Added Values or Propensities to
Buy.* South Bank Business School.

Ehrenberg, A.S.C., Goodhardt, G. J. and Barwise, T. P. (1990). 'Double Jeopardy
revisited'. *Journal of Marketing,* 54 (July): 82–91.

Eubank, S. K. (1993). 'Understanding brand equity: a volumetric model'. ARF Brand
Equity Research Day, New York, October, in *Exploring Brand Equity.* New York:
ARF, 1995.

Feldwick, P. (ed.) (1991). *Advertising Works 6.* Henley on Thames: NTC Publications.

Feldwick, P. and Bonnal, F. (1995). 'Reports of the death of brands have been greatly
exaggerated'. *Marketing and Research Today,* 23 (2) May: 86–95.

Gardner, B. B. and Levy, S. J. (1955). 'The product and the brand'. *Harvard Business
Review,* March–April: 33–39.

Jones, J. P. (1986). *What's in a Name: Advertising and the Concept of Brands.* Lexington,
MA: Lexington Books.

Jones, J. P. (1991). 'Over-promise and under delivery'. *Proceedings of the ESOMAR
Seminar, What do we know about how advertising works and how promotions work?*
Amsterdam, April, pp. 13–27.

Kamakura, W.A. and Russell, G.J. (1993). 'Measuring brand value with scanner data'. *International Journal of Research in Marketing*, 10 (1) March: 9–22.

Kapferer, J.N. (1992). *Strategic Brand Management: New Approaches to Creating and Evaluating Brand Equity*. London: Kogan Page. Translated from Les Marques, *Capital de l'enterprise*. Paris: Les Editions D'Organisation, 1991.

King, S. (1970). *What is a Brand?* London: J. Walter Thompson.

Light, L. (1994). *The Fourth Wave: Brand Loyalty Marketing*. New York: Coalition for Brand Equity.

Lockwood, T. C. (1994). 'The confessions of a brand equity junkie'. ARF Annual Conference, in *Exploring Brand Equity*. New York: ARF, 1995.

McQueen, J., Foley, C. and Deighton, J. (1993). 'Decomposing a brand's consumer franchise into buyer types'. In Aaker and Biel, pp. 235–246.

McWilliam, G. (1993). 'A tale of two gurus'. *International Journal of Research in Marketing*, 10 (1) March: 105–111.

Moran, W. T. (1994). 'Brand equity: the durability of brand value'. ARF Brand Equity Workshop, New York, February, in *Exploring Brand Equity*. New York: ARF, 1995.

Murphy, J. (1990). 'Assessing the value of brands'. *Long Range Planning*, 23 (3): 23–29.

Owen, S. (1993). 'The Landor Image Power Survey: a global assessment of brand strength'. In Aaker and Biel, pp. 11–30.

Pioche, A. (1992). 'A definition of brand equity relying on attitudes and validated by behaviour'. *Proceedings of the ESOMAR Seminar: the Challenge of Branding Today and in the Future*, Brussels, October, pp. 2740.

Reeves, R. (1961). *Reality in Advertising*. New York: Alfred A. Knopf.

Roth, S. (1991). 'Pricing, profits and equity'. 3rd ARF Advertising and Promotions Workshop, New York, February, in *Exploring Brand Equity*. New York: ARF, 1995.

Taylor, J. A. (1992). 'Brand equity; its meaning, measurement and management'. *Proceedings of the ESOMAR Seminar: the Challenge of Branding Today and in the Future*, Brussels, October, pp. 55–75.

ACKNOWLEDGEMENTS

I am very grateful to Patrick Barwise and Simon Broadbent who read a draft of this paper and made many helpful comments.

9

Shifting Perspectives on Organizational Memory: from Storage to Active Remembering

*Liam J. Bannon and Kari Kuutti**

INTRODUCTION

In many interdisciplinary endeavors, there are certain general concepts that serve an orienting function for the community, even if the very concept itself is often found to be problematic, or capable of multiple interpretations, leading to serious misconceptions among members of the particular community. Indeed, we have elsewhere examined how the concept of 'interface' for the human–computer interaction community and 'co-operative work' for the computer supported co-operative work community are two such concepts, which serve both a unifying function for their respective fields yet on closer analysis are revealed as complex composites that can be viewed in multiple, even conflicting lights (cf. Kuutti and Bannon, 1991, 1993; Bannon, 1997; Bannon and Schmidt, 1991).

We are of the opinion that the topic under discussion here, namely 'organizational memory', is yet another example of a concept that has served a useful function in orienting people from a variety of disciplines to a set of issues concerning the way organizations use and maintain knowledge in various forms. At the same time, on an initial trawl through the literature where this concept is mentioned, a neophyte might question its very utility, given the variety of definitions that are available in the published literature. This hoary old chestnut can be found in such different fields as administrative studies, organizational theory, change management, psychology, sociology, design studies, concurrent engineering, and software engineering. Indeed, the term seems recently to have gained increasing prominence, with a number of workshops and panels devoted to it at a variety of disciplinary meetings. The fact that such a concept is appealed to across a wide range of studies, even if its definition is disputed, is testimony to the fact that even if people cannot

* Reprinted from *Proc. HICSS '96: 29th Hawaii International Conference on System Sciences, Vol. III, Collaboration Systems and Technology*, January 1996, IEEE Computer Society Press.

agree on what exactly the term means, there must be some set of issues that can be subsumed under its umbrella that people feel are important and worth discussing.

The intent of this chapter is once again to examine the concept of 'organizational memory' in an effort to disentangle some of the mixed views on the topic. Some people argue that the term itself is somewhat meaningless, and is an example of the 'fallacy of misplaced concreteness' in that only people, and not organizations, can be considered to have memories, but for our purposes here [we] wish to see how the term is actually used in practice, and what aspects of organizational life it uncovers, with a particular emphasis on differing conceptions of 'memory'. In the next section we start our hunt for the meaning of organizational memory through examining certain papers in administrative and information studies that utilize the concept. Having noted some of the definitions which have a strong emphasis on the 'storage' metaphor, we then take a pragmatic stance and switch our focus to systems applications that attempt to support some form of organizational memory, culling examples from a variety of disparate sources. The increasing recognition of the importance of treating information and knowledge in organizations as 'living' and active, rather than simply as a passive collection of records, is the aspect of organizational memory which we wish to pursue here, as we believe that this perspective has important implications for the kinds of computer support tools that might be required for keeping information accessible and relevant within an organization over time. We pursue the active approach to memory through the work of psychologists from an earlier period and show that the distinction between memory as a passive store and memory as a constructive act, which has a long history, might open up some new issues for the role of technology support in the area of organizational 'memory', where the focus is on memory as a construction, and not simply as a pointer to a data repository.

A SAMPLING OF VIEWS ON ORGANIZATIONAL MEMORY

One of the features of the work on organizational memory is the many and varied places where this term can be found: it does not exclusively 'belong' to any particular research area or discipline. A recurring theme is the idea that the knowledge and experience that resides within the organization needs to be 'preserved' somehow – for instance as members of the organization retire or move on – and also 'shared' among organizational members. The intention is to allow current and future projects to benefit from the experience of other projects, both current and previous, and allow for organizational competencies to be continually reconstituted. For example:

> The sharing of an organization's knowledge resources among knowledge workers is essential from two standpoints. First, it avoids duplication of effort in knowledge collection and maintenance. Second, it promotes consistent decision-making since

all knowledge workers have access to the same body of knowledge (or subsets thereof). The shared knowledge may be centralized and/or distributed. In any case, knowledge management software must be capable of ensuring the integrity of shared knowledge, enforcing security restrictions that apply to various classes of knowledge workers, and supporting reasonable access speeds. (Holsapple and Whinston, 1987: 82)

The essential feature of CM/1 is that it uses a graphical hypertext system to capture the full richness and depth of the team's interactions on the problem – whether it takes place over two weeks or two years. It is easy to track and view the flow of the process, which includes the background and *rationale* for the decisions, thus creating an *organizational memory*. (Conklin and Yourdon, 1993: 5)

Organizational learning is achieved through the acquisition, distribution, interpretation, and storage of information. Learning should lead to more effective information processing and thus more effective functioning and performance. A key component of learning relates to the memory component of this information processing. (Hoffer and Valacich, 1993: 229)

A need exists to organize, integrate, filter, condense, and annotate collaborative data and other relevant information and place it in a common repository that is easily accessible by team members, managers, and other interested (and authorized) personnel. (Morrison, 1993: 123)

Probably the largest body of literature on the concept can be found in the field of organization studies. Given the shortage of space in this chapter, this is not the place to provide an exhaustive or even extensive reference to the evolving literature on the theme. Rather, we will refer to a recent major review paper on the topic (Walsh and Ungson, 1991) which collates much of the early material and provides a useful context for our subsequent remarks. Thereafter we switch our attention to the more pragmatic concerns of systems builders, and their attempts to implement systems that support various aspects of organizational memory.

Organizational analyses

In the organizational and administrative studies literature, one can find at least two distinct approaches to organizational memory (cf. Cook and Yanow, 1993). One focuses on the individual cognitive capabilities of people and views organizational learning and memory as simply defining the learning or memory of *individuals* in the organization; a second view presents organizational memory as some cognitive property of an *organizational collective entity* that itself can be viewed as learning and memorizing.[1] We would agree with Cook that neither of these alternatives seems satisfactory. The former tends to eschew analysis of the real organizational context of the activity, whereas the latter lends itself to an anthropomorphism which is distinctly problematic and unhelpful, leading us to search for the location of engrams in the basements of an organization.

Another notion of organizational memory is the idea that everything in organizations contains some information and is thus comparable with a 'memory':

> Organizational memory, broadly defined, includes everything that is contained in an organization that is somehow retrievable. Thus storage files of old invoices are part of that memory. So are copies of letters, spreadsheet data stored in computers, and the latest strategic plan, as well as what is in the minds of all organizational members. (Kim, 1993)

One of the best known and widely cited conceptions of organizational memory is presented by Walsh and Ungson (1991). In their review paper Walsh and Ungson develop a model of the structure of organizational memory from the administrative science point of view that synthesizes a large number of previously presented conceptions. The fundamental component of this model consists of five 'retention bins', around which both acquisition and retention take place. The 'bins' identified are as follows (pp. 63–66):

1 *Individuals.* Individuals store information about their organizations in their own capacity to articulate and remember experience, and they keep records and files as memory aids.
2 *Culture.* Culture embodies past experience that can be useful in dealing with the future. The cultural information is seen to be stored in different ways, for example in language, in shared frameworks, in symbols or in stories.
3 *Transformations.* Transformations embody the logic that guides the transformation of an input (e.g. raw material, a new recruit, an insurance claim) into an output (correspondingly a finished product, a company veteran, an insurance payment).
4 *Structures.* Different roles within an organizational structure provide a repository in which organizational information can be stored.
5 *Ecology.* The actual physical arrangement of a workplace also embodies information about the organization that can be decoded.

The conceptual framework proposed by Walsh and Ungson is comprehensive, but it suffers from an attempt to include virtually everything, so that one is left wondering exactly what, within organizations, is not a part of organizational memory? The attempt to ensure completeness results in an overly complex and unwieldy conception of organizational memory. There is also a distinct bias towards a storage model of 'memory' in their paper, despite the occasional references to active features of using memories. This is another point that we will return to later. So, what of our perspective on the concept of organizational memory? Our own position is that, given the very loose and non-overlapping definitions of the term, we are not particularly enthusiastic about its use as a coherent conceptual construct in the literature. On the other hand, given its wide usage, we are concerned to point out certain features of memory, in humans or organizations, which we believe have not received sufficient prominence to date in the debate about organizational memory, which could reorient some of the work done under its banner. So, for the rest of the chapter we will use the term *organizational memory* as a general category, without further equivocation, despite our conceptual concerns.

Let us now turn to see how another disciplinary background has brought people to a somewhat different conception of organizational memory.

Computer-based systems to support organizational memory

While it is important not to reify this concept of 'organizational memory', and since the term has been used in a wide and at times confusing way in much of the organizational theory literature, the label still serves as a useful heuristic to describe a set of concerns about how information is collated, stored, accessed, accreted, updated, and used in organizations. Some theorists express the view that with appropriate information technology, we can make good the deficiencies of human memory in organizations. Huber (1990) provides a particularly explicit example of such a perspective:

> Given what is known about the many factors contributing to inaccurate learning and incomplete recall and to motivational distortions in sharing information, it is not at all surprising that the human components of organization memories are less than satisfactory. . . . In the future, smart indexing or artificial intelligence will facilitate retrieval of transaction information and will result in computer-resident organizational memories with certain properties, such as completeness, that are superior to the human components of organizational memories. (Huber, 1990: 60)

This represents a fairly standard view of the human as the fallible element in the system, and the possibility of supplementing or even replacing the human element with computers. We will later question this particular viewpoint, and show that there is a lot more to the concepts of human and organizational remembering than simply accessing large data stores.

Within the computing community, a number of pilot and even some commercial systems have been developed to provide a form of what has been termed organizational memory (the pioneering work of Engelbart and the NLS team on the NLS Journal system and 'community handbook' (Engelbart, 1963, 1988)). There is also work in engineering design concerning shared memory (Konda et al., 1992), while others have tried to develop systems to support the software development process through maintaining a design rationale (Conklin and Begemen, 1988) or a design knowledge base (Terveen et al., 1993) or more general systems support (Ackerman, 1994b) and organizational support (Fuchs and Prinz, 1993). Let us now briefly characterize some of the contributions at the level of systems before we go further into our analysis of the concept. The intent here is to illustrate a variety of attempts to embed aspects of what is commonly called organizational memory into software systems. The examples chosen are not exhaustive or necessarily representative, but illustrate a variety of approaches which the authors have come across over the years that seem of interest, and which we present for further examination.

Doug Engelbart's vision One of the few people who foresaw the revolutionary potential of the computer as a medium for improving idea development and group and organizational communication was Doug Engelbart, who conceived a project entitled 'Augmenting the Human Intellect' at Stanford Research Institute in the early 1960s (Engelbart, 1963). This work of Doug Engelbart and his group has had, and indeed is still having, a profound impact on the development of interactive computing and our interfaces to computers (Engelbart, 1988; Bannon, 1989). Engelbart's vision encompassed a new kind of computerized working environment in which the emphasis was on how people could achieve significant gains in productivity as a result of the computerized support made available to them. Integral to Engelbart's scheme was the provision of computerized support to enhance communication and collaboration between people. As well as providing electronic mail facilities on his system, users could link their screens and thus work in a shared space mode, often with a telephone connection as well, so that they could discuss and change the joint document they were viewing. With regard to the concept of an organizational or community memory, the system provided a journal facility for archiving messages and reports to serve this function. Items in this record could be directly referenced in messages, and the receiver could get access directly to the referenced document if required. As well as simple archiving features such as the NLS Journal, he had an explicit design intention to provide in the planned ARPANET Network Information Center (NIC) a centre that would support the community by integrating and facilitating dialogue and evolving what he refers to as a community handbook, which is a 'system designed to support collaboration in a community of knowledge workers'. This would allow for the creation, modification, transmission, etc. of messages supporting cross-referencing, cataloguing and indexing and 'should also support managing externally generated items'. In a more recent exposition of what he had in mind, even though this aspect never really came to fruition, Engelbart and Lehman discuss the vision of this dynamic database or superdocument:

> Tools for the responsive development and evolution of such a superdocument by many (distributed) individuals within a discipline- or project-oriented community could lead to the maintenance of a 'community handbook,' a uniform, complete, consistent, up-to-date integration of the special knowledge representing the current status of the community. The handbook would include principles, working hypotheses, practices, glossaries of special terms, standards, goals, goal status, supportive arguments, techniques, observations, how-to-do-it items, and so forth. An active community would be constantly involved in dialogue concerning the contents of its handbook. Constant updating would provide a 'certified community position structure' about which the real evolutionary work would swarm.

As noted elsewhere (Schmidt and Bannon, 1992) the notion of 'a uniform, complete, consistent, up-to-date integration' of community knowledge is hardly realistic. Interpretative work remains to be done by the actors accessing the community handbook. It could indeed be a valuable *resource* for developing what Schmidt and Bannon term a 'common information space' with other actors, but due to the distributed nature of co-operative work the handbook will be necessarily incomplete and partial. However, given the time period, the ideas and implementation of Engelbart's group were quite far-sighted, and his work is still worth reading today in order to understand the breadth and depth of his vision. Only relatively recently have other researchers begun to reinvestigate this work in the context of the newly emerging field that has been labelled CSCW – Computer Supported Co-operative Work.

The 'Answer Garden' project – a more modest proposal? We now turn to discuss a prototype system with a focused objective of making recorded knowledge in a narrow domain retrievable for future use. The system, called 'Answer Garden', was initially developed by Mark Ackerman as an MIT dissertation project in the early 1990s, and has developed further since then. Answer Garden is one of the few organizational memory systems that have been developed to the stage where they are actually usable in practice. Answer Garden is a hypermedia network system that combines database-like and communication features:

> In the standard configuration of Answer Garden, users seek answers to commonly asked questions through a set of diagnostic questions or other information retrieval mechanisms. . . . If an answer is not found or is incomplete (or if the user becomes confused or lost) the user may ask the question through the system. Answer Garden then routes the question to an appropriate human expert. . . . The expert then answers the user via electronic mail, and if the question is a common one, the expert can insert the question and its answer back into the database. (Ackerman, 1994b: 244–245)

The first application developed by using the Answer Garden Substrate – the database and communication 'engine' – was aimed to serve as an X Window help system (Ackerman, 1994b); another reported usage is to help astrophysicists cope with a multitude of different software packages through which they have to run their research data (Ackerman and Mandel, 1995). The early papers on Answer Garden had grand visions (Ackerman and Malone, 1990), but later papers are more modest, when it comes to the scope of application of the system. Ackerman has acknowledged the problems involved in interpreting preserved data (Ackerman, 1994a) due to contextual factors, and in his latest paper (Ackerman and Mandel, 1995) he explicitly advocates 'memory-in-the-small' – task-based data that is so local and short-term that there should be no problems in interpreting it.

Jeff Conklin's work on IBIS and CM/1   The work of Jeff Conklin and others on capturing design rationale using the IBIS (Issue Based Information System) framework within a computer-based hypertext framework has been described in several papers (Conklin and Begemen, 1988; Yakemovic and Conklin, 1990; Conklin and Yakemovic, 1991). This viewpoint attempts to capture the existing conversations and information flows as a source of design rationale.

Yakemovic and Conklin claim that:

> The IBIS structure of Issues (which state questions or problems), Positions (which state possible resolutions of an Issue) and Arguments (which state pros and cons of Positions) is one form of the natural, intuitive structure of decisions: some choice to be made, some set of alternatives, some trade-off analysis among the alternatives (optional), and a commitment to some resolution. (Yakemovic and Conklin, 1990)

In earlier work at MCC, Conklin and colleagues developed a computer-based graphical IBIS. The intent was that this system would help groups to capture the design rationale of their projects in the course of actually making the design. Experiences of the use of this system in groups are reported in Yakemovic and Conklin, 1990, and in Selvin, 1994. In the former case, in a commercial software development project over an extended period, the authors claim that the method was an improvement over unstructured notes and had several beneficial side effects. CM/1 is the PC-based commercial product developed by Conklin's Corporate Memory Systems, Inc. – a spin-off company specializing in technology to provide for organizational memory and learning through 'living documentation'. According to CMS, its products for organizational learning are based on two technical insights. The first is that decisions, assumptions, and open issues (i.e. events surrounding the making of intellectual commitments) are the pivotal elements on which an organization's actions turn, that this information is never systematically recorded, and that it can be naturally and powerfully captured using a simple method. The second is that for organizational memory to be effective it must dwell within a 'living document', that is, it must be embedded in the everyday tools and practices of the organization in a way that makes adding information to it and retrieving information from it easy, natural and compelling.

Selvin discusses issues concerning the facilitation of meetings with CM/1, and notes some of the problems that can occur in trying to use the system in real time at meetings, such as the problem of classifying the rhetorical type of an utterance and placing it on the decision map (issue net) in an appropriate place quickly enough not to inhibit the conversations. He also notes that the 'culture' of specific groups can be different, as to their acceptance of the new language and way of discussing issues that is required in using such a tool. In some cases, it has been noted that people who are supportive of the methodology will code up discussions in this formalism after the meetings, rather than having group acceptance and collective use of the tool. In terms of our immediate interest in organizational memory, while this approach is claimed to have the potential for the management of longer-term group memories, it has not yet been fully supported in the tools, to our knowledge, and to date there is little information available on subsequent re-use of this information.

'Living design memory'   A recent paper by software developers at AT&T Bell Labs provides an interesting and thoughtful discussion of issues surrounding the concept of an organizational memory as well as a description of the development and use of a prototype system to serve as a 'living design memory' (Terveen et al., 1993). Like many others in the area of software development, the authors are concerned with the high cost of developing software and have developed their tool in an effort to integrate local design knowledge, rules of thumb, heuristics, lessons learned from previous designs, etc., into a knowledge base that is constantly evolving through use. What is striking in the account of what they learned in the process is the fact that the relevant knowledge exists in the form of 'folklore' rather than being enshrined in formal organizational procedures, and their recognition of the need to integrate their system into the everyday organizational practice of the community if it is to serve any function: 'the members of the community in which a system is to be deployed must *own* the system' (Terveen et al., 1993, original italics). Contrary to many in the field of information systems, they recognize that 'knowledge of *facts* is not enough: it also is necessary to know *how the knowledge is to be used*' (ibid., original italics).

   Thus early attempts promising a corporate memory involving on-line structured text files encountered problems due to the fact that the information was not organized for efficient access (the problem of indexing), there was no way to ensure compliance and no natural way to ensure the evolution of documents. Their solution was to develop a design knowledge base and a designer assistant program which interfaces between the designer and the system, giving advice which the human designer should incorporate into their design document. At design review further information produced is fed back into the design knowledge base. The paper is very interesting because it provides an account of the iterative design of the system based on experiences of use of the prototype. At the same time, however, we should note that many users still have problems with the current system. The authors claim that this work, while related to that of Conklin described above, goes beyond capturing design rationale and does not stop at integrating a tool into design practice, as with IBIS, but also integrates it into existing organizational processes, modifying these processes as necessary.

Design engineering   Konda et al. (1992) have written an interesting paper on organizational memory from the viewpoint of engineering design; in it they explicitly address the problem of contextuality we have pointed out above. They trace the variety and development of different design theories and come to the conclusion that universal design methods have a multitude of problems and that if they are to be used they should be contextually evaluated using collected historical experiences. To facilitate this process, they suggest the necessity of a 'shared memory'. This shared memory concept can be divided into two forms: vertical and horizontal. Vertical shared memory is the collected corpus of knowledge within one professional group or sub-discipline within such group. This knowledge is more or less universal, collected in textbooks and advanced by research. Horizontal shared memory is a corpus of knowledge with a consensus and meaning shared by different professional groups and disciplines participating in a particular design project. Konda et al. insist that some form of shared horizontal memory is a necessity for any design project. Thus they not only recognize the importance of the maintenance of the contextuality of information, they make it a prerequisite. We will return to some of their concerns in the final section of this chapter.

Summary

What we have seen from the brief accounts of the systems described above are wide disparities in the conceptual frameworks employed, and in the empirical evidence in support of the systems developed, yet undoubtedly these researchers have tapped a rich vein, as they all are of the opinion that some form of shared memory is of importance to organizational development, even if there is still profound disagreement and confusion about exactly what kind of computer support might be possible to enhance this. For example, note that both ECSCW'91 and CSCW'94 had panels on the concept of organizational memory, both of which, in the opinions of most of the audience, generated more questions than answers. While a large part of the work within the Computer Supported Co-operative Work (CSCW), especially in the area of software development, has to date focused on synchronous interactions, it is likely that in the long term support for various forms of information gathering and dissemination activities will come to be seen as having a much greater impact on organizational functioning. Now that we have examined a variety of approaches to understanding and implementing the idea of organizational memory, it is time to return to a more fundamental re-examination of the metaphors of memory that are implicit in these perspectives.

THE CONCEPT OF MEMORY REVISITED

> Remembering is not the re-excitation of innumerable fixed, lifeless and fragmentary traces. It is an imaginative reconstruction, or construction, built out of the relation of our attitude towards a whole active mass of organized past reactions or experience, and to a little outstanding detail which commonly appears in image or in language form. It is thus hardly ever really exact, even in the most rudimentary form of rote recapitulation, and it is not at all important that it should be so. (Bartlett, 1932)

While 'memory 'is one of the central concepts that has interested psychology since its foundation as an area of academic study, and even well before (cf. the

Greek work on mnemonists' strategies, and the analysis of the Method of Loci for memorization), over the past 30 years much psychological theorizing has been influenced by work in computer science, in particular artificial intelligence, due to an interest in possible mechanisms underlying human cognitive abilities. It is not the place here to critique this turn of events, but it is important that its formative influence on much psychological theorizing be understood as it had serious implications for the way in which conceptions of human memory became intertwined with models of computer storage. Thus, there developed a very direct and concrete linkage between the human act of remembering and some function-retrieving information from a computer store. Note that no longer is the computer simply a metaphor for human cognition but rather, 'cognition is computation' (Pylyshyn, 1984).

The result of this take-over has been the casting out of an alternative conception of memory – which also has had a long lineage from ancient times – that stresses the active act of remembering over the notion of some form of simple table lookup. One can see these two contrasting perspectives from the early days of psychology proper as well, with the less well known views of Franz Brentano and others concerning 'act' psychology being defeated by the empiricist associationists. However, the concerns underlying the alternative view have never been completely discarded, and can be seen in what is unquestionably a landmark book in psychology by the eminent British psychologist, Sir Frederic C. Bartlett: *Remembering* (note: not Memory!) back in 1932. For many people who may have despaired of the meagre results and methodological nitpickings that characterize much of the dust-bowl empiricist behaviourist psychological work from the 1920s to the 1960s, this book will be a relief. It is full of insightful observations, clever experimentation, and thoughtful conceptualizations. Of interest here is its repeated emphasis on the view of human memory as anything but a passive store, but of remembering as a constructive act – 'remembering appears to be far more decisively an affair of construction than one of mere reproduction. . . . condensation, elaboration and invention are common features of ordinary remembering' (1932: 205).

During the 1970s and 1980s the information-processing perspective in cognitive psychology was so dominant that its metaphors became a part of everyday talk and for the layman – including non-psychological researchers – it was synonymous with psychology. Thus Bartlett's work was not as influential as it should have been at this time. We do find renewed interest in the late 1970s, when aspects of the computer model were called into question, and more emphasis was given to ecological factors in human cognition which did not accord well with simple computational accounts of phenomena (cf. Neisser, 1982). It is important to remember that, even in the domain of cognition, information processing psychology is just one of the many traditions of psychology. Some of the other traditions have a distinctively different view on cognition and memory and it might be worthwhile to recall some of them because they offer a more realistic starting point for the discussion about memory and remembering.

One psychological tradition that shares Bartlett's concerns with the active nature of human memory processes, emphasizing remembering as purposeful action in some definite context, is Russian cultural-historical psychology, founded by L. S. Vygotsky in the 1920s. Cultural historical psychologists see remembering as processes of structuring and storing past experience to enable its use in activities. It is a purposeful action relying on the use of socially developed signs and depending on the goals and motives of the activity within which it takes place. One of the best known memory researchers within the tradition is a contemporary of Bartlett, P. I. Zinchenko:

> Within this framework, memory processes can be viewed neither as a mechanical coupling, as a connection, of subjective images and experiences, nor as external relations. To treat them as the function of some metaphysical capacity for memory, a capacity to preserve and reproduce impressions, is also unacceptable. Nor can they be viewed as a metaphysical capacity of the brain, of the brain conceptualized outside the actual process of the subject's life. Memory processes must be understood as processes that constitute the content of a specific action. They must be understood as remembering or recollection responsive to and functioning in a particular task. (Zinchenko, 1983: 76)

Each action of memorizing or storing information and each action of recalling and remembering takes place in the context of an activity. If storing context and recalling context are the same activity, the interpretation of the material may not be problematic. But if remembering takes place in a different activity where material has been stored, the material will be reinterpreted with respect to the new object of activity, and there is no automatic guarantee that the material is relevant any more in the same way as it was when it was stored. We believe that this problem of contextuality has been somewhat neglected in the studies of re-use, design rational etc. mentioned earlier.

The import of this work for our discussion of the much broader concept of organizational memory is that in the vast majority of cases, underlying any mention of the term 'memory' is a view of memory as a passive register of experience. Yet we now know that this view is certainly not appropriate to human memory. This does not of course imply that providing some register of events or some form of storage is inappropriate in an organization, as of course we are required for legal reasons alone to maintain such records, but it does become important in situations where people are designing systems that are supposed to allow people in organizations to store and later retrieve accounts of experiences which can hopefully be shared throughout the organization. So, what are the consequences of taking such an approach to organizational memory? In the next and final section, we begin the process of reconstructing this concept according to this alternative perspective, and hint at possible questions that are raised, and issues that need to be explored more fully.

IMPLICATIONS/CONSEQUENCES OF OUR POSITION

> Co-operative work is not facilitated simply by the provision of a shared database, but requires the active construction by the participants of a common information space where the meanings of the shared objects are debated and resolved, at least locally and temporarily. Objects must thus be interpreted and assigned meaning, meanings that are achieved by specific actors on specific occasions of use. (Schmidt and Bannon, 1992)

The purpose of this chapter has been to survey a number of quite disparate activities in a variety of fields concerned with the theme of organizational memory and learning. We have shown how much of the work in the organizational field has been based on an implicit, if not explicit, view of organizational memory as akin to human memory. Models of human memory that tend to be discussed emphasize human memory as the storing of experience, so memory is viewed as a storage bin. How to 'capture' information in the organization, and then recirculate it becomes simply a matter of developing suitable hypertext and electronic communication systems to help in the 'input' and 'output' of the engrams, traces, or information nuggets that exist in the organization. It is in a sense a great irony that in much of this work we have a circular set of concepts and definitions – computer systems are used by information-processing psychologists to develop theories of human memory, these models of human memory in turn influence organization theorists in their views of organizational memory, and in turn are the basis for computer systems!

We have examined briefly some computer systems that have been developed to support aspects of organizational memory, and noted some of their features, positive and negative. While some of these systems have been developed with a limited pragmatic purpose in mind, in the majority of cases there is still an implicit perspective of 'capture' of relevant information. What we have attempted to show is that there is an alternative conceptualization of memory which has a long tradition focusing on the active constructive aspects of remembering. In our view, this perspective is not only of import for psychological or sociological theory, but has implications for the construction of computer 'support' systems for any such processes. For example, a number of information systems projects that attempt to capture all the activities of groups within an organization would appear to be going up a blind alley, as such data capture is unlikely to be able to be interpreted and reworked to be useful for a later situation. Time passes, and the people, settings and context in which the original 'information' was produced also change. Thus the likelihood of being able to characterize what kinds of information in an organization are potentially significant and worth keeping is an impossible task, as we must take into account the fact that people are actively making sense of the information presented, either intra- or intersubjectively. At another level, the very idea of what is required in order to make people in organizations function more effectively, i.e. access to more information, is open to question on a number of counts. For example, the study by Kidd (1994) makes a number of interesting observations about how knowledge workers learn, and emphasizes that it is the act of making notes, rather than the resulting notes, that are of value in many situations, a finding that has major implications in the current context.[2]

How do we 'capture' the meanings that are required in order to make sense of any situation or fact? Our very concepts for discussing such issues are not well developed, although recently there has been work from a variety of quite different sources which at least acknowledges the problem, and offers some suggestions as to what direction we might head. For example, in an ambitious and important programme of work briefly discussed earlier (Konda et al., 1992), a group at Carnegie-Mellon University in Engineering Design are involved in the building of a shared memory, but in contradistinction to much of the work in the area, they have taken on board some of the concerns expressed here. They are aware that collaboration does not simply consist of a transfer of information between parties but that for any sort of shared memory to be developed there must be shared meanings: 'one cannot have a meaningful shared memory without shared meaning, since a memory that is neither accessible nor understandable can hardly be called sharable' (Konda et al., 1992). This view is strikingly reminiscent of comments made in another paper, concerning the notion of a 'shared information space' (Bannon and Schmidt, 1991) or more recently, a 'common information space' (Schmidt and Bannon, 1992): 'A common information space encompasses the artefacts that are accessible to a co-operative ensemble *as well as* the meaning attributed to these artefacts by the actors.' The authors elaborate: 'Objects must thus be interpreted and assigned meaning, meanings that are achieved by specific actors on specific occasions of use. Computer support for this aspect of co-operative work raises a host of interesting and difficult issues that have not been fully addressed within the field to date.'

The implications of these views for building corporate repositories of information is only beginning to be addressed. In both cases, the problem resides in the fact that information does not simply exist 'out there', but is produced by specific people in specific contexts for specific purposes. While this does not imply that it is bound solely to that whole context, it does mean that one cannot in any straightforward way extract and abstract from this web of signification items of 'information' which can be stored in some central resource for later use without having some conception of this whole 'context' question. What is good information changes depending on the time, the originator, the context, etc. . . . and without these cues, the relevance of items of 'information' becomes deeply problematic. The views of the Carnegie-Mellon group, Bannon and Schmidt, and the authors of the present chapter are that no universal language will be possible for encoding information, nor is there any algorithm to determine 'relevance'. Information is always produced in a context, and must be reinterpreted in other contexts. Understandings, either between people or between artefacts or information and people, are achieved, not given. Neither human remembering, nor human interaction simply occurs; it is an outcome that is dependent on the interplay of many factors.[3]

Within the field of CSCW, increasing attention is being given to the issue of how people construct understandings based on texts and artefacts produced by others. As noted by Schmidt and Bannon,

> the focus is on how people in a distributed setting can work co-operatively in a common information space – i.e. by maintaining a central archive of organizational information with some level of 'shared' agreement as to the meaning of this information (locally constructed), despite the marked differences concerning the origins and context of these information items. The space is constituted and maintained by different actors employing different conceptualizations and multiple decision making strategies, supported by technology. (1992)

What is surprising is that there has been little focus among the various disciplinary groups concerned with organizational memory on the details of how organizations actually develop and use organizational memories – the ways in which procedures embed knowledge, the possibilities for changing organizational routines as a result of organizational learning, the ways in which artefacts and their uses can inculcate a particular way of doing things throughout the organization, the care and evolution of corporate information repositories, the role of gossip and the grapevine in contributing to organizational memory, etc. The material that does bear on such issues is often developed by people from outside this community. For example, the work of JoAnne Yates on the history of managerial control and communication mechanisms in American organizations (Yates, 1989) provides a rich historical analysis of material of relevance here. Likewise, from a cultural-historical activity perspective, the work of Engeström and his colleagues, e.g. (Engeström et al., 1990) is concerned with the historical analysis of work activities as a part and parcel of the developmental work research tradition. Also, there are numerous ethnographic studies of work that provide important insights into how people use records, documents and artefacts of all kinds to accomplish their work activities, and engender shared ways of viewing the world within specific communities (see e.g. Suchman, 1987; Hughes et al., 1993; Sachs, 1994). The role of 'war stories' that are swapped among various groups, detailing interesting, difficult problems with equipment and their resolution, is relevant here. While our aim here has been to bring to the attention of researchers on organizational memory a relatively neglected body of psychological literature that provides a reframing of the nature of human memory and of the 'memory' concept *per se*, it is also important to note that within the field of sociology there is also a strong body of work that emphasizes the constructive aspect of remembering as a social phenomenon rather than memory as some passive store (Hughes et al., 1995). Both sets of views reinforce the position that, at a pragmatic level, computer-based support systems for organizational memories that simply consist of some passive capturing, storage and eventual replay of information will have very limited if any use for the practical accomplishment of activities within an organization.

In recent years we have witnessed the development of a variety of accounts of phenomena that, taken together, present a very strong case for the importance of the contingent nature of human activities, that stress the role of talk and interaction as the basis for mutual understanding and intelligibility. There is an increased interest in the role of stories and narratives as methods for encoding and disseminating information in all aspects of human life. It is not the stories *per se* but the discussion and debate that they stimulate that is important in developing real understanding. Wynn notes: 'In an office as it presently operates, the knowledge which is both means and product is dependent on interaction between people for its quality, relevance and appropriateness. These interactions are in turn dependent on social practices' (Wynn, 1979: 165). More recently, Blacker notes: 'Talk about computer-mediated information and the transformation of isolated problem-solving attempts into a shared activity are crucial to the effective operation of the "informated" organization. It is only through such processes that the process of collective interpretation can be reached' (Blackler, 1994: 12). Within the CSCW community, the work of Julian Orr on story-telling as an important practice in learning on the job has attracted attention: 'Diagnosis is observed to have a strong narrative component in the integration and assessment of known facts; the technicians tell themselves what they know about the machine. This narration prepares them to tell others of their experience, either in asking for help or telling of a new problem, and stories of interesting problems circulate quickly through the community. These stories inform the community; they also demonstrate and celebrate the competent practice in maintenance of the service situation which is the basis of the community' (Orr, 1992: 6). As Brown and Duguid note:

> In some form or another the stories that support learning-in-working and innovation should be allowed to circulate. The technological potential to support this distribution – e-mail, bulletin boards, and other devices that are capable of supporting narrative exchanges – is available. But narratives, as we have argued, are embedded in the social system in which they arise and are used. They cannot simply be uprooted and repackaged for circulation without becoming prey to exactly those problems that beset the old abstracted canonical accounts. (Brown and Duguid, 1991: 54)

In contradistinction to the explicit socially sanctioned role of story-telling, we also see an emphasis on the importance of talk in work settings: '[the] important function served by serendipitous talk about work is its importance in constructing and maintaining an up to date "intelligence" concerning the current activities of the team. This working "intelligence" or "memory" can be seen to be collectively constituted in the team's conversations' (Middleton, 1988: 14). As Bannon (1991) notes:

These stories not only impart information, they also provide a context for use of the information, and they also serve as a way of bonding the group together. They are vehicles for group cohesiveness and identity, and as such cannot be replaced with simple factual information about the original problem that is the basis of the story. Can such stories be put into a community information base without losing their dual function as both information bearing and social bonding entities? We must admit we cannot answer that question at this stage. What are the pre-conditions for having people commit to contributing and sustaining such a system? Can the motives be completely altruistic? What are the rewards, both personal, social, organizational, for those that contribute to this information repository, either directly, or when explicitly asked? What kind of support structures, either embedded in the computer network itself, or external to it, might be of use to support this kind of co-operative learning and exchange of information? Are there software needs that can be identified that would assist in the development of such a community memory?

CONCLUDING REMARKS

In this chapter we have provided some commentary on the concept of organizational memory, arguing that its current uses are so broad as to render it of little use as a conceptual construct. At the same time, the term serves an orienting function among a range of disciplines towards concerns about the preservation of information and the re-use of knowledge within organizations. We have attempted to go beyond the prototypical conception of memory as a storage facility and stressed the active, constructive aspect of remembering in human activity at both a personal and a collective level. This perspective has implications in the context of organizational memory, as it puts the spotlight on the ways in which information is initially produced and stored and subsequently interpreted and understood by other people, in other settings, at other times. For example, while records can be stored, on each occasion of 're-use', actors must develop a common information space in which meanings are developed, and computers might support the development of such interpretations through allowing access not just to the physical artefacts or records but possibly to the actors themselves and to a richer picture of the context for which the information was originally produced. To end on a somewhat provocative and reflexive note, perhaps what is now required of all of us within the information systems community is more involvement in analysing the ways in which organizational memory – in whatever form it is conceptualized – and its computer support is built and used in real organizations by human actors in particular settings, rather than in developing additional corollaries or hypotheses about the nature of the beast![4] It is to this task that our future work in the field will be dedicated.

NOTES

The authors would like to acknowledge the following projects for supporting this work: EU Esprit Basic Research Action 6225 (COMIC); EU Human Capital and Mobility Programme (ENACT); COST-14 CoTech Action (Project #2: Common Information Spaces and Organizational Memory). We especially thank all our colleagues on these projects for stimulating discussions.

1. This links into the literature that refers to organizations as 'giant brains'.
2. Our thanks to Yvonne Rogers for pointing us to this reference and providing other useful comments.
3. In discussing human remembering, Bartlett refers to this set of factors as a 'schema' although he was well aware of the possible misuses of this term, and certainly his notion is far removed from later AI attempts to reify this concept (Minsky, Schank).
4. It is interesting to speculate about the relationship between the ideas of business process re-engineering (BPR), or at least one variant of it, that argues for doing away with traditional practices in a wholesale fashion, on the one hand, and the concern with aspects of organizational memory, the preservation of aspects of organizational tradition, on the other. Investigating this paradox would take us too far afield however, but see Bannon, 1994 and Kuutti et al., 1995 for some further comments.

REFERENCES

Ackerman, M. S. (1994a) 'Definitional and contextual issues in organizational and group memories', in *27th Hawaii International Conference on System Sciences (HICSS-27)* (pp. 191–200). Maui, Hawaii, January: IEEE Computer Press.

Ackerman, M. S. (1994b) 'Augmenting the organizational memory: a field study of Answer Garden', in *CSCW'94* (pp. 243–252). Chapel Hill, NC: ACM Press.

Ackerman, M. S. and Malone, T. W. (1990) 'Answer garden: a tool for growing organizational memory', in *ACM Conference on Office Information Systems* (pp. 31–39). Cambridge, MA: ACM Press.

Ackerman, M. S. and Mandel, E. (1995) 'Memory in the small: an application to provide task-based organizational memory for a scientific community', in *28th Annual Hawaii International Conference on System Sciences (HICSS-28)*, IV (pp. 323–332). Maui, Hawaii, 3–5 January: IEEE Computer Press.

Bannon, L. (1989) 'The pioneering work of Douglas C. Engelbart', in Z. Pylyshyn and L. Bannon (eds), *Perspectives on the Computer Revolution* (pp. 301–306). Norwood, NJ: Ablex.

Bannon, L. (1991) 'Community technology? Issues in computer supported work', *Mutual Uses of Cybernetics and Science, Special Issue of Systemica – Journal of the Dutch Systems Group*, 8 (2): 23–41.

Bannon, L. (1994) 'Computer supported co-operative work: challenging perspectives on work and technology', Invited paper, in W. Baets and R. Galliers (eds), *Conference on Information Technology and Organizational Change*, Nijenrode University (The Netherlands Business School), Breuklen, The Netherlands, April.

Bannon, L. (1997) 'Dwelling in the "Great Divide": the case of HCI and CSCW', in G. Bowker, L. Star, W. Turner and L. Gasser (eds), *Social Science, Technical Systems and Co-operative Work*. Princeton, NJ: L. J. Erlbaum.

Bannon, L. J. and Schmidt, K. (1991) 'CSCW: four characters in search of a context?' in J. M. Bowers and S. D. Benford (eds), *Studies in Computer Supported Co-operative Work. Theory, Practice and Design* (pp. 3–17). Amsterdam: North-Holland.

Bartlett, F. C. (1932) *Remembering*. Cambridge: Cambridge University Press.

Blackler, F. (1993) 'Knowledge and the theory of organizations: organizations as activity systems and the reframing of management', *Journal of Management Studies*, 30(6): 863–884.

Blackler, F. (1994) 'Knowledge, knowledge work and organizations. An overview and interpretation', in *Workshop on European Competitiveness in a Knowledge Society*, Lyon, 30 Nov.– 2 Dec.

Brown, J. S. and Duguid, P. (1991) 'Organizational learning and communities of practice: toward a unified view of working, learning and innovation', *Organization Science*, 2(1): 40–57.

Conklin, J. and Begemen, M. L. (1988) 'IBIS: a hypertext tool for exploratory policy discussion', in *CSCW'88* (pp. 140–152). Portland: ACM Press.

Conklin, J. and Yakemovic, K. C. B. (1991) 'A process-oriented approach to capturing design rationale', *Human-Computer Interaction*, 6: 357–391.

Conklin, J. and Yourdon, E. (1993) 'Groupware for the new organization', *American Programmer*, September: 3–8.

Cook, S. D. N. and Yanow, D. (1993) 'Culture and organizational learning', *Journal of Management Inquiry*, 2(4): 373–390.

Engelbart, D. C. (1963) 'A conceptual framework for the augmentation of man's intellect'. In P. Howerton and D. Weeks (eds), *Vistas in Information Handling* (pp. 1–29). Washington, DC: Spartan Books.

Engelbart, D. C. (1988) 'The augmented knowledge workshop', in A. Goldberg (ed.), *A History of Personal Workstations*. New York: ACM Press.

Engelbart, D. and Lehman, H. (1988) 'Working together', *Byte*, December: 245–252.

Engeström, Y., Brown, K., Engeström, R. and Koistinen, K. (1990) 'Organizational forgetting: an activity-theoretical perspective', in D. Middleton and D. Edwards (eds), *Collective Remembering*. London: Sage.

Fuchs, L. and Prinz, W. (1993) 'Aspects of organizational context in CSCW', in L. Bannon and K. Schmidt (eds), *Issues of Supporting Organizational Context in CSCW Systems. COMIC Deliverable 1.1.* Lancaster: Lancaster University.

Hoffer, J. A. and Valacich, J. S. (1993) 'Group memory in group support systems: a foundation for design', in L. M. Jessup and J. S. Valacich (eds), *Group Support Systems: New Perspectives* (pp. 214–229). New York: Macmillan.

Holsapple, C. W. and Whinston, A. B. (1987) 'Knowledge-based organizations', *The Information Society*, 5: 77–90.

Huber, G. P. (1990) 'A theory of the effects of advanced information technologies on organizational design, intelligence, and decision making', *Academy of Management Journal*, 15(1): 47–71.

Hughes, J., King, V., Mariani, J., Rodden, T. and Twidale, M. (1993) 'Paperwork and its lessons for database design', in *12th Schärding International Workshop on Design of Computer Supported Co-operative Work and Groupware*, Schärding, Austria, 1–3 June.

Hughes, J., O'Brien, J. and Rouncefield, M. (1995) 'Organizational memory, or, how can we sack Mavis but keep her brain?' in *COST 14 CoTech (Project 2: Common Information Spaces and Organizational Memory) Meeting*, Limerick, Ireland, January.

Kidd, A. (1994) 'The marks are on the knowledge worker', in *Proceedings of CHI'94*, (pp. 186–191). New York: ACM Press.

Kim, D. H. (1993) 'The link between individual and organizational learning', *Sloan Management Review*, Fall: 37–50.

Konda, S., Monarch, I., Sargent, P. and Subrahmanian, E. (1992) 'Shared memory in design: a unifying theme for research and practice', *Research in Engineering Design*, 4: 23–42.

Kuutti, K. and Bannon, L. (1991) 'Some confusions at the interface: re-conceptualizing the "interface" problem', in M. Nurminen and G. Weir (eds), *Human Jobs and Computer Interfaces* (pp. 3–19). Amsterdam: North-Holland.

Kuutti, K. and Bannon, L. (1993) 'Searching for unity among diversity: exploring the interface concept', in *Proceedings ACM/IFIP Conference InterCHI'93* (Human Factors in Information Systems) (pp. 263–268). Amsterdam, April.

Kuutti, K., Virkkunen, J. and Young, K. (1995) '"Activity" instead of "process"? Questioning the unit of analysis in BPR', *COMIC Report Oulu-1–4*. Lancaster: Lancaster University.

Middleton, D. (1988) 'Talking work. Argument in co-ordination, commemoration and improvisation in team work', in *Summer Conference on 'Work and Communication'*. UCSD, San Diego, 11–15 July.

Morrison, J. (1993) 'Team memory: information management for business teams', in *HICSS-2*, Hawaii, January. IEEE Press.

Neisser, U. (Ed.) (1982) *Memory Observed. Remembering in Natural Contexts*. San Francisco: W. H. Freeman.

Orr, J. (1986) 'Narratives at work: story telling as diagnostic activity', in *Proceedings CSCW'86* (pp. 62–72). Austin, TX: ACM.

Orr, J. E. (1992) 'Ethnography and organizational learning: in pursuit of learning at work', in *NATO Advanced Research Workshop 'Organizational Learning and Technological Change'*, Siena, Italy, 22–26 September.

Pylyshyn, Z. W. (1984) *Computation and Cognition. Toward a Foundation for Cognitive Science*. Cambridge, MA: MIT Press.

Sachs, P. (1994) 'Transforming work: the role of learning in organizational change', in L. Suchman (ed.), *Representations of Work*. Honolulu: HICSS Monograph.

Schmidt, K. and Bannon, L. (1992) 'Taking CSCW seriously. Supporting articulation work', *Computer Supported Co-operative Work (CSCW)*, 1(1–2): 7–40.

Selvin, A. M. (1994) 'Meeting facilitation with GDSS: reflections on skill development', in *Proceedings of Conference on Computer-Supported Co-operative Work 1994 (CSCW'94)*. New York: ACM.

Suchman, L. (1987) *Plans and Situated Actions*. Cambridge: Cambridge University Press.

Terveen, L. G., Selfridge, P. G. and Long, M. D. (1993) 'From "folklore" to "living design memory"', in *Interchi'93* (pp. 15–22). Amsterdam, April: ACM Press.

Toulmin, S. (1990) *Cosmopolis. The Hidden Agenda of Modernity*. Chicago: University of Chicago Press.

Walsh, J. P. and Ungson, G. R. (1991) 'Organizational memory', *Academy of Management Review*, 16(1): 57–91.

Wynn, E. (1979) 'Office conversation as an information medium'. Unpublished Ph.D. dissertation, University of California, Berkeley, CA.

Yakemovic, K. C. B. and Conklin, E. J. (1990) 'Report on a development project use of an issue-based information system', in *Proceedings of the Conference on Computer-Supported Co-operative Work 1990 (CSCW'90)* (pp. 105–118). New York: ACM.

Yates, J. (1989) *Control through Communication. The Rise of System in American Management*. Baltimore: John Hopkins University Press.

Zinchenko, P. I. (1983) 'The problem of involuntary memory' [originally published in Russian 1939], *Soviet Psychology*, 22(2): 55–111.

Part III Communicating and Sharing Knowledge

The opening parts of this book have presented the context and characteristics of knowledge creation and of the resources and capabilities needed to bring knowledge to its point of application. The readings in this part deal with the related issues of the communication processes and the supporting structures needed to manage knowledge. The contributors share a concern for the dynamics of knowledge flows within organizations.

The first three chapters address the role of language in the dissemination of knowledge within organizational settings. The interaction between verbal and non-verbal aspects of communication and the culturally embedded nature of communication are addressed. The remaining chapters look at the creation and maintenance of appropriate organizational structures and the processes required to ensure that knowledge can be applied within and between organizations.

Condon and Yousef addressed their concerns over the cross-cultural dimension of communication in their 1975 book *An Introduction to Intercultural Communication*. Their chapter on communication perspectives is reproduced here. This presents a range of both verbal and non-verbal sources of miscommunication in cross-cultural situations. They endorse Edward Hall's view that culture itself is a form of communication and that effective communication must take account of its setting by paying due regard to both the verbal and non-verbal expectations within a particular context.

Condon and Yousef provide examples relating to intercultural situations which we can appreciate as an increasing hazard within a globalizing world economy. However, cultural dimensions are also present within national boundaries, not just between geographical regions, but also across industries and between occupational groups. The cautionary tale of the contradictory cues given by the informal public dress of Mexican priests provides an example of implicit assumptions about social roles which is relevant to situations within a dominant culture. Within organizations, different groups may stereotype one another, and unwittingly impoverish communication.

Mary Goodyear looks at the consequences of the issues delineated by Condon and Yousef from a different perspective. The ubiquitous presence of high profile brands is the most visible evidence of a globalizing economy. Brands can communicate reputation and value. The history of marketing and advertising is replete with examples of cross-cultural misunderstandings, even within the narrower range of European markets. However, Goodyear demonstrates that the diffusion of established practice itself is far from unproblematic. The adoption of a variety of technical terms from primarily North American sources by marketing teams across the globe is no guarantee that meaning is shared beyond a superficial level. She provides evidence that marketing itself is not necessarily perceived as a distinct activity, separate from selling. This criticism can be applied to firms and sectors within developed economies as well as to developing ones. The neat evolutionary models of market development have been upset by the emergence of global brands supported by global production and distribution networks.

Roos and von Krogh, in two related articles, provide a concise treatment of epistemology in relation to language and knowledge in business organizations. They identify language as a strategic resource, and regard conversation as the backbone of businesses. They identify both strategic conversations, concerned with the creation of knowledge, and operational conversations which are concerned with the exploitation of knowledge. They provide guidance on the effective management of strategic conversations to maximize knowledge creation. Their view complements that of other writers, such as Stewart Clegg who monitored the contestation over language and meaning, where, for example, the operational definition of contractual terms had a direct bearing on the cost of a building contract (Clegg, 1975).

The remaining chapters in this part move to a consideration of the organizational frame for managing knowledge. They raise the question of what organizational processes and characteristics are appropriate to knowledge-intensive work.

Amidon and Skyrme examine the 'learning organization'. They explore the overlap between this term which has become popular particularly in Europe, and the notion of 'knowledge-based companies'. They provide a range of definitions linked to the defining texts of Chris Argyris, Donald Schon and Peter Senge. Several views of learning are identified, and Senge's model of five disciplines essential to learning is mapped onto knowledge considerations to provide an explanation of their popularity among knowledge practitioners.

The next chapter moves further into the realm of practice. Isherwood summarizes the practical outcome of a specific process of organizational learning. This is in the form of a concise overview of one company's use of a technical resource: Lotus Notes, which was seen as the key resource in the facilitation of the collaborative working strategy that they had identified as the key to retaining competitive advantage. For Isherwood, this represents an organizational transformation achieved through the use of groupware. This experience has allowed the identification of ten critical success factors which are seen as the key to the successful alignment of technology and user capabilities.

In the concluding chapter of this part, Miles et al. put forward a much broader argument that major periods of business history can be related to particular organizational forms. Such forms reflect the overall logic shaping of a firm's strategy structure and management and are in turn a response to the pull of prevailing market forces. The authors identify an era of standardization amply investigated in the work of Alfred Chandler. This is contrasted with a succeeding, but overlapping period of customization. Market segmentation gave rise to the divisional form of organization that could address either products or geographical markets, however, efficient customization requires mixed forms such as the matrix organization. For Miles et al. we are facing the point at which a new form, already present in knowledge-intensive sectors such as biotechnology, is required to meet a new economic era: the knowledge age. For them this form is best represented by the cellular organization which they describe here.

REFERENCE

Clegg, S. (1975) *Power, Rule and Domination: a Critical and Empirical Understanding of Power in Sociological Theory and Organizational Life*. London: Routledge and Kegan Paul.

10
Communication Perspectives

*J. C. Condon and F. S. Yousef**

THE AMBASSADOR'S DANDRUFF

We were talking with some Japanese students in Tokyo about a former US ambassador to Japan, whose knowledge of the Japanese language and culture was widely praised. One girl remarked, 'Yes, he was excellent, but . . . I think his wife was not such a good wife, if you know what I mean.' We didn't know. Was this some gossip from one of the notorious Japanese weekly magazines? No, the girl said, it was nothing like that. She simply had seen the ambassador interviewed on television a few times and 'noticed he had dandruff on his shoulders'. That was the end of the explanation. But it was sufficient for the other students, who agreed that, yes, perhaps his wife was not such a good wife. To this writer, an outsider at that time, these were *non sequiturs*; the 'explanation' made no sense. So they all patiently explained that in Japan a good wife is responsible for her husband's personal appearance. If he is not well groomed, obviously it is his wife's fault. But what did the girl remember hearing the ambassador *say* when he was interviewed? She said she couldn't remember anything he said – just that dandruff. *Moral*: One speck of dandruff is worth a thousand words – in some situations, and in some cultures.

Here the US ambassador communicated something to this Japanese girl.[1] What he communicated was neither what he said nor what he intended to communicate; he was not even aware of that girl or her reaction. Still, we can say that there was communication if we are referring to any behavior that is perceived and interpreted by another, whether or not it is spoken or intended or even within the person's conscious awareness. This concept of human communication, different from many other uses of the word, is the concept we will employ in this chapter.

Perhaps it is safe to say that most of what is communicated in any encounter between people, even those from the same culture, is not spoken, not interpreted as it was intended, and largely occurs outside of their awareness. That does not mean, of course, that speaking is unimportant or that we should be satisfied with any interpretation that is made of our behavior.

Some writers have extended this concept to the point of stating, as a principle, that it is impossible *not* to communicate.[2] Their logic is simply that if 'communication' embraces all human behavior, then it is impossible *not to communicate* because it is impossible *not to behave*. It is possible to avoid certain behaviors, such as speaking, but the very absence of behavior, if behavior is expected, still communicates. Not answering a person usually is a far more powerful 'message' than anything that might be said. 'No news' may or may not be 'good news,' but if one is expecting news – a letter, a word of thanks, any response – then that kind of 'no news' is also news; it communicates something.

The implications of this view of communication may be discomfiting at first, especially in intercultural communication, where each party is likely to feel more uncertain about how his behavior is observed and interpreted than he would in his own society. Probably it is especially disturbing to persons who like to feel that they have full control of a situation and want others to accept them on their own terms. But for these very reasons we need a broad concept of communication when considering what transpires between people of different cultural backgrounds. Without it we will be left with the confusions and protestations that so often have characterized discussions of international and intercultural communication, with each blaming the other for misunderstanding: 'That's not what I said,' and 'That's not what I meant.' Without a broader understanding we will continue to try to 'improve communication' merely by repeating the same thing in a louder voice.

This word 'communication' often is used in many different ways; some persons equate it with *agreement*, saying that two people who disagree about something are 'not communicating'. But if people are disagreeing and know it, they must be communicating; it seems far more accurate and less pretentious merely to say that they disagree. The word 'communication' is also used to mean 'understanding,' quite apart from agreement. The American in a Paris café tells the waiter that he will have the *soupe du jour*; the waiter informs him that it is tomato soup; and the American snaps back, 'I know that – I studied French in college.' They are having difficulty understanding, perhaps, but they are communicating nevertheless.

Two other uses seem as unhelpful as they are common. One is the use of 'more communication' or 'less communication' not as a measure of the frequency of speech or other communicative acts, but as an equivalent of positive impact. Just as some people say that one person has 'more personality' than somebody else, they may say that a particular individual 'communicates more' or 'really communicates'. The dullest conversationalist 'really communicates' too, even though he may seem to be tedious company. This usage is especially annoying when used to describe different societies; for example, Italians 'communicate more' than the Swedes. A related use is that which limits 'communication' to something that is viewed as positive, productive, or at least satisfying. Thus some people may say that when people stop talking and start fighting, they have ceased to communicate. But a fight is just as much a kind of communication as a speech or a song or flecks of dandruff.

PERSPECTIVES

In thinking about intercultural communication, we are considering two of the broadest and most abstract categories we could possibly link together. Like other terms at such a high level of abstraction, the two tend to blend into each other. Much of what is called 'patterns of communication' could be – and is, in other contexts – called 'cultural patterns'. It is not surprising, therefore, that one writer has said that 'culture is communication',[3] and that others have said that at a certain point, principles of communication and anthropological statements about a culture are identical.[4] Nevertheless, there are important differences in the study of 'communication' and the study of 'culture'; academically, despite sharing of data and insights, researchers have pursued different approaches, and different contributions have resulted. We would like to begin by presenting a very limited number of non-technical observations or 'perspectives' from the eclectic field of interpersonal communication. And, though it will not be easy, we would like to do so without cultural bias.

As just noted, it is often difficult to distinguish between a general communication pattern and a more limited cultural pattern. Many, or perhaps most, of the learned principles of communication are culturally limited. If these are principles learned informally (such as looking at the person you are talking to) they may seem to be universal because everybody else around us follows the same rules. It is only when we go outside of our familiar territory that we realize not everybody behaves in the same way and that, indeed, good advice at home may be very bad advice elsewhere. If these principles result from academic studies, particularly those carefully controlled experimental studies with impressive neutrality of statistics, we may also feel we have described something basic about 'human behavior'. But of course, as social scientists have come to realize, much that is described about 'human behavior' does not apply outside the society in which the study was conducted and may not even describe much more than the kind of 'college culture' where the study took place. This also seems to be true of some of the grand theories which have gained international recognition. A Mexican colleague, who is a psychiatrist, remarked of Freud, 'Freudian theory does not work so well here; he speaks of repression, but we Mexicans remember *everything*!'

We believe that to be sensitive to intercultural communication we must have some understanding of at least rudimentary concepts of interpersonal communication, as well as some understanding of some aspects of culture. A book claiming to fully encompass either of these might be suspect; thus a book attempting to relate both might seem outrageous. But to avoid saying something about each as they are linked together seems, in the middle of the twentieth century, unduly cautious. We begin with a few insights from the field of interpersonal communication.

SIX MEN IN A DIALOGUE

We usually identify the person with whom we are talking simply by saying his or her name or perhaps by giving a physical description ('that tall blond guy') or perhaps by describing an activity ('that woman having coffee'). But if we think for a moment, we realize that these perceptions are dangerously oversimplified.

Person A does not just communicate with person B; he or she communicates with his 'image' of person B, an image which may change during the communication. And, similarly, person B has an image of person A, which influences how he speaks to A and how he interprets what A says. This is most apparent when a person in conversation discovers the identity (or status) of another; for example, in Mexico, where clergymen are forbidden to wear clerical garb in public, many Roman Catholic priests have experienced a dramatic change in a conversation with a stranger who has just told a dirty joke and asks 'What do you do?' The response, 'I'm a priest,' produces a sudden change of expression and a series of embarrassing comments and apologies ('Oh . . . Father, I didn't know . . . why didn't you . . . I hope you'll forgive what I . . . oh, my God!').

To a much greater extent than we may realize, we communicate not with flesh-and-blood people, but with roles, with positions of status, with representatives of the social structure. Across cultures, obviously, this realization is of great significance. Not only are the classifications which influence our communicative behavior likely to be different from what we are familiar with, we are also likely to lack the information and clues which tell us 'who is who'. If a newly arrived German medical doctor calls upon the mayor of an Indian town, the doctor is likely to talk to his image of an Indian mayor, not that particular Indian 'who happens to be mayor'. But how does the information that 'this man is the mayor' assist the doctor in speaking differently than he would to any other person? If nothing else, the recognition of role and status somehow causes us to alter communication, but we may not know how best to alter it. At any rate, the two flesh and blood people, plus the image each has of the other, adds up to 'four people' in the dialogue. It becomes even more complex when more changes occur in image and situation: suppose, for example, the mayor is the doctor's patient or suppose the doctor wishes to beg a favor of the mayor.

We must add at least two (the geometry suggests still more) when we realize that each of these parties has his own self-image, his own self-concept in this particular situation. The doctor is not just another person – he never is. As 'a medical doctor,' he may wish to be treated in a particular manner, and he has his own image of how he should be seen by the mayor or whomever he is talking with. But in different cultures it is probably difficult for him to know what his image is to those people: another Schweitzer, perhaps – until he learns that the mayor never heard of Schweitzer (which might also alter his image of the mayor); perhaps as a 'typical German' or 'a typical European' or even a typical 'Englishman,' depending on the mayor's experience; or perhaps as a miracle worker (it is his skill and not his ethnicity which shapes the image – perhaps); perhaps as an intruder; perhaps as an outcast from his own society ('why has he come *here*?'). It would be very difficult for this visitor, as for any visitor, ever to know quite what his image is; he can only guess, based on the reports he has heard and the behavior which he observes and interprets.

In a mobile society which espouses egalitarian values, such as the United States, persons may wish to minimize the role and status image of themselves and of others. A father may prefer to be thought of just as his son's 'buddy', the President may wish to be thought of as 'the voters' friend'. Persons from such cultures may like to think of the influence of images and self-concepts as masks, and as essentially harmful to good communication. They may feel that 'true communication' occurs only when six men in the dialogue are levelled to the 'basic two'.

In countless popular American novels, dramas, and films, this conflict between 'the real self' and the image has been emphasized to show that the images are prejudicial and distort communication. American psychotherapists such as Maslow and Rogers stress similar views.[5] In communication studies the emphasis on such projects as role-playing exercises, T-group experience, and sensitivity training has also sought not merely to recognize the influence of such images but apparently to do away with them entirely in order to achieve 'true communication'. The American student of communication is likely to regard 'status', 'rank', and other categories as essentially harmful to communication. But intercultural communication is more likely to be effective if all 'six-plus men' are recognized and accommodated; indeed, those fifth and sixth persons in the dialogue are often more important than the first two.

ONE OF *THOSE* PEOPLE

A very strong influence in a person's self-concept and in his image of the other's self-concept is what is sometimes called 'the reference group concept'. This refers to a larger grouping with which people identify themselves or others, and it often serves as a guide to action and as a basis of comparison. The most obvious of such reference groups are identified by broad semantic categories, including nationality, sex, age, region ('a Texan' or 'a Parisian', for example), and race. In intercultural communication, confusions in reference group identification are very common.

For example, in Kenya, as in most African nations, there are many tribes, often quite unrelated in languages spoken, physical appearance, and cultural values. A member of the Luo tribe in Kenya may think of himself first as a Luo, secondly as a citizen of Kenya. He may or may not, at times, identify himself as an African, or as a member of 'the third world'. But if he travels to Europe or to the United States to study, he is more likely to be identified first as 'an African' (an extraordinary grouping perhaps comparable to an American being identified as a 'Northern Hemisphere Person') and secondly as a Kenyan. At times he may be grouped as 'black' or 'Negro.' It is unlikely that many persons, apart from those who have visited or studied Kenya will classify him as a Luo. He is likely to be invited to meetings and parties with people with whom he feels little or no commonality ('the foreign students') – including, perhaps, a Muslim from Morocco, a Coptic Christian from Egypt, a South African white, a political refugee from Angola and the daughter of an Ismaeli trader from Malawi. Semantically all of these people may legitimately be classified as 'Africans', but in terms of reference group identification, it is possible that none of these 'Africans' had ever thought of themselves as being members of the same group.

The reference group concept cuts across many basic principles of communication: it may help to explain differing psychological 'sets' of people in communication, it is certainly related to self-concepts and images of others, and it often suggests some of the structures which will be imposed upon the fluid process of communication. Moreover, a person's changing reference group identification is often an indication of the influence of communication: our Luo student may come to think of himself as 'an African' because he is so often called upon to represent 'Africans' and to answer questions and give opinions on matters he had never considered previously.

In rhetorical theory, the reference group identification has always been important. For a rhetorical theorist such as Kenneth Burke, 'identification' rather than 'persuasion' is the key term in the study of rhetoric.[6] Certainly the facile persuader is likely to seek any plausible form of identifying himself with his audience; thus Nixon in political campaigns was alternately 'a Quaker', 'a former soldier', 'a child who knew poverty, too', 'an established lawyer', 'a Californian', 'a New Yorker', and so forth, depending on which identification was more likely to match that of his audience. And the audience are not likely to feel that these identifications are inconsistent.

It seems that Americans, for reasons to be discussed later, feel rather free to associate and dissociate themselves from different groups, and they may wish to be treated as 'individuals' rather than being considered as a member of any single group or even as 'Americans'. Younger persons, especially, are likely to try to dissociate themselves from their country and to assert their individuality or their commonality with 'youth'. Perhaps most Americans abroad will remark, 'Of course I am not a typical American.' And this may be true, for typically most Americans are not found abroad; but it may also be true that to say 'I am not a typical American' is a typically American thing to say.

Inappropriate reference grouping has long been noted by sociologists, and the chances of misclassifying unfamiliar cultures are even greater than they are for the same culture. 'You Mexicans and Puerto Ricans all seem the same to me,' remarks a person who is surely not a member of either group. A third-generation German-American objects to a black political activist, who can trace his family lines back to before the *Mayflower*, and says 'I don't know why you people are always complaining – you have more advantages here than in Africa!' Such irrelevant comparisons are the product of ignorance, and as we are likely to be more ignorant about other cultures than about our own, we must expect to observe many more such reactions in intercultural communication.

As we will note in discussing language and culture, the common word stock may predispose us to make certain groupings and not others. In Swahili the three main racial-social categories are *Mafrika* ('Black Africans', usually); *Mhindi* ('Asian', usually applied to the merchant and professional group of Indian ancestry which has comprised the bulk of the East African business and professional community); and *Mzungu* (usually translated as 'European' but including all 'whites'. Significantly, 'Mzungu' historically refers to the lost 'white man' seen wandering around). There are, of course, words for all nationalities, religions, and other ethnic distinctions. In Japanese there are two broad groupings: *Nihonjin*, the Japanese, and *Gaijin*, meaning, usually, 'white' foreigner or 'Westerner'. For other national groups there are specific words but no word which would group *Nihonjin* with other Asians in a way that 'Asian' might in English. American categories, of course, are different still. Often they appear to be relatively precise: 'third generation Polish Catholic'. Rarely is a word like 'European' used, but 'Latin American' is a net that captures millions. And 'Latin', which may have some linguistic value, is more likely to group persons according to imagined emotional behavior. Thus the influence of a person's available word stock may be influential in his choice of reference groups, and his own semantic distinctions are likely to be very different from those of another who speaks a different language.

Not only language influence but the sheer necessity of categorization may make such reference groupings inevitable. The prevalence of deductive reasoning requires broad categories from which specifics may be deduced: in our own culture, so long as we talk and think in terms of Ms Owen, the coed; Mr Smith, the politician; and Dr Russell, the philosopher, we may continue to talk of Mr Diaz, the Mexican, and Miss Lee, the Korean. Ignorance, too, leads us into false categories: so long as people believe there are tigers in Africa (there are none, except in zoos) or that Africa is mostly jungle (about 5 percent is jungle), we should not be surprised that 'Africans' are grouped as basically the same throughout the continent. In intercultural communication our ignorance affects the entire process of communication. Too often we add insult to ignorance.

SORTING THINGS OUT

The mental processes with which we perceive and interpret human behavior make any analysis of interpersonal communication difficult, since we can only guess how another person is thinking and because we are by no means fully aware of how we ourselves are reacting. Thus for many years communication scholars in a number of related fields have sought means of analysing overt behavior: primarily speech but, increasingly, nonverbal behavior as well. Any such attempt involves certain 'models' or diagrams which represent the structure of the interaction. Many of these identify a speaker or 'sender', a listener or 'receiver', and many attempt to show with grids or arrows the 'flow of communication'. Other scholars, while recognizing the need for some structure for purposes of identification, have objected to communication models which are static and linear in form. They argue that communication is a fluid process, 'multi-linear' at least ('a speaker' is also a listener – even when he is speaking), and impossible to diagram adequately without greatly distorting what is going on. Even with the addition of a term like 'feedback' – that all-purpose word in communication theory – one is assuming a great deal, oversimplifying, and ignoring the process of communication. In the West the traditional emphasis given to verbal communication may demand a directional interpretation: two people 'talking at once' suggests 'no communication'. But in forms of communication which are defined as multi-personal (as in many dances), the parties interact so completely that it is difficult to identify a leader and follower, a sender and a receiver. Such an image is likely to be a better model for intercultural communication than the linear models.

For example, a young girl is likely 'to communicate a smile' not as the start of communication or even as acknowledgement of receipt of communication but as a point in the process. The smile originates in several places (his remark, her upbringing, their relationship) and reflects and directs all of these at the same time. If one is at a funeral, one probably does not laugh – but not primarily because of concern for the others' reaction (the feedback?) but because of reasons shared by all members. It may be best not to think of beginnings, middles, and ends, or of senders and receivers.

If communication is process, different persons are likely to impose different structures on the 'same process' based on different backgrounds, assumptions, and purposes. The person in a discussion group says, 'I am only silent because they do not invite me to speak', but the others say, 'we have given up on this person because he never wants to speak though we have shown him through our example that speaking is important.' The foreign technical advisor says, 'Their childish attitudes made me give up trying to help them,' but those who would be 'helped' say 'his treating us like children makes us wish he would go away'. These and other typical patterns illustrate the difficulty of trying to structure the process of communication – except from the individual viewpoints of the persons involved.

Nevertheless, to stress that communication is a process that we enter into is not sufficient for interpreting the process. We need to impose some kind of structure, even though the attempt may result in a chicken-and-egg dilemma – particularly in Samuel Butler's formulation, 'Is the chicken the egg's way of creating another egg, or is the egg the chicken's way of creating another chicken?' That is, we are more often interested in guessing intention and reaction than in speculating on which event came first.

So long as we recognize that as participants or observers in the process of communication we are imposing the structure, and that there are alternative ways of giving structure to the otherwise fluid process, we may proceed. Some theorists have referred to this as the act of 'punctuating' the process, using the analogy of writing symbols which mark beginnings and endings, questions and exclamations.[7] The analogy seems especially appropriate for cross-cultural communication, since upon first hearing a foreign language we think that the words are all seemingly run together. Only with acquired skill do we learn to perceive beginnings and endings. Similarly with much larger aspects of cultural patterns of behavior, experience leads us to comprehend meaningful patterns.

It is hoped that some of the basic concepts of interpersonal communication, such as self-images and reference groups, will be helpful in providing clues to the structure of the communication process. Even more helpful, when we consider interaction across cultures, will be our awareness of differing value orientations, nonverbal patterns, and structures of argument.

Within the realm of interpersonal communication theory, there is one principle of structure, a principle first proposed by Gregory Bateson,[8] which we believe to be most helpful in interpreting intercultural encounters. This says that every spoken 'message' may be interpreted on two levels: *what* is said and *how* it is said. The 'how' is much less precise and includes nonverbal behavior (which could be classified as part of the 'what'), vocal inflection (paralanguage), setting, timing, and much more. In Bateson's terminology, there are two aspects of each intended communication: 'the report' (the what) and 'the command' (the how and why). Like the distinction between 'denotation' and 'connotation,' however, there are basic problems of identification and definition.

Perhaps the distinguishing characteristic is that the 'report' is largely verbal and recognized and is the sort of datum that would appear in a printed text. The 'how' is largely nonverbal, sometimes paralinguistic, and often is more difficult to describe. Our descriptions of the 'how' are likely to be imprecise – 'He didn't seem serious when he said it' – but can be made relatively precise ('He said it at a distance of about twenty-one feet with his eyes looking downward and with a voice we would use to communicate embarrassment').

Normally, we expect that these two aspects are consistent with each other, and conventionally the 'command' aspect has been treated as a complement of the report aspect. In information theory, which usually conceives of communication as verbal ('systematic') behavior, the command elements of communication may be ignored, or may be classified as functionally redundant elements, or, in some analyses, may be classified as part of the 'noise' factor which interferes with the message. That is, many studies of interpersonal communication disregard nearly all aspects of communication except the verbal; communication is rendered into a kind of playwright's script and the analysis begins here. Other studies pay attention to facial expressions, gestures, vocal inflection, to the extent that the actions 'say the same thing' as the words; thus the actions are functionally redundant in the sense that if a listener does not hear every word spoken or does not know the meaning of a particular word, he may still be able to understand, or 'fill in', on the basis of these nonverbal and paralinguistic expressions. Such expressions may also be regarded as dysfunctional or treated as elements of 'noise' (an all-purpose term for any kind of interference in the 'channel' which disrupts or garbles the 'message'). Thus, a speaker's nervous twitch, his cracking of knuckles, or pacing back and forth while speaking, is noticed to the extent that it seems to threaten the verbal message and make clear reception difficult.

Often if there is a conflict between report and command we are likely to pay more attention to the command aspect, or the nonverbal, than to what was said. A mother scolding her child and demanding, 'Now, you say "I am sorry"' will not be satisfied if the child says 'I am sorry' while laughing at his mother. The child can claim, 'But I said it, didn't I?' However, she may feel that he didn't mean it.

Conflicts between the report and command functions of communication are sometimes noted, sometimes not. Paradoxes can be noted in any newspaper any day: a monument to Joyce Kilmer, the poet who penned 'Trees', was built after several dozen trees had been chopped down. Government officials have been found to be violating the law in order to arrest persons for violating the law; and so on. Those who notice such paradoxes may become cynical or at least receive a message quite different from the one intended.

The effect of inconsistency between report and command across cultures is less often noticed by the party who is inconsistent. In many parts of the world, the American Peace Corps volunteer hopes to convey the meaning of idealism, self-sacrifice, and identification with the people he has come to serve. And yet he is often paid a stipend considerably higher than the average earnings of the people he serves, and is provided with supplies, perquisites, and a round-trip ticket – all of which can be seen as quite inconsistent with his espoused values of 'sacrifice'. Elaborate government aid programs to developing nations are often clearly of greatest benefit to the donor nation. And – as with some inconsistencies observed within a single culture – the reactions abroad are likely to be critical, if not cynical.

But it is at the level of interpersonal communication and not government policy that we wish to be most concerned about inconsistencies between the *what* and the *how*, the *report* and the *command*. Edward T. Hall, following publication of *The Silent Language*, has been credited with an extremely significant contribution to intercultural communication, a contribution which can be interpreted in terms of *report* and *command*. He has stressed that on one level, the report communication can convey one meaning, while on another level – the nonverbal, *command* level – a very different meaning can be conveyed. The result of such inconsistencies is neither 'good communication' nor 'no communication'; the result might be called 'miscommunication': something is communicated, even though it is not what was intended and often it is not what was thought to have been communicated. The Englishman, Jones, and the Mexican, López, are likely to prefer being positioned at different distances from each other: Jones prefers a bit more distance between himself and another person, while López's preference is 'too close' for Mr Jones's comfort. Jones, speaking fluent Spanish, may express in words his feeling of friendship, but by standing away from López he also communicates (to López) aloofness, something very different from his words. López is also friendly and 'easygoing' in what he says, but as he moves closer to Jones so that he, López, feels more comfortable, he seems to Jones to be 'pushy', 'aggressive'. A kind of dance may ensue, with Jones retreating a bit each time to feel comfortable, and neither is likely to recognize what is happening. Both may feel awkward and uncomfortable even though the verbal content seems relaxed and friendly. Because of Hall's writings, this kind of problem is now perhaps the most widely discussed by students of intercultural communication, but it remains as only one example of report–command inconsistency and there is no proof that spacial pattern differences are the most important barrier to intercultural communication. There is a tempting danger for students of intercultural communication to feel that if a person stands a certain distance from his counterpart, arrives at the appropriate time, and casts his eyes in the right direction, he surely will be effective. Though these elements are important in communication – and so often have been ignored in the past – they are still but part of communicative behavior. Moreover, as we shall consider later, it is even easier to miscommunicate when all of these behaviors are 'correct' while other elements – spoken language and, particularly, values, for example – are inconsistent. It is even possible, as many Japanese have indicated, that the foreigner who adjusts too much and behaves nonverbally too much like a Japanese is considered quite strange and miscommunicates for this reason!

ACTORS ALL

Although we can never be sure what aspects of our behavior will be observed and interpreted in ways not at all intended, most of what we say and do is directed toward particular individuals in particular situations to create a particular interpretation. Not only what we say, but also where and when we say it, how we are dressed, and much more contribute to creating the impression we hope to convey. This suggests a perspective of performance, of consciously acting – with props and costumes in an appropriate setting – for the benefit of a selected audience. The dramatic metaphor is used to provide insight, not to be interpreted so literally that people seem to be calculating and insincere.

It is interesting that in recent years, the 'actor–audience' model of communication has been largely neglected, possibly because the sender–receiver, encoder–decoder mechanical models have been stressed. And yet for over 2,000 years, the actor–audience assumption was the basis for the study of 'persuasion' which was *the model* of interpersonal communication. 'Analyse your audience' is the first lesson of rhetoric, followed by 'adapt to your audience'. This was such a familiar approach to communication that it is odd that it has fallen out of favor. The social science tradition, by and large, has not emphasized this relationship, perhaps because the ancient notion of rhetorical 'art' evoked a Neoplatonic reaction among some social scientists. As an 'art' there has been no progress expected of 'science' (and perhaps, too, it is not even an 'art' but a kind of knack, as Plato argued, thus receiving the abuse of both artist and scientist). Probably, too, there is a feeling that there is something unjust, dishonest, and demeaning about always trying to adapt to an audience, of always playing a part. For whatever reasons, the performance view of communication largely has been ignored in the mechanical models.

A notable exception is the sociologist, Erving Goffman, whose works have stressed that acting or performance is a part of almost all of our behavior.[9] Like a modern Aristotle, he has sought to describe in general, nonexperimental terms, the strategies of 'impression management'. Goffman's first and best-known book, *The Presentation of Self in Everyday Life*, provides examples that can be easily recognized: even though hospital nurses often run out of things to do, either officially or practically, they don't dare sit down or look unoccupied when they have finished their appointed rounds. Because nurses are seen as curative personnel, such 'relaxed' behavior would upset the patients; thus they are often required to scurry about looking busy – filling out charts on clipboards, demonstrating their roles as helpers, even though this busyness is largely performance. Their audience demands it and their role as nurses is largely defined in terms of that bedridden audience. A baseball umpire must often decide, very quickly, whether a runner is 'out' or 'safe', and even if he feels unsure, he must appear to be decisive. As Goffman makes clear, we not only acquiesce to such performances, we expect them, demand them. We would not *praise* a nurse or an umpire who behaved otherwise; we would say they were poor in executing their duties.

Every day we all must make similar performances for similar reasons. We do so out of social necessity, not because we are cynical. And we do so even knowing, sometimes, that our audience is aware that we are playing our role.

The view of communication as performance is extremely important in considering intercultural communication. For one thing, perhaps the most frequent communications across cultures are those of self-conscious perfor-mance. A person arriving in another country or welcoming a guest in his own country assumes an extremely predictable role: that of advisor, the teacher, the student, and perhaps most often, the vague role of 'guest'. Until some routine is established, until the formality becomes more personal, predictable performances are to be expected and understood. Until some routine is established, there are probably more little ceremonies – welcoming speeches, orientation meetings, dinner parties and the like, all quite performance centered – enacted across cultures than within our own culture, or at least it might seem so to Americans. Not quite knowing how he is seen in a new culture, the visitor has great difficulty in knowing how to act – serious, casual, or flip; intimate or aloof. And the visitor's cultural background and values are likely to direct even this attempt. Likewise, he does not know how to judge the 'audience reaction': 'They seemed pleasant, but was that for me, or are they always that way?' Or, 'They seemed unfriendly by my standards; is that "expected", is that their impression of *me*, or am I in such a state that I cannot tell their real reaction?' Cross-culturally, there is difficulty in interpreting the success of performance.

Standards of acting and even the value of performance are likely to vary from culture to culture, a problem likely to affect Americans, especially. A recent trend in communication education in the United States is manifest in a variety of ways, such as 'sensitivity training' or expressions such as 'Tell it like it is.' While we do not wish to be unduly critical, this trend is really very 'American', for Americans are likely to dislike status differences, formality, host–guest roles and anything that looks like older and therefore (in the American way) more rigid systems. North Americans want to get down to 'brass tacks', to 'reality', to 'business', to 'the nitty gritty' – the terms change but this value or value orientation or complex of value orientations seems to have remained remarkably consistent over the years. Such values eschew the idea of *performing*. And yet ceremony, speeches (even in an extremely nonspeech-oriented society such as Japan), and social amenities of all kinds are expected, even demanded. The American is often unprepared for this, both in experience and in cultural values.

Later we will discuss the difficulty that many non-Americans encounter in dealing with the informality in the USA. But briefly we might note here that the apparent absence of performance and ceremony in much of American communication – 'Be frank', 'Make yourself at home', 'Help yourself' – is equally disturbing for many non-Americans unaccustomed to directives which seem to require performances without rules or standards. It is not surprising, therefore, that residents or students from other countries often appraise the United States as open, free, and friendly, but also as confusing, cold, and cruel.

Our behavior, then, often is based on performance for a particular audience, and the form of performance – as well as its value – varies across cultures. One cannot be 'just oneself', or 'do what comes naturally' when one is suddenly in the strange surroundings of a new culture and far away from the familiarity of one's own culture.

A FUNCTIONAL APPROACH

A young French couple may spend an evening in which they first have a deep philosophical discussion, followed by a violent argument, followed by a long period of silence. The amount of communication between the two has not changed; rather, the form of communication has changed. But even in the lapses they are communicating clearly, if not loudly. In the Japanese romantic tradition, a couple may sit together for hours and exchange no more than a half-dozen words while communicating as much and as well as their more verbal counterparts in other societies. Should the young man observe to his fiancée, 'How beautiful is the moon', he will have communicated a proposal of marriage at least as clearly as his French counterpart would through many more words all related to the romantic prospects ahead. Similarly, college students in the United States complain that they and their parents 'never really communicate; we just talk about trivial things'. It is not so much that the students and their parents have or have not 'communicated'; it is more likely that their respective styles and functions of communication differ, in this case to their mutual dissatisfaction.

Across cultures this problem of contrasting or conflicting functions of communication is especially troublesome. Not only is the word 'communication' used so promiscuously as to make it difficult to identify more specific problems of interaction, but the form and style of communication across cultures is often so contrastive that, in the more popular sense, people often cannot tell if they are 'communicating' or not.

And so it may be helpful to identify at least some broad functions of communication and in the process perhaps suggest other functions which might be added. Characterizing kinds of expression on the basis of apparent or intended function is useful for at least two reasons: one, we can often, though not always, find 'failures to communicate' when there are different functions expected or perceived by the parties involved; and in addition, we may be able to suggest preferred orders and frequencies of the functions in different cultures.

For example, in the US a public speaker is likely to begin a speech on almost any subject with a joke ('A funny thing happened to me on the way to . . . '). He does this partly because he has learned that this is a good way to begin a speech and also to suggest that he is a friendly guy (important in establishing his ethos in his own culture, but it may not be important in a host culture). In a culture other than his own, when he tells his joke, he may do so with a 'straight face' (in keeping with his culture's standards: 'Don't laugh at your own jokes'). But his audience may not be able to tell if this was a joke or not, and it is very likely that, to be safe, his audience will not laugh, for even those who suspect they heard a joke may prefer to seem slow rather than be rude by laughing at a comment that might have been serious. Though part of the problem in this hypothetical case is one of value differences, much of the problem may be interpreted as a conflict between the intended and the perceived (or those which are expected) functions of communication. In this way it is misleading to blame either this unfortunate speaker or the audience for 'failing to communicate'. The speaker may say so after the speech, of course, but this simply means he did not get the response he expected and does not know why. The significance of this distinction may be clearer if we consider occasions such as this: A speaker tells a joke which the audience does not think is funny but the people laugh anyway because they understand the purpose of the joke and what is expected of them. To not laugh would be rude and surely would discomfit the speaker just as much as would laughing at something not intended to be funny.

The functional approach alerts us to potential problems in communication. When something intended as small talk, such as 'Stop in and see me whenever you are in the neighborhood', is taken by a stranger to be a genuine request, both parties are embarrassed when the stranger does indeed stop by. In school and college classrooms we expect the transmission of information to be a central function, so that most students take notes on what is said; even if the

227

information is not personally meaningful, it will be functionally useful in answering examinations. But the student who spends six hours a day taking notes on what is said within the classroom rarely takes notes outside of class, even if the information outside is more relevant. The atheist may dismiss most of religion as 'mere ritual', while the faithful may or may not stress ritual as a value but may see religious services as serving more functions than ritual alone. A pert English lady calls her new male friend, 'Love', but probably if this friend attaches some literal significance to that sobriquet he will feel deceived. In Brazil *dotor* (doctor) may be applied to almost any mature Brazilian as an expression of respect and affection (a cartoon in Brazil several years ago showed a person calling out 'Hello Doctor,' whereupon everybody in the street turned around and waved!). To assume that the Brazilian 'doctor' is the product of years of professional university training would be to misinterpret the function of that name.

There are several common and important functions of communication which we will describe below.

SMALL TALK

Expressions which show an openness or a desire to enter into conversation take many forms and have been given several names by communication theorists: small talk, 'phatic communion' (a name coined by the anthropologist Malinowski for a more limited function of communication, but often extended to the great range of 'small talk') and others. Though this function would seem to be universal, it varies from culture to culture in several aspects. For one thing, the expressed forms are so idiomatic and diverse as to mislead any dictionary-minded visitor unfamiliar with them. Many are even odd grammatical constructions within their own language ('How do you do?'); many are set patterns (as when two people meeting exchange the greeting, 'Hello'); and very many are questions and answers, but they are questions which require no thought and answers which meet no test of accuracy (what we sometimes refer to as the 'rhetorical' question). Thus many cultures have an expression which is the equivalent of 'How hot it is!' but do not have equivalents of 'How hot is it?' In the former, the person addressed needs only to agree ('It sure is!') while in the latter he needs to have more detailed and accurate information. On the other hand, unless one is familiar with the form and function of such patterns, it may seem difficult to answer some questions which are meant to serve this function. English speakers may be surprised to learn that some non-native speakers of English will pause and think about answering a question like 'How are you?' or 'How are things!' It has taken some Americans in Japan a long time before discovering that in Japan the question 'Where are you going?' functionally means the same things as 'How are you?' and requires neither thought nor honesty for a functionally appropriate answer; the standard answer is *'Chotto soko made'* – 'Just over there.'

Viewed functionally, a remark or question which might seem absurd if taken too seriously ('It looks like it's raining, doesn't it?' said when it is just starting to rain) might be perfectly appropriate, whereas a reply which is honest and accurate might be wrong because it is not what is expected.

Two other aspects of this first function may also vary: (1) the length of time devoted to such functions before passing into a different level of communication; and (2) the frequency with which such expressions are exchanged between the same persons during a period of a day or week. The first of these reflects that even this function may be regarded as serving many additional functions, especially between strangers: exchanging 'small talk' may reveal considerable information about the character and personalities of the individuals, of their language abilities (across cultures, at least), of their desire to talk about other subjects, and may even provide some clues as to which other subjects might be appropriate. Also, in a sense, because the forms are so predictable, easily interpreted, and therefore require so little thought as to content, the persons are able to take in a great deal of information about such traits as voice tones, rate, and volume, which is extremely important in preparing for further conversation.

The length of time taken in exchanging small talk varies across cultures, but the reason is not simply one of convention or custom; rather, this is related to pace of living, many values concerning individuals and activity, and, of course, values associated with time itself. If people from the United States seem to 'want to get down to business' more quickly than most other people in the world, it is probably due in part to the American's distinction between the individual and his role or job, and thus we do not have to 'test' through small talk the personal worth of, say, a plumber or electrician – for we don't care about such things. Literally, 'that is none of our business'. In much of the world, however, this distinction is not so clear-cut, and so it is important to be able to judge this individual as a person before accepting him in his particular function. Thus another functional conflict in communication occurs when persons from one culture expect and desire to move on to another function, while the persons from the other culture seem to want to remain at the same level of communication.

Similarly, cultural patterns may differ in the frequency of small talk exchanges between the same persons within a given period of time. In the United States, if two friends happen to see each other four times within one day, the extent of their small talk is likely to decrease with each successive meeting, so that by the fourth time or even by the third, almost no comment need be exchanged. In much of Latin America, on the other hand, nearly the same pattern of greetings may be repeated each time ('How are you, how is your mother, how is your father . . . ?').

RELATING AND RECEIVING INFORMATION

When people travel across cultures, they appear to give more attention to this function than they might at home, which is interesting in itself. This is the function we are referring to when we speak of taking a phrase literally. Usually, instructions or directions on how to get somewhere is the kind of information involved in this function. This, too, is the function most often associated with the popular view of 'communication'.

Some observations about this function are especially important in cross-cultural communication. One has been suggested several times previously: information is often *not* to be taken literally, but cross-culturally – particularly if we are not fully confident of the language and especially if we are unfamiliar with customs – we are likely to 'take literally' most of what is said, ignoring the functional approach to meaning. Moreover, in a new situation we are sometimes likely to perceive as *information* kinds of behavior which other members of the culture ignore and which we would also ignore in our own culture. Sometimes we are also likely to ignore or be incapable of perceiving as information what is intended as information. Partly for this reason, there seems to be some truth in the familiar attitude that newcomers or strangers have a clearer insight into some aspects of a culture than do members of the culture or even foreign residents of several years. The problem, of course, is that the newcomer is never really sure how significant his observations are: they may be different, but that does not make them profound or even accurate interpretations.

This function of relating and receiving information may also serve other functions. When one gives information, for example, he may also be saying something about himself ('See what I know?') and something about his attitude toward the other person ('I know more than you' or 'I want to help you'). That strangers often appear to be so curious in a new culture, asking questions about every possible subject, may also suggest that we tend to resort to this form of communication as a substitute for small talk expressions with which we are unfamiliar.

CATHARSIS OR TENSION RELEASE

A mixed category, tension release includes laughter; exclamations of surprise and other emotions ('Oh, wow!'); expressions of anger (swearing); and a variety of autistic mannerisms (such as snapping our fingers when we are trying to think – or have suddenly thought – of something). Of all the functions of communication, this one would seem to be the most instinctive and personal, minimally influenced by language and culture. And yet there are significant differences cross-culturally in the form and frequency of catharsis.

Expressions of anger are instructive of cultural differences. In most languages there appears to be a range of expressions to coincide roughly with the degree of anger to be expressed (or the degree of tension to be released);

there are also likely to be differences according to the speaker's age, sex, background, role and the social setting in which the anger is expressed. And, as with the other functions, this form may serve more than the immediate and apparent function: a person may swear because he or she is angry; a man may swear to show that he is a man – or, perhaps, to convey other information. Moreover, any person who has learned to speak another language probably realizes that foreign swear words are not likely to express his anger as effectively as his native language does. In this sense, it may be more difficult to communicate with ourselves in a foreign language than it is to communicate with others.

As suggested above, it may be especially risky to express some forms of tension in the language of another culture; not only may the speaker be ignorant of the specific social implications of such expressions, his phrase – even if semantically correct – may strike his hosts as being odd, false, a performance.

Cathartic expressions are often confusing across cultures because we are likely to assume that they are universal when clearly they are not. Laughter, for example, in most Western cultures is usually associated with humor – whether it's nonsensical, clever, gentle, or cruel. In Japan, laughter is often an indication of embarrassment, so that misunderstandings often occur when, for example, a European expresses anger and this anger embarrasses his Japanese counterpart, who then expresses his embarrassment through laughter. If the European is ignorant of this custom, he is likely to become even angrier as a result of feeling he is being laughed at. In Tanzania, President Nyerere sometimes begins a speech with a kind of gentle laugh which is echoed by the audience and then repeated by the President, and so on, until a 'laughing relationship' is established. For one accustomed to a Western view of laughing, this performance is most puzzling. No Swahili dictionary will give the meaning of that laughter.

RITUAL

Of all of the functions of communication, perhaps none has received as much attention by anthropologists as that of the ritual. There are a number of reasons for this attention: rituals often express the ethos of a culture better than do most other forms of communication; also, in rituals the outside observer is able – and probably compelled – to remain detached and therefore able to make objective observations; and rituals help to direct the sense of community, the sense of permanence. Originated so long ago, most rituals cannot be explained easily by those who participate in them, and often the explanations are rationales conjectured by participants first confronted with the question, 'Why do you do this?' Thus, the advantage of detached observations may carry an ironic disadvantage: while we may be able to collect objective, detailed information on certain rituals, our exclusion might make it impossible to relate this information to our behavior when we are in a new culture.

Nevertheless, visitors are often invited to observe, if not participate in directly, the rituals of their host country. To attend a wedding, funeral, feast, saint's day, national holiday, or local festival is usually desired by visitors, since it is something special and memorable and possibly even a candidate for slides or tape recordings for the mechanized traveller. Travel agencies, too, play up many large festivals and encourage tourists to visit during the festive season.

Rituals are likely to be awkward occasions for communication; the visitor feels like an outsider but wants to participate to some extent; he may know how to behave appropriately but knows also that appropriate behavior during some rituals may be very different from the usual day-to-day behavior; he's appreciative of the special food, the dress, the dances, and yet feels that true appreciation is impossible for one who is not a member of the community.

For a resident – in the United States, especially – ritual as a communicative function may be difficult to appreciate in his own country. As will be noted later, values which direct us toward the future, encourage change, or minimize formality tend to relegate ritual, when perceived as such, to a primitive category: 'mere ritual'. In addition, it is often difficult to recognize rituals within our own culture. Thus Americans may think of fireworks on the Fourth of July as ritualistic but may forget that birthday parties (with ice cream and cake, games, presents, candles) are also little rituals for marking ages. And Americans may be surprised when they discover that in much of the world, birthdays are not celebrated.

Deciding what to categorize as ritual is somewhat more difficult than it might first appear to be. What of the dress, music, dancing, and life-style of 'youth'? These customs would seem to have great ritualistic value in distinguishing people who like the same music and style of clothing and hair from 'the straight people' who are outside of this community. One of the striking things about the 'youth revolution' or 'the counterculture' of the late 1960s and the 1970s is its universality: that young persons throughout the world could express membership in the same kind of community. Apart from some religious rituals which are similar in many parts of the world, this phenomenon is historically unique. Therefore, on the basis of this functional approach, a shift from the 'hippie revolution' to the 'Jesus revolution' in the United States does not seem so surprising.

AFFECTIVE COMMUNICATION

The function of affective (not effective) communication is to express emotions toward another person, and as such it suffers the cultural distinction between 'head and heart', *reason* and *emotion*. Even though there are affective elements in almost all other functions of communication, the ill-definable category of affective communication is useful in examining communication across cultures.

Considerable attention has been given to theory and research on the need for balance between reason and emotion and also to the view that persons, subcultures, and cultures which have been deprived of either reason or emotion have stressed the other. Some small-group research, conducted primarily in the United States, suggests that every group discussion will, over a time, produce a balance between 'task-oriented' comments and 'socioe-motional expressions'.[10] Advice to administrators often warns against a too businesslike attitude which does not show enough concern for the personal feelings of the staff. Aristotelian rhetoric recommends a balance between *logos* and *pathos*, appeals of *reason* and *emotion*. Latin American philosophers have stressed the spirit of *la raza*, with strong affective sentiments as something better than the cold, calculating cultures of Northern European origin, including England and the United States. (The analogy of Ariel and Caliban is frequently cited.) Japanese are fond of comparing their aesthetic and soulful (located in the belly, it would seem) culture with that of 'the rational West'.

In popular American mythology today, the most affectively typified people are the poor, the humble, the uneducated, the rural and just about anybody 'in the good old days'. Suburbanites even more than their urban neighbors have no 'soul', are mechanized, distant, unfeeling. Nearly anybody who is affluent is suspected of lacking human affective qualities, at least in this popular view. In this country, success American-style either requires a lack of feeling or destroys feeling. This is a constant theme in much literature throughout the world, it would seem. It is difficult to find a credible financial success who is compassionate and nearly as difficult to find an interesting impoverished character who is highly 'rational'. Part of the remarkable popularity of John Kennedy, who would seem to be an exception to this pattern (in much of the world his image towers above Lincoln's), was that he had close family ties, was handsome and witty, and was Roman Catholic, a religion regarded as 'irrational' by many Protestants.

Affective communication is the communication of feelings, of honest, heart-felt emotions. And much of intercultural communication is based on goals in which such expressions are minimized, if not discouraged altogether. That is, in business, in technical assistance programs, in foreign study and research work, and in diplomatic negotiations, the conveying of information and the instrumental (see below) functions receive first priority. When a culture's values and reasoning patterns (and even aspects of language) clearly distinguish these, the affective qualities of communication may suffer. Former Secretary of State John Foster Dulles's comment that 'The US does not have friends, it has interests' is bitterly remembered by Latin American critics (with Mr Dulles sometimes called 'Mr Dollars'), as is the rhetorical question asked a number of years ago by a congressional representative, 'Now that we have spent billions of dollars in foreign aid, how many friends have we bought?'

Note that the category of affective communication includes insults as well as compliments, dislike as well as love. Perhaps more so than most of the other general functions, affective elements are often expressed nonverbally (hugs, kisses, a pat on the back, an angry gesture), and this accounts for additional problems across cultures. If it were possible to line up cultures on a continuum beginning with the most perceivably expressive, those which seem to be most expressive might also seem to be the most affective. In this case, a hypothetical bookkeeper from Honduras might seem to have more 'soul' than a Vermont Saint.

INSTRUMENTAL COMMUNICATION

When words or gestures are used as *instruments* in helping to achieve some result, we may identify them as instrumental. As in previous categories, such a broad definition of function might seem to include nearly all of what we call *communication*. But in attempting to keep these categories broad enough for a wide variety of uses, we can say that some gestures and expressions are more clearly instrumental than others: commands and requests ('Open the door', 'Do not smoke') especially seem instrumental and quite distinct from other functions, with the possible exception of conveying information. A weather report would seem to be classified as 'conveying information', but upon interpretation it may be instrumental in suggesting what kind of clothing to wear, or whether or not to carry an umbrella.

As suggested in the previous category, instrumental expressions are often contrasted with affective expressions: if one's most frequent expressions are highly instrumental, one is likely to be regarded as lacking in feelings. It may be that there is a status differential which influences these two forms when the same goal is intended; that is, a person with authority may legitimately express his role through instrumental communication ('Do this, don't do that'), whereas a person who lacks power in any situation must achieve goals through indirection (flattery, cajoling). Thus in many cultures, the husband is the acknowledged authority in the home, giving the orders and speaking in a less affective style. (By extension, this may be part of the explanation for cultural distinctions between the head and the heart, as the 'heart' is more affective and most often associated with the powerless.)

In the Judeo-Christian tradition, the Old Testament God is highly instrumental. Indeed, it would be difficult to find more striking examples of instrumental communication than in Genesis, where God's every word turns into reality. Christ, however, added an affective style, with values centred on God's love, forgiveness, compassion. In Roman Catholicism in many cultures God remains aloof and instrumental, while Mary is the affective soulful go-between, who intercedes. An interesting study revealed that the style of communication between a male saint and the Virgin Mary in Mexican churches perfectly mirrored communication between a child and his parents in the Mexican home.[11] The author described these parallel differences in terms of instrumental and affective communication.

In intercultural communication the recognition of instrumental or directive communication may be difficult. In time, a child learns that when his mother says 'I don't think so' she often means 'No'; likewise, across cultures and languages it takes time to learn the functional equivalents for instrumental goals. When a person's ability to speak a second or third language is weak, he is likely, lacking the skills in affective language, to sound more blunt, more directive than he intends. Cultural value differences also complicate the problem: the American's values both of frankness and of minimization of status differences may appear to be too blunt or crude in cultures where indirectness is valued, while they may not be directive enough in cultures where a person of higher status is expected to give commands as if he were an army general. Moreover, roles ascribed according to sex often are reflected in a female-affective style and a male-instrumental style. Compared to many societies, however, American men and women speak in about the same style, and this means that in some cultures the American woman is likely to sound insufficiently affective ('demanding', 'aggressive', 'masculine' in the eyes of her host-culture counterparts), while the American male may seem too affective (and, therefore, weak, unmasculine).

While there are other functions which could be listed here, our purpose is only to provide a representative and suggestive list of categories. Thus we are including only the six given previously. Any one function is likely to be expressed in other functional styles and interpreted across cultures as having still different functional intents. And these differences reflect and are yet further complicated by the presence of different values, nonverbal behavior, language predispositions, and the other perspectives mentioned earlier. Even this complex composition might be analysed if a speaker always had one functional intention in mind and could express this function distinct from other functions. However, although we have separated functions for purposes of explanation, most expressions are likely to serve several functions at the same time, and often the speaker does not have a single goal in mind. Even such a commonplace airport greeting as, 'Welcome, we've all been looking forward to your visit', may represent the following functions: (1) *Small talk* – a conventional way of acknowledging the presence of another; (2) *Transmission of information* – implying that preparations have been made involving an unstated number of persons; (3) *Catharsis* – it may be that many greetings on occasion result in part from the tension which has developed in preparation and waiting for the visit; (4) *Ritual* – at least in an extended sense of ritual, such as Goffman uses to describe such everyday interactions; (5) *Affective communication* – clearly this appears to be a compliment to the visitor; (6) *Instrumental* – the comment may direct the guest to reply in kind ('I've been looking forward to this visit, too').

For the sake of brevity, most of our examples have been limited to the expressions of a single speaker or a single interchange between two persons. Using a larger unit of discourse for analysis, such as an hour of behavior, the functional division may be still easier, for we can discover patterns in the expressions of each person and in the total field of communication established between the two.

Confusion frequently occurs when a listener knows the literal meaning of what is said but still is not sure 'what it means' and therefore does not know how to respond. An American greets the friend of a non-American in a way that seems insulting; should the non-American ignore this, defend his friend, or add his own insult? The Tokyo housewife tells her dinner guest that there is nothing to eat; should the guest say he isn't hungry, be puzzled since he was invited to dinner, or treat this as conventional politeness? A functional approach to communication alerts us to such varied interpretations of the same 'reports'.

Communication is still a fuzzy concept, used sometimes to describe intentional 'one-way' expressions and at other times to describe a complex phenomenon which exists whenever persons are mutually aware of the presence of others. Keen scholarly writing does not result from fuzzy concepts, but at the current stage of communication studies it would be worse to be more precise or even to be thoroughly consistent. After all, one basic assumption is that the structural process of communication is considered differently by different persons, and we would like to leave the door open for as many structures as possible, depending on the needs, interests, and knowledge of each reader.

If nothing else, perhaps these perspectives remind us of the enormous complexity of communication, even apart from any differences in the cultural backgrounds of those who are communicating. Now a cliché in the field of communication is the belief that complete understanding between any two persons is impossible, and that misunderstanding occurs to a far greater degree than we usually assume. That we do as well as we do may be cause for some satisfaction. But in the global context today, the knowledge that we do so poorly must be cause for deep concern.

NOTES

1. Some might also feel that the unseen wife 'communicated' to the girl, too.
2. P. Watzlawick, J. Beavin and D. D. Jackson, *The Pragmatics of Human Communication* (New York: W.W. Norton, 1967), pp. 48–51.
3. E. T. Hall, *The Silent Language* (New York: Doubleday, 1959), p. 37.
4. J. Ruesch and G. Bateson, *Communication: Social Matrix of Psychiatry* (New York: W.W. Norton, 1951), p. 8.
5. See A. H. Maslow, *Toward a Psychology of Being*, 2nd edn (New York: Van Nostrand Reinhold, 1968), and C. R. Rogers, *On Becoming a Person* (Boston: Houghton Mifflin, 1961).
6. K. Burke, *A Grammar of Motives* (New York: Prentice-Hall, 1955).
7. Watzlawick et al., *Human Communication*, pp. 54–59.
8. Ibid., pp. 179–81.
9. See E. Goffman, *The Presentation of Self in Everyday Life* (New York: Doubleday, 1959) and *Encounters* (Indianapolis: Bobbs-Merrill, 1961).
10. See, for example, R.F. Bales, *Interaction Process Analysis* (Cambridge: Addison-Wesley, 1950).

11. C. Nelson, 'Saints and sinners: parallels in the sex-role differentiation in the family of saints and in the family of man in a Mexican peasant village', mimeographed, n.d.

11

Divided by a Common Language: Diversity and Deception in the World of Global Marketing

*Mary Goodyear**

Global marketing is a complex task with the potential for much misunderstanding and friction.

The overt practicalities of working across cultures are often compounded by the human factor. Problems arise, for example, from using the processes of marketing to help integrate corporate structures and systems that were not originally designed to cope with global, or even regional initiatives.

Which international researcher has not felt like the messenger bearing bad news, when caught in the power struggle between the local operating company and head office?

There is also the ever-present problem of language. The translation of advertising copy or of new product concepts usually becomes an expensive, iterative process involving translators, advertising agencies and, sometimes, consumers.

Issues like these have been well chronicled in discussions of globalization and solutions are well known, even if not always employed.

However, there is another aspect of international marketing that is dangerous and troublesome, all the more because it is a problem in disguise.

The disguise that cloaks the problem is the language of marketing and research: those words that outsiders would call jargon, but which insiders think of as the tools of the trade. Most of this language originated in the world's biggest and most sophisticated marketplace, the USA. Terms like 'brand', 'brand positioning', 'advertising concept', 'segmentation', 'unique selling proposition', 'focus groups', etc., were spawned in the USA and are now common parlance in marketing and research communities worldwide.

The problem lies in the meanings of those terms; behind the language lies a world of diversity and deception. Take the word 'marketing'. The American Marketing Association has a straightforward description:

* Reprinted from *Journal of the Market Research Society*, Vol. 38, No. 2, April 1996, The Market Research Society.

Marketing = the process of planning and executing the conception, pricing promotion and distribution of ideas, goods and services to create exchanges that satisfy individual and organizational goals.

The Macmillan *Dictionary of Marketing and Advertising*, however, claims there is no single universally agreed definition of marketing. Michael Baker (1984), the editor, lists some of the main definitions and he also refers to an article by Keith Crosier (1975) in the *Quarterly Review of Marketing* where Crosier reviewed over 50 definitions and categorized them as falling (or being pushed) into three major groups:

- marketing as an activity or process;
- marketing as a concept or philosophy of business – the idea that marketing is a 'social exchange process involving willing consumers and producers';
- marketing as an orientation 'present to some degree in both consumers and products; the phenomenon which makes the concept and the process possible'.

Even in the UK alone, one can see the complexity behind the simple term. When one introduces an international perspective, the matter gets even more complex.

Here in the West, I think most marketers would make a distinction between 'selling' and 'marketing', viz. Ted Levitt's (1960) definition of them both in *Marketing Myopia*:

Selling is preoccupied with the seller's need to convert his product into cash; marketing with the idea of satisfying the needs of the consumer by means of the product, and the whole cluster of things associated with creating delivery and finally consuming it.

Yet in many countries, neither consumers nor those engaged in selling goods make that distinction. 'Marketing' itself does not yet seem to have been sufficiently developed as a discipline/activity/art to be readily differentiated from the act of selling.

In Africa 'marketing' often refers to going shopping, either to buy or sell in an exchange market. So it is not too surprising that in African companies the marketing manager is often the man in charge of the sales force. The same is true in many Asian countries, where marketing is so heavily dependent on getting a strong distribution network that, again, the marketing manager is the man who looks after distribution. Marketing can have a slightly different set of associations in those former communist countries which are now developing a market economy. In Vietnam, for example, the term *marketing* can be used to refer to the act of filling out an import form.

Closer to home, the distinction between marketing and selling is barely made in those companies which traditionally have been less marketing-orientated. For example, marketing in financial services, in agrochemicals, in pharmaceuticals, and in the oil business is still focused on selling product, rather than 'satisfying individual goals' (AMA) or 'satisfying the needs of the consumer' (Levitt).

Many companies in those sectors do not even know their consumers' needs. They are still more concerned with finding out how to sell what they make, rather than make what will be bought.

Yet in mature marketing environments, current definitions are breaking down the concept of marketing as a discrete function and recommending, instead, that it become a way of doing things, and of thinking about customers (whether internal or external), that is diffused throughout all the company's activities: positioning marketing as a way of life.

Even more leading-edge thinking is incorporating marketing and the commercial world into corporate missions for good citizenship, and the satisfaction of the whole man beyond his economic identity.

Let us take another apparently simple word that is used, and confused, across cultures: 'brand'. There are differences of interpretation here that have already become part of the public discourse on branding and brand management. For example, at what level of the corporate/product hierarchy can brand values be said to 'belong'?

In the Western world there has been a tendency to focus communication on product ('classic') brands such as, say, Persil or Lux, sometimes to the exclusion of reference to the corporate owner (Unilever). In Japan and Korea, for historical reasons, 'brand' tends to refer to the corporate entity and, consequently, becomes part of a system that is evaluated on a much longer time horizon: cf. McCallum and Hasegawa (1995).

> . . . the role of the brand. So often the raison d'être of much market research is different in Japan where the main brand is that of the corporation e.g. Kao, Shiseido, Ajinimoto, Sony, Matsushita, Toyota, etc. Hence the orientation is that of total *corporate* share of market, rather than individual brand. Those individual brands can come and go.

The concept of brand architecture has been developed in recent years by brand positioning specialists, such as Kapferer in France and Alcock et al. in the UK (cf. Kapferer, 1992): 'The (product) brand is not only mouthpiece of an enterprise . . . there are four distinct levels of communication: enterprise, institutional, brand and product – each having their own specific purpose, target, content and style').

But there are other differences in the way countries think about brands that have not received much attention: these bob up to the surface, nevertheless, in the guise of various discrepancies which confuse the global picture. One of these differences relates to the *role brands play* and the value they have for consumers in a particular culture. Global marketing needs a model to explain why fmcg[1] brand positioning is largely product attribute based in, say, Germany, and more likely to be based on psychological end-benefits in Italy or the UK. There are clearly differences in each country in the meaning invested in brands, and their significance for both consumer and marketer.

The term 'consumer segmentation' is another easy façade, behind which lie many different assumptions. In most countries the consumer is seen as a fixed entity whose attitudinal set and (ensuing) purchasing strategy are equally unchanging. Against such a static background 'segmentation' is similar to cutting a cake or counting out different coloured beans: all the tertiary-educated in one pile, all the over-50s in another.

From the States came the idea of segmentation based not on external demographics but 'internal', psychologically driven and attitudinally defined sectors, like the consumer typologies of the VALS system.[2] More recently, however, studies of the link between attitude and behaviour reveal that in certain markets it is not appropriate to think of consumers as stable targets, either in terms of their education or what kind of residential area they live in, or in terms of their values and attitudes overall. None of these ways of describing the consumer seems to help predict purchase, or explain the apparent lack of consistent loyalty patterns.

In highly competitive, mature fmcg markets this apparent unpredictability and promiscuity of behaviour has led to the concept of a modal consumer and needs-related marketing. To quote from Jon Francis and Nina Davidson of the Henley Centre (1995):

> segmenting consumers according to demographics, psychological or life-style factors may no longer be sufficient to be able to understand a market and to predict behaviour. A market may also need to be analysed on an occasion-by-occasion basis.

The underlying construct here borrows from a number of modern ideas:

- Post-modernism and the disappearance of restrictive social norms. People today feel free to buy what they want, and use it when they like, without acknowledging conventions.
- Psychology and the challenge to the concept of personality as anything other than a learned predisposition to respond, and react, in certain ways.
- Maslow's hierarchy of needs, which suggests that after basic physiological needs have been taken care of, desires and wants take over. Today's affluent consumers, operating at the higher end of the hierarchy, often play with goods, sometimes getting their sense of identity from them.
- Micro-marketing – competition between companies is the spur to offering greater and more personalized customer satisfaction. Technological innovation makes possible customizing of products to ever-smaller target groups.

Segmentation on an occasion-and-needs-determined basis is now extensively used in the UK and USA. But in much of the rest of the world, consumers are still being identified and targeted as if they were stable and predictable types of people.

Advertising and research offer plenty of scope for similar misunderstandings, despite the common language. Researching an advertising concept

can mean creative development of a basic written proposition or an evaluation of several alternative pieces of finished artwork with copy. The less
sophisticated the marketing environment, the more likely it is that the various
processes involved in creating advertising and reality checking with
consumers will be concentrated into the one stage.

Within research itself, the term 'focus group discussion' is commonly used
across all continents, yet it subsumes approaches that are discretely different.
There are two main schools of thought: the one being cognitive, concerned
with external information; the other being conative, focused on inner feelings.
The Americans, for example, have a largely cognitive tradition which borrows
format and interviewing style from quantitative research. 'American-style
groups' is shorthand in the UK for large groups (10 respondents on average),
a structured procedure and a strong element of external validation. They are,
indeed, groups 'focused' on specific issues with all the disciplines that follow
from convergent thinking and control. The analysis or articulation of the
problem has been worked on before, and so the interview is largely a question
of confirming or expanding known issues.

In Europe, the term 'focus group' is in common usage but assumes a
different intellectual starting point, one that emphasizes exploration, with the
analysis taking place during and after the group. The difference in styles is
like the difference between a mirror (what you see is what you get) and an
iceberg. Which approach is employed has many implications for costings,
timing and the choice of personnel (see Figure 11.1) and when the two cultural
styles come together there is an obvious need to negotiate.

	Cognitive	Conative
Purpose	demonstration	exploration
Sample size	10–12	6–8
Duration	1 hour	1–4 hours
Interviewing	logical sequence	opportunistic
Questions	closed	open
Techniques	straight questions	probing
	questionnaires	facilitation
	hand shows	projectives
	counting	describing
Response required	give answers	debate issues
Interviewer	moderator	researcher
Observer's role	to get proof	to understand
Transcripts	rarely necessary	usually full
Analysis	on the spot	time-consuming
Focus of time	pre-planning	post-fieldwork
Accusation of other style	'over-controlling'	'formless'
Type of problem suited for	behavioural	attitudinal
	confirmatory	exploratory
	evaluative	creative
Output	information	understanding

FIGURE 11.1 *The two schools of thought about 'focus group discussions'*

While I was writing this paper a colleague from India sent me a fax in which, coincidentally, she describes the cognitive/conative clash:

> I've just completed the most amazing set of group discussions (if one can call them that!) . . . it was like dealing with a set of robots whose main message was 'we're paying you to do quali research our way'. We finally had to sit the respondents in a row and ask rapid-fire questions of each and 'answer to the point please and not a word more!'
>
> Even more amazing, the client was horribly *pleased* with this and wanted no analysis. . . .

The rest of the world's qualitative researchers tend to have adopted one or other of the styles, dependent on the history of the development of the sector and also the main constituents of their trading profile. It is usually not worthwhile offering a conative style if the client and his marketing department can only work with a cognitive approach.

An enquiring mind asks why all these differences occur.

When these points of dissension happen it is tempting to take a snapshot of the event and attribute the differences to culture: i.e. the Americans or the Japanese or the Italians interpret these words differently because they are from different cultures. However, if you have the opportunity to work in the international arena for some years and can take several snapshots *over time*, what emerges is a picture of an organizing principle that is working in an evolutionary way. The principle can be said to produce a 'continuum of consumerization'.

Consumerization is the evolution of the dialogue and the relationship between the manufacturer (and service agencies) and the consumer. It is a confluence of different streams of marketing activity which progress over time with increasing sophistication and sensitivity. The progress of the different elements within this broad stream of development are interrelated and interdependent. As the market becomes more competitive, the consumer becomes more discriminating. As the consumer gains power, so the advertiser must become more subtle in trying to keep one step ahead. As the transmission and interpretation of advertising becomes more sophisticated, so research must adapt its methodologies and interpretation in order to stay perceptive and useful. If one accepts the concept of the survival of the fittest in the context of the behaviour of society (Herbert Spencer's 'Darwinian socialism'), then the natural tendency is for economic growth: 'Progress is not an accident but a necessity' (H. Spencer, 1851).

The assumption underlying consumerism is that markets grow with affluence and industrialization, from being manufacturer- and product-led towards being consumer-orientated and brand-driven. During the course of this evolution the significance and orientation of certain elements in the marketing mix ('brand', 'segmentation', 'loyalty', etc.) also change, even though the language stays the same. Thus, even though we use the same term 'brand' or even 'marketing' in countries as far apart in marketing sophistication as say, America and Russia or the Ivory Coast, the interpretation of those terms is different. *And this difference needs to be identified and understood before any kind of cross-cultural 'harmonization' can take place.*

The process is a process, but decisions tend to be about concrete issues like pack designs, media selection, and the development of creative advertising. This is my rationale for describing the continuum in terms of various discrete stages. Of course they are neither properly defined stages, nor properly discrete, but they *are* proposed as an aid to recognition, so that the reader can bring his or her own international experience into the frame for comparison.

Let us look a little more closely at this evolutionary maturation process, starting off with the less developed economies.

Stage 1 – seller's market

In the seller's world of under-supply, packaged goods of any kind are in such high demand that customers will beat a track to the manufacturer's door to buy. There is no need to create attractive packaging, or develop branding, or to define target groups, or to spend on advertising or research. The manufacturer has the power and he sells.

Stage 2 – marketing

Marketing starts when the manufacturer is faced with more competition. Customers begin to have choice. They start to discriminate and the manufacturer is forced into finding ways of creating differentiation: of making his products stand out in a way that is unique and attractive. He may be forced along a strategy ladder before he commits to classic branding. Many countries and industries are at this early stage of marketing.

One of the early stages on the ladder is to make a superior product (a better mousetrap). This can only succeed for as long as competitors stay dormant. When product performance tends to reach parity across the market sector then further action is required.

In some countries and some sectors (for example the gemstone market) there are attempts to monopolize the supply of raw materials or to control distribution. Government intervention (as in Communism) and industrial networking (as in the Keiretsu and Chaebol systems in Japan and Korea) can also protect sectors from competition, and, thereby, the need for higher-order branding.

Some cultures which are less interventionist may use price as their weapon, wiping out the competition by price wars. This tends to be the adversarial style adopted by some of the big American corporations.

Another stratagem at this level is to differentiate functionally, to find some way of changing the product so it no longer has direct competition.

If competition pursues the manufacturer into this new sector, then branding may be the only answer.

It is at this stage of the transition from product marketing to classic brand marketing that the marketer is admitting that, instead of selling, his job has become one of *persuading the customer* to buy. The task has changed and the tools for the new job take time to be used with skill. Many financial services, business equipment, agro-chemical, pharmaceutical, oil and even drinks companies are functioning at this level of branding. Typically they are managed by a generation whose ideas about their industry were formed when it was a seller's market. It takes a younger team, usually from middle management, to be able to recognize the need for brand marketing and to be willing to cede a personal sense of control for corporate survival.

Stage 3 – classic brand marketing

Typically, the development of 'three-dimensional brands', supported by emotive advertising and conative research, starts first in the fmcg sector where purchases are frequent and often of less import and interest. This allows the consumer to have a more playful and experimental attitude towards purchase. Classic branding has been the mainstay of the British marketing world since the 1960s.

Stage 4 – customer-driven marketing

As the marketplace becomes even more saturated with brands, it takes those with more resources to take the final step towards icon branding. This is the stage of managing products with added values that have become meaningful symbols for whole sectors of society. They are associated with primary motivational drives like caring (Persil), aggression/winning (Nike), machismo (Marlboro), harmony with nature (Body Shop), etc., and are used by consumers to express those values to society, and reaffirm them to themselves.

At this stage the brand is in the public domain. The consumer 'owns' it as much as does the marketer; it may even become a 'sacred' object, linked with some treasured set of commonly held values. Consider the battle between Classic Coca-Cola and new Coca-Cola. It was not just a new recipe that consumers were rejecting, but the removal of part of their daily existence.

HOW LONG DOES THE PROCESS TAKE?

The journey from commodity to fully supported brand can take decades; for example, 60 years ago most British households used ordinary paper, often newspaper, in the WC. Then, gradually, a branded market evolved, from products like Izal and Jeyes flat pack through to fully branded soft and coloured brands like Andrex and Kleenex. Now the toilet tissue market is a multimillion-pound branded business and is supported by award-winning advertising.

Or the process can take less than a year. Consider how privatization has 'branded' the water supply.

Obviously the process is made easier in an environment where branded goods constitute the bulk of goods and services purchased: the retail structure and systems are in place, and the media and consumer understanding are all present.

HOW IS CONSUMERIZATION MADE MANIFEST?

How can a country or market be assessed in terms of its consumerization rating?

The following factors seem to be key indicators:

- the proportion of goods that are branded overall;
- the role that brands play within the marketplace;
- the extent to which brand equity has both hard (financial) as well as soft measures;
- the extent to which segmentation is defined by external measures (such as SES) or based on internal means (e.g. needs-mapping);
- the level of advertising literacy and the prevailing model of 'how advertising works';
- the level of market research literacy and whether it is driven by a need to measure or to understand the consumer.

Let us look at each in some detail:

Proportion of branded goods

Developing countries have a much smaller proportion of branded goods in the weekly shopping bag than highly consumerized countries. Some idea of how branding spreads within markets over time can be gained from the recognition that as little as 35 years ago in the UK products such as eggs, bread, butter, biscuits, milk, sugar, etc., were bought loose as commodities. Now they are all packaged and branded. Even individual oranges more often than not have labels with a brand name or the importer's name and country of origin.

It is relevant here to ask what is meant by 'branded'. It is not quite the same as packaged, even packaged with a name. If brands are products with added values, and if those values are intangible, then they need to be *supported by advertising*, either above or below the line. So it is not enough for a market to have a lot of named and packaged goods; those goods need to be supported in order to start the branding dialogue with the consumer.

The role of brands

Brands start off as labels on products (Stage 1) and end up as icons of meaning (Stage 4). The various roles they play along that path are identified in Figure 11.2.

In low consumerized markets, people's appreciation of brands and the role they play is centred on the product, usually as a sign of quality. At this stage the brand is a reference, indicating maker's ownership (as with branding of cattle).

As consumerization proceeds, and the manufacturer is forced to look for differentiation, the brand's role changes. In addition to being seen as an identification of source and as the seal of quality the brand name, logo-style and packaging are imbued with an emotional component, *as a promise to the consumer*. This added value forms part of the brand's communication. If the market situation and the promise is apposite, the added values acquire character and personality – this development helps involve the consumer, either as a means for identification or as some form of compensation. (This distinction is often overlooked. An illustration would be, say, the identification of a male driver with his Mercedes whilst the female driver of the same marque might feel that the masculine values compensated for her feelings of vulnerability on the road.)

In environments when the impact of the media is high this encourages the development of icon brands imbued with significance at the societal level.

Brand equity

All the added values in the world will only be taken seriously if they add value to the bottom line. In the 1980s, formulae were developed to measure the

Classic branding

Unbranded	commodities, packaged goods
	major proportion of goods in non-industrialized context
	minor role in Europe/USA
	supplier has power
Brand as reference	brand name often name of maker
	name used for identification
	any advertising support focuses on rational attributes
	name over time becomes guarantee of quality/consistency
Brand as personality	brand name may be 'stand-alone'
	marketing support focuses on emotional appeal
	product benefits
	advertising puts brand into context
Brand as icon	consumer now 'owns' brand
	brand taps into higher-order values of society
	advertising assumes close relationship
	use of symbolic brand language
	often established internationally

FIGURE 11.2 *Role of brands*

financial equity of brands, a sure sign that branding had come home to manufacturers, and had been promoted from the marketing department to the boardroom. The development of this monetary evaluation of a brand's worth only takes place in highly consumerized environments where brands have, indeed, become capable of sustaining preference, premiums and thereby profitability over time. The presence of financial brand equity suggests a marketplace where consumerization is at Stage 3 or 4.

New forms of segmentation

When a market sector is richly furnished with consumer choice, then consumers (excluding the 'role-relaxed' and the brand-weary) become more proactive and promiscuous in their behaviour. They pick and choose which brands they want, deploying a repertoire of products and brands to suit the needs of the moment: the moment of purchase or of consumption.

These needs can be mapped against a coherent framework, so that the total needs system can be understood, as well as the relationship between one need-state and another. Because needs-mapping is based on psychology, it is constant across different cultures, and across demographics, attitude clusters and personality archetypes. It is segmentation at source, at the conative level, before the constructs of personality, life stage, and socio-demographics.

Needs-mapping is used to position brands and identify communication requirements; at all stages the marketer is working with the raw stuff of human needs and motivations, the most solid material from which to create customer-driven marketing.

Needs-related marketing is the sophisticated and sensitive culmination of promiscuity on the part of the consumer and seduction from the manufacturer. It can only come after a period of more prosaic and clumsy courtship.

Advertising literacy

As consumers become more sophisticated and their choices more prolific, so advertising spend increases to maintain the brand's share.

Exposure to advertising creates a 'literacy' amongst consumers, an ability to understand the conventions of the media (how to 'read' film, for example) and the devices used by advertisers to surprise, inform, entertain, and persuade. This literacy is one part of the consumerization continuum; the stages of literacy (Figure 11.3) are arbitrary and not discrete, but they all follow the same pattern of a shift of focus, from the manufacturer and his product to the consumer.

Advertising literacy is a subject that has been described in detail by various authors and a short summary of the various states and trends will suffice here.

The overall development is from products to brands, from rational to emotional messages, from attributes to benefits; from the concept of the consumer as passive 'victim' to that of 'active' participant, and from the real and particular, to the abstract and general (Figure 11.4).

1	Straight sell	rational
		product attributes
		pack shots, salesperson
		role = to inform
2	Hard sell	rational, emphatic
		comparative product attributes
		role = to convince
3	Metaphor	message rational, medium emotional
		consumer benefits, usually functional
		metaphor used to enhance brand performance
		role = to persuade
4	Endorsement	message rational, messenger persuasive
		product functional benefits
		famous personality (shifts to 'typical' consumer)
		role = to persuade
5	Life-style	message emotional
		focus on psychological and functional benefits
		brand (if shown) in consumer world (shifts from 'idealized' to 'realistic')
		role = to encourage identification
6	Symbolic	message emotional
		focus on higher order values
		shorthand symbols developed from brand language
		role = to create respect *for* user
7	Post-modern	message rational or emotional
		focus on advertising itself
		de-bunking references to brand and commercial world
		role = to gain respect *from* a 'knowing' audience

The stages are arbitrary. Literacy is a continuum from dialectic to conspiracy.

FIGURE 11.3 *Advertising literacy stages of development*

The value of studying advertising literacy is to enable international advertisers, especially those with global or regional intentions, to anticipate their audience and produce leading-edge creative work which is familiar enough to be recognized and new enough to have saliency.

Low consumerization		*High consumerization*
product attributes	→→→	product benefits
focus on product	→→→	focus on usage
rational	→→→	emotional
realistic	→→→	symbolic
fact	→→→	metaphor
maker's language	→→→	brand language
salesman	→→→	consumer
pack shot	→→→	consumption
left brain	→→→	right brain
'masculine'	→→→	'feminine'
selling	→→→	buying

These two columns represent the elements in advertising and the gradual evolution that takes place over time from low consumerization to high.

FIGURE 11.4 *Advertising literacy*

Market research literacy

As branding and advertising become more sophisticated, so must research methodologies become more sensitive in order to offer relevant information and recommendations. An interviewing approach that fails to acknowledge the intangible, emotionally driven aspects of brands will not be able to satisfy the brand manager or the advertiser who is working at a more sophisticated level. The researcher will not know what he is looking for, nor how to recognize it when it is offered.

Similarly, a researcher from a sophisticated environment may need to adjust – if not his methodological approach at least his interpretation – if he works in markets or market sectors lower down the consumerization continuum.

For example, the projective techniques that are regularly used throughout Europe are less popular in some countries in the Far East. They were also unusual in the USA until the last few years. Why is that? One hypothesis that has been put forward is that the Chinese, for example, prefer not to express their feelings in a group. If one accepts the consumerization concept, however, perhaps a more appropriate hypothesis is that neither consumer, nor researcher, nor manufacturer in the Chinese market has yet reached the stage of thinking about brands in that way.

In some environments, consumers are ready long before the manufacturers, advertisers or researchers. Fifteen years ago I carried out some interviews in New York using a battery of projective techniques as a demonstration to an agency and some of their clients. The consumers 'performed' brilliantly, responding with enthusiasm and openness to every question I asked. But at the end of four days, eight group discussions and a dozen depth interviews, both agency and clients said, 'Interesting, but what can we do with it?' Their management systems were not designed to work with the kind of material that European-style research was generating. Their concept of 'brand', or 'persuasive advertising', and of 'focus groups' was at a different stage of consumerization.

The 'literacy level' of the research culture, then, can be good indication of the country's position on the continuum.

How does consumerization – the maturing of the consumer's relationship with the market – help explain the discord and discrepancies underlying the common marketing language?

Different country-cultures and certain product sectors tend to have different interpretations of marketing language because of their level of development within the consumer environment. Although there may be certain traditional cultural factors that influence their interpretations, my thesis is that the proposed consumerization process is largely independent of those cultural variables. This means that those countries which now think of brands as 'reference', and where the advertising style is largely focused on product attributes rather than consumer benefits, will gradually evolve towards more classic marketing.

The speed of a country's movement along the continuum is influenced by a number of economic and cultural factors.

What factors predispose a country towards rapid marketing maturity?

- A competitive market economy is a pre-condition. Centrally planned economies which control supply and reduce competition prevent the duplication of products and, therefore, the need for manufacturers to struggle for differentiation. There were no real brands in Communist Russia and researchers there, along with consumers, had to learn their significance and structure after perestroika.
- Affluence and a buoyant economy *is* another factor stimulating maturity. The consumer must have choice amongst product equals before the need for branding occurs.
- Branding, persuasive advertising and wooing the consumer require a business culture that can accommodate the concept of emotions being brought into play in marketing. A very strongly rational environment, with low tolerance of ambiguity, may find this mixing of 'thinking and feeling' unacceptable.
- Strong communication through the media is also important. If brands are to symbolize values and meaning, then it is essential that those meanings can be made widely known. In societies where the media are censored or where social contact is still the main messenger of culture, branding cannot be so rapidly established.
- Cultures based on trading and services rather than primary production (whether agricultural or industrial) find it easier to move away from product values and deal with the impressions, opinions and preferences of the consumer. They are used to the concept of satisfying needs.
- Customer-driven marketing is based on the art of listening, and providing what is desired. This is a passive and, traditionally speaking, feminine role. The manufacturer's and, particularly, the marketer's role has always been that of aggression and hard sell, a story of the marketing man's victory over the (female) consumer.

Adjustment to this new, rather more passive, role will perhaps come more easily to those societies where aggression is not an axiomatic aspect of masculinity.

IS THERE LIFE AFTER CLASSIC BRANDING?

There comes a time when consumers become so literate about marketing and communication that they 'see through' the conventions and devices used to ensnare them. If they are persuaded at all at this level of sophistication it is only with their knowing acceptance. The loss of belief in the authority of any established body or institution has been described as one of the characteristics of post-modernism. The indications are that after classic branding the next stage of consumer maturation is akin to post-modernism (see Figure 11.5).

All classic branding roles, plus:

Brand as company	brands have complex identities
	consumer assesses them all
	need to focus on corporate benefits to diverse 'customers'
	integrated communication strategy essential through-the-line
Brand as policy	company and brands aligned to social and political issues
	consumers 'vote' on issues through companies
	consumers now 'own' brands, companies and politics

FIGURE 11.5 *Post-modern branding*

The first indication of this next stage is the change in consumers' attitudes and behaviour. As they realize their power, they start to challenge the marketer's message; armed with product knowledge and political convictions they bring a new framework to the appraisal of brands. Their reaction takes different forms of purchasing strategies: some shop aggressively for benefits of lower cost, others on the basis of political correctness or the absence of 'E' numbers.

These super-consumers have been described by Faith Popcorn as 'vigilante consumers', informed and fighting back against duplicity:

> Consumers became their own product investigators, researching product quality before they made their choice. After a few years, this work-intensive consuming began to breed resentment . . . the corporate aura of power and omniscience has been demystified. For years we couldn't see the man at the top of the corporate ladder. Now we want him out front, and held accountable.

The emergence of the knowing, and sometimes feisty, consumer seems likely to affect all the strands of consumerization: new relationships will need to be formed through different media and with a different style of communication.

In some areas of consumption, branding will play a diminished role, maybe no role at all. In other areas, classic brands, with all their dreams and promises intact, will continue to persuade and please, simply because this is the relationship the consumer demands.

In some areas, branding could play a much bigger role, creating meaning for consumers and upholding values in the wider social and cultural environment.

As Gabriele Morello, Professor Emeritus of Marketing, Vrije University, Amsterdam, says: 'We have moved from products as bundles of utilities to products as bundles of meaning' (Morello, 1993).

The role of brands is already beginning to embrace more than mere economic values. In lieu of respected institutions, manufacturers, retailers and the media are becoming the cultural authorities. It is they who determine modern-day values. You are what you consume: product *and* brand values.

More, then, will be demanded of companies, than just goods, choice and information. They can expect to play a part (by choice or force) in the socio-

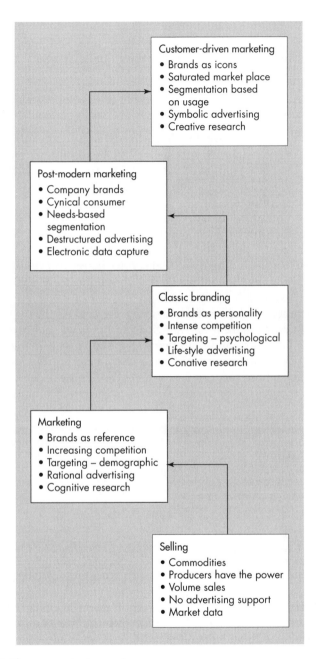

FIGURE 11.6 *The consumerization continuum*

political life of today. Already one can see some companies embracing this new larger responsibility (Body Shop and Benetton, for example) whilst others (like Shell perhaps) are being pulled into the spotlight whether they want it or not.

253

The new deregulation of institutional life coupled with the glorification of the economics of consumption seem likely to add new meanings to the marketing lexicon and new problems for the global marketer.

CONCLUSIONS

The common language of marketing hides the diversity of meaning associated with elements of the marketing mix, as well as the disciplines of advertising and research. The covert nature of this diversity, the fact that it is hidden by an almost universal language, can exacerbate the problems inherent in marketing across cultures.

Although some traditional aspects of culture may explain why these differences exist, another more dynamic factor seems to be at work. A continuum of consumerization is proposed, an evolving development of the dialogue between marketers (including those that service them) and consumers. It is a market's position along the continuum that determines how marketing terms will be interpreted (Figure 11.6).

The importance of the consumerization concept is that it provides a framework for understanding, and anticipating, between-country differences. The marketer who understands the overall shape and nature of the continuum is no longer working in the dark with an unknown culture, but moving along a well-worn track whose very familiarity gives confidence to decision-making.

NOTES

1. Fast moving consumer goods.
2. SRI Consulting's Values and Lifestyle questionnaire.

REFERENCES

Baker, Michael J. (ed.) (1984) *Macmillan Dictionary of Marketing and Advertising*. New York: Nichols Publishing.

Crosier, Keith (1975) 'What exactly is marketing', *Quarterly Review of Marketing*, 1 (2): 21–5.

Francis, J. and Davidson, N. (1995) 'From consumer marketing to modal marketing. Proceedings of the ESOMAR/JMA/ARF Conference', New York.

Kapferer, J. N. (1992) *Strategic Brand Management*. London: Kogan Page.

Levitt, T. (1960) 'Marketing myopia', *Harvard Business Review*, 38, July–August: 45–56.

McCallum, David and Hasegawa, Paul H. (1995) 'The role of research in Japan's post-bubble era. Proceedings of the ESOMAR/JMA/ARF Conference', New York.

Morello, G. (1993) 'The hidden dimensions of marketing', *Journal of the Market Research Society*, 35 (4): 293–314.

Popcorn, F. (1992) *The Popcorn Report: Targeting Your Life*. London: Arrow.

Spencer, H. (1851) *Social Statics*. London: Chapman.

12

The New Language Lab – Parts 1 and 2

*Johan Roos and Georg von Krogh**

PART 1

The urgent need to understand 'knowledge-workers' and to create 'learning organizations' is an important preoccupation for the current generation of managers. But the challenge is daunting due to the lack of clear and useful frameworks for how knowledge is created by individuals – and within groups – engaged in business enterprises.

Epistemology is the field of science that deals with the creation of knowledge and we have found that it contains numerous insights for management that will accelerate the pace with which companies can develop and make use of knowledge. Three of the most powerful concepts within the domain of corporate epistemology are:

- *Self-reference*: the observation that each of us carries our own unique frame of references which is the source of both group creativity and group confusion. Because these frames are so individualized, you cannot force self-reference to happen through the exercise of authority; it must be voluntary.
- *Languaging*: the process through which we both create new meaning and share meaning and frames of reference in language.
- *Self-similarity*: when the same basic patterns of interaction recur at different scales within the company – individual, group, strategic business unit and so on. This is one of the key features of the most powerful knowledge-development processes and management systems.

WHAT YOU SEE DEPENDS ON WHO YOU ARE

Traditionally in companies, directions have been decided on and resources allocated very much as a parent gives guidance and boundaries to a child. A hierarchy of authority underpins this process.

* Reprinted from Bickerstaffe, G. (ed.) *Financial Times Mastering Management*, Pitman Publishing, a division of Pearson Professional Ltd.

The company chief executive gains the backing of investors based on his or her understanding of the commercial environment, the corporation develops a strategy based on this understanding and gets it accepted throughout the organization by virtue of its authority over the various businesses. In like manner, managers impose this strategy on their subordinates by virtue of their authority, and so on down the hierarchical line.

Underpinning this process is the assumption that when exposed to a new experience, we all see it as the same thing. In the authority-based company, it really does not matter who gathers the data, does the analysis and/or draws the conclusions. The higher up one is in the hierarchy, the more information/knowledge one is supposed to have. So, with a higher position in the hierarchy came the privilege of strategic thinking.

Of course this does not reflect the needs of a business environment in which technology is creating new industries requiring radically new knowledge and skills. Nor does it reflect the strategic priorities of empowerment, organizational learning and foresight. Nor does it reflect the fact that authority in companies no longer rests on a profound knowledge base that has been rigorously tested and validated throughout a long corporate career.

Self-referencing refers to the commonsense, everyday observation that each of us has a unique set of experiences that makes us see and react to things differently. What you see depends on who you are. Through this continuous self-reference we develop new knowledge that will always be unique to each one of us. In turn, our private knowledge makes us see new things others do not. This is why it matters who did the industry analysis, who made the claim about emerging technology or who did the market segmentation.

Although the differences between people's views eventually converge and become trivial on routine matters, they are the essential building blocks for the creation of new knowledge. This is also why every company always develops an ever-changing knowledge base.

While the exercise of command authority (where one individual tells another individual what to do) is sometimes necessary, excessive reliance on authority is an enormous barrier to the availability and creation of knowledge within a company. It prohibits individuals from successfully self-referencing.

Management also needs to understand norms, beliefs, values and world views of employees, groups, units and the whole company. All of those form the basis from which to see the future and to decide what new knowledge is legitimate and what is not. This goes beyond alluding to vision/mission statements, job descriptions, organizational charts and other artefacts of the company. People participate in, and contribute their knowledge to, many organizations simultaneously, such as the company, the family and the basketball team. All of these experiences influence who they are and, therefore, what knowledge they develop and contribute to their companies.

LANGUAGE AS STRATEGIC RESOURCE

It is obvious that without language, knowledge could not flow from person to person within a company. It is equally obvious that if people speak different languages, then communication is stifled.

What is not always obvious is that due to self-referencing, people are constantly in the process of creating new language and new meanings, even if they share the same mother tongue. On the high value-added boundaries of knowledge creation, the ability to 'make' new language – and rapidly diffuse it through a company – is a strategic advantage. The strategic significance of language is discussed in detail in Part 2.

MAKING MANAGEMENT SIMPLE SO THE BUSINESS CAN BE COMPLEX

Businesses are turning Frederick Taylor's rules of management upside down. Work groups are autonomous and decide for themselves how and when to fulfil orders; employees are multi-functional so that they can participate in different teams and work units.

This is a traditional manager's nightmare. Policies that are productive in one setting may be disruptive in another. In the extreme case, specific policies and action plans might need to be different for each individual worker. To the traditional manager, this looks like anarchy, like chaos.

The new-style manager looks for a hidden order behind the throes of knowledge creation. He or she takes a clue from the repeating patterns observed in nearly all things in nature. When patterns or processes recur at different levels within a system they are said to be 'self-similar'. The notion has been popularized by colorful pictures of geometric shapes – so-called 'fractals' – and by books on chaos theory, ironically enough. But the good news for managers is that self-similarity seems to be nature's way of reducing one form of complexity while giving other forms of complexity – including knowledge – the means to flourish.

People, groups and companies have the capacity to self-reference and 'language' the way we have described. For example, if a company can simplify its management systems so that essentially the same process is used to make individual, team, business unit and corporate management decisions, then the artificial limits to the size or shape of that company might be eliminated, i.e. it can become as large or as small as it needs to be. At the same time it increases the number of different markets in which a company might be able to operate effectively – all without increasing the complexity of managing the company.

This is precisely how a manufacturing and financial services company in the US has set out to improve its strategic management capability. It defines management responsibilities in terms of a small number of key functions: to develop new knowledge in the form of new options; to decide on which options are relevant; and to implement these options.

The model is designed to be replicated at any level in the organization. Middle managers use it in their daily activities as do foremen in the manufacturing plant.

CONCLUSION

In a knowledge-driven society where more and more employees are seen as knowledge workers, management is not what it used to be. In this section we have offered some 'food for thought' for a different managerial frame in the guise of three new concepts: languaging, self-reference and self-similarity. These are old concepts; they have been part of human culture for tens of thousands of years. Still, they are taking on a new life as strategic tools in the hands of managers in the knowledge age.

The meaning of these concepts in management is not only about reassessing how we collectively and individually use language and stimulate self-reference but rethinking how we view power, trust and co-operation as well as how we develop foresight and set directions. On a more profound level, however, it requires us to rethink what is knowledge, how we view work and what it means to be employed.

One thing is certain: managers who have ability, guts and the humility constantly to reassess and challenge their management thinking and practice will be more valuable to their employers than those who do not.

SUMMARY

Three of the most important concepts within the domain of corporate epistemology are 'self-referencing', 'languaging' and 'self-similarity'. Self-referencing refers to the everyday observation that each of us has a unique set of experiences which is the source of both group creativity and confusion. Differences between people's views are essential building blocks for the creation of new knowledge – excessive reliance on authority in a company is an enormous barrier to this process. Languaging is the process through which we create and share meaning and frames of reference. The ability to 'make' new language (and rapidly diffuse it through an organization) is a strategic advantage. When patterns of processes recur at different levels within a system they are said to be 'self-similar'. This seems to be nature's way of reducing one form of complexity while giving other forms of complexity (including knowledge) the opportunity to flourish. Artificial limits to a company's size can thereby be eliminated, and the number of markets in which a company can operate effectively can be increased.

PART 2

Conversations are the backbone of business. Nothing gets done in a business without at least two people talking about it, and if they do not understand each other, things can go terribly wrong.

Every company has its own unique set of concepts and phrases – its own language – that cannot be easily translated or adopted by anyone else. Unless you are part of the conversations that made the language, and continually remake it, important meanings can be totally missed.

The success of a company in taking on a new product or market is directly related to its ability to create new language and rapidly diffuse it into operations. As Peter Drucker, management writer, has noted: 'Knowledge has become the key economic resource and the dominant, if not the only, source of comparative advantage'.

Since language is the currency of knowledge, it is the only means through which that advantage can be institutionalized and exploited. Given the centrality of language to both the routine operation and the future success of business, it is ironic how few managers pay the slightest attention to it – or to the *conversations* that give rise to it. We have yet to see a strategic planning document with 'Manage the business conversations better' as a major bullet point, but the time has come to put it near the top of the list.

STRATEGIC AND OPERATIONAL CONVERSATIONS

There is a useful distinction to be made between the conversations that are primarily focused on executing existing routines within a business and those trying to create a space for something new to take shape.

The former covers issues that have been talked about previously. Perhaps these issues were new to everyone at some time in the past and once required more extensive conversation, but not any longer. The latter calls for people to move into new and unfamiliar territory, perhaps talking about things that have never been talked about before.

Operational conversations are about exploiting the knowledge gained in the past and present. Strategic conversations are about creating the knowledge – and the language to diffuse it – that will be necessary for a successful future.

Managers instinctively seem to do a better job on the operational conversations than the strategic ones. Consider the following illustration: a general manager calls an afternoon meeting to discuss how to bring down the costs of maintenance on a production line. The discussion is lively and contentious but at the end a decision is hammered out and everyone leaves feeling that they accomplished something.

The following weekend the same group of managers gets together to talk about long-term strategy. The setting is a beautiful retreat center in the mountains; the company has spared no expense. There are long conversations about 'corporate culture', 'core competencies' and 'foresight' but the resulting statements feel fairly abstract and the managers' minds wander to a troubling employee or a contract that needs to be finalized. Most leave the meeting feeling that they wasted a lot of time and that nothing really will change.

This scene repeats itself with frustrating regularity. Managers who are proficient at talking about the day-to-day challenges in their businesses have trouble translating that success into their strategic conversations. 'Strategy sessions' end up focusing on day-to-day operational details or become over-structured, boring and political – a waste of time. The exceptions to this pattern are fondly remembered but remain exceptions.

In the days when a company's strategy took years to unfold and was tied to a fairly stable set of products, this limitation did not carry a great cost. Now they are under pressure to change directions in a matter of weeks or months. Like the obsolescence of computer equipment, a strategy has a very short shelf life. If managers are not proficient at talking about the future, their company will not have one.

One reason that managers have less success with strategic conversations is that they try to utilize the same rules and tools that they do in operational conversations. At first glance, one might think that the skills were transferable. A conversation is just a conversation, after all. Unfortunately, it does not work that way.

MANAGING STRATEGIC CONVERSATIONS

In most companies, operational and strategic conversations are two very different undertakings. Many common elements of operational conversations are in fact active barriers to successful strategic conversations. Managers need to abandon many of their well-worn habits and take a decidedly different course. This is not impossible but it takes discipline and attention to at least the following four basic rules:

Focus on building shared meaning, not on 'who's right'

In an operational conversation, a manager can request: 'Mary, make sure our new French client receives our standard marketing packet' without fear of being seriously misunderstood. This confidence is based on numerous conversations that have gone on before, between the manager and Mary as well as a history of conversations among all the other workers before them. Over time, the words and phrases develop widely shared meanings and a whole operational 'language' emerges that is as brief, clear and static as possible. There are clearly right and wrong interpretations of the language.

Newcomers are trained in the use and meaning of the language so that routines go smoothly. When people disagree, they strenuously advocate their own versions of 'the truth' to see whose version will prevail.

Strategic conversations have a decidedly different purpose. The future of the company does not yet exist; it must be created. The language surrounding the future of the company does not yet exist; it too must be created.

Not all of the conversations that will eventually give rise to operational routines have taken place. There are no right or wrong answers yet. There is very little meaning that is shared. An executive may say: 'We must become a learning organization'. But everyone might understand the phrase in a different way. If that fuzziness is allowed to persist, the routines that eventually result may not support each other and may even conflict. No one is right or wrong yet. Knowledge and perspectives must be shared before a powerful image of the future can be refined.

Strategic conversations must be a dialogue for understanding rather than advocacy for agreement. If an adversarial tone is allowed into strategic discussions then the creation of new knowledge and language will stop and the future shape of the company may turn out more like the present than it may need to be.

Leave authority at the door

Authority usually derives either from a manager's responsibility for a specific set of business operations (routines) or because an individual is known to possess a special knowledge to which others should defer. A general manager has the former, a technical expert has the latter, for example.

If a strategic conversation is sufficiently future-oriented, then it is impossible to know just what knowledge will be most important or what operational routines will result. Authority will be created 'along with' the future of the company, not beforehand. Managers who jump the gun and try to 'take control' will greatly limit what the future of the company might be. So while one's current organizational authority is relevant to operational conversations, it is meaningless to strategic ones.

As a result, as soon as authority is used in a discussion, it ceases to be a strategic conversation and becomes operational.

More extreme uses of power, such as threats and intimidation, are even less compatible with strategic conversations and may even be disruptive to operational discussions.

Keep strategy conversations exclusively for strategy

The incompatibility between authority and strategy makes it extremely difficult to mix strategic and operational conversations.

For example, the management team of a major newspaper once decided to set aside three hours for a strategy meeting. They met at 11 a.m. in the boardroom of the company, a very prestigious and beautiful room. At 11.10, everybody had arrived – well, almost everybody. The editor-in-chief was still missing. The managing director of the newspaper suggested the meeting should start but the others indicated they would prefer to wait.

More small talk. Even more coffee. Everybody looked at their watches. At 11.20 the editor-in-chief arrived, red-eyed, furious and with puffs of cigar smoke following in his wake. He slammed the day's newspaper on the table and exclaimed: 'Have you seen this?!? Pages two and five are completely missing. Our best stories have vanished. Our best advertisers have had their expensive advertisements erased. Who is responsible?' As might be guessed, there was no conversation about strategy that day. Attention shifted immediately to operational concerns. The next time a strategy meeting was called, people winced and came prepared to talk about operations. It does not take such a radical departure from the agenda to undercut strategic conversations. We have seen situations where an innocuous discussion about choosing a secretary, buying a new coffee machine or fixing a doorbell has had the same effect.

It is theoretically possible, of course, for an intensely knowledge-oriented company that is organized in a highly non-hierarchical manner to be able to blur the lines between strategic and operational conversations. But since most companies are still struggling with more rudimentary forms of decentralization, empowerment and shared decision-making, the exceptions to this rule are hardly worth noting.

Remove time pressure

Time is a scarce commodity in modern business and most managers typically seek a fast resolution to any discussion. Action is wanted, not words. If it were possible, some managers might prefer to eliminate conversation entirely, relying on the fewest possible words to communicate the desired results. Speed and efficiency are the watchwords of the operational environment and are in fact the goal of most operational conversations and language.

Strategy works to a different clock. Prematurely closing off strategic conversations only leads to poorer strategies and less successful operations. Ideally, strategic conversations have no 'beginning' or 'end'. The task of inventing the future of a company is ongoing, and cannot be moulded to artificial deadlines. There is no simple rule to determine how much time is too much or too little.

The essential question, therefore, is how to use 'well' the time that is devoted to strategic conversations. The four rules above serve only as a starting point. Each company must invent its own best method of managing its strategic conversations.

THE STRATEGY OF CONVERSATIONS

The development and diffusion of knowledge in a modern company are all about the development and diffusion of language. And the development and diffusion of language are all about the art of conversation. A word or phrase may embody a marvellous idea but it cannot really be called 'language' until it is successfully used in conversation with others.

The management of conversation needs to be a central concern of every manager who wishes to succeed in a knowledge-intensive age. The process through which we both create new meaning and share meaning and frames of reference in language is at the heart of knowledge development in organizations. It is a powerful concept within the domain of corporate epistemology. It is about the future of management.

Since the successful management of conversations still rests in the future for most companies, an interesting circularity arises: one of the first strategic conversations upon which a company must embark is how to engage in strategic conversations. Without this knowledge and a language to diffuse it, there can be no progress. There is no logical way out of this loop, one must simply start talking about it – and talk about it as if the future depended on it. It does.

SUMMARY

Language is the currency of knowledge and the time has come to put 'managing business conversations' near the top of the agenda. A distinction should be made between operating conversations (about exploiting knowledge gained in the past and present) and strategic conversations (creating new knowledge). Managers are instinctively better at the former. At a time when strategic shelf lives are getting shorter, though, not to address the latter will be costly. There are four basic rules. Focus on building 'shared meaning', not on who is right (strategic conversations should be a dialogue for understanding). Do not try to take control – current organizational authority is not relevant. Do not mix the two types of conversation. Remove time pressures and remember that strategy works to a different clock than operational discussions.

All this mostly rests in the future so there is an important circularity for companies. One of the first strategic conversations they will need to have is how to engage in strategic conversations.

SUGGESTED FURTHER READING

Roos, J. and von Krogh, G. (1995) *Organizational Epistemology*. London: Macmillan.
Roos, J. and von Krogh, G. (1996) *Managing Knowledge: Perspectives on Co-operation and Competition*. London: Sage.

13
The Learning Organization

D. J. Skyrme and D. M. Amidon*

The 'learning organization' is one of those terms that has gained in acceptance over the last few years, especially in Europe. Our research found significant overlap and correlation between knowledge-based companies and the 'learning organization'. Some interviewees saw one as part of the other (but a different one depending on where they were coming from!), some as related but different. Thus to Glaxo Wellcome and Anglian Water, their main initiative was a learning organization initiative from which knowledge management has evolved as a key component. On the other hand, Monsanto and CIBC each had knowledge as a part of a balanced triumvirate of initiatives, while Skandia drive management through intellectual capital and see learning as a vital support. Whatever your perspective, though, our research found that applying the concepts and principles of the 'learning organization' is an important ingredient of any 'rounded' knowledge management programme.

What is a learning organization? There are almost as many definitions as there are of culture. Some of those that resonated with the views of our interviewees are the following:

> The essence of organizational learning is the organization's ability to use the amazing mental capacity of all its members to create the kind of processes that will improve its own learning capacity. (Nancy Dixon, 1994)

> A Learning Company is an organization that facilitates the learning of all its members and continually transforms itself. (Pedler et al., 1991)

> Organizational learning occurs through shared insights, knowledge and mental models . . . and builds on past knowledge and experience – that is, on memory. (Stata, 1989)

> Organizations where people continually expand their capacity to create the results they truly desire, where new and expansive patterns of thinking are nurtured, where collective aspiration is set free, and where people are continually learning to learn together. (Senge, 1990)

* Reproduced from *Creating the knowledge – Based Business* by Debra M. Amidon and David J. Skyrme, © Business Intelligence, Third Floor, 22–24 Worple Road, Wimbledon, London, SW19 4DD, www.business-intelligence.co.uk.

A learning organization is an organization skilled at creating, acquiring and transferring knowledge, and at modifying its behaviour to reflect new knowledge and insights. (Garvin, 1993)

One of the problems identified by several respondents is that the 'learning organization' label has been misappropriated in several quarters. Often, it is identified with individual learning and even then applied to conventional training. Michael McMaster, a management consultant, says that use of the term implies that many organizations may be deemed by default to be 'not learning', which is patently not true. The issues, he says, are to improve the capacity to learn, and to apply the learning. The real challenge is to move these up from the individual to the organization as a whole.

David Garvin, a professor at Harvard Business School, has suggested five building blocks of a learning organization:

1 systematic problem solving;
2 experimentation with new approaches;
3 learning from own experience and past history;
4 learning from the experience and best practices of others (e.g. in benchmarking);
5 transferring knowledge quickly and efficiently.

He thus starts drawing a correlation with factors we identify as key to knowledge management. In the methods to improve the learning experience and transfer of knowledge (Table 13.1) he gives several examples [. . .]

TABLE 13.1 *Methods to improve organizational learning*

Aspect of learning	Methods and tools
Learning from experience	Processes that force managers to review success and failure, e.g.
	Boeing's lessons from developing the 727/747 and applying them to the 767
	Jamborees (events, exhibitions) where examples of best practice are displayed
	Post-appraisal unit to review lessons of a completed project e.g. BP
	Lessons learned database
Learning from others	Benchmarking as a disciplined process
	Customer visits to see product in action
	Contextual enquiry (ethnography)
	First delivery teams
Tools for transferring knowledge	Written reports
	Videos
	Presentations
	Site visits and tours
	Job rotation
	Education and training linked implementation

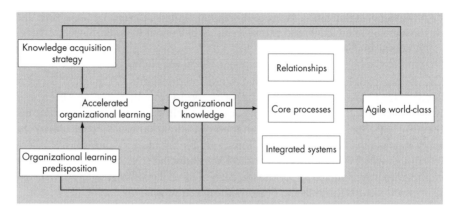

FIGURE 13.1 *Relationship of knowledge and organizational learning (Roth et al., 1994)*

Another group that has drawn the links between organizational learning and knowledge is Roth and colleagues at North Carolina (Roth et al., 1994). They portray learning capabilities as complementing rapid acquisition and deployment of knowledge to create world-class operations (Figure 13.1).

They argue that organizations need to understand how core knowledge drives their business – its philosophy, systems, approaches to problem solving and decision making – and how to develop the skills to acquire, organize, codify and deploy knowledge. They offer seven key principles:

1   A *learning philosophy* contributes to the development of knowledge around the organization.
2   Improved *rates of learning* create more choices and opportunities; they need boundary spanning.
3   Adoption of '*stretch goals*'.
4   '*Safe-failing*', i.e. providing opportunities that encourage risk taking, but where damage from risk [is minimal] (see for example the use of simulation and games).
5   Systems for encouraging *knowledge and learning*.
6   Stimulating core *knowledge processes*.
7   Systems that *cross functional boundaries* e.g. teams and networks.

Fundamental to the new perspective is viewing products and processes in terms of their information, expertise and knowledge.

Another useful model is also provided by Nevis, DiBella and Gould, who likewise demonstrate the links between the learning organization and knowledge, this time in a 'systems model' (Figure 13.2).

Within the learning system, knowledge is processed through three stages. The diagram shows what 'facilitating factors' support the core knowledge processes of acquisition, dissemination and use. The specific 10 factors they

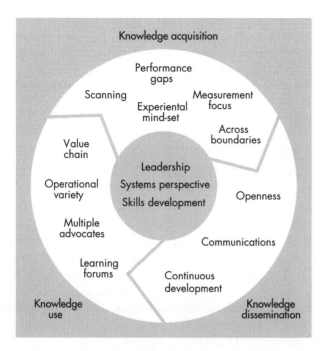

FIGURE 13.2 *Systems model linking knowledge and learning (adapted from 'Understanding organizations as a learning system', Nevis, DiBella and Gould, Sloan Management Review, Winter 1993)*

listed fall neatly into the groups covered in this report and covered by architectural models and frameworks such as KMAT and EMSA [. . .], thus:

- *Measurement* – performance gaps, measurement focus;
- *Processes* – scanning, operational variety;
- *Leadership* – involved leadership, multiple advocacy, continuous education, systems perspective;
- *Culture* – openness, experiential mind-set.

Throughout our research we found such perspectives being reinforced. Worthy of comment here are the two factors listed under process, which in our research were not as evident as perhaps they should be.

The first factor requiring more attention is sensing. The effective knowledge-based (and learning) organization is one that senses and adapts to changes in its environment. The 'systems model' portrayed here emphasizes the boundary with vital external knowledge, such as market and customer knowledge. This needs continuous scanning, and implies developing good market and competitor intelligence systems, as well as various interfaces with the external environment such as Steelcase's customer knowledge channel. Our sense is that many knowledge management programmes could benefit from a stronger orientation to developing these systematic sensing mechanisms.

The second factor is operational variety. The organization that can respond better to change will need a greater diversity of responses. The explicit documentation of core business processes is often focused on the 'standard' process rather than the exceptions. This is where human knowledge and skill must supplement standard processes. A knowledge base should therefore capture this variety in its various 'cases'. At CIGNA additional knowledge and pointers to knowledge were encapsulated in the underwriter's workstation. The pitfall that knowledge managers should be wary of is that through the process of systematization of knowledge, in the interests of efficiency and standardization of formats, variety becomes diminished.

FIVE DISCIPLINES

It is appropriate here to review the role of Senge's five disciplines in knowledge management terms. Senge and colleagues' book *The Fifth Discipline Fieldbook* was heavily cited by our knowledge practitioners. Although the focus of this book is on learning, explicit links are made to knowledge, for example: 'Learning in organizations means the continuous testing of experience, and the transformation of that experience into knowledge – accessible to the whole organization, and relevant to its core purpose.'

The authors then pose these four questions:

1 Do you continually test your experiences?
2 Are you producing knowledge?
3 Is the knowledge shared?
4 Is the learning relevant?

In several places in the book knowledge is referred to as the 'capacity for effective action', in effect a collective capability developed through learning. But what of the five disciplines, where knowledge is rarely mentioned? Our views of how they relate to knowledge skills are shown in Table 13.2.

There is thus significant correspondence between some of Senge's learning disciplines and those of knowledge processes described by Nonaka and Takeuchi.

We found organizations like Glaxo Wellcome and Monsanto applying many of Senge's techniques in the context of their learning organization and knowledge programmes. Although our research shows growing awareness of the links between learning and knowledge, we suspect that most knowledge management programmes have yet to make these links explicit at the operational or technique level as implied by Table 13.2.

TABLE 13.2 *Relationship of Senge's five disciplines to knowledge*

Discipline	Contribution to knowledge management
Systems thinking – structures, relatedness, systemic (holistic perspectives); the specific methods of systems dynamics.	This discipline is about widening and deepening knowledge: 'seeking out interrelationships never discussed (or noticed) before'. Thus, systems dynamics helps people gain insights into what is often counter-intuitive behaviour of a system (such as a supply chain). It's like Garvin's know-why knowledge.
Personal mastery – developing greater understanding of personal goals and today's reality, values and reality, interdependence with others.	This is self-knowledge. It is about making sense of your own position, by being more explicit. It is about articulating your knowledge in ways that are helpful to others.
Mental models – the models in your mind that shape actions and decisions. Two key tools are reflection and inquiry. Argyris and Schon's (1974) 'ladder of inference' and action science are described, as is 'the left hand column' (Beers, 1995). The most difficult discipline but the one with the greatest leverage, according to Senge.	Here the book makes an explicit link to knowledge. Mental models are 'the tacit knowledge in personal cognitive maps'. The 'left hand column' is 'what I'm thinking' (vs the right hand column: 'what is said'). The processes of enquiry and reflection aid the surfacing [of] tacit knowledge, making tacit knowledge explicit. This correlates with Nonaka and Takeuchi's 'knowledge spiral'.
Shared vision – this is the bringing together in shared processes of a collective vision – co-creating the future: 'bringing together multiple visions in an organic interdependent whole'. Dialogue is an important tool. The book described a shared vision as a tacit shared sense of purpose.	This is very much about knowledge building through knowledge sharing. It is moving personal knowledge into team knowledge and ultimately organizational knowledge. It requires a common language so that diverse perspectives can contribute to the overall whole and sense of purpose.
Team learning – developing a collective understanding and capability, alignment so that the team acts as a whole. Unity since each member 'knows each other's hearts and minds'. Dialogue and skilful discussion are its two key methods.	This represents two aspects – the processes of tacit to explicit and vice versa, and the diffusion of individual knowledge to collective knowledge. It relates mostly to Nonaka's processes of socialization, though to some extent externalization.

LESSONS LEARNED

An important explicit link between organizational learning and knowledge we encountered several times during our research was that of capturing 'lessons learned' knowledge. As shown in Figure 13.1, a key aspect is to accelerate organizational learning. It is essential to expedite the process whereby one part of the organization, when it learns something of value, then makes this knowledge widely available.

Project assignments at several of the major management consultancies are not considered complete until participants have reflected on the key lessons and these have been elicited and added to their knowledge base. One difficulty reported frequently is how to get the stories and also how to portray them honestly. For example, Ernst and Young in describing Mobil's experience, tells of the difficulties of 'capturing the truth', since on the one hand they wanted to avoid 'bragging' and on the other 'there was an aversion to being associated with a 'failure'of any kind'. In Mobil's case the lessons were developed in a shared workshop setting, that brought participants from several perspectives together (Argyris, 1990).

Garvin (1996) sets forth five conditions that should be present for organizations to learn from their past experience:

1   Ensure that the learning is purposeful.
2   Set aside the time to conduct these activities.
3   Cultivate a culture that encourages self-assessment and critical thinking.
4   Create performance measurement and evaluation systems that recognize this and do not penalize employees for mistakes.
5   Build mechanisms to convert learning into policy and practice.

He outlines 'lessons learned' approaches that operate at several levels – individual, project team and organization. They include the debriefing of skilled performers, post-project reviews and case studies. He cites the US Army Center for Lessons Learned as a good example of capturing and applying lessons learned at the organizational level.

CASELET – US ARMY

The 'lessons learned' approach

In the US Army no action or project is considered complete until it has been systematically reviewed. This 'learning after doing' philosophy started around 1985 and has now become established as an integral part of day to day activity in every unit. It is seen as part of a learning organization system that equips the US Army for the constantly changing environment and battle scenarios of the twenty-first century. Known as AAR (After Action Review), its key features are:

- *Immediacy* – it starts as soon as possible after the activity; this may be at the end of the day in a battle situation.
- *All key people participate* – those in the front line as well as commanding officers.
- *It is done in a climate of openness* – full and frank discussion of experiences is encouraged (personal comments about individuals, while recorded in the experiences, do not go into an individual's personal record).
- *A set procedure is followed*, so that the process is easily remembered and reproducible.
- *It is recorded*, again in a predetermined format, so that lessons from different theatres of activity can be compared.

What happened, what was supposed to happen, what went wrong, how to reinforce success, and recommendations for fixing problems are all part of the review. Time is rigorously allocated as follows: 25 per cent for what happened; 25 per cent for why it happened and 50 per cent for what to do about it. This is deliberate, since the natural tendency is to jump straight into diagnosis and solutions without reviewing the past, which accounts for half the time in the AAR process.

REFERENCES

Argyris, C. (1990) *Overcoming Organizational Defenses.* Allyn and Bacon.

Argyris, C. and Scho, D. (1974) *Theory in Practice.* Jossey Bass.

Beers, M. C. (1995) *Knowledge Transfer at Mobil: Using Success Stories for Organizational Learning.* Ernst and Young Field Profile (May).

Dixon, N. (1994) *The Organizational Learning Cycle.* McGraw-Hill.

Garvin, D. A. (1993) 'Building a learning organization', *Harvard Business Review,* July–Aug.: 78–88.

Garvin, D. A. (1996) 'Learning from experience', paper presented at *Knowledge Management 96* Conference, Business Intelligence (December).

Pedler, M., Burgoyne, J. and Boydell, T. (1991) *The Learning Company: A Strategy for Sustainable Development.* McGraw-Hill.

Roth, A.V., Marucheck, A.S., Kemp, A. and Trimble, D. (1994) 'Knowledge factory for accelerated learning processes', *Planning Review,* 22 (3) May/June: 26–33.

Senge, P. (1990) *The Fifth Discipline: the Art and Practice of the Learning Organization.* Doubleday.

Senge, P., Kleiner, A., Roberts, C., Ross, R. and Smith, B. (1994) *The Fifth Discipline Fieldbook.* Doubleday.

Stata, R. (1989) 'Organizational learning: the key to management innovation', *Sloan Management Review,* Spring: 63–73.

14

Intel Corporation (UK) Ltd: 10 Critical Success Factors for Notes Adoption

*Dene Isherwood**

BACKGROUND

In 1993, microprocessor manufacturer Intel reported net revenues of $5.8 billion, had 26,000 employees worldwide and was one of the world's fastest growing companies. Yet Intel felt that however well it was doing, it should do better.

As part of its efforts to retain competitive advantage, the company introduced an efficiency improvement programme in its sales and marketing operations. One aim of the programme, called 'Intelligence', was to reduce the existing proliferation of approaches to information technology, such as the range of software packages and information formats. The overriding purpose was to make it possible to share information around the organization.

Dene Isherwood, European Programme Manager at Intel at the time, explains the problem: 'Intel is proud of the proportion of income it pumps back into the company, particularly in research and development and capital spending. This has been particularly true in our factories and our engineering offices. Yet we have made little use of personal computers in the business. Those employees who had them found it hard to share information, because their colleagues were often using different applications software.'

COMPUTER-SUPPORTED COLLABORATION

Intel operates in a business environment where its operations are global and where customer service is a key issue. 'We needed to get rid of the "I'll get back to you" response to customers,' says Mr Isherwood. 'In 1993, Intel decided to become a "just in time" business, through the use of computer-supported collaboration.'

* Reprinted from Lloyd, P. and Whitehead, R. (eds) *Transforming Organizations through Groupware*, © Springer-Verlag London Limited, 1996.

The company saw certain issues as being fundamental to the successful implementation of a collaborative working strategy.

- The processing power of its computers had to be sufficient to take advantage of new developments, such as sending video clips over networks. It also had to provide the sort of response times that people had become used to with their personal and home computers.
- The system had to cater for mobile workers, both those travelling with laptop or notebook computers and those who worked at home using desktop computers.
- The system had to be available to everyone who wanted to be part of it. Mr Isherwood felt that such a system could only be useful if 100% of a group that needed it had it.

THE LOTUS NOTES SOLUTION

The company decided to use Lotus Notes and developed a full range of applications within the USA; later introducing it across Europe. Intel set up pilot projects to test the value of Notes in a variety of business environments, including sales, marketing, factory planning and information systems.

Discussion databases, which allow wide participation in discussions on projects, proved to be particularly successful. The Northern Europe management team, for example, can work closely together through Lotus Notes, despite being based in different countries. 'These databases are successful,' says Mr Isherwood, 'wherever there is a business need for cross-company discussion.'

Lotus Notes has many other uses within the organization:

- It has been especially successful in problem tracking at the company help desk.
- It has also allowed customer support staff to respond immediately to queries, finding out whether a problem has occurred before and getting problems fixed quickly.
- The pan-European market development team, which keeps in touch and reports through a Notes database, has become a keen user of the system. So, too, has a team of five sales people based in the Milan office.

The information systems (IS) team itself uses Lotus Notes for keeping track of the complex training programmes developed for users. By carrying this database on their laptop computers, team members can answer users' queries about their individual programs at any time. The IS team has also found it useful to have a directory of users within Lotus Notes, giving name, address, phone and fax number, for easy identification.

Dene Isherwood points out that the value of Lotus Notes as a reference library is often overlooked. In Intel, users can access technical information, and also product updates, customer information and competitive information. The diverse and often confidential information available within these databases calls for extensive use of Notes's security features, allowing different users access at various levels.

As well as putting in their own information, users can view data fed from external services into Lotus Notes. Intel also uses Lotus Notes to broadcast large amounts of internal information across the organization. These can be presentations or files with video clips inserted, for example.

Because some users work from home or in hotels, it is not always convenient for them to download large files of data through modems. To address this problem, Intel makes use of the Notes's File Transfer Databases feature. This allows a user to send out a mail to other users, telling them a file is available. Interested parties can then download the file to their machines when they have a high-speed link available.

IMPLEMENTATION

There are now Lotus Notes servers in every main Intel sales office, each containing current versions of the appropriate databases. Desktop personal computers on networks are linked directly with the Lotus Notes servers in each office.

Automatically scheduled replication of the databases across the world is carried out every two hours, using Intel's local and wide area networks. Information inputted in the European headquarters in Munich takes just six hours to filter around Europe and eight hours to reach the US and Japanese offices.

Laptop and notebook computer users maintain replicated databases on their personal computers and initiate the replication procedure themselves. 'We needed to persuade these users to do updates regularly,' says Dene Isherwood. 'It's like brushing your teeth – do it once in the morning and once at night. If you leave it much longer than that the information to be transferred builds up rapidly.'

By the end of 1993, there were 5,000 Lotus Notes users in the company, roughly a fifth of its employees. A corporate team of 10 people provides them with worldwide support. This team also administers the addition of users to the system and validates the use of software and hardware within the company. Field and strategic intelligence groups, comprising about 54 people worldwide, support the user applications. Users in Europe found that there were many ways in which they needed the applications to be customized because Intel developed its first applications in the USA.

MAXIMIZING VALUE

According to Dene Isherwood the successful take-up of Lotus Notes can be attributed to a number of reasons. First was that senior business managers drove the implementation top-down, rather than from the information systems department.

Secondly, the programme met with the warmest welcome in groups where people were not only enthusiastic about the new technology, but also had a genuine business need for using it.

The third reason for Notes's success was that the company provided thorough and appropriate training in the use of computer technology. This ensured that staff understood their working environment and could maximize their value from it. Dene Isherwood emphasizes that, for Intel, training was crucial. 'Lotus Notes isn't difficult,' he says, 'but it builds on a great deal of knowledge that needs to be acquired first.'

After a false start using just internal trainers, the company started again with a programme developed with the help of consultants and Lotus Development itself. Each member of staff was first given three months to build a thorough understanding of his or her personal computer, starting with finding the way around the keyboard and working through the elements of Lotus's SmartSuite bundle of desktop applications software.

Once ready for Lotus Notes training, each user attended a course tailored to his or her job function. The length of the course ranged from one to three-and-a-half days, depending on the mixture of training required. Professional trainers gave the courses, with Intel system staff in attendance.

The Notes team ran courses in Paris, Munich and Swindon, training over 300 people in the first quarter of 1993. Fewer than 10 required additional training.

THE WISDOM OF HINDSIGHT

Two years later, by which time Intel's revenues had reached $11.5 billion, Dene Isherwood looked back on the sales and marketing 'Intelligence' programme, and on the use of Lotus Notes throughout Intel generally. He discussed his experiences and observations at a meeting of the 'Trading Post' groupware forum, in London, in May 1995. What follows is a summary of what he said, set out in the form of a scorecard.

(To use the scorecard, one should first select the relevant answer for each of the ten questions set out below. Add up the scores indicated – the weightings of which were decided by the members of the March 1995 forum – to produce an overall total. From that, one can see which of the four bands it falls into. The resulting advice is given entirely tongue in cheek – Editors.)

TEN CRITICAL SUCCESS FACTORS

Dene Isherwood said that, in his mind, 10 factors are critical to the successful adoption of groupware throughout any enterprise.

1 **Business pressure**. How much of a competitive threat exists against your company?

- Acknowledged serious threat – score 10
- Acknowledged threat – score 5
- No perceived threat – score 0

Many people in strong, successful companies have never known failure. Everything they do 'turns to gold'. If someone proposes something revolutionary, which challenges the way they are doing things, they see no reason to change. They tend to argue that if they change anything, they are likely to kill the goose that lays the golden eggs.

A better approach, feels Dene Isherwood, is to ask, 'How is your company differentiating itself in the marketplace?' It might not be (or feel) under competitive threat, but it might want to differentiate its products or services from a competitor's. One way to achieve this is by moving information around faster and by sharing it out to customers. 'Groupware obviously helps with this. On the other hand, if it's not necessary to your business, then you're not going to get very far with it.'

2 **Long-term thinking**. Over what timescale do you normally plan your work?

- Two years – score 9
- One year – score 6
- Six months – score 3
- Less than six months – score 0

'Project managing a specific groupware project is a recipe for disaster, because you're dealing with a timescale of typically a week or a month. The people who are power-playing around you are basically setting things in motion and putting stakes in the ground well in advance. They can put insurmountable obstacles in your way, which you don't even see until you walk straight into them.

'A long-term vision as to where one is going and how one is going to get there is essential if one is going to be successful with groupware. Groupware cannot be introduced in six months or less, unless your company is just five people strong. And even then two will want to leave.'

3 **Seniority**. How senior are you in your organization?

- Managing director/chief executive, IT director/CIO – score 8

- One level down – score 6
- Two levels down – score 4
- Three levels down – score 2
- Four levels down – score 1
- More than four levels down – score 0

'Groupware projects in companies tend to start small; consequently, relatively junior staff are held responsible. This is not a recipe for success. Senior staff should be actively involved in all aspects of groupware implementation planning, since the business impact of this blend of technologies is far greater than the technical effort required.

'The more political power the individual has, the greater chance of success there is. In particular, the managing directors of small companies seem to have the highest chance of success.'

4 **Business champion**. Are you, or have you identified, a senior business champion for the Notes approach? Does he or she use Notes?

- Yes, and is on the board – score 8
- Yes, and is a senior manager – score 4
- No – score 0

'If the company champion for groupware sits in the IT function, then there is a very strong need for a senior business person to take a strong and active interest in the implementation projects and process. Without a business-oriented champion, groupware will be relegated to the "nice to haves" and will not tackle the core business problems of the enterprise.

'The problem with core business problems is that they need to be well defined and this cannot easily be done by people with little business experience.'

5 **Business process change**. How willing is your organization to undergo significant business process change?

- Always changing business processes – score 6
- Sometimes changes business processes – score 3
- Never changes business processes – score 0

'If the business thinks that it is always getting things right, then it will not easily consider making business process changes. But unless you change some of the business processes, you are not going to get much reward for all your effort. You need to look for examples of previous projects that have tried to change the way parts of the enterprise functions. Did these succeed?'

6 **Influence**. How much influence (over people, budget, etc.) do you have within IT applications development?

- Full control of all IT application development – score 5
- Partial control – score 3
- No control – score 0

'If you control the applications development environment and you are a Notes champion, your chances of success are greatly enhanced. If you don't control the application development environment, make sure you positively influence the person who does.'

7   **Technical capability**. Has your organization experience of supporting any large scale client/server system or infrastructure?

- Much experience (for example, in client/server email) – score 5
- Limited experience – score 2
- No experience – score 0

'The technical capability that exists within a typical IT support department is very important. Groupware depends on Intel-based or Apple personal computers being around in large quantities. If you haven't already built a large scale client/server system, you're going to have to spend two or three years building that up in most large companies.

'You need to be able to support this diverse personal computer environment across your entire company. If you can't do that across the whole infrastructure, then you can't bring up the groupware product because it needs everyone communicating to function fully.'

8   **Business trade-off**. Are your business users prepared to put up with second best in return for a very fast IT response to today's problems?

- Yes, most of the time – score 3
- Yes, some of the time – score 1
- No – score 0

'The business is used to IT projects taking six to nine months, with three to six people involved. And that's on little projects. The big projects would require 10 to 12 people for, perhaps, four years!

'With Notes you can go in and say to them, "Look again at your requirements. Don't give me all the bells and whistles, just what do you really need to do. Give me that brief and I'll go away and do it, and I'll do it in a week." They don't believe you and often they are not prepared to accept second best. They want the bells and whistles; they want the traffic lights in the bottom right hand corner of the screen – going red, red–yellow, green, yellow and then red – rather than some information presented in a relatively simple manner.

'If your business and your IT developers are not prepared to sacrifice Graphical User Interface (GUI) appeal for speed of development, then you're in trouble.'

9   **Office politics**. How do you rate yourself in handling office politics?

- High – score 2
- Medium – score 1
- Low – score 0

'When people actually look out for themselves in companies, they don't do what's right for the companies, they do what's right for them. Some senior managers seem to acknowledge this fact and go along with it as well. You have to have a little bit of trust in the system, that it tends to self correct, but you can end up the victim. So you have to be astute in handling this, and if you are not very good at this then implementing any enterprise-wide programme will be difficult for you. You must always search for the "win–win" solution, although sometimes there will be losers.'

10 **Notes expertise**. How much Notes expertise are you able to muster?

- Plenty of expertise available – score 2
- Some expertise available – score 1
- No expertise readily available – score 0

'If you can't get hold of this you are pretty well sunk. You can always buy it in, but how deep are your pockets? Do you have people in IT that can be trained up rapidly in this environment? It doesn't take a long time to take effect. If you are in charge of the IT development department, you can send 30% of your developers off on a course. They can pick it up within weeks.

'If you're not in charge, then it is much more of a problematical issue. You are going to have to buy in contractors and the contractors are going to have to learn your business processes. They then leave, which is not good. So, try to muster as much Notes expertise as you can.'

Scoring

Can you succeed?

- Total score of 40+ – Yes, go full steam ahead. Work to score 100% (58 points).
- Total score of 30+ – Tread with extreme caution on exposed areas.
- Total score of 20+ – Increase score to 50% (29 points) before starting seriously.
- Total score below 20 – Leave the company or move on to another task.

15

Organizing in the Knowledge Age: Anticipating the Cellular Form

Raymond E. Miles, Charles C. Snow, John A. Mathews, Grant Miles and Henry J. Coleman, Jr*

Since the Industrial Revolution, the United States economy has moved through the machine age into the information age and now stands at the threshold of the knowledge age. The locus of organizational exemplars has shifted from capital-intensive industries, such as steel and automobiles, to information-intensive industries, such as financial services and logistics, and now toward innovation-driven industries, such as computer software and biotechnology, where competitive advantage lies mostly in the effective use of human resources.

This evolution has been simultaneously powered and facilitated by the invention of a succession of new organizational forms – new approaches to accumulating and applying know-how to the key resources of the day. The contribution of each new form has been to allow firms to use their expanding know-how to adapt to market opportunities and demands, first for standardized goods and services, then to increasing levels of product and service customization, and presently toward the expectation of continuous innovation. Certain trends visible in the coevolution of markets and organizations make it possible to predict the shape and operation of the twenty-first-century organization. A number of pioneering firms are already demonstrating the organizational characteristics suggested by those trends, especially a growing reliance on entrepreneurship, self-organization, and member ownership of firm assets and resources.

THE EVOLUTION OF ORGANIZATIONAL FORMS

An organizational form is an overall logic shaping a firm's strategy, structure and management processes into an effective whole. In each historical era,

* Reprinted from *Academy of Management Executive*, Vol. 11, No. 4, © Academy of Management Executive.

market forces *pull* forth new organizational forms as managers seek new ways of arranging assets and resources to produce the products and services that customers want and expect. At the same time, some companies accumulate more know-how than their present operating logic allows them to utilize. Those excess capabilities *push* managers to experiment with new organizational arrangements that, in turn, stimulate the search for new markets and/or new products or services. The continuing interaction of these push–pull forces has been visible in the major eras that have characterized the US economy over the past hundred-plus years (see Table 15.1).

TABLE 15.1 *Organizational evolution*

Historical era	Standardization	Customization	Innovation
Organizational form	Hierarchy	Network	Cell
Key asset	Capital goods	Information	Knowledge
Influential manager	Chief operating Officer	Chief Information Officer	Chief knowledge Officer
Key capability	Specialization and segmentation	Flexibility and responsiveness	Design creativity

Era of standardization

The era of standardization saw hierarchical forms of organization used to apply know-how primarily to the use of such physical assets as raw materials, capital equipment, and plant facilities. In the late nineteenth and early twentieth centuries, the pioneering companies of that time learned to efficiently mass produce standardized products (e.g. steel and automobiles) and services (e.g. transportation and communications).[1] The period's dominant organizational form, the functional organization, used a centrally co-ordinated, vertically integrated structure to manage employees in highly specialized jobs. By focusing on limited product and service lines, firms moved down the learning curve, using their accumulating know-how to produce time and cost reductions that constantly added value to employed resources and allowed the United States to mass produce its way to a position of global economic power.

Early customization

As illustrated in Figure 15.1, the era of customization actually began during the earlier period of standardized production. That is, by the middle of the twentieth century (and even before in industries such as automotive and retailing), markets had generally become more demanding, and some firms had accumulated know-how that could not be fully utilized in the production of their existing goods and services. Thus, markets pulled companies to diversify their offerings, and their underutilized know-how and resources pushed them toward new markets where expansion was possible.[2] Those forces coalesced in the invention of a new organizational form, the divisional,

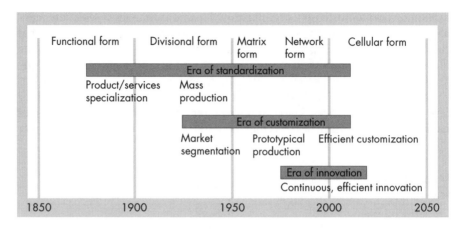

FIGURE 15.1 *Coevolution of economic era and organizational form*

which allowed companies to serve related markets with differentiated goods and services. In the divisional form, know-how that accumulated in one market could be utilized by a newly created, semi-autonomous division to provide products or services to different but related markets. Corporate-level executives sought new market opportunities for the creation of new divisions and used the current revenue streams to invest know-how and resources in these new arenas. Although each division typically produced a standard product (e.g. autos at General Motors), the divisional form enabled companies to achieve limited amounts of customization (market segmentation).

The movement from standardization to customization continued into the late 1960s and 1970s, as firms adopted mixed organizational forms, such as the matrix, that allowed a dual focus on both stable and emerging market segments and clients.[3] For example, by employing a matrix organization, an aerospace firm such as TRW could produce differentiated but standard products for the civilian and military markets in one or more divisions, while simultaneously transferring some resources from those units into project groups that designed and built prototypical products for space exploration. The matrix organization provided companies with a more finely grained mechanism for exploiting their know-how across a wider range of both standardized and customized products and services.

Full, efficient customization

By the 1980s, the pull toward customization intensified as a rapidly growing number of firms around the world used their know-how to enter an increasingly deregulated global marketplace.[4] New entrants competed for customer attention with lower prices, improved quality and distribution, and seemingly endless choices among styles and models. However, many existing companies initially found it difficult to unleash their competencies and know-how to meet the new market opportunities and pressures. Divisional and matrix organizations, designed for less challenging and turbulent markets, were better suited to internal co-ordination needs than to rapid forays into new markets.

Once again, a new organizational form was needed in order to help firms use and extend their capabilities. The model that evolved from the late 1970s into the 1990s was the network organization.[5] The key contribution of the network form was not just its ability to respond rapidly to market demands for differentiated products and services, but to do so efficiently by extending the chain, from raw materials, to parts and component production, to manufacture and assembly, to distribution and final sale. In their search for flexibility and responsiveness, most traditional companies began by downsizing and then refocusing on those areas where their assets and know-how added the greatest economic value. As companies downsized and reengineered, they began to outsource non-core operations to upstream and downstream partner firms whose capabilities complemented their own. As multiform networks proliferated, numerous potential partners around the world began to occupy points along industry value chains, offering increased overall flexibility and therefore more opportunities for customization. The expanded number of competent firms kept prices in check, improved product and service quality, and pressured all firms to adopt better information and production technologies.

Most importantly from an organizational point of view, companies began to realize that success in the age of efficient customization again demanded a higher level of know-how and resource utilization than existing internal management processes allowed. Increasingly, firms turned to network structures in which empowered teams managed not only their internal work processes, but also external relationships with upstream and downstream partners. In many networks of the 1990s, it became difficult to determine where one organization ended and another began, as cross-firm teams resolved interface issues, representatives of important customers were invited to participate in new product development processes, and suppliers were given access to large firms' scheduling and accounting processes through electronic data interchange systems.

In little more than a century, the pull of market forces and the push of underutilized company know-how carried the US economy through the era of mass standardization into the era of efficient customization. Throughout this period, firms faced increasingly complex market and technological environments. In response, firms themselves became more complex, by creating new organizational means of adding economic value.

Functional firms, as shown in Table 15.2, primarily utilized increased operating know-how to add economic value, with only top managers providing co-ordination and entrepreneurial direction. The divisional form utilized operating knowledge and also developed and applied knowledge of how to invest money, people, and systems in related markets – so-called diversification know-how. In the process, divisional firms brought not only corporate managers, but an expanding group of divisional managers, into organizational and business decision processes.

TABLE 15.2 *Location of managerial know-how in alternative organizational forms*

	Operational know-how	Investment know-how	Adaptation know-how
Functional	Top, middle, lower	Top	Top
Divisional	Top, middle, lower	Top, middle	Top
Matrix	Top, middle, lower	Top, middle	Top, middle
Network	Top, middle, lower	Top, middle	Top, middle, lower
Cellular	Top, middle, lower	Top, middle, lower	Top, middle, lower

Matrix organizations were designed to add value not only through the application of operating and investment know-how, but also through their adaptation capabilities – the frequent refocusing of underutilized assets on the needs of temporary projects and new market opportunities. In those organizations, top managers, division managers, and project managers were all involved in entrepreneurial and organizational decisions.

The network form allowed value to be added across as well as within firms along the value chain, combining the operational, investment, and adaptation know-how of individual firms and achieving higher levels of overall utilization through their freedom to link rapidly with numerous upstream and downstream partners. The network organization's dependence on decision-making teams, both within and across firms, dramatically increased involvement in organizational and entrepreneurial decisions in all firms at all levels.

In sum, across this entire period of organizational evolution, certain trends are clearly evident. First, as each new organizational form was created, it brought an expectation that more and more organization members would develop the ability to self-organize around operational, market, and partnering tasks. Second, each new form increased the proportion of members who were expected to perform entrepreneurial tasks – identifying customer needs and then finding and focusing resources on them. Third, each new organizational form increased member opportunities to experience psychological ownership of particular clients, markets, customized products and services, and so on. Also, because performance measurement now occurred at more points and organizational levels, the opportunity for reward systems to promote financial ownership increased, mostly in the form of bonuses and stock-purchase plans. These key trends, we believe, can be used to forecast the main characteristics of twenty-first-century organizational forms.

THE TWENTY-FIRST CENTURY: ERA OF INNOVATION

In tomorrow's business world, some markets will still be supplied with standard products and services, while other markets will demand large amounts of customization. However, the continued pull of market forces, and the push of ever-increasing know-how honed through network partnering, is already moving some industries and companies toward what amounts to a continuous process of innovation. Beyond the customization of existing designs, product and service invention is becoming the centerpiece of value-adding activity in an increasing number of firms. So-called knowledge businesses – such as design, including software design, health care, and consulting – not only feed the process of innovation but feed upon it in a continuous cycle that creates more, and more complex, markets and environments.[6] Indeed, for companies in such businesses, both by choice and by the consequences of their choices, organizational inputs and outputs become highly unpredictable.

For example, according to the CEO of a biotechnology firm, the potential inputs to the firm are spread across hundreds and even thousands of scientists worldwide. Around each prominent researcher is a cluster of colleagues, and each cluster is a rich mix of talent held together by a set of connecting mechanisms, including shared interests, electronic mail systems, and technical conferences. Connecting devices are not co-ordinated by plan but rather are self-organizing, reflecting the knowledge needs and data-sharing opportunities recognized by members of the various clusters. The overall challenge of the biotechnology firm is to maintain close contact with as much of this continuously evolving knowledge field as it can. A similarly complex pattern is visible at the output interface of the firm, as myriad alliances and partnerships are formed to take partially developed products (and by-products) through the stages of final design, testing, and marketing. Clearly, a biotechnology firm that is rigidly structured will not be able to muster the internal flexibility required to match the complexity of its environment.

A new organizational form for a new economic era

Similar elements of complexity are visible in a growing number of industries. In computer software, for example, there are few limits on potentially profitable product designs, and a vast array of independent designers move in and around software companies of every size. The choices firms face at both the input and output ends of their operation are thus large and constantly changing. Faced with these opportunities, and projecting the evolutionary trends discussed above, one would expect the twenty-first-century organization to rely heavily on clusters of self-organizing components collaboratively investing the enterprise's know-how in product and service innovations for markets that they have helped create and develop.

Such firms can best be described as cellular.[7] The cellular metaphor suggests a living, adaptive organization. Cells in living organisms possess fundamental functions of life and can act alone to meet a particular need. However, by acting in concert, cells can perform more complex functions. Evolving characteristics, or learning, if shared across all cells, can create a higher-order organism. Similarly, a cellular organization is made up of cells (self-managing teams, autonomous business units, etc.) that can operate alone but that can interact with other cells to produce a more potent and competent business mechanism. It is this combination of independence and interdependence that allows the cellular organizational form to generate and share the know-how that produces continuous innovation.

Building blocks of the cellular form

In the future, complete cellular firms will achieve a level of know-how well beyond that of earlier organizational forms by combining entrepreneurship, self-organization, and member ownership in mutually reinforcing ways. Each cell (team, strategic business unit, firm) will have an entrepreneurial responsibility to the larger organization. The customers of a particular cell can be outside clients or other cells in the organization. In either case, the purpose is to spread an entrepreneurial mind-set throughout the organization so that every cell is concerned about improvement and growth. Indeed, giving each cell entrepreneurial responsibility is essential to the full utilization of the firm's constantly growing know-how. Of course, each cell must also have the entrepreneurial skills required to generate business for itself and the overall organization.

Each cell must be able to continually reorganize in order to make its expected contribution to the overall organization. Of particular value here are the technical skills needed to perform its function, the collaborative skills necessary to make appropriate linkages with other organizational units and external partner firms, and the governance skills required to manage its own activities. Application of this cellular principle may require the company to strip away most of the bureaucracy that is currently in place and replace it with jointly defined protocols that guide internal and external collaboration.

Each cell must be rewarded for acting entrepreneurially and operating in a businesslike manner. If the cellular units are teams or strategic business units instead of complete firms, psychological ownership can be achieved by organizing cells as profit centers, allowing them to participate in company stock-purchase plans, and so on. However, the ultimate cellular solution is probably actual member ownership of those cell assets and resources that they have created and that they voluntarily invest with the firm in expectation of a joint return.

TOWARD THE CELLULAR ORGANIZATION

Examples of cellular organizations, where the individual cellular principles and their interconnectedness are clearly seen, are rare. We have attempted to identify and track those companies that appear to be at the leading edge of organizational practice, and our interviews and observations to date have uncovered one example of a complete cellular organization, Technical and Computer Graphics of Sydney, Australia. Also, The Acer Group, a rapidly growing personal computer company, is a significant user of cellular principles on a global scale. There are many examples of companies around the world that are partial users of the cellular form, relying on one or more of its key building blocks to achieve impressive innovative capabilities.

TCG: a complete cellular organization

Technical and Computer Graphics (TCG), a privately held information-technology company, is perhaps the best example of the cellular approach to organizing. TCG develops a wide variety of products and services, including portable and hand-held data terminals and loggers, computer graphics systems, bar-coding systems, electronic data interchange systems, and other IT products and services. The 13 individual small firms at TCG are the focus of cellularity. Like a cell in a large organism, each firm has its own purpose and ability to function independently, but it shares common features and purpose with all of its sister firms. Some TCG member firms specialize in one or more product categories, while others specialize in hardware or software.

At TCG, the various firms have come into the group with existing high levels of technical and business competence. However, the operating protocol at TCG ensures that systemwide competence will continue to grow. The process is called triangulation, and it is the means by which TCG continually

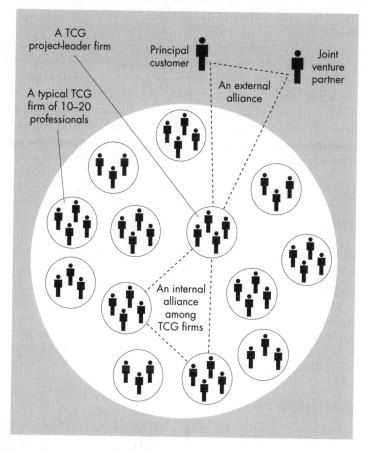

FIGURE 15.2 *TCG's cellular organization*

develops new products and services.[8] Triangulation is a three-cornered partnership among (a) one or more TCG firms, (b) an external joint-venture partner (e.g. Hitachi) that also provides equity capital to the venture, and (c) a principal customer (e.g. Telstra, an Australian telephone company) whose large advance order wins it contractual rights as well as providing additional cash to the venture. (See Figure 15.2.)

Each TCG firm is expected to search continually for new product and service opportunities. When a particular venture shows concrete promise, the initiating firm acts as project leader for the remainder of the venture. The first step in the triangulation process is to identify and collaborate with a joint-venture partner, a firm with expertise in the proposed technology. TCG receives partial funding for the project from the joint-venture partner, and it also gains access to technical ideas and distribution channels. Next, the project leader firm identifies an initial large customer for the new product. TCG also collaborates with the customer in the sense that it agrees to custom-design a product for that client. By working together with the joint-venture partner and the principal customer, TCG is able to efficiently develop a state-of-the-art product that is tailor-made to the principal customer's specifications.

According to TCG's governance principles, the project leader firm is also expected to search among the other TCG companies for additional partners – not only because they are needed for their technical contribution, but also because the collaboration itself is expected to enhance overall organizational know-how. The process of internal triangulation thus serves a dual purpose. It produces direct input to the project, and it helps to diffuse competence in areas such as business development, partnering, and project management. The three principles of cellularity are tightly interconnected at TCG, mutually reinforcing each other and producing a strong overall organization. First, acceptance of entrepreneurial responsibility is required for admission to the group and is increasingly enhanced by the triangulation process. Second, self-organization gives the individual firm both the ability and the freedom to reach deeply into its own know-how to create responses to a continuously evolving set of customer and partner needs. Third, each firm's profit responsibility, as well as its opportunity to own stock in other TCG firms, provides an ongoing stimulus for the growth and utilization of know-how.

To this point, TCG has pushed its version of the cellular organizational approach to a modest size (approximately 200 staff in 13 small firms). Whether TCG's particular approach can be used to propel its growth to medium or large size is not yet clear. It may well be that some modification of its self-organizing abilities and reward system may be required.

Acer: a global cellular company

An attempt to build a large-scale cellular organization is evident at The Acer Group, where co-founder Stan Shih has created a vision of a global personal computer company.[9] Shih's design, like that at TCG, calls for a federation of self-managing firms held together by mutual interest rather than hierarchical control. Shih's driving slogan is '21 in 21' – a federation of at least 21 independent firms located around the world by the twenty-first century, each operating in what Shih calls a 'client–server' mode. That is, each firm, depending on the type of transaction involved, is either a client or a server of the other firms in the federation. Some firms, called Regional Business Units (RBUs), are operated primarily as marketing organizations – advertising, selling, and servicing computers according to particular national or regional needs. Other firms, called Strategic Business Units (SBUs), are primarily R&D, manufacturing, and distribution units. For the most part, RBUs are clients that receive products from servers, the SBUs. However, RBUs are required to submit on an ongoing basis short-, medium-, and long-term forecasts of their product needs. In this mode, the SBUs are the clients of the RBUs – depending on each RBU's knowledge of its local market to provide information that will drive product development and manufacturing.

Although each firm has a core task to perform, new product concepts can and do originate anywhere in the federation. For example, Acer America (an RBU) wanted a stylish yet affordable PC for the North American market. It contracted with Frog, an outside industrial design firm, to assist it in the development of the highly acclaimed Acer Aspire. Manufacturing was done by Acer SBUs, and the marketing campaign was jointly developed by Acer America and Acer International, another RBU based in Singapore. Other Acer units are free to borrow from the Aspire design or to create unique designs suited to their respective markets. Every new product proposal is evaluated as a business venture by the federation's partner firms.

Shih's vision for the Acer federation of companies, however, appears to go one step beyond that of TCG in terms of reinforcing both the responsibility of the individual firm for its own destiny and the responsibility of all firms for the long-term success of the total organization. At TCG, the value of each of the member firms is calculated through an internal stock market, and firms are free to leave the group if they so choose. At Acer, the firms are each jointly owned by their own management and home-country investors, with a (usually) minority ownership position held by Acer Inc., the parent firm. Shih intends that Acer firms around the world will be listed on local stock exchanges and be free to seek capital for their own expansion. He believes that local ownership unleashes the motivation to run each business prudently.

With all Acer firms enjoying the freedom to both operate and expand, the value of their membership in the federation is the capacity of the 'cells' to continue to serve one another in an increasingly competitive global marketplace. Acer has developed the competence to efficiently produce all its products for just-in-time assembly and distribution. With minimal inventories, the latest models are available at all times at every sales site.

As yet, Acer's operating protocols are not as explicitly geared to the diffusion of know-how as they are at TCG. Nevertheless, Acer's business model provides the opportunity for each firm to draw on federation partners as preferred providers or clients. Currently, Acer's worldwide training programs are being used to translate Shih's global vision into action programs at the local firm level.

Partial uses of the cellular approach

Even those firms that have not yet moved to a complete cellular model appear to obtain benefits from using one or more of its three main building blocks. For example, Kyocera relied heavily on the principle of self-organization to improve its manufacturing process. Each of its cells consists of a small group of machines and a team of highly trained employees who collaborate in the production of a well-defined set of products for a specific group of customers. As opposed to the functional organization of manufacturing, where machines are grouped according to task performed, and products or parts are produced using specialized batch methods, the cellular approach divides the stream of production into parallel flows, giving the members of each cell responsibility for planning their own operations, ensuring that the quality of their output meets specified performance standards, interfacing with their suppliers and customers, and responding to unusual circumstances.[10]

Oticon, the Danish hearing aid manufacturer, has carefully reengineered its organization using approaches similar to the cellular principles of self-organization and entrepreneurship. First, it dramatically and systematically removed many of the bureaucratic barriers that plagued organization members. It eliminated rules, reports, and forms, achieving in the process a paperless workplace. It reduced the need for planning and supervision by allowing employees to choose their project teams. Such voluntarism also served to stimulate entrepreneurship, as the most successful projects were those which were widely regarded as compelling ideas.[11] Thus, self-managing teams now have responsibility for both the identification and organization of new business projects.

At Semco, the Brazilian industrial-equipment manufacturer, management places great emphasis on the principles of member ownership and entrepreneurship. Work teams within all of Semco's plants have a standing invitation to take their operations outside the company and form their own business firms. If the new outside firm uses Semco equipment, the company will lease that equipment to the firm at very favorable rates. If the new firm provides a product or service desired by Semco, it can do business with its former employer. Even if the new firm later wishes to rejoin Semco, it can propose to do so, and the decision will be treated just like any other business proposal. All of these actions are encouraged because Ricardo Semler, Semco's former CEO, believes that employee ownership is the best means of achieving a competitive business. Although it is a privately held company, Semco shares almost a quarter of its profits with managers and employees.[12]

Adding value by using the cellular form

A close examination of cellularly structured firms such as TCG and Acer indicates that they also share some of the features of earlier organizational forms. Indeed, each new form, as we noted earlier, incorporates the major value-adding characteristics of the previous forms and adds new capabilities to them. Thus, the cellular form includes the dispersed entrepreneurship of the divisional form, customer responsiveness of the matrix form, and self-organizing knowledge and asset sharing of the network form.

The cellular organizational form, however, offers the potential to add value even beyond asset and know-how sharing. In its fully developed state, the cellular organization adds value through its unique ability to create and utilize knowledge. For example, knowledge sharing occurs in networks as a by-product of asset sharing rather than as a specific focus of such activity. Similarly, matrix and divisionalized firms recognize the value that may be added when knowledge is shared across projects or divisions, but they must create special-purpose mechanisms (e.g. task forces) in order to generate and share new knowledge. By contrast, as illustrated at TCG, the cellular form lends itself to sharing not only the explicit know-how that cells have accumulated and articulated, but also the tacit know-how that emerges when cells combine to design unique new customer solutions.[13] Such learning focuses not on the output of the innovation process, but on the innovation process itself: it is know-how that can be achieved and shared only by doing.

Beyond knowledge creation and sharing, the cellular form has the potential to add value through its related ability to keep the firm's total knowledge assets more fully invested than do the other organizational forms. Because each cell has entrepreneurial responsibility, and is empowered to draw on any of the firm's assets for each new business opportunity, high levels of knowledge utilization across cells should be expected. Network organizations aspire to high utilization of know-how and assets, but upstream firms are ultimately dependent on downstream partners to find new product or service uses. In the cellular firm, the product/service innovation process is continuous and fully shared.

IMPLEMENTING THE CELLULAR ORGANIZATION

Many organizational variations using some or all of the cellular principles are likely to emerge in the years ahead.[14] While the direction of the evolution is clear, however, companies that attempt implementation of the complete cellular form face several significant challenges. It is certain that cellularly structured firms will not just happen. Our interviews with leaders of cellular firms make it clear that such a firm is the product of a bold managerial vision and, even more importantly, of a unique managerial philosophy.[15] The ability to envision and build the entrepreneurial, self-organizing, and ownership components of cellular organizations must be undergirded with a philosophy that emphasizes investment in human capabilities and the willingness to take substantial risks to maximize their utilization.

The first requirement is a willingness to invest in human capability that goes well beyond simply providing for current education and training. The concept of investment calls for expenditures to build the capabilities needed to respond to the future demands that will be placed on the organization, even those that cannot be easily forecast. Training to meet current needs is not an investment, because the requirement is clear, and the costs and benefits can be easily calculated. Building competencies for future needs *is* an investment because risk is involved – not every return can be predicted and, moreover, not everyone whose skills are enhanced will remain with the firm.

Companies such as Chaparral Steel, for example, make heavy investments in building know-how even though not all returns can be easily measured. Chaparral invests up to one third of every member's time annually in one form or another of continuous education and skill development. Chaparral views growing know-how as the basic source of members' ability to add economic value in a highly competitive industry.[16] The competencies visible in firms such as Kyocera, Oticon, Semco, Acer, and TCG are the products of similar investments.

It is worth noting that the basic notion of achieving competitive advantage through people is far from new. In the late 1950s, Edith Penrose focused on managerial competence as the principal engine of organizational growth, and in the 1960s, Rensis Likert advocated careful accounting for investments in human resources and the costs of managerial actions that might deplete them. The 1990s have brought a renewed awareness among managers and management scholars that building know-how is the primary means by which firms create economic value.[17] The difference today, however, is that continuing investment in the competence of organization members is no longer merely an option; it is an economic must.[18]

The concept of investment always involves risk, which is usually proportional to the level of possible return. The biggest challenge facing most firms that are considering the use of a cellular form of organization is not just the investment required to build key competencies; it is the willingness to allow the levels of self-governance necessary to fully utilize that competence. For example, Oticon takes what many firms would view as an extraordinary risk in allowing members to choose their own work assignments on projects where their capabilities can be most effectively used. Others would regard the firm (cell) autonomy allowed at TCG and Acer to involve even bigger risks, since co-ordination is largely voluntary, and agreed-upon protocols and responsibilities are used instead of hierarchical controls.

Perhaps even more challenging than making investments and taking risks, however, is the long-term requirement for sharing with organization members the returns of their knowledge utilization. If organization members are to accept professional levels of responsibility, traditional reward schemes such as bonus plans are not likely to be sufficient. Perhaps the future structure of return-sharing will follow the philosophies expressed by Stan Shih and Ricardo Semler – that the long-run pursuit of an increasingly competent organization may require innovative mechanisms providing real ownership and profit-sharing, mechanisms that give members' intellectual capital the same rights as the financial capital supplied by stockholders.

Given the required levels of investment, risk taking, and member ownership, many companies will not – and need not – move completely to the cellular organizational form. Firms that produce standard products or services to forecast or order may still be most productive if arranged in at least shallow hierarchies. Groups of such firms may be linked into networks for greater speed and customization. The push toward cellular approaches, as noted earlier, is appearing first in firms focused on rapid product and service innovation – unique and/or state-of-the-art offerings. However, while cellular firms are most easily associated with newer, rapidly evolving industries, the form lends itself to firms providing the design initiative in virtually any type of industry. Within a network of companies in a mature business, it is the cellularly structured firms that are likely to provide leadership in new product and service development.

CONCLUSION

Across national and regional economies, the overlapping eras of standard-ization, customization, and innovation will continue to evolve, and new variations of hierarchical, network, and cellular organizational forms will continue to emerge. Decades of experimentation honed the functional, divisional, matrix, and network forms, clarifying their operating logics and highlighting their costs and benefits. A similar pattern can be expected to occur with the cellular form. Throughout the evolutionary process of organizational form, one constant has been the search for ever-increasing effectiveness and efficiency in the ability to fully apply know-how to resource utilization. Firms willing to take the risks to lead this search have been and will continue to be economic leaders.

NOTES

This chapter reflects the authors' continuing conversations with managers in leading-edge firms in the United States, Europe, Asia and Australia. We wish to thank those managers for their insights into the process of building cellular organizations. We are also grateful for research funding from the Carnegie Bosch Institute for Applied Studies in International Management.

1. For excellent accounts of the evolution of organizational forms during this period, see A.D. Chandler, Jr., *Strategy and Structure: Chapters in the History of the American Industrial Enterprise* (Cambridge, MA: MIT Press, 1962); and P.R. Lawrence and D. Dyer, 'Generation of self-managing human systems', *Human Systems Management*, 9 (1990): 57–59.
2. A discussion of 'excess managerial capacity' as the engine of corporate growth can be found in E.T. Penrose, *The Theory of the Growth of the Firm* (Oxford: Basil Blackwell, 1959). A new edition of this book, with a foreword by Professor Penrose, was published in 1995.

3. For a discussion of matrix organizations, see S.M. Davis and P.R. Lawrence, *Matrix* (Reading, MA: Addison-Wesley, 1977).
4. For a discussion of the globalization process, see M.E. Porter (ed.), *Competition in Global Industries* (Boston, MA: Harvard Business School Press, 1986).
5. The multifirm network organization was first identified and described by R.E. Miles and C.C. Snow, 'Fit, failure and the Hall of Fame', *California Management Review*, 26 (3) (1984): 10–28. For descriptions of the major types of network organization used today, see R.E. Miles and C.C. Snow, *Fit, Failure and the Hall of Fame: How Companies Succeed or Fail* (New York: Free Press, 1994), Chs 7–9.
6. S. Kauffman, *At Home in the Universe* (New York: Oxford University Press, 1995).
7. We did not invent the cellular label. The concept of cellular structures has been discussed at least since the 1960s. For a review, see J.A. Mathews, 'Holonic organizational architectures', *Human Systems Management*, 15 (1996): 1–29.
8. J.A. Mathews, 'TCG R&D networks: the triangulation strategy', *Journal of Industry Studies*, 1 (1993): 65–74.
9. J.A. Mathews and C.C. Snow, 'The expansionary dynamics of the latecomer multinational firm: the case of The Acer Group', Conference on 'The emerging East Asian multinational', organized by *Asia Pacific Journal of Management*, National University of Singapore, February 1997.
10. M. Zeleny, *Amoebae: the New Renewing American Industry* (New York: Free Press, 1983).
11. L. Kolind, 'Creativity at Oticon', *Fast Company*, (1996): 5–9.
12. R. Semler, *Maverick* (New York: Time Warner Books, 1993).
13. I. Nonaka and H. Takeuchi, *The Knowledge-Creating Company: How Japanese Companies Create the Dynamics of Innovation* (New York: Oxford University Press, 1995).
14. Many of these experiments will involve various forms of strategic alliances and/or joint ventures. See A.C. Inkpen, 'Creating knowledge through collaboration', *California Management Review*, 39 (1996): 123–40.
15. J.A. Mathews and C.C. Snow, 'A conversation with Taiwan-based Acer Group's Stan Shih on global strategy', *Organizational Dynamics*, Summer 1998: 65–74.
16. G.E. Forward, D.E. Beach, D.A. Gray, and J.C. Quick, 'Mentofacturing: a vision for American industrial excellence', *Academy of Management Executive*, 5 (1991): 32–44.
17. Penrose, op. cit.; R. Likert, *The Human Organization* (New York: McGraw-Hill, 1967); and J. Pfeffer, *Competitive Advantage through People* (Boston, MA: Harvard Business School Press, 1994).
18. For an example of a firm that seriously and creatively attempted to calculate the value of its intellectual capital and other intangible assets, see L. Edvinsson and M.S. Malone, *Intellectual Capital: Realizing Your Company's True Value by Finding Its Hidden Brainpower* (New York: Harper Business, 1997).

EXECUTIVE COMMENTARY

Jeff Koeppel, Becton Dickinson and Co.

Imagine an organization that replicates the biological building blocks of life uniquely adapted to its environment, conducting all essential functions to meet its basic needs, and by acting in concert with others, performing more complex functions. In an evolutionary sense, this organization is capable of learning, continuous growth and innovation. This is the simple, yet elegant analogy of the 'cellular organization', a vision of what the twenty-first century business enterprise ought to look like.

Evolution is a useful perspective for understanding organizations. The vertically integrated, functionally specialized hierarchies of the Machine Age were designed for mass standardization. Today, many of us refer to the remnants of this era in our current organizations as dinosaurs, whether they be manufacturing plants, management processes, or the mindsets of people.

The movement from standardization to customization took us through divisional and matrix organizations, more highly evolved structures for co-ordinating internal resources and decision-making. In the last ten years, we have heard much about network organizations, multifirm confederations of partners designed for the efficient customization required by global markets in the Information Age.

The authors argue that each organizational form has been well suited to the market forces of its time, but by virtue of its limitations, gives rise to the next. The cellular form is emerging because it is better suited to compete more aggressively around continuous learning and innovation, where design skills and creativity are at a premium. There is familiar and persuasive logic here.

Cellular firms are designed to maximize entrepreneurship, self-organization, and member ownership of firm assets and resources – factors that drive and reinforce the inventiveness needed to go beyond incremental extension of current products and services.

None of these factors is particularly new to organizational designers or managers. Most modern corporations have been grappling with ways to stimulate entrepreneurial initiative for years. The same is true for self-managed business teams and broad-based employee ownership plans. What may be unique is the manner in which cellular organizations are able to integrate and implement the factors to create and utilize knowledge faster and better than their competitors.

The authors cite a few examples of cellular organizations in pure or partial forms, primarily technology companies developing hardware and software, advanced electronics, and industrial equipment. They tend to be small to mid-size, globally focused, knowledge-driven businesses. TCG is the most striking example because it is a 'complete' cellular organization. Its triangulation process for ensuring collaboration among its project-led businesses with joint-venture partners and customers is well defined and consistent with the principles of cellularity.

While the other companies mentioned, including Acer, Kyocera, and Semco, have adopted some elements of the cellular model, collectively they do not yet provide compelling proof of the case. But they do provide a series of data points that are starting to form an intriguing pattern. We have the sense that something's out there, we're just not sure what it is and where it's going.

If the cell form is the organizational blueprint of the future, we should expect to see a much greater number of people with the know-how to participate in operational, investment, and strategic decisions at all levels of the enterprise. This is not a subtle distinction; it means a very different set of expectations and skills from what most companies are accustomed to today. Where will the people with these skills come from? Clearly there are major implications for the selection, development, and retention of a firm's key associates, internal and external. It is also possible that many of the entrepreneurs who set out on their own to avoid the pitfalls of corporate life, may find themselves now drawn towards (or back to) more attractive relationships with self-organizing, member-owned cellular firms. We can all dream.

Tamar Elkeles and Dan Sullivan, QUALCOMM Corporate Learning Center
The cellular organizational form proposed by the authors has its origins in the research and study of cybernetics. The term *cybernetics* was coined in the 1940s by Nobert Wiener, the MIT mathematician who studied the processes of information exchange through which machines and organisms engage in self-regulating behavior in order to maintain a steady state.

Forty-five years later, Gareth Morgan noted that cybernetics leads to an organizational theory based on the ability of a system to (a) sense, monitor, and scan the environment; (b) relate this information to the operating norms guiding system behavior; (c) detect deviations from these norms; and (d) initiate corrective action when discrepancies are detected.

The cellular metaphor provides a contemporary image grounded in past literature that is useful for thinking about organizational systems and states in high-tech organizations. One significant point relates to the role and impact of connecting devices in cellular organizations as facilitators of data sharing and knowledge creation. Knowledge sharing is especially critical in businesses whose operations are dispersed as a result of growth or geographic separation where spanning time and space is a considerable challenge. In such firms, face-to-face interaction between employees is augmented by the use of technology that creates a virtual environment, such as the Internet, for electronic interactions.

While solving one problem, virtual environments have created another. Even as people and departments have become more linked via networks and computers, we are seeing a growing lack of human connectedness, which can directly affect the success of the cellular form in organizations. In addition, the sharing of meaningful information has suffered. Consideration of this reality is particularly important in companies such as QUALCOMM, where we are engaged in efforts to promote and enhance knowledge sharing and information on an organization-wide basis.

QUALCOMM is a leader in digital wireless communications, growing from $81 million in revenue in fiscal year 1996 to over £2 billion in 1997, with over 8,000 employees. Throughout the firm, we believe that we are better as a collective whole than as distinctive parts. Therefore, we want to foster employee sharing and communication so that critical ideas are freely and widely distributed. Within QUALCOMM, employees use electronic mail lists to communicate with a wide audience on a particular topic. An extensive

Intranet also promotes sharing of information and ideas. Additionally, we foster interpersonal communication through engineering lectures, education expositions, internal business seminars, and breakfast meetings with senior management. Whatever the format, it is important to ensure opportunities for organizational communication.

The purpose of sharing learning across cells is, of course, to make the organization more flexible and, as a result, more competitive as it works to anticipate and adapt to changing customer demands. Employees who work in such organizations generally have more flexibility, creative freedom, and autonomy but are also encouraged to work collaboratively. This is quite different from organizations of the past, where silos operated on the theory that knowledge is power and that sharing information is threatening.

Since there are remnants of this mentality in many organizations, it may be of benefit to those moving toward the cellular form to offer incentives or rewards for sharing information and connecting with others across the organization. The building blocks of the cellular form – entrepreneurship, self-organization, and member ownership – seem indicative of organizations in the twenty-first century. A growing reliance on entrepreneurship in high-tech firms is not unique to the cellular form, but is rather a compelling business requirement for high-tech organizations in general.

Entrepreneurship has enabled more adaptive technologies and innovative ideas to flourish, making it a critical component in organizational success. The authors mention the importance of spreading an entrepreneurial mindset across the company as a way to encourage entrepreneurship. In promoting entrepreneurialism, the organization must take steps to ensure that employees have the dispositions and skill sets to function in such a culture. At QUALCOMM, we have a complex hiring process in which we try to find employees who fit our entrepreneurial culture. Employees who do not have an ownership mindset usually don't survive our environment. As a result, we would argue that entrepreneurship is a function both of employees and of the organizational environment, realizing that not everybody is comfortable working in a cellular form of organization.

Self-organization, another building block of the cellular form, creates another set of challenges for many high-tech, high-growth organizations. When companies are hiring rapidly, there are many preconceived notions about what organizational climate, policies, and procedures should be. QUALCOMM prefers guidelines over the imposition of strict policies around organizational standards. We consistently regulate bureaucracy as we strive to maintain a flexible, adaptive organization. The protocols described by the authors to guide collaboration are excellent examples of how fluid cellular organizations need to be.

Member ownership, both psychological and monetary, is integral to the cellular form. It is virtually impossible to hold an entrepreneurial mindset in an organization without employee ownership. Rewards and recognition are a monumental component of managing employee performance because they reinforce the norms, values, and goals of the organization. Psychological ownership, however, goes beyond stock purchase plans and can incorporate everything from implementation of ideas to autonomous decision making. Employees who feel their input is valued, and that they are trusted to make decisions, achieve the psychological ownership of organizations. Psychological ownership could, in some cases, be damaged by lack of trust or rigorous structure, even if an employee did own company stock.

Finally the authors comment on a handful of organizations that either add value by using the cellular form, partially use the cellular approach, or are complete cellular organizations. We believe this list is far from complete. Most high-tech companies utilize some form of the cellular approach. In the wireless communications sector alone, our market has evolved so rapidly that the cellular form is represented by a majority of companies. Additionally, with the expansion of the international marketplace, more organizations are rapidly moving to even newer ways of doing business. Thus, as business continues to change, new organizational forms and business structures will further evolve, calling for even newer terminology. What comes after cellular?

Part IV Knowledge, Innovation and Human Resources

One of the key factors in the growth of interest in knowledge management in the 1990s was the *re*discovery that employees have skills and knowledge that are not available to (or 'captured' by) the organization. It is perhaps no coincidence that this rediscovery of the central importance of people as possessors of knowledge vital to the organization followed an intense period of corporate downsizing, outsourcing and staff redundancies in the West in the 1980s. Organizations that downsized and introduced early retirement packages for older workers in the 1980s found they had lost much of their organizational memory or intellectual capital. Rather than innovating, firms found themselves 'reinventing the wheel' and repeating the mistakes of the past. So too, the notion of 'knowledge work', and 'knowledge workers', first articulated by Peter Drucker in the 1960s, has received increasing attention in the last decade as traditional industries and jobs moved from the West to the newly industrializing economies.

In Part IV we explore a range of approaches to the 'human factor' as addressed in the new literature on intellectual capital and knowledge management. A major theme is the people-centred nature of knowledge creation and innovation, and the human resource strategies and practices required to encourage and sustain these. The chapter explores the notion of people as the locus of intellectual capital; the idea that knowledge work, and even knowledge workers, somehow require different human resources strategies; and the key question of the relationship between the individual as possessor of knowledge, and the wider organization.

The first chapter is 'Brainpower' by Thomas A. Stewart, editor of *Fortune* magazine. Originally a front-page feature article, it acted as a catalyst for the popularization of the idea of managing employee knowledge and intellectual capital. It raises a number of key issues surrounding the identification of knowledge assets, the notion of knowledge-intensive businesses, and the management of knowledgeable workers. Stewart identifies organizational intellectual capital with knowledge held by individuals: 'It's the sum of everything everybody in your company knows that gives you a competitive edge in the marketplace.' For Stewart, the management challenge is to capture, capitalize on and leverage this 'free-floating brainpower'.

In Chapter 17 Schuler and Jackson then present an analysis of the link between strategic human resource management (SHRM) and innovation strategy. The authors emphasize the need for creativity and thinking differently, which can be facilitated by a human resource strategy that includes bringing in outsiders to enrich the knowledge pool. The human resource practices required for an innovation strategy are compared with cost-reduction strategies and a strategy of differentiation based on quality, the authors suggesting that each of these has different SHRM characteristics.

Schuler and Jackson argue that innovation requires workers to have high morale, feelings of autonomy and high commitment. The SHRM implications include: careful selection of highly skilled people; job design ensuring that employees are given considerable autonomy and discretion, using minimal managerial controls; investing in training and development; making resources available for experimentation; tolerance of a certain degree of failure; and performance evaluation over a long rather than short period. A business strategy based on innovation and creativity requires a long-term rather than a short-term focus, relatively high levels of co-operative and interdependent behaviour, and a high tolerance of ambiguity. Innovation will not be achieved by encouraging people to work *harder* or even to work *smarter* on the same tasks, but by requiring people to work *differently*.

The chapter by Quinn et al., 'Managing Professional Intellect: Making the Most of the Best', argues that little attention has been paid to the management of professional intellect, even though it creates the most value in the new economy. The HRM implications include the renewal and development of intellect and expertise through recruitment of the best people, intensive early development, constant increase in challenges, and the design of appropriate forms of evaluation and appraisal. The chapter gives examples of organizations where professional intellect can be leveraged by capturing knowledge in systems and software. The authors argue for the value of a form of self-organizing network structure known as a 'spider's web', which involves experts forming teams to address a specific issue and then disbanding when the project is completed.

According to Quinn et al. companies that are successful innovators are characterized by common patterns: they contain 'visionaries', they have conducive 'atmospheres', they have staff who are market-focused, they have flat structures, encourage 'skunkworks', facilitate interactive learning, and they have a conscious strategy for innovation. However these generalizations are qualified by the observation that in practice, innovation tends to be opportunistic, non-linear and interactive in its unfolding.

In Chapter 19, Storey further relates human resource requirements to organizational structure. Storey suggests that the challenges of the competitive environment are leading many organizations to seek new organizational forms, and that different organizational forms are associated with different human resource management challenges. These organizational forms include outsourcing, strategic alliances and collaborations, networks and virtual organizations. In theory these provide new ways to ensure the organization has the necessary and appropriate mix of knowledge and intellectual capital, without necessarily having to retain this by means of traditional employment strategies. Such organizational forms may confer greater flexibility and speed of response, compared to in-house organic growth of resources.

Storey explores the ways in which outsourcing and other non-hierarchical forms of organization require new human resources strategies and practices. For example, where outsourcing arrangements prevail, the priority may shift from managing an internal hierarchy to attempting to ensure quality performance from staff who are not direct employees of the organization. Moreover, the network or virtual organization raises concerns about the core knowledge and intellectual capital that must be retained. The dangers of 'hollowing out' the organization, with the loss of capabilities, expertise and knowledge, may threaten the organization's ability to innovate or to learn. The chapter posits the idea that human resource strategy must now attempt to operate beyond the conventional boundaries of the organization, within and across the network or supply chain, because that is where many of the essential knowledge resources are located.

The final chapter in this part is by David Straker, a manager with Hewlett-Packard in the UK, as well as an author. His focus is on the means by which an innovative company can sustain innovation, even when that company is well into maturity. Straker draws on Crosby's idea of 'maturity levels', first developed in relation to quality management, in order to conceptualize the changes to management style relevant to innovation. Five levels of innovation maturity are described: suppressed, enabled, encouraged, educated and enlightened. For each level Straker describes the features of the organization in terms of culture and management style. In particular he is concerned with the ways in which mature organizations can continue to encourage creativity and indeed cope with creative people. As we move up the scale away from suppressed innovation we can see an increase in worker autonomy, encouragement for creativity and increased reflective thinking about the innovation process itself. His account is enriched by the inside knowledge of Hewlett-Packard, which provides many examples that illustrate the practical measures discussed.

Whether we subscribe to the view that organizational knowledge is equivalent to the sum of professional intellects in that organization – i.e. all the knowledge in all the heads of all the employees – or whether organizational knowledge is somehow greater than that because of the knowledge that becomes embedded in systems, routines, technologies and culture, it is clear that the management of people is central to any aspiration to manage knowledge.

16
Brainpower

*Thomas A. Stewart**

Intellectual capital is becoming corporate America's most valuable asset and can be its sharpest competitive weapon. The challenge is to find what you have – and use it.

Brainpower has always been an essential asset. It is, after all, why *Homo sapiens* rules the roost. But it has never before been so important for business. Every company depends increasingly on knowledge – patents, processes, management skills, technologies, information about customers and suppliers, and old-fashioned experience. Added together, this knowledge is intellectual capital. Pope John Paul II recognized it in his encyclical writing (of 1991) of a new, important form of ownership: 'the possession of know-how, technology, and skill'. Hugh Macdonald, house futurologist for ICL, the big British computer maker, calls it 'knowledge that exists in an organization that can be used to create differential advantage'. In other words, it's the sum of everything everybody in your company knows that gives you a competitive edge in the marketplace.

Such collective knowledge is hard to identify and harder still to deploy effectively. But once you find it and exploit it, you win. Says Dr P. Roy Vagelos, CEO of Merck and Co.: 'A low-value product can be made by anyone anywhere. When you have knowledge no one else has access to – that's dynamite.' Dynamite, indeed. Merck, voted five years in a row America's most admired company in *Fortune*'s annual survey, has invented more new medicines than any other US pharmaceutical company.

Intellectual capital has always been most visible and most valued on the leading edge of science, whether in smelting bronze 5,500 years ago or in writing software today. 'We guard our research even more carefully than our financial assets,' says Vagelos. You can also see it clearly in professional services. Your lawyer doesn't charge $375 an hour because his physical assets – his desk, his bust of Oliver Wendell Holmes – are so costly. Many corporations sell little else but knowledge: think of database publishers, software houses, syndicators and program packagers, consultants, advertising agencies.

* Reprinted from *Fortune*, 3 June 1991. Figure p. 304: Aluminium Association; Figure p. 311: MIT Sloan School of Management.

Today the intellectual content of even mundane human activities is multiplying, as Figures 16.1 to 16.5 show. A mere piece of information – John Doe's address, say – isn't an asset, any more than one brick in a factory wall is. You can, however, make an asset out of your list of a thousand households to which you delivered pizza with anchovies last year. To picture intellectual capital at work, consider these three examples:

- Helios, a new medical imaging system from Polaroid Corp., will reach the market this year, after just three years in development. That's twice as fast as wild-eyed optimists in the company had predicted. The reason: interdisciplinary teamwork in the labs. 'Our researchers are not any smarter,' says CEO I. MacAllister Booth, 'but by working together they get the value of each other's intelligence almost instantaneously.'
- At Pioneer Hi-Bred International, scientists breed special strains of corn for disease resistance, high yield, or specific attributes like oil content. A decade ago such work ate up hundreds of acres of farmland and consumed untold numbers of man-hours. These days they can do it by manipulating the plant's DNA directly, using a petri dish. Apart from the cost savings, the company expects to knock two years off the seven- to ten-year time it takes to develop a new hybrid. Moreover, Pioneer now can focus on individual customers – breeding strains rich in cornstarch for industrial users or in specific oils for food processors. The upshot, says Research Vice-President Rick McConnell: 'Corn is no longer a commodity.'
- IDS Financial Services, the financial planning subsidiary of American Express Co., codified the expertise of its best account managers in a software program called Insight. 'Now even the worst of our 6,500 planners is better than our average planner used to be,' says Chairman Harvey Golub. One result: in four years the percentage of clients who leave has dropped by more than half.

These companies have learned to exploit their intellectual capital. In Pioneer Hi-Bred's case, brainpower is replacing land – the elemental form of wealth. IDS has turned the talent of a few employees into an asset available to all its planners. Polaroid is managing its knowledge to dramatically shorten development time.

In most companies the management of intellectual capital is still uncharted territory, and few executives understand how to navigate it. They may know about the assets that take tangible form, like patents and copyrights. They may have an inkling of the value of others, such as the computer software that runs their information systems. They may even intuit that training and the experience gained on the learning curve belong somehow in their asset base.

But talent is intellectual capital too. The value of a lab, for instance, includes its scientists' ability to make new discoveries in the future. How do you put a pricetag on that? Or on intangibles like design, service, and customizing, which distinguish winners from losers? Even cost competition increasingly turns less on how many machines you own than on how well you use them. These intellectual assets sometimes behave in ways that defy ordinary rules. Managing know-how is not like managing cash or buildings, yet intellectual investments need to be treated every bit as painstakingly. Besides, as Ted Smith, Director of Knowledge-based Systems at Baby Bell US West, says, 'Managing knowledge as an asset spawns whole new disciplines.' It alters how executives think about economics, technology, human resources, and planning.

The first step in getting more fun from your intellectual assets is to find them. Ask your CFO how much cash you have in the bank or the value of your land and buildings, and she won't even have to put you on hold to get the answer. Ask what you should spend to replace the old lathes in the Provo plant, and you'll have the number by noon. Lots of luck, though, if you inquire about your intellectual capital. How much could you get if you sold the R&D that doesn't bear fruit? You know what your payroll is, but what's the true replacement cost of your people – the value of the skills you'd have to replenish if they left tomorrow?

Odds are, no one even knows what those skills are, says Jeffrey Staley, Vice-President of Scientific Generics, a management consulting firm. Staley, an alumnus of Arthur D. Little and Digital Equipment Corp., helps companies map their technology assets – that is, locate them, define them, and lay out routes for getting them to other parts of the company. Often his clients are startled to learn how much intellectual capital they have. One division of AMP, for example, knows how to drill minuscule holes in ultra-thin plastic and metal rings to make connectors for fiber-optic cables. Its drillers are the best in the world, and the precision of their work allows AMP to make some connectors for half its competitors' cost. Yet it wasn't until the company, working with Staley, mapped its technology assets that AMP learned how to transfer the skill to making connectors for copper wiring systems.

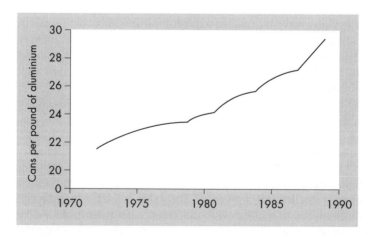

FIGURE 16.1 *I think, therefore I can. The beer has a head, but the can has brains. Technology lets manufacturers make more containers from the same amount of metal.*

Surprises like that are typical of intellectual assets. Explains Virgil Barry, a consultant at the A.T. Kearney firm: 'When you buy a machine, you know exactly how much value it adds. When you hire a researcher or develop a new process, you don't know where it will lead.'

Step two is matching the company's intellectual needs with its strategic plan. Polaroid is chockablock with scientists who know all there is to know about the chemistry of film. But the age of digital photography is dawning, and Polaroid needs electronics experts. To get them, the company revamped its human resources management. First, it made a sophisticated model of its hiring requirements; the forecast combines historical employee-turnover trends with data about the current workforce, such as probable retirement dates, to estimate how many people with what skills will leave in the next decade. (Even with low turnover, new hires will number in the thousands.) That information is then meshed with the company's long-range plan to show whether departing workers should be replaced by newcomers with similar or different training – a chemist by a chemist, or by a software engineer.

That's not all. Polaroid wants the present workforce to equip itself for those jobs. Lots of companies reimburse employees who take job-related courses. Polaroid has them piped into its offices from nearby Harvard, MIT, and Northeastern, and has hooked up a satellite relay from the National Technological University – a consortium of 39 institutions – to offer advanced degrees in disciplines like materials science. As an added incentive, Polaroid pegs raises and promotions to acquiring new skills. A worker who masters a skill that his department needs gets a raise, whether or not a promotion comes with it. Says Sam Yanes, Director of Corporate Communications: 'The old system had no way of compensating employees who invest intellectually in the future of the company. Now we've connected human-resource planning to business planning.'

Polaroid is far ahead of the pack. In most places, intellectual capital enters the strategic planning process – if at all – some time after the decision about who gets the fourth corner office. Even if scientists and engineers come to strategy meetings, says Staley, 'they sit in the back of the room. If the boss asks "What do you think about this idea?" they say, "Yeah, I guess we can do that."' Rarely is there a systematic attempt to find out what technologies the company will need to carry out the plan, or to analyse the strategic implications of technology gaps, such as whether to make or buy a critical component.

Once you've got a handle on your intellectual assets, how do you package them? Most companies are filled with intelligence, but too much of it resides in the computer whiz who speaks a mile a minute in no known language, in the brash account manager who racks up great numbers but has alienated everyone, or in files moved to the basement. Or it's retired and gone fishing. The challenge is to capture, capitalize, and leverage this free-floating brainpower.

One way is to automate it. Till now, says Dennis Yablonsky, CEO of Carnegie Group, a software design company in Pittsburgh, 'the time and energy invested in computers has gone into automating systems that relate to tangible assets – like payroll and inventory – not knowledge assets. Knowledge has been too hard to get to: it's in people's heads, it's unstructured.'

As technology gets more powerful, that is changing. At Xerox, when a repairman finds a part that failed, he logs the fact into an information base that will guide engineers to problem areas when they design a new copier. Carnegie Group has formed a joint venture with US West, Digital Equipment, Ford Motor, and Texas Instruments called the Initiative for Managing Knowledge Assets (IMKA). IMKA's aim is to make intellectual assets available through software that links databases, artificial intelligence, and plain old rules of thumb.

IMKA software just installed at Ford keeps track of the equipment and processes used to make electronic components at every manufacturing plant around the globe – down to such details as how solder flows across a circuitboard. Why should that matter? When employees in a plant in Brazil tried to speed up production by rotating the boards made there 90 degrees, the failure rate jumped. Flowing at a new angle, the solder shorted out the circuits. IMKA software could have told them that would happen before they wasted time and money trying.

Automation, however, isn't the only way to capture intellectual capital – and often isn't even the best. Sometimes ordinary storytelling works better, says management consultant David Nadler, President of Delta Consulting Group. Take Xerox again: a study by the company's Palo Alto Research Center revealed that repairmen learn most about fixing copiers not from company manuals but from hanging around swapping stories. 'Most managers would say those guys are wasting time,' says Nadler. Instead of busting up the gang by the water cooler, companies should make opportunities for storytelling at informal get-togethers and loosely organized off-site meetings, and through videotapes and bragging sessions.

Make no mistake: harnessing your intellectual capital is not easy. It will force you to think hard about what kind of outfit you run, and maybe even change it significantly. 'You can't just take a stodgy organization, hire smart guys, and expect good things to happen,' says Julio Rotemberg, an MIT economist who is studying how management style affects innovation. Getting results from investing in knowledge, Rotemberg's studies show, requires a corporate culture that allows it to flow freely, which means breaking down hierarchies and scrapping rules that stifle new ideas.

His colleague Roger Samuel, program director of a five-year MIT study of information technology management, cites a company in which two accounting groups bought the same computers and software. One group's boss told its people exactly how to use the new equipment; the other, while providing guidelines, encouraged them to fiddle around. Asks Samuel, 'Guess which one had the successful experience?'

Measuring such successes presents a whole new set of problems. Managers and accountants carefully calculate physical inputs like ore and labor; economists monitor money flows. 'When I was a kid in the bank, the most important economic indicator we looked at was freight car loadings,' says retired Citicorp Chairman Walter Wriston. 'Who the hell cares about them now? What we ought to have is something that measures the knowledge people bring to what they do.' But we don't. Intellectual assets appear on no balance sheet, flash on no Quotron. One reason people give intellectual capital short shrift is that they can't see the brain gain – the returns on their investment.

The problem with trying to measure intellectual capital directly, says Robert S. Kaplan, a professor of accounting at the Harvard business school, is that it mostly consists of 'self-created assets'. Standard accounting practices don't capture them; indeed, most disappear into the welter of the expense budget. 'We don't even have a nonfinancial number to measure enhanced ability that would work for a broad spectrum of companies,' Kaplan says. Seldom does a market ascribe value to intellectual assets. Book publishers are one exception, because they capitalize the advances they pay writers. These rarely correspond to the authors' eventual earnings – in 1989 the publishing division of Paramount wrote off $20 million in unearned advances. But at least the payments result from a market transaction that ascribes a value to the author's talent.

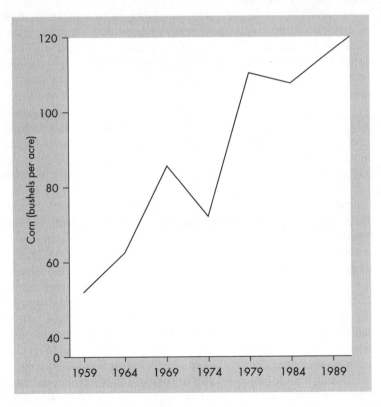

FIGURE 16.2 *Corny but wise. Intelligent plant breeding produces corn hybrids whose yields per acre are still growing.*

By contrast, Dun and Bradstreet's databases, worth billions, appear on no balance sheet. At American Airlines, jetliners show up as assets. However, the information system that runs Sabre – the reservation service that analysts figure makes more money than the planes do – is almost entirely an intangible asset, and that is nowhere to be seen on the balance sheet. That's fine for the Securities and Exchange Commission (SEC), which holds that the fewer intangibles on the balance sheet, the better. (Some intellectual capital does show up after an acquisition, as part of goodwill.)

But what about enlightened managers who want to evaluate the return on their intellectual capital and know whether it is growing? There is help. Since these invisible assets cast long shadows, the best technique for tracking them may be to measure the shadows themselves.

One surrogate measure, says David Teece, an economist at Berkeley, is Tobin's q. That's the ratio between a company's market value (stock price times shares outstanding) and the replacement value of its physical assets. The ratio was invented by James Tobin, a Nobel Prize-winning economist at Yale, who used it to analyse why companies make capital investments. But, says Teece, it also 'reflects something the market values that's not on the balance sheet, part of which is intellectual capital'.

As you'd expect, high-tech companies have a higher q than basic industries. In 1990, Carnegie Group compared market value with book value (a number like replacement value, but more forgiving because it depreciates physical assets) for 100 companies. Says Dennis Yablonsky: 'Generally the more high tech, the higher the ratio of market to book value.' For software leader Microsoft it was nearly 8 to 1; for Emerson Electric, the ratio was 2 to 1.

Tobin's q can give only a relative measure of brainpower, because it shows much else: takeover talk, a company's market clout, general bullishness. (The q can be less than 1 in bear markets, which doesn't mean a company is moronic.) But taken with enough salt, Tobin agrees, his ratio reflects knowledge assets. For example, you can gauge whether you are closing or widening the gap with a competitor by comparing q's.

In companies that depend heavily on R&D, the value of intellectual assets can be approximated by measuring the results of research. Take Merck. The company generated a 1990 return on assets, as usually measured, of 22.2%. (The median for the Fortune 500 industrial companies: 4.8%.) Says Senior Vice-President Frank Spiegel: 'On a financial accounting model, it looks as if we have excess profits.' But as Merck and other drug companies would like critics of their 'greed' in Congress to understand, that model ignores the cost of the knowledge that produces those expensive drugs. Last year Merck sank $854 million into R&D – almost half what it spent on materials and manufacturing. This year it will invest $1 billion. Internally, Merck counts R&D as capital spending. Most other companies treat it as an expense.

To track R&D, Merck calculates the net present value of its patents, using discounted cash flows tied to the cost of capital. The company also factors in product life cycles, which are getting shorter as competition intensifies. Viewed this way, says Spiegel, 'we look pretty normal' in terms of Return on

Assets (ROA). More important, the model lets Merck make sure it is investing enough in R&D to replenish its intellectual capital.

Why not just tote up the raw cost of R&D? Not good enough, says Kaplan: 'The value of these investments only loosely correlates with what you spend. A company might put $100 million into R&D and get nothing – or get a billion a year for ten years. It's like drilling for oil.' Also, research depreciates. At Westinghouse, says R&D chief Isaac Barpal, the average technology becomes obsolete in five to seven years – at the company's electronic systems group, in just two or three years.

Other knowledge assets can be defined and treated the same way as R&D. Motorola calculates returns on its employee training costs; the company says some programs yield $33 in cash flow for every dollar spent. US West breaks its technology investments into two classes: those that create knowledge assets (such as expert systems that embody problem-solving techniques) and those that simply automate support functions like payroll. The payoff on the former is about twice the payoff on the latter.

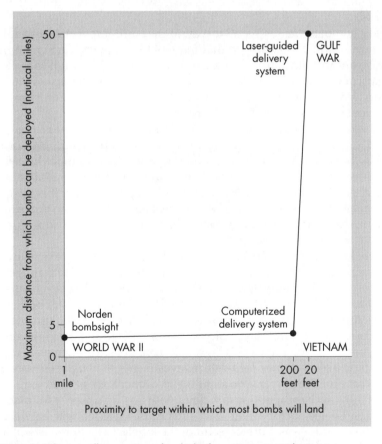

FIGURE 16.3 *Military intelligence. Smart bombs hit faraway targets with pinpoint accuracy. Result: fewer bombs needed, fewer pilots – and civilians – killed.*

Once you understand the value of knowledge assets, you can start using them in earnest to increase returns on physical assets – earning more bucks from the bricks. Failure to manage know-how is one reason capital-intensive industries show low returns on assets, says Alcoa's President, C. Fred Fetterolf. 'Our engineers have really been capital managers,' he notes, spending pots of money on machinery and not enough brainpower on improving processes. To change that, companies need to track organizational learning.

Whether charting learning curves, defect rates, or some other intellectual standard, the key is to measure not only *how much* improvement but *how long* it takes to achieve it. Argues Ray Stata, Chairman of Analog Devices, an electronic components maker: 'The rate at which individuals and organizations learn may become the only sustainable competitive advantage.'

Take on-time delivery – an important way brainpower can increase profits. Analog Devices logged the monthly percentage of late shipments for each of its seven divisions for a year. One division cut the number in half every four months. Others were barely improving; that is, they weren't learning. By tying bonus plans to these results, the company rewarded winners and motivated laggards.

Every company needs its own way to measure intellectual capital and the returns on it. The expertise that matters to a supermarket chain might be irrelevant to a stockbroker or a carmaker. Says ICL's Hugh Macdonald: 'It almost doesn't matter what the bloody metrics are, so long as you can know that this thing, whatever it is, is getting better or worse. If you don't keep your intellectual capital refreshed, it will erode.'

The economic landscape of knowledge-intensive business can differ markedly from the familiar neoclassical world. 'Buy land,' Will Rogers advised; 'they ain't makin' any more of it.' But we make more knowledge every day. Considered as capital, knowledge has other peculiarities. For instance, you can sell it to someone and still keep it yourself. It is also more flexible than physical capital. Says MIT's Roger Samuel: 'You can turn a farmer into an investment banker more easily than you can turn an auto assembly plant into an electronics factory.'

Where knowledge is the main ingredient in a product or service, up-front costs tend to be enormous, marginal costs relatively low. The average R&D outlay for a new drug approved in the 1980s was $231 million; seven out of ten drugs that made it to market never recovered their research cost. The marginal manufacturing cost for a typical prescription, however, is just a few dollars. 'Home runs matter a lot,' says Spiegel. Merck CFO Judy Lewent invented a video game, based on high tech's high-risk economics, in which players place their bets on a set of chancy high-return investments, then try to survive as the results come in. The player who stints on investment doesn't last long.

Often high-tech competition is vicious, with no purse money for place and show. The US-led victory over Iraq – the most lopsided war between big armies on record – was a direct result of the intellectual supremacy of allied arms and doctrine, not superior numbers of troops or tons of TNT. Its winner-take-all outcome has parallels in less lethal struggles. The VHS videocassette player virtually wiped out the Betamax format, because JVC quickly shared its VHS technology with others and that format became the one in which most prerecorded videocassettes were made. To avoid a fate like that of Betamax, Citibank tied into the Cirrus automatic teller network in New York, after years of a go-it-alone strategy. DEC joined the Open Software Foundation, having concluded that its proprietary VAX operating system would be worth more if it was compatible with the other systems too.

In all these cases, the companies grabbed for what are called network externalities, meaning that a network's value grows faster than the number of participants in it. Take a non-network business: imagine two candy bar makers each with 50 customers, who all buy one candy bar for $1 apiece. If one adds five customers, his revenue is 10% greater than his rival's. Now consider two discrete phone systems, each with 50 customers who call all the others at a buck a pop. Because each phone connects to 49 others, each network generates $2,450 for its owner. But if one signs up 10% more customers, they can call 55 times 54 people, or 2,970. That's 21% more potential revenue for the successful company. In networks, you can violate the law of diminishing returns for years without getting caught.

When a network gets big enough, its value can become so overwhelming that its competitors must join or die. Says Anthony Oettinger, head of Harvard's Program on Information Resources Policy: 'The map of the United

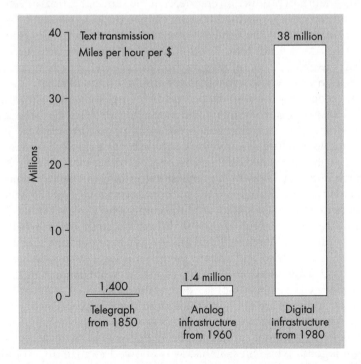

FIGURE 16.4 *Sending data smarter. A page of text zips from New York to Chicago faster and cheaper than ever. The message may be no more intelligent, but the means of transmission are.*

311

States is littered with old river towns, canal towns, and railroad towns that died because of new networks like interstates and airline hubs.' Network power can even lock in inefficiencies: soda cans, for example, could be made more cheaply if they were squat or tall and skinny – but they wouldn't work with the network of vending machines.

Fine, you say, but I'm in the candy bar business; what's in it for me? Simply this: network economics is available to anyone who wants to get the greatest returns out of their intellectual capital. Point-of-sale information sent through an electronic network can tell you instantly which candies are moving at which stores, helping you sharpen inventory management and marketing. Knowledge can be organized into the ultimate network: expensive to create, cheap and fast to use, accessible from any point at any time, valuable in geometric relation to the number of its parts. Says MIT's Roger Samuel: 'In theory, everybody in an organization could add value to everybody everywhere – and the organization could get the exponential returns of a network.'

The greatest challenge for the manager of intellectual capital is to create an organization that can share the knowledge. Like money in a mattress, says Hugh Macdonald, 'intellectual capital is useless unless it moves. It's no good having some guy who is very wise and sits alone in a room.' By finding ways to make knowledge move, an organization can create a value network – not just a value chain. It can link customers and suppliers to wipe out inventory, or put designers and production engineers at the same table (real or electronic) so that they can design products that are easy to build. Costs can be stripped out or value added to the total system, not just one part. 'Polaroid grew functionally,' says CEO Mac Booth. 'Now we're trying to create cross-disciplinary teams without diluting the functional excellence. Networking can do that in a hurry – and how fast that system can build value!'

Merck recognizes the importance of diffusing knowledge through the company. Research, development, and marketing all share the same mission. Says Vagelos: 'The marketing and production people are brought into the planning for a new drug so early you can hardly see a ripple. Scientists know that they haven't succeeded till their discovery is on the market.' Merck makes that clear in its reward system. It grants stock options to scientists who invent potential new drugs. Unlike regular stock options that vest on predetermined dates, these cannot be exercised until the compound passes various hurdles on its way to government approval. When research doesn't result in a marketable product, Merck will find other ways to reward the scientist if the information is published and adds to the general store of knowledge.

When a company turns expertise into capital, it creates something enduring. Take IDS. Says CEO Harvey Golub: 'Few of our portfolio managers are stars, but our mutual funds are often top ranked. And it's not because of patents or unique products. There's a value that's not just financial.'

What is it? Intellectual capital can be as ephemeral as the Holy Grail. In Arthurian legend, when Sir Galahad was allowed to gaze directly into the Grail's divine mysteries, he renounced the material world and was borne aloft on angels' wings. That won't do for a business executive, who needs to make

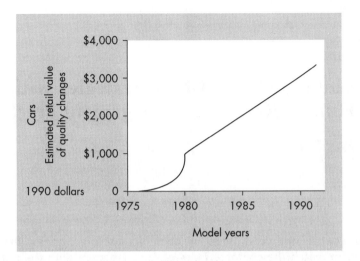

FIGURE 16.5 *The Automotive IQ. The cumulative value of quality improvements in new cars partly reflects intellectual investments in safety, fuel economy, emission controls, and other features.*

intellectual mysteries serve material purposes. Golub gropes to describe them. 'There's something about the culture – not just the knowledge but the way it gets applied – that gives the organization skills beyond the talent of the people.'

When skills belong to the company as a whole, they create competitive advantages that others can't match. The organization becomes more than the sum of its parts.

17

Linking Competitive Strategies with Human Resource Management Practices

*Randall S. Schuler and Susan E. Jackson**

Over the past several years there has been increased recognition that there is a need to match the characteristics of top managers with the nature of the business. According to Reginald H. Jones, former Chairman and CEO of the General Electric Company, 'When we classified . . . [our] . . . businesses, and when we realized that they were going to have quite different missions, we also realized we had to have quite different people running them.'[1]

Within academia there has been similar growing awareness of this need. Although this awareness is being articulated in several ways, one of the most frequent involves the conceptualization and investigation of the relationship between business strategy and the personal characteristics of top managers.[2] Here, particular manager characteristics such as personality, skills, abilities, values, and perspectives are matched with particular types of business strategies. For example, a recently released study conducted by Hay Group Incorporated, in conjunction with the University of Michigan and the Strategic Planning Institute, reports that when a business is pursuing a growth strategy it needs top managers who are likely to abandon the status quo and adapt their strategies and goals to the marketplace. According to the study, insiders are slow to recognize the onset of decline and tend to persevere in strategies that are no longer effective; so, top managers need to be recruited from the outside.

> Recruiting outsiders as a part of strategy has been successful for Stroh Brewing Co., once a small, family-run brewery in Detroit. Some 20% of its senior management team of 25 executives, including President Roger T. Fridholm, have been brought into Stroh since 1978. They've been instrumental in transforming it into the third-largest U.S. brewer.[3]

The result of such human resource staffing practices has been rather significant:

* Reprinted from *Academy of Management Executive*, Vol. 1, No. 3, copyright © The Academy of Management Executive, 1987. By permission of The Copyright Clearance Center.

Growth companies that staffed 20% of their top three levels with outsiders exceeded their expected return on investment by 10%. Those that relied on inside talent fell short of their goals by 20%. The same holds true for companies in declining industries: companies with outsiders in one out of every five top management jobs exceeded expected returns by 20%; those with a low proportion of outsiders fell 5% short.[4]

Outsiders, of course, are not always helpful. When a business is pursuing a mature strategy, what is needed is a stable group of insiders who know the intricacies of the business.

The results of the Hay study suggest that the staffing practices of top management be tied to the nature of the business because different aspects of business demand different behaviors from the individuals running them. The implication, then, is that selecting the right top manager is an important staffing decision.

Another perspective holds that top managers are capable of exhibiting a wide range of behavior, and all that is needed is to match compensation and performance appraisal practices with the nature of the business. Peter Drucker, commenting on the relationship between compensation and a strategy of innovation, observed that:

> I myself made this mistake [thinking that you can truly innovate within the existing operating unit] 30 years ago when I was a consultant on the first major organizational change in American history, the General Electric reorganization of the early 1950s. I advised top management, and they accepted it, that the general managers would be responsible for current operations as well as for managing tomorrow. At the same time, we worked out one of the first systematic compensation plans, and the whole idea of paying people on the basis of their performance in the preceding year came out of that.
>
> The result of it was that for ten years General Electric totally lost its capacity to innovate, simply because tomorrow produces costs for ten years and no return. So, the general manager – not only out of concern for himself but also out of concern for his group – postponed spending any money for innovation. It was only when the company dropped this compensation plan and at the same time organized the search for the truly new, not just for improvement outside the existing business, that GE recovered its innovative capacity, and brilliantly. Many companies go after this new and slight today and soon find they have neither.[5]

Similar results illustrating the power of performance appraisal and compensation to affect individual behavior have been reported in the areas of reinforcement, behavior modification, and motivation theories.[6] However, while much has been written on matching the behavior of top managers with the nature of the business, less attention has been given to the other employees in the organization. Nevertheless, it seemed reasonable to assume that the rest of the workforce would also have to be managed differently, depending on the business. This, then, became our focus of attention.

A critical choice we had to make in our study concerned which aspects of the business we were going to use. Consistent with previous studies, we decided to use the general notion of organizational strategy.[7] On the basis of previous studies that looked at strategy and human resource practices, we decided to adapt Porter's framework of competitive strategy.[8] Using the competitive strategy framework, we developed three archetypes of PHRM (Personnel and Human Resource Management) practices combinations. These were derived from the literature, secondary sources, and our previous research. We then examined each of the three archetypes in depth, using additional secondary data and field results, and addressed issues regarding implementation and revision of the archetypes. All are presented in this chapter.

First, we shall review the nature and importance of competitive strategy, and then we shall describe the concept of needed role behavior that enabled us to link competitive strategies and HRM practices.

COMPETITIVE STRATEGIES

Crucial to a firm's growth and prosperity is the ability to gain and retain competitive advantage. One way to do this is through strategic initiative. MacMillan defines 'strategic initiative' as the ability to capture control of strategic behavior in the industries in which a firm competes.[9] To the extent one company gains the initiative, competitors are obliged to respond and thereby play a *reactive* rather than proactive role. MacMillan argues that firms that gain a strategic advantage control their own destinies. To the extent that a firm gains an advantage difficult for competitors to remove, it stays in control longer and therefore should be more effective.

The concept of competitive advantage is described by Porter as the essence of competitive strategy.[10] Emerging from his discussion are three competitive strategies that organizations can use to gain competitive advantage: innovation, quality enhancement, and cost reduction. The *innovation strategy* is used to develop products or services different from those of competitors; the primary focus here is on offering something new and different. Enhancing product and/or service quality is the primary focus of the *quality enhancement strategy*. In the *cost reduction strategy*, firms typically attempt to gain competitive advantage by being the lowest-cost producer. Although we shall describe these three competitive strategies as pure types applied to single business units or even single plants or functional areas, some overlap can occur. That is, it is plausible to find business units, plants, or functional areas pursuing two or more competitive strategies simultaneously. This, and how to manage it are discussed later.

COMPETITIVE STRATEGY: NEEDED ROLE BEHAVIORS

Before developing a linkage between competitive strategy and HRM practices, there must be a *rationale* for that linkage. This rationale gives us a basis for predicting, studying, refining, and modifying both strategy and practices in specific circumstances.

Consistent with previous research, the rationale developed is based on what is needed from employees apart from the specific technical skills, knowledge, and abilities (SKAs) required to perform a specific task.[11] Rather than thinking about task-specific SKAs, then, it is more useful to think about what is needed from an employee who works with other employees in a social environment.[12] These needed employee behaviors are actually best thought of as needed role behaviors.[13] The importance of roles and their potential dysfunction in organizations, particularly role conflict and ambiguity, is well documented.[14]

Based on an extensive review of the literature and secondary data, several role behaviors are assumed to be instrumental in the implementation of the competitive strategies. Figure 17.1 shows several dimensions along which employees' role behaviors can vary. The dimensions shown are the ones for which there are likely to be major differences across competitive strategies. This can be illustrated by describing the various competitive strategies and their necessary organizational conditions in more detail, along with the needed role behaviors from the employees.

INNOVATION STRATEGY AND NEEDED ROLE BEHAVIORS

Because the imperative for an organization pursuing an innovation strategy is to be the most unique producer, conditions for innovation must be created. These conditions can be rather varied. They can be created either formally

1	Highly repetitive, predictable behavior	. . . Highly creative, innovative behavior
2	Very short-term focus	. . . Very long-term behavior
3	Highly co-operative, interdependent behavior	. . . Highly independent, autonomous behavior
4	Very low concern for quality	. . . Very high concern for quality
5	Very low concern for quantity	. . . Very high concern for quantity
6	Very low risk taking	. . . Very high risk taking
7	Very high concern for process	. . . Very high concern for results
8	High preference to avoid responsibility	. . . High preference to assume responsibility
9	Very inflexible to change	. . . Very flexible to change
10	Very comfortable with stability	. . . Very tolerant of ambiguity and unpredictability
11	Narrow skill application	. . . Broad skill application
12	Low job (firm) involvement	. . . High job (firm) involvement

FIGURE 17.1 *Employee role behaviors for competitive strategies (adapted from R. S. Schuler, 'Human resource management practice choices,' in R. S. Schuler, S. A. Youngblood, and V. L. Huber (eds), Readings in Personnel and Human Resource Management, 3rd edn, St Paul, MN: West Publishing, 1988)*

through official corporate policy or more informally. According to Rosabeth Moss Kanter:

> Innovation [and new venture development] may originate as a deliberate and official decision of the highest levels of management or there may be the more-or-less 'spontaneous' creation of mid-level people who take the initiative to solve a problem in new ways or to develop a proposal for change. Of course, highly successful companies allow both, and even official top management decisions to undertake a development effort benefit from the spontaneous creativity of those below.[15]

To encourage as many employees as possible to be innovative, 3M has developed an informal doctrine of allowing employees to 'bootleg' 15% of their time on their own projects. A less systematic approach to innovation is encouraging employees to offer suggestions for new and improved ways of doing their own job or manufacturing products.

Overall, then, for firms pursuing a competitive strategy of innovation, the profile of employee role behaviors includes (1) a high degree of creative behavior, (2) a longer-term focus, (3) a relatively high level of co-operative, interdependent behavior, (4) a moderate degree of concern for quality, (5) a moderate concern for quantity, (6) an equal degree of concern for process and results, (7) a greater degree of risk taking, and (8) a high tolerance of ambiguity and unpredictability.[16]

The implications of pursuing a competitive strategy of innovation for managing people may include selecting highly skilled individuals, giving employees more discretion, using minimal controls, making a greater investment in human resources, providing more resources for experimentation, allowing and even rewarding occasional failure, and appraising performance for its long-run implications. As a consequence of these conditions, pursuing an innovation strategy may result in feelings of enhanced personal control and morale, and thus a greater commitment to self and profession rather than to the employing organization. Nevertheless, benefits may accrue to the firm as well as the employee, as evidenced by the success of such innovative firms as Hewlett-Packard, the Raytheon Corporation, 3M, Johnson and Johnson, and PepsiCo.

Thus, the innovation strategy has significant implications for human resource management. Rather than emphasizing managing people so that they work *harder* (cost-reduction strategy) or *smarter* (quality strategy) on the same products or services, the innovation strategy requires people to work *differently*. This, then, is the necessary ingredient.[17]

QUALITY-ENHANCEMENT STRATEGY AND NEEDED ROLE BEHAVIORS

At Xerox, CEO David Kearns defines quality as 'being right the first time every time'. The implications for managing people are significant. According to

James Houghton, Chairman of Corning Glass Works, his company's 'total quality approach' is about people. At Corning, good ideas for product improvement often come from employees, and in order to carry through on their ideas Corning workers form short-lived 'corrective action teams' to solve specific problems.

> Employees [also] give their supervisors written 'method improvement requests,' which differ from ideas tossed into the traditional suggestion box in that they get a prompt formal review so the employees aren't left wondering about their fate. In the company's Erwin Ceramics plant, a maintenance employee suggested substituting one flexible tin mold for an array of fixed molds that shape the wet ceramic product baked into catalytic converters for auto exhausts.[18]

At Corning, then, quality improvement involves getting employees committed to quality and continual improvement. While policy statements emphasizing the 'total quality approach' are valuable, they are also followed up with specific human resources practices: feedback systems are in place, team work is permitted and facilitated, decision making and responsibility are part of each employee's job description, and job classifications are flexible.

Quality improvement often means changing the processes of production in ways that require workers to be more involved and more flexible. As jobs change, so must job classification systems. At Brunswick's Mercury Marine division, the number of job classifications was reduced from 126 to 12. This has permitted greater flexibility in the use of production processes and employees. Machine operators have gained greater opportunities to learn new skills. They inspect their own work and do preventive maintenance in addition to running the machines.[19] It is because of human resource practices such as these that employees become committed to the firm and, hence, willing to give more. Not only is the level of quality likely to improve under these conditions, but sheer volume of output is likely to increase as well. For example, in pursuing a competitive strategy involving quality improvement, L. L. Bean's sales have increased tenfold while the number of permanent employees has grown only fivefold.[20]

The profile of employee behaviors necessary for firms pursuing a strategy of quality enhancement is (1) relatively repetitive and predictable behaviors, (2) more long-term or intermediate focus, (3) a modest amount of co-operative, interdependent behavior, (4) high concern for quality, (5) a modest concern for quantity of output, (6) high concern for process (*how* the goods or services are made or delivered), (7) low risk-taking activity, and (8) commitment to the goals of the organization.

Because quality enhancement typically involves greater employee commitment and utilization, fewer employees are needed to produce the same level of output. As quality rises, so does demand, yet this demand can be met with proportionately fewer employees than previously. Thanks to automation and a co-operative workforce, Toyota is producing about 3.5 million vehicles a year with 25,000 production workers – about the same number as in 1966 when it was producing one million vehicles. In addition to having more productive workers, fewer are needed to repair the rejects caused by poor quality. This phenomenon has also occurred at Corning Glass, Honda, and L.L. Bean.

COST-REDUCTION STRATEGY AND NEEDED ROLE BEHAVIORS

Often, the characteristics of a firm pursuing the cost-reduction strategy are tight controls, overhead minimization, and pursuit of economies of scale. The primary focus of these measures is to increase productivity, that is, output cost per person. This can mean reduction in the number of employees and/or a reduction in wage levels. Since 1980, the textile industry's labor force decreased by 17%, primary metals, almost 30%, and steel, 40%. The result has been that over the past four years, productivity growth in manufacturing has averaged 4.1% per year, versus 1.2% for the rest of the economy.[21] Similar measures have been taken at Chrysler and Ford and now are being proposed at GM and AT&T. Reflecting on these trends, Federal Reserve Governor Wayne D. Angell states, 'We are invigorating the manufacturing sector. The period of adjustment has made us more competitive.'[22]

In addition to reducing the number of employees, firms are also reducing wage levels. For example, in the household appliance industry where GE, Whirlpool, Electrolux, and Maytag account for 80% of all production, labor costs have been cut by shifting plants from states where labor is expensive to less costly sites. The result of this is that a new breed of cost-effective firms are putting US manufacturing back on the road to profitability.[23]

Cost reduction can also be pursued through increased use of part-time employees, subcontractors, work simplification and measurement procedures, automation, work rule changes, and job assignment flexibility. Thus, there are several methods for reducing costs. Although the details are vastly different, they all share the goal of reducing output cost per employee.

In summary, the profile of employee role behaviors necessary for firms seeking to gain competitive advantage by pursuing the competitive strategy of cost reduction is as follows: (1) relatively repetitive and predictable behaviors, (2) a rather short-term focus, (3) primarily autonomous or individual activity, (4) modest concern for quality, (5) high concern for quantity of output (goods or services), (6) primary concern for results, (7) low risk-taking activity, and (8) a relatively high degree of comfort with stability.

Given these competitive strategies and the needed role behaviors, what HRM practices need to be linked with each of the three strategies?

TYPOLOGY OF HRM PRACTICES

When deciding what human resource practices to use to link with competitive strategy, organizations can choose from five human resource practice 'menus'. Each of the five menus concerns a different aspect of human resource management. These aspects are planning, staffing, appraising, compensating, and training and development.

A summary of these menus is shown in Figure 17.2. Notice that each of the choices runs along a continuum. Most of the options are self-explanatory, but a rundown of the staffing menu will illustrate how the process works. A more detailed description of all menus is provided elsewhere.[24]

Planning choices

Informal	. . .	Formal
Short term	. . .	Long term
Explicit job analysis	. . .	Implicit job analysis
Job simplification	. . .	Job enrichment
Low employee involvement	. . .	High employee involvement

Staffing choices

Internal sources	. . .	External sources
Narrow paths	. . .	Broad paths
Single ladder	. . .	Multiple ladders
Explicit criteria	. . .	Implicit criteria
Limited socialization	. . .	Extensive socialization
Closed procedures	. . .	Open procedures

Appraising choices

Behavioral criteria	. . .	Results criteria
Purposes: development, remedial, maintenance		
Low employee participation	. . .	High employee participation
Long-term criteria	. . .	Short-term criteria
Group criteria	. . .	Individual criteria

Compensating choices

Low base salaries	. . .	High base salaries
Internal equity	. . .	External equity
Few perks	. . .	Many perks
Standard, fixed package	. . .	Flexible package
Low participation	. . .	High participation
No incentives	. . .	Many incentives
Short-term incentives	. . .	Long-term incentives
No employment security	. . .	High employment security
Hierarchical	. . .	High participation

Training and development

Short term	. . .	Long term
Narrow application	. . .	Broad application
Productivity emphasis	. . .	Quality of work life emphasis
Spontaneous, unplanned	. . .	Planned, systematic
Individual orientation	. . .	Group orientation
Low participation	. . .	High participation

FIGURE 17.2 *Human resource management practice menus (adapted from R. S. Schuler, 'Human resource management practice choices,' in R. S. Schuler, S. A. Youngblood, and V. L. Huber (eds), Readings in Personnel and Human Resource Management, 3rd edn, St Paul, MN: West Publishing, 1988)*

Recruitment

In each of these areas, a business unit (or a plant) must make a number of decisions; the first choice involving where to recruit employees. Companies can rely on the internal labor market, e.g., other departments in the firm and other levels in the organizational hierarchy, or they can rely on the external labor market exclusively. Although this decision may not be significant for entry-level jobs, it is very important for most other jobs. Recruiting internally essentially means a policy of promotion from within. While this policy can serve as an effective reward, it commits a firm to providing training and career development opportunities if the promoted employees are to perform well.

Career paths

Here, the company must decide whether to establish broad or narrow career paths for its employees. The broader the paths, the greater the opportunity for employees to acquire skills that are relevant to many functional areas and to gain exposure and visibility within the firm. Either a broad or a narrow career path may enhance an employee's acquisition of skills and opportunities for promotion, but the time frame is likely to be much longer for broad skill acquisition than for the acquisition of a more limited skill base. Although promotion may be quicker under a policy of narrow career paths, an employee's career opportunities may be more limited over the long run.

Promotions

Another staffing decision to be made is whether to establish one or several promotion ladders. Establishing several ladders enlarges the opportunities for employees to be promoted and yet stay within a given technical specialty without having to assume managerial responsibilities. Establishing just one promotion ladder enhances the relative value of a promotion and increases the competition for it.

Part and parcel of a promotion system are the criteria used in deciding who to promote. The criteria can vary from the very explicit to the very implicit. The more explicit the criteria, the less adaptable the promotion system is to exceptions and changing circumstances. What the firm loses in flexibility, the employee may gain in clarity. This clarity, however, may benefit only those who fulfil the criteria exactly. On the other hand, the more implicit the criteria, the greater the flexibility to move employees around to develop them more broadly.

Socialization

After an employee is hired or promoted, he or she is next socialized. With minimal socialization, firms convey few informal rules and establish new procedures to immerse employees in the culture and practices of the organization. Although it is probably easier and cheaper to do this than to provide maximum socialization, the result is likely to be a more restricted psychological attachment and commitment by the employee to the firm, and perhaps less predictable behavior from the employee.

Openness

A final choice to be made in the staffing menu is the degree of openness in the staffing procedures. The more open the procedures, the more likely there is to be job posting for internal recruitment and self-nomination for promotion. To facilitate a policy of openness, firms need to make the relevant information available to employees. Such a policy is worthwhile; since it allows employees to select themselves into jobs, it is a critical aspect of attaining successful job–person fit. The more secret the procedures, the more limited the involvement of employees in selection decisions, but the faster the decision can be made.

A key aspect of the choices within the staffing activity or any other HRM activity is that different choices stimulate and reinforce different role behaviors. Because these have been described in detail elsewhere, their impact is summarized below.

HYPOTHESES OF COMPETITIVE STRATEGY-HRM ARCHETYPES

Based on the above descriptions of competitive strategies and the role behaviors necessary for each, and the brief typology of HRM practices, we offer three summary hypotheses.

Innovation strategy

Firms pursuing the innovation strategy are likely to have the following characteristics: (1) jobs that require close interaction and co-ordination among groups of individuals, (2) performance appraisals that are more likely to reflect longer-term and group-based achievements, (3) jobs that allow employees to develop skills that can be used in other positions in the firm, (4) compensation systems that emphasize internal equity rather than external or market-based equity, (5) pay rates that tend to be low, but that allow employees to be stockholders and have more freedom to choose the mix of components (salary, bonus, stock options) that make up their pay package, and (6) broad career paths to reinforce the development of a broad range of skills. These practices facilitate co-operative, interdependent behavior that is oriented toward the longer term, and foster exchange of ideas and risk taking.[25]

Quality-enhancement strategy

In an attempt to gain competitive advantage through the quality-enhancement strategy, the key HRM practices include (1) relatively fixed and explicit job descriptions, (2) high levels of employee participation in decisions relevant to immediate work conditions and the job itself, (3) a mix of individual and group criteria for performance appraisal that is mostly short-term and results oriented, (4) relatively egalitarian treatment of employees and some guarantees of employment security, and (5) extensive and continuous training and development of employees. These practices facilitate quality enhancement by helping to ensure highly reliable behavior from individuals who can identify with the goals of the organization and, when necessary, be flexible and adaptable to new job assignments and technological change.[26]

Cost-reduction strategy

In attempting to gain competitive advantage by pursuing a strategy of cost reduction, key human resource practice choices include (1) relatively fixed (stable) and explicit job descriptions that allow little room for ambiguity, (2) narrowly designed jobs and narrowly defined career paths that encourage specialization, expertise, and efficiency, (3) short-term, results-oriented performance appraisals, (4) close monitoring of market pay levels for use in making compensation decisions, and (5) minimal levels of employee training and development. These practices maximize efficiency by providing means for management to monitor and control closely the activities of employees.

AN INNOVATIVE STRATEGY: ONE COMPANY'S EXPERIENCE

Frost, Inc., is one company that has made a conscious effort to match competitive strategy with human resource management practices. Located in Grand Rapids, Michigan, Frost is a manufacturer of overhead conveyor trolleys used primarily in the auto industry, with sales of $20 million.[27] Concerned about depending too heavily on one cyclical industry, President Charles D. 'Chad' Frost made several attempts to diversify the business, first into manufacturing lawn mower components and later into material-handling systems, such as floor conveyors and hoists. These attempts failed. The engineers didn't know how to design unfamiliar components, production people didn't know how to sell them. Chad Frost diagnosed the problem as inflexibility. 'We had single-purpose machines and single-purpose people,' he said, 'including single-purpose managers.'

Frost decided that automating production was the key to flexibility. Twenty-six old-fashioned screw machines on the factory floor were replaced with 11 numerical-controlled machines paired within 18 industrial robots. Frost decided to design and build an automated storage-and-retrieval inventory control system, which would later be sold as a proprietary product, and to automate completely the front office to reduce indirect labor costs. The new program was formally launched in late 1983.

What at first glance appeared to be a hardware-oriented strategy turned out to be an exercise in human resource management. 'If you're going to reap a real benefit in renovating a small to medium-size company, the machinery is just one part, perhaps the easiest part, of the renovation process,' says Robert McIntyre, head of Amprotech, Inc., an affiliated consulting company Frost formed early in the automation project to provide an objective, 'outside' view. 'The hardest part is getting people to change.'

Frost was clearly embarking on a strategy of innovation. As it turns out, many of the choices the company made about human resource practices were intended to support the employee role behaviors identified as being crucial to the success of an innovation strategy.

For example, the company immediately set out to increase employee identification with the company by giving each worker 10 shares of the closely held company and by referring to them henceforth as 'shareholder-employees'. The share ownership, which employees can increase by making additional purchases through a 401(d) plan, are also intended to give employees a long-term focus, which is another behavior important for an innovation strategy to succeed. Additional long-term incentives consist of a standard corporate profit-sharing plan and a discretionary profit-sharing plan administered by Chad Frost.

Frost's compensation package was also restructured to strike a balance between results (productivity) and process (manufacturing). In Frost's case, the latter is a significant consideration, since the production process is at the heart of the company's innovation strategy. Frost instituted a quarterly bonus that is based on companywide productivity, and established a 'celebration fund' that managers can tap at their discretion to reward significant employee contributions. The bonuses serve to foster other needed employee role behaviors. By making the quarterly bonus dependent on companywide productivity, the company is encouraging co-operative, interdependent behavior. The 'celebration fund' meanwhile, can be used to reward and reinforce innovative behavior. (Even the form of the celebration can be creative. Rewards can range from dinner with Chad Frost to a weekend for an employee and spouse at a local hotel, to a belly dancing performance in the office.)

Frost encourages co-operative behavior in a number of other ways as well. Most offices (including Chad Frost's) lack doors, which is intended to foster openness of communication. Most executive perks have been eliminated, and all employees have access to the company's mainframe computer (with the exception of payroll information) by way of more than 40 terminals scattered around the front office and factory floor.

In our view, a vital component of any innovation strategy is getting employees to broaden their skills, assume more responsibilities, and take risks. Frost encourages employees to learn new skills by paying for extensive training programs, both at the company and at local colleges. It even goes further, identifying the development of additional skills as a prerequisite for advancement. This is partly out of necessity, since Frost has compressed its 11 previous levels of hierarchy into four. Because this has made it harder to reward employees through traditional methods of promotion, employees are challenged to advance by adding skills, assuming more responsibilities, and taking risks.[28]

HONDA'S QUALITY-ENHANCEMENT STRATEGY

We can identify those human resource practices that facilitate product quality by examining Honda of America's Marysville, Ohio plant.[29] With a current workforce of approximately 4,500, this plant produces cars of quality comparable to those produced by Honda plants in Japan. Although pay rates (independent of bonuses) may be as much as 30–40% lower than rates at other Midwest auto plants, Honda has fewer layoffs and lower inventory rates of new cars than its competitors. How is this possible?

One possible explanation is that Honda knows that the delivery of quality products depends on predictable and reliable behavior from its employees. In the initial employee orientation session, which may last between three and four hours, job security is emphasized. Employees' spouses are encouraged to attend these sessions, because Honda believes that spouse awareness of the company and its demands on employees can help minimize absenteeism, tardiness, and turnover. Of course, something so critical to quality as reliable behavior is not stimulated and reinforced by only one human resource practice. For example, associates who have perfect attendance for four straight weeks receive a bonus of $56. Attendance also influences the size of the semi-annual bonus (typically paid in spring and autumn). Impressive attendance figures enhance an employee's chances for promotion. (Honda of America has a policy of promotion from within.)

In addition to getting and reinforcing reliable and predictable behavior, Honda's HRM practices encourage a longer-term employee orientation and a flexibility to change. Employment security, along with constant informal and formal training programs, facilitate these role behaviors. Training programs are tailored to the needs of the associates (employees) through the formal performance appraisal process, which is developmental rather than evaluational. Team leaders (not supervisors) are trained in spotting and removing performance deficiencies as they occur. To help speed communication and remove any organizational sources of performance deficiencies, the structure of the organization is such that there are only four levels between associates and the plant manager.

At Honda, co-operative, interdependent behavior is fostered by egalitarian HRM practices. All associates wear identical uniforms with their first names embossed; parking spaces are unmarked, and there is only one cafeteria. All entry-level associates receive the same rate of pay except for a 60-cents-an-hour shift differential. The modern health center adjacent to the main plant is open to all. These practices, in turn, encourage all associates to regard themselves collectively as 'us' rather than 'us' versus 'them'. Without this underlying attitude, the flexible work rules, air-conditioned plant, and automation wouldn't be enough to sustain associate commitment and identification with the organization's goal of high quality.

The success of Honda's quality enhancement strategy goes beyond concern for its own HRM practices. It is also concerned with the human resource practices of other organizations, such as its suppliers. For example, Delco-Remy's practice of participative management style, as well as its reputation for producing quality products at competitive prices, was the reason why Delco was selected by Honda as its sole supplier of batteries.[30]

A COST-REDUCTION STRATEGY AT UNITED PARCEL SERVICE

Through meticulous human engineering and close scrutiny of its 152,000 employees, United Parcel Service (UPS) has grown highly profitable despite stiff competition. According to Larry P. Breakiron, the company's Senior Vice-President of Engineering, 'Our ability to manage labor and hold it accountable is the key to success.'[31] In other words, in an industry where 'a package is a package', UPS succeeds by its cost-reduction strategy.

Of all paths that can be taken to pursue a cost-reduction strategy, the one taken by UPS is the work standard/simplification method. This method has been the key to gains in efficiency and productivity increases. UPS's founder, James E. Casey, put a premium on efficiency. In the 1920s, Casey hired pioneers of time and motion study such as Frank Gilbreth and Fredrick Taylor to measure the time each UPS driver spent each day on specific tasks. UPS engineers cut away the sides of UPS trucks to study how the drivers per-formed, and then made changes in techniques to enhance worker effectiveness. The establishment of effective work standards has led not only to enormous gains in efficiency and cost reduction; it actually makes employees less tired at the end of the day. During the day, the employees engage in short-term, highly repetitive role behaviors that involve little risk taking. Because specialists identify the best way to accomplish tasks, employee participation in job decisions is unnecessary.

Through the use of time and motion studies, UPS has established very specific ways for workers to perform their jobs. The company also monitors closely the performance of the workers. More than 1,000 industrial engineers use time and motion study to set standards for a variety of closely supervised tasks. In return, the UPS drivers, all of whom are Teamsters, earn approxi-mately $15 per hour – a dollar or so more than the drivers at other companies. In addition, employees who perform at acceptable levels enjoy job security.

IMPLEMENTATION ISSUES

These descriptions of Frost, Honda, and UPS illustrate how a few organizations systematically match their HRM practices not only with their articulated competitive strategies, but also with their perceptions of needed role behavior from their employees. Although only a beginning, the success of these firms suggests that HRM practices for all levels of employees are affected by strategic considerations. Thus, while it may be important to match the characteristics of top management with the strategy of the organization, it may be *as* important to do this for *all* employees.

Although the results of these examples generally support the three major hypotheses, they also raise several central issues: which competitive strategy is best? Is it best to have one competitive strategy or several? What are the implications of a change of competitive strategy?

Which competitive strategy is best?

Of the three competitive strategies described here, deciding which is best depends on several factors. Certainly customer wants and the nature of the competition are key factors. If customers are demanding quality, a cost-reduction strategy may not be as fruitful as a quality improvement strategy. At the Mercury Marine division of Brunswick and at Corning Glass works, the issues seem to be quality. According to McComas, 'Customers, particularly industrial trial buyers, would have been no more inclined to buy their products even if the manufacturer could have passed along savings of, say, 10% or even 20%.'[32]

If, however, the product or service is relatively undifferentiated, such as the overnight parcel delivery industry, a cost-reduction strategy may be the best way to gain competitive advantage. Even here, though, there is a choice. United Parcel Service, for example, is pursuing the cost-reduction strategy through work process refinements such as work clarification, standardization, measurement, and feedback. Roadway, in contrast, pursues the same strategy by combining employee independence and ownership (drivers own their own trucks, of various colors; UPS drivers do not own their brown trucks) with as much automation as possible.[33] The advantage of these latter approaches to cost reduction, compared with such approaches as wage concessions or workforce reductions, is the amount of time required to implement them. Cost reduction through wage concessions or employee reductions, though painful, can be relatively straightforward to implement. As a consequence, it can be duplicated by others, essentially eliminating the competitive advantage gained by being able to offer lower prices. The adoption of two-tiered wage contracts within the airline industry is a good example: soon after American Airlines installed a two-tier wage system for its pilots, Eastern, United, and Frontier Airlines negotiated similar contracts with their employees.

There may, however, be some external conditions that might permit the success of a strategy of cost reduction to last. After four straight years of losses and a shrinkage in the number of stores from nearly 3,500 in 1974 to a little more than 1,000 in 1982, the Great Atlantic and Pacific Tea Company (A & P) and the United Food and Commercial Workers (UFCW) saw the writing on the wall: either reduce costs and be competitive, or go out of business. According to a *Business Week* article:

> In an experimental arrangement negotiated with the . . . UFCW at 60 stores in the Philadelphia area, workers took a 25% pay cut in exchange for an unusual promise: If a store's employees could keep labor costs at 10% of sales – by working more efficiently or by boosting store traffic – they'd get a cash bonus equal to 1% of the store's sales. They'd get a 0.5% bonus at 11% of sales or 1.5% at 9.5% of sales. It was a gamble in the low-margin supermarket business, but it worked.[34]

The result? An 81% increase in operating profits in 1984 and a doubling of A & P's stock price. Although the UFCW agreed with the incentive compensation scheme at A & P, the union appears unwilling to see this practice spread. Consequently, competitors of A & P, such as Giant Food Inc., would have difficulty implementing the same scheme.[35]

By contrast, a quality improvement strategy, whether by automation or quality teams, is more time consuming and difficult to implement. As the US auto industry has experienced, it is taking a long time to overcome the competitive advantage gained by the Japanese auto industry through quality improvement. The J. D. Powers 1986 Consumer Satisfaction Index of automobiles suggests, however, that Ford's dedicated approach to quality enhancement may be reaping benefits.

One competitive strategy or several?

Although we focused on the pursuit of a common competitive strategy in our examples, this may be oversimplifying reality. For example, at Honda in Marysville, associates are encouraged to be innovative. Each year the group of associates that designs the most unique or unusual transportation vehicle is awarded a trip to Japan. At UPS, teamwork and co-operation are valued and at Frost, Inc., product and service quality are of paramount importance. Lincoln Electric is recognized as one of the lowest cost *and* highest quality producers of arc welders. While these examples indicate that organizations may pursue more than one competitive strategy at a time, it may be that organizations actually need to have multiple and concurrent competitive strategies. Using multiple strategies results in the challenge of stimulating and rewarding different role behaviors while at the same time trying to manage the conflicts and tensions that may arise as a consequence. This may be the very essence of the top manager's job. According to Mitchell Kapor of Lotus Development Corporation:

> To be a successful enterprise, we have to do two apparently contradictory things quite well: We have to stay innovative and creative, but at the same time we have to be tightly controlled about certain aspects of our corporate behavior. But I think

that what you have to do about paradox is embrace it. So we have the kind of company where certain things are very loose and other things are very tight. The whole art of management is sorting things into the loose pile or the tight pile and then watching them carefully.[36]

Perhaps, then, the top manager's job is facilitated by separating business units or functional areas that have different competitive strategies. To the extent that this separation is limited or that a single business unit has multiple strategies, effective means of confrontation and collaboration need to exist. However, even with this issue under control, there is another equally significant challenge.

Change of competitive strategies

By implication, changes in strategy should be accompanied by changes in human resources practices. As the products of firms change, as their customers' demands change, and as the competition changes, the competitive strategies of firms will change. Consequently, employees will face an ever-changing employment relationship. A significant implication of this is that employees of a single firm may be exposed to different sets of human resource practices during the course of employment. Thus, employees may be asked to exhibit different role behaviors over time and they may be exposed to several different conditions of employment. Although it remains to be seen whether all employees can adjust to such changes, it appears that many can and have. For those who wish not to, firms may offer outplacement assistance to another firm, or even to another division in the company. For those who have problems changing, firms may offer training programs to facilitate the acquisition of necessary skills and abilities as well as needed role behaviors.

Another implication is that all components of a system of human resource practices need to be changed and implemented simultaneously. The key human resource practices work together to stimulate and reinforce particular needed employee behaviors. Not to invoke a particular practice (e.g., high participation) implies invoking another (e.g., low participation) that is less likely to stimulate and reinforce the necessary employee behaviors. The likely result is that employees will experience conflict, ambiguity, and frustration.

CONCLUSION

The recent attack on US firms for failing to keep costs down, not maintaining quality, and ignoring innovation are misdirected, given what many firms like Frost, Honda-Marysville, UPS, Corning Glass, A & P, 3M, and Brunswick are doing.[37] These firms and others are pursuing competitive strategies aimed at cost reduction, quality improvement, and innovation. The aim in implementing these strategies is to gain competitive advantage and beat the competition – both domestically and internationally. While cost and market conditions tend to constrain somewhat the choice of competitive strategy, the constraint appears to be one of degree rather than of kind. Consequently, we can find firms pursuing these three competitive strategies regardless of industry.

Not all firms are seeking to gain competitive strategy. Not doing so, however, is becoming more of a luxury. For those attempting to do so, the experiences of other firms suggest that effectiveness can be increased by systematically melding human resource practices with the selected competitive strategy. Certainly, the success or failure of a firm is not likely to turn entirely on its human resource management practice, but the HRM practices are likely to be critical.[38]

NOTES

The authors wish to thank John W. Slocum, Jr., C. K. Prahalad, and John Dutton for their many helpful suggestions, and the Human Resource Planning Society, the Center for Entrepreneurial Studies, New York University, and the University of Michigan for their financial support of this project.

1. L. J. A. Byrne and A. Leigh Cowan, 'An interview with Reginald Jones', *Organizational Dynamics*, Winter 1982: 46.
2. D. C. Hambrick and P. A. Mason, 'Upper echelons: the organization as a reflection of its top managers', *Academy of Management Review*, 9 (1984): 193–206; A. K. Gupta, 'Contingency linkages between strategy and general manager characteristics: a conceptual examination', *Academy of Management Review*, 9 (1984): 399–412; A. K. Gupta and V. Govindarajan, 'Build, hold, harvest: converting strategic intentions into reality', *Journal of Business Strategy*, 4 (1984a): 34–47; A. K. Gupta and V. Govindarajan, 'Business unit strategy, managerial characteristics, and business unit effectiveness at strategy implementation', *Academy of Management Journal*, 9 (1984b): 25–41; M. Gerstein and H. Reisman, 'Strategic selection: matching executives to business conditions', *Sloan Management Review*, Winter 1983: 33–49; D. Miller, M. F. R. Kets de Vries and J. M. Toulouse, 'Top executives' locus of control and its relationship to strategy-making, structure, and environment', *Academy of Management Journal*, 25 (1982): 237–253; A. D. Szilagyi and D. M. Schweiger, 'Matching managers to strategies: a review and suggested framework', *Academy of Management Review*, 9 (1984): 626–637; and J. D. Olian and S. L. Rynes, 'Organizational staffing: integrating practice with strategy', *Industrial Relations*, 23 (1984): 170–183.
3. L. J. A. Byrne and A. Leigh Cowan, 'Should companies groom new leaders or buy them?' *Business Week*, 22 September: 94–95.
4. Ibid.
5. A. J. Rutigliano, 'Managing the new: an interview with Peter Drucker', *Management Review*, January 1986: 38–41.
6. D. Q. Mills, *The New Competitors*, New York: Free Press, 1985; and M. Beer, B. Spector, P. R. Lawrence, D. Q. Mills, and R. E. Walton, *Managing Human Assets*, New York: Macmillan, 1984; R. M. Kanter, 'Change masters and the intricate architecture of corporate culture change', *Management Review*, October

1983: 18–28; and R. M. Kanter, *The Change Masters*, New York: Simon and Schuster, 1983.

7. J.L. Kerr, 'Diversification strategies and managerial rewards: an empirical study', *Academy of Management Journal*, 28 (1985): 155–179; J. W. Slocum, W. L. Cron, R. W. Hansen, and S. Rawlings, 'Business strategy and the management of plateaued employees', *Academy of Management Journal*, 28 (1985): 133–154; D. C. Hambrick and C. C. Snow, 'Strategic reward systems', in C. C. Snow (ed.), *Strategy Organization Design and Human Resources Management*, Greenwich, CT: JAI Press, 1987.

8. For detailed examples of how firms use their human resource practices to gain competitive advantage, see R. S. Schuler and I. C. MacMillan, 'Gaining competitive advantage through human resource management practices', *Human Resource Management*, Autumn 1984: 241–255; R. S. Schuler, 'Fostering and facilitating entrepreneurship in organizations: implications for organization structure and human resource management practices', *Human Resource Management*, Winter 1986: 607–629; and M. E. Porter, *Competitive Strategy*, New York: Free Press, 1980, and M. E. Porter, *Competitive Advantage*, New York: Free Press, 1985.

9. For an extensive discussion of competitive initiative, competitive strategy, and competitive advantage see I. C. MacMillan's 'Seizing competitive initiative', *Journal of Business Strategy*, 1983: 43–57.

10. McComas (1986), Porter, 1980, 1985.

11. B. Schneider, 'Organizational behavior', *Annual Review of Psychology*, 36 (1985): 573–611.

12. D. Katz and R. L. Kahn, *The Social Psychology of Organizations*, 2nd edn, New York: John Wiley, 1978.

13. J. C. Naylor, R. D. Pritchard, and D. R. Ilgen, *A Theory of Behavior in Organizations*, New York: Academic Press, 1980; T. W. Dougherty and R. D. Pritchard, 'The measurement of role variables: exploratory examination of a new approach', *Organizational Behavior and Human Decision Processes*, 35 (1985): 141–155.

14. J. R. Rizzon, R. J. Hose, and S. I. Lirtzman, 'Role conflict and ambiguity in complex organizations', *Administrative Science Quarterly*, 14 (1970): 150–163; S. E. Jackson and R. S. Schuler, 'A meta-analysis and conceptual critique of research on role ambiguity and role conflict in work settings', *Organizational Behavior and Human Decision Processes*, 36 (1985): 16–78.

15. R. M. Kanter, 'Supporting innovation and venture development in established companies', *Journal of Business Venturing*, Winter 1985: 47–60.

16. H. DePree, *Business as Unusual*, Zeeland, MI: Herman Miller, 1986.

17. The following discussion is based on our survey and observations, and findings reported on by others. For a review of what others have reported, see R. S. Schuler's 'Human resource management practice choices,' *Human Resource Planning*, March 1987: 1–19.

18. M. McComas, 'Cutting costs without killing the business', *Fortune*, 13 October 1986: 76.

19. For a detailed presentation of Marine Mercury's program to improve quality, see ibid.

20. S.E. Prokesch, 'Bean meshes man, machine', *The New York Times*, 23 December 1985: 19, 21.

21. S. E. Prokesch, 'Are America's manufacturers finally back on the map?' *Business Week*, 17 November 1986: 92, 97.

22. Ibid., 92.

23. Ibid., 97. For more on Electrolux's human resource practices, see B. J. Feder's 'The man who modernized Electrolux,' *The New York Times*, 31 December 1986: 24.

24. Schuler, 1987.

25. E. E. Lawler III, 'The strategic design of reward systems', in R. S. Scholer and S. A. Youngblood (eds), *Readings in Personnel and Human Resource Management*, 2nd edn, St Paul, MN: West Publishing, 1984, pp. 253–269; and R. S. Schuler, 'Human resource management practice choices', in R. A. Schuler, S. A. Youngblood, and V. L. Huber (eds), *Readings in Personnel and Human Resource Management*, 3rd edn, St. Paul, MN: West Publishing, 1988. Other factors that can influence the human resource practices are top management, hierarchical considerations, what other firms are doing, what the firm has done in the past, the type of technology, size and age of firm, unionization status, and the legal environment and its structure (see R. K. Kazanjian and R. Drazin, 'Implementing manufacturing innovations: critical choices of structure and staffing roles', *Human Resource Management*, Fall 1986: 385–404).

26. P. F. Drucker, *Innovation and Entrepreneurship*, New York: Harper and Row, 1985; K. Albrecht and S. Albrecht, *The Creative Corporation*, Homewood, IL: Dow Jones-Irwin, 1987.

27. P.F. Drucker, 'Quality means a whole new approach to manufacturing', *Business Week*, 8 June 1987: 131–143; P. F. Drucker, 'Pul-eeze! Will somebody help me?' *Time*, 2 February 1987: 48–57; and R. L. Desatnick, *Managing to Keep the Customer*, San Francisco: Jossey-Bass, 1987.

28. This description is expanded upon in detail by S. Galante, 'Frost, Inc.', *Human Resource Planning*, March 1987: 57–67.

29. For additional collaborating information, see J. Merwin, 'A tale of two worlds', *Forbes*, 16 June 1986: 101–105; and S. Chira, 'At 80, Honda's founder is still a fiery maverick', *The New York Times*, 12 January 1987: 35.

30. As reported in Schuler and MacMillan, 'Gaining competitive advantage', 1984: 249–250.

31. D. Machalaba, 'United Parcel Service gets deliveries done by driving its workers', *The Wall Street Journal*, 22 April 1986: 1, 23.

32. M. McComas, 'Cutting costs without killing the business', *Fortune*, 13 October 1986: 77.

33. Ibid.

34. M. McComas, 'How A&P fattens profits by sharing them', *Business Week*, 22 December 1986: 44. For an excellent discussion of the difficulties to be overcome in dealing with changing from human resource practices based on hierarchy or status to those based on performance or what's needed, see R. M. Kanter, 'The new workforce meets the changing workplace: strains, dilemmas, and contradictions in attempts to implement participative and entrepreneurial management', *Human Resource Management*, Winter 1986: 515–538.

35. For a discussion of relevant issues, see D. Q. Mills, 'When employees make concessions', *Harvard Business Review*, May–June 1983: 103–113; and R. R. Rehder and M. M. Smith, 'Kaizen and the art of labor relations', *Personnel Journal*, December 1986: 83–94.

36. *The Boston Globe*, 27 January 1985.

37. Recent attacks on public and private firms have been summarized by the use of the word 'corpocracy'. A description of corpocracy is found in M. Green and J. F. Berry's 'Takeovers, a symptom of corpocracy', *The New York Times*, 3 December 1986.

38. The application of these human resource practices to strategy can be done by a firm on itself and even upon other firms that may be upstream or downstream of the local firm. For a further description, see Schuler and MacMillan, 'Gaining competitive advantage', 1984.

18

Managing Professional Intellect: Making the Most of the Best

James Brian Quinn, Philip Anderson and Sydney Finkelstein*

In the postindustrial era, the success of a corporation lies more in its intellectual and systems capabilities than in its physical assets. The capacity to manage human intellect – and to convert it into useful products and services – is fast becoming the critical executive skill of the age. As a result, there has been a flurry of interest in intellectual capital, creativity, innovation and the learning organization, but surprisingly little attention has been given to managing professional intellect.

This oversight is especially surprising because professional intellect creates most of the value in the new economy. Its benefits are immediately visible in the large service industries, such as software, health care, financial services, communications and consulting. But in manufacturing industries as well, professionals generate the preponderance of value – through activities like research and development, process design, product design, logistics, marketing or systems management. Despite the growing importance of professional intellect, few managers have systematic answers to even these basic questions: What is professional intellect? How can we develop it? How can we leverage it?

WHAT IS PROFESSIONAL INTELLECT?

The true professional commands a body of knowledge – a discipline that must be updated constantly. The professional intellect of an organization operates on four levels, presented here in order of increasing importance:

Cognitive knowledge (or know-what) is the basic mastery of a discipline that professionals achieve through extensive training and certification. This knowledge is essential, but usually far from sufficient, for commercial success.

* Reprinted by permission of *Harvard Business Review,* March/April 1996. Copyright © 1996 by the President and Fellows of Harvard College. All rights reserved.

Advanced skills (know-how) translate 'book learning' into effective execution. The ability to apply the rules of a discipline to complex real-world problems is the most widespread value-creating professional skill level.

Systems understanding (know-why) is deep knowledge of the web of cause-and-effect relationships underlying a discipline. It permits professionals to move beyond the execution of tasks to solve larger and more complex problems – and to create extraordinary value. Professionals with know-why can anticipate subtle interactions and unintended consequences. The ultimate expression of systems understanding is highly trained intuition – for example, the insight of a seasoned research director who knows instinctively which projects to fund and exactly when to do so.

Self-motivated creativity (care-why) consists of will, motivation and adaptability for success. Highly motivated and creative groups often outperform groups with greater physical or financial resources. Without self-motivated creativity, intellectual leaders can lose their knowledge advantage through complacency. They may fail to adapt aggressively to changing external conditions and particularly to innovations that make their earlier skills obsolescent – just as the techniques of molecular design are superseding chemical screening in pharmaceuticals today. That is why the highest level of intellect is now so vital. Organizations that nurture care-why in their people can simultaneously thrive in the face of today's rapid changes and renew their cognitive knowledge, advanced skills and systems understanding in order to compete in the next wave of advances.

Intellect clearly resides in the brains of professionals. The first three levels can also exist in the organization's systems, databases or operating technologies, whereas the fourth is often found in its culture. The value of intellect increases markedly as one moves up the intellectual scale from cognitive knowledge to self-motivated creativity. Yet most enterprises focus virtually all their training attention on developing basic rather than advanced skills and little or none on systems or creative skills.

Most of a typical professional's activity is directed at perfection, not creativity. Customers primarily want professional knowledge delivered reliably and with the most advanced skill available. Although there is an occasional call for creativity, most of the work done by accounting units, hospitals, software companies or financial service providers requires the repeated use of highly developed skills on relatively similar, though complex, problems. People rarely want surgeons, accountants, pilots, maintenance personnel or nuclear plant operators to be very creative. Managers clearly must prepare their professionals for the few emergencies or other special circumstances that require creativity, but they should focus most of their attention on delivering consistent, high-quality intellectual output.

Because professionals have specialized knowledge and have been trained as an elite, they often tend to regard their judgement in other realms as sacrosanct as well. Professionals generally hesitate to subordinate themselves to others or to support organizational goals not completely congruous with their special viewpoint. That is why most professional firms operate as partnerships and not as hierarchies, and why it is difficult for them to adopt a unified strategy.

Members of every profession tend to look to their peers to determine codes of behaviour and acceptable standards of performance. They often refuse to accept evaluations by those outside their discipline. Many doctors, for example, resist the attempts of HMOs and insurance companies to tell them how to practise medicine. Such a posture is the source of many professional organizations' problems. Professionals tend to surround themselves with people who have similar backgrounds and values. Unless deliberately fractured, these discipline-based cocoons quickly become inward-looking bureaucracies that are resistant to change and detached from customers. Consider the many software or basic research organizations that become isolated inside larger organizations, creating conflicts with other professional groups such as marketing or manufacturing departments.

DEVELOPING PROFESSIONAL INTELLECT

At the heart of the most effective professional organizations we have observed are a handful of best practices for managing intellect that resemble successful coaching more than anything else.

Recruit the best

The leverage of intellect is so great that a few topflight professionals can create a successful organization or make a lesser one flourish. Marvin Bower essentially created McKinsey and Company; Robert Noyce and Gordon E. Moore spawned Intel; William H. Gates and Paul Allen built Microsoft; Herbert W. Boyer and Robert A. Swanson made Genentech; and Albert Einstein put Princeton's Institute for Advanced Study on the map. But even such organizations must find and attract extraordinary talent.

It is no accident that the leading management consultants devote enormous resources to recruiting and that they heavily screen the top graduates of the leading business schools. Microsoft interviews hundreds of highly recommended people for each key software designer it hires, and its gruelling selection process tests not only cognitive knowledge but also the capacity to think about new problems under high pressure. The Four Seasons Hotels often interview 50 candidates to make one hire. Venture capital firms, recognizing talent and commitment as the most critical elements for their success, spend as much time selecting and pursuing top people as they do making quantitative analyses of projects.

Because the most qualified professionals want to work with the best in their field, leading organizations can attract better talent than their lesser competitors. The best commercial programmers, for example seek out and stay with Microsoft largely because they believe Microsoft will determine where the industry will move in the future and because they can share the excitement and rewards of being at that frontier. But second-tier organizations are not destined always to lag behind. Managers who understand the importance of the right kind of talent can pull a jujitsu reversal on industry leaders by acquiring such talent. When CEO Marshall N. Carter led State Street Bank's entry into the rapidly emerging custodials business, he hired world-class data processing managers to seed his new organization. Today State Street handles $1.7 trillion in custodial accounts, and virtually all its senior managers have data processing rather than traditional banking backgrounds.

Force intensive early development

Professional know-how is developed most rapidly through repeated exposure to the complexity of real problems. Thus for most professionals, the learning curve depends heavily on interactions with customers. Accordingly, the best companies systematically put new professionals in contact with customers, where they work under the watchful eye of an experienced coach. Microsoft, for example, assigns new software developers to small teams of three to seven people. Under the guidance of mentors, the developers participate in the design of complex new software systems at the frontier of users' needs.

The legendary 80-hour weeks and all-nighters that give investment bankers and software developers their bragging rights serve a more serious developmental purpose: they enable the best talent to move up a learning curve that is steeper than anyone else's. On-the-job training, mentoring and peer pressure can force professionals to the top of their knowledge ziggurat. Although burnout can be a problem if people are pushed too far, many studies show that intensity and repetition are critical to developing advanced skills in fields as diverse as the law and piloting aircraft.

People who go through these intensive experiences become noticeably more capable and valuable – compared with their counterparts in less intensively managed organizations – within six months to a year. If they are properly coached, they also develop a greater in-depth feel for systems interactions (know-why) and identify more with the company and its goals (care-why). The most successful organizations ensure such growth through constantly heightened (preferably customer-driven) complexity, thoroughly planned mentoring, substantial rewards for performance, and strong incentives to understand, systematize and advance the discipline. The great intellectual organizations all seem to develop deeply ingrained cultures that emphasize these values. Most others do not.

Constantly increase professional challenges

Intellect grows most when professionals buy into a serious challenge. Leaders of the best organizations tend to be demanding, visionary and intolerant of halfhearted efforts. They often set almost impossible 'stretch goals' – as did Hewlett-Packard's William R. Hewlett (improve performance by 50%), Intel's Gordon Moore (double the number of components per chip each year), and

Motorola's Robert W. Galvin (achieve six sigma quality). Some professionals may drop out in response to such demands. Others will substitute their own even higher standards. The best organizations constantly push their professionals beyond the comfort of their book knowledge, simulation models and controlled laboratories. They relentlessly drive associates to deal with the more complex intellectual realms of live customers, real operating systems, and highly differentiated external environments and cultural differences. Mediocre organizations do not.

Evaluate and weed

Professionals like to be evaluated, to compete, to know they have excelled against their peers. But they want to be evaluated objectively and by people at the top of their field. Hence, heavy internal competition and frequent performance appraisal and feedback are common in outstanding organizations. As a result, there is a progressive winnowing of talent. For example at Andersen Consulting, only 10% of the carefully selected professional recruits move on to partnerships – a process that takes 9 to 12 years. Microsoft tries to force out the lowest-performing 5% of its highly screened talent each year. Great organizations are unabashed meritocracies; great organizations that fail are often those that forget the importance of objective praise and selective weeding.

LEVERAGING PROFESSIONAL INTELLECT

Conventional wisdom has long held that there are few opportunities for leverage in professional activities. A pilot can handle only one aircraft at a time; a chef can cook only so many different dishes at once; a researcher can conduct only so many unique experiments; a doctor can diagnose only one patient's illness at a time. In such situations, adding professionals at the very least multiplies costs at the same rate as benefits. In the past, growth most often brought diseconomies of scale as the bureaucracies co-ordinating, monitoring or supporting the professionals expanded faster than the professional base. Universities, hospitals, research firms, accounting groups and consultancies all seemed to pay the price.

For years, there were only two ways in which many organizations could create leverage: by pushing their people through more intensive training or work schedules than their competitors or by increasing the number of 'associates' supporting each professional. The latter practice even became the accepted meaning of the term *leverage* in the fields of law, accounting and consulting.

But new technologies and management approaches are changing the traditional economics of managing professional intellect. Organizations as diverse as Merrill Lynch, Andersen Worldwide and NovaCare have found effective ways to link new software tools, incentive systems and organizational designs in order to leverage professional intellect to much higher levels. Although each organization has developed solutions tailored to the specific needs of its business, there are a handful of common underlying principles.

Boost professionals' problem-solving abilities by capturing knowledge in systems and software

The core intellectual competence of many financial organizations – such as Merrill Lynch and State Street Bank – lies in the human experts and the systems software that collect and analyse the data that are relevant to investment decisions. A few financial specialists working at headquarters leverage their own high-level analytical skills through close interactions with other specialists and 'rocket scientist' modellers and through access to massive amounts of data about transactions. Proprietary software models and databases leverage the intellect of those professionals, allowing them to analyse markets, securities, and economic trends in ways that otherwise would be beyond their reach. Software systems then distribute the resulting investment recommendations to brokers at retail outlets who create further value by customizing the centre's advice in order to meet the needs of individual clients. If one thinks about this organization as a centre connected to customers at multiple points of contact, or nodes, leverage equals the value of the knowledge multiplied by the number of nodes using it. Value creation is enhanced if experimentation at the centre increases know-why and incentive structures stimulate care-why.

Merrill Lynch's retail brokerage business follows the basic structure outlined above. Roughly 18,000 Merrill Lynch brokers operate out of more than 500 geographically dispersed offices to create custom investment solutions for clients. The typical retail broker is not a highly skilled financial professional with years of advanced training. Yet the firm's brokers serve millions of clients worldwide with sophisticated investment advice and detailed, up-to-date information on thousands of complex financial instruments. Information systems make this extraordinary leverage possible.

Electronic systems capture Merrill Lynch's aggregate experience curve, quickly enabling less-trained people to achieve performance levels ordinarily associated with much more experienced personnel. The firm's computer network ensures that the retail brokers' cognitive knowledge is current and accurate. Merrill Lynch's information technologies allow the centre to capture and distribute to the brokerage offices information about transactions, trading rules, yields, securities features, availability, tax considerations and new offerings. Proprietary software, available on-line, serves as an instant training vehicle. It ensures that all brokers adhere to current regulations, make no arithmetic or clerical errors and can provide customers with the latest market information. Capturing and distributing the firm's knowledge base through software allows Merrill Lynch to leverage the professional intellect at its core.

Information technology allows a large modern brokerage to be both efficient and flexible. At the centre, it can achieve the full information power and economies of scale available only to a major enterprise. Yet local brokers can manage their own small units and accounts as independently as if they alone provided the service on a local basis. Their reward system is that of local entrepreneurs. The centre functions primarily as an information source, a communications co-ordinator, or a reference desk for unusual inquiries. Field personnel connect with the centre to obtain information to improve their performance, rather than to ask for instructions or specific guidance. At the same time, the centre can electronically monitor local operations for quality and consistency. Most operating rules are programmed into the system and changed automatically by software. Electronic systems replace human command-and-control procedures. They can also eliminate most of the routine in jobs, free up employees for more personalized or skilled work and allow tasks to be more decentralized, challenging and rewarding.

Overcome professionals' reluctance to share information

Information sharing is critical because intellectual assets, unlike physical assets, increase in value with use. Properly stimulated, knowledge and intellect grow exponentially when shared. All learning and experience curves have this characteristic. A basic tenet of communication theory states that a network's potential benefits grow exponentially as the nodes it can success-fully interconnect expand numerically. It is not difficult to see how this growth occurs. If two people exchange knowledge with each other, both gain information and experience linear growth. But if both then share their new knowledge with others – each of whom feeds back questions, amplifications and modifications – the benefits become exponential. Companies that learn from outsiders – especially from customers, suppliers and specialists such as advanced design or software firms – can reap even greater benefits. The strategic consequences of exploiting this exponential growth are profound. Once a company gains a knowledge-based competitive edge, it becomes ever easier for it to maintain its lead and ever harder for its competitors to catch up.

Overcoming professionals' natural reluctance to share their most pre-cious asset, knowledge, presents some common and difficult challenges. Competition among professionals often inhibits sharing, and assigning credit for intellectual contributions is difficult. When professionals are asked to collaborate as equals in problem solving, slow response is common as specialists try to refine their particular solutions to perfection. Because professionals' knowledge is their power base, strong inducements to share are necessary.

Even then, the tendency of each profession to regard itself as an elite with special cultural values may get in the way of cross-disciplinary sharing. Many professionals have little respect for those outside their field, even when all parties are supposedly seeking the same goal. Often, in manu-facturing companies, researchers disdain product designers, who disdain engineers. In health care, basic researchers disdain physicians (because 'they don't understand causation'). Physicians disdain both researchers (who 'don't understand practical variations among real patients') and nurses (who 'don't understand the discipline'). Nurses disdain both doctors and researchers (who 'lack true compassion'). And all three groups disdain administrators (who are 'nonproductive bureaucrats').

To facilitate sharing, Andersen Worldwide has developed an electronic system linking its 82,000 people operating in 360 offices in 76 countries. Known as ANet, the T1 and frame-relay network connects more than 85% of Andersen's professionals through data voice and video interlinks. ANet allows Andersen specialists – by posting problems on electronic bulletin boards and following up with visual and data contacts – to self-organize instantly around a customer's problem anywhere in the world. ANet thus taps into otherwise dormant capabilities and expands the energies and solution sets available to customers. Problem-solving capacity is further enhanced through centrally collected and carefully indexed subject, customer-reference and resource files accessible directly through ANet or from CD-ROMs distributed to all offices.

Initially, Andersen spent large sums on hardware, travel and professional training to encourage people not only to follow up on network exchanges but also to meet personally to discuss important problems – with disappointing results. Major changes in incentives and culture were needed to make the system work. Most important, participation in ANet began to be considered in all promotion and compensation reviews. To stimulate a cultural shift toward wider use of ANet, senior partners deliberately posed questions on employees' email files each morning 'to be answered by 10'. Until those cultural changes were in place ANet was less than successful despite its technological elegance.

Organize around intellect

In the past, most companies aimed to enhance returns from investments in physical assets: property, plant and equipment. Command-and-control structures made sense when management's primary task was to leverage such physical assets. For example, the productivity of a manufacturing facility is determined largely by senior managers' decisions about capital equipment, adherence to standardized practices, the breadth of the product line and capacity utilization. With intellectual assets on the other hand, individual professionals typically provide customized solutions to an endless stream of new problems.

INVERTING ORGANIZATIONS

Many successful enterprises we have studied have abandoned hierarchical structures, organizing themselves in patterns specifically tailored to the particular way their professional intellect creates value. Such reorganization often involves breaking away from traditional thinking about the role of the centre as a directing force.

Consider NovaCare, the largest provider of rehabilitation care and one of the fastest-growing health-care companies in the United States. Its critical professional intellect resides in its more than 5,000 occupational, speech and physical therapists. As professionals, they work alone to customize their expertise for individual patients at 2,090 locations in 40 states. To be of greatest value, they must be highly trained and constantly updated on the best practices in their fields.

By organizing around the work of its therapists, NovaCare achieves considerable leverage. To focus their time on serving patients' needs, the organization frees the therapists from administrative and business responsibilities by, for example, arranging and managing their contracts with care facilities, scheduling and reporting on treatments they give, handling their accounting and credit activities, providing them with training updates and increasing their earnings through the company's marketing capabilities.

NovaCare's software system, NovaNet, captures and enhances much of the organization's systems knowledge, such as the rules with which therapists must comply and the information they need about customers, schedules and billing; it highlights for executives those trends or problem areas most pertinent to future operations. NovaNet collects information from all therapists about, for example, their costs and services, techniques that have worked well and changing care patterns in different regions. This information is vital for recruiting, training, motivating and updating therapists.

To facilitate the collection and analysis of knowledge NovaCare records its therapeutic care activities in 10-minute blocks. This detailed information creates a database that can be used by a diverse group of stakeholders: caregivers, hospitals, clinics, payers, government agencies, executives and outside financial and regulatory bodies. NovaCare utilizes extensive peer and customer reviews in evaluating its therapists' work and (based on the time units captures in NovaNet) rewards them on the amount and quality of the care they deliver.

NovaCare's professionals are highly self-sufficient; they have tremendous autonomy on questions involving patient care. Therapists can give orders to all intermediate line organizations. The company's regional and functional specialists in accounting, marketing, purchasing and logistics exist primarily to support the therapists. Even CEO John H. Foster refers to the therapists as 'my bosses'. The leverage of NovaCare's organizational structure is 'distributive' – that is, the support organization efficiently distributes logistics, analysis and administrative support to the professionals. But it does not give them orders.

NovaCare has thus inverted the traditional organization. The former line hierarchy becomes a support structure, intervening only in extreme emergencies – as might the CEO of a hospital or the chief pilot of any airline. The function of former line managers changes: instead of giving orders, they are now removing barriers, expediting resources conducting studies and

Individual professionals

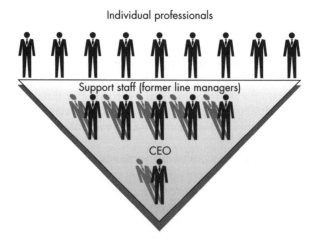

Support staff (former line managers)

CEO

FIGURE 18.1 *In Inverted Organizations, Field Experts Become Bosses.*
The center provides support services that leverage the professionals in the field. Inverted
organizations are appropriate when individual professionals have enough expertise to be
self-sufficient and can act independently to meet specific customer needs. Many health-care
providers, technical troubleshooting units, and universities are inverted organizations

acting as consultants. They support and help articulate the new culture. In effect, line managers evolve into staff people. (See Figure 18.1)

Inverted organizations like NovaCare make sense when individual experts embody most of the organization's knowledge, when they do not have to interact with one another to solve problems and when they customize their knowledge at the point of contact with customers. The software behind inverted systems must serve two somewhat conflicting goals: rules enforcement and professional empowerment. First, because professionals often resist regimentation, the software forces NovaCare's therapists to provide information in a consistent format, to comply with corporate rules and external regulations and to originate the information necessary to monitor quality, costs and trends for the organization's overall operation. Second, the software captures and distributes to professionals all the knowledge the company has built up over time so they can do their jobs better or more efficiently. That knowledge includes information about customers, professional databases, analytical models, successful solutions to problems and access to specialized sources of knowledge.

Inverted organizations pose some unique managerial challenges. The apparent loss of formal authority can be traumatic for former line managers. And field people who are granted formal power may tend to act more and more like specialists with strictly 'professional' outlooks and to resist any set of organizational rules or business norms. Given those tendencies and without a disciplining software, field people often don't stay current with details about their organization's own complex internal systems. And their empowerment without adequate information and controls embedded in the company's technology systems can be dangerous. A classic example is the rapid decline of People Express, which consciously inverted its organization and enjoyed highly empowered and motivated point people but lacked the systems or the computer infrastructures to enable them to adapt as the organization grew.

If such organizations fail, it is usually because – despite much rhetoric about inversion – their senior managers did not support the concept with thoroughly overhauled performance-measurement and reward systems. Inverted systems rarely work until field people largely determine their 'support people's' wages, promotions and organizational progress. Former line people are reluctant to take this last crucial step. In our studies of more than 100 major structural changes in 60 large service organizations, less than 20% of the organizations had changed their performance-measurement systems significantly, and only about 5% had changed their reward systems.[1] Without such changes, the complications were predictable. People continued to perform according to the traditional measures.

CREATING INTELLECTUAL WEBS

In NovaCare's business, the professional therapists who create value are largely self-sufficient individual contributors. The inverted organization, coupled with the right software and incentives allows NovaCare to enhance its therapists' productivity while giving them the operating autonomy they need. In other businesses, professional intellect is called on to create value by solving problems that exceed the capabilities of any solo practitioner. When problems become much more complex or less well defined, no one person or organization may know exactly what their full dimensions are, where key issues will ultimately reside, or who may have potential new solutions.

To tackle such problems – and to leverage their own intellectual assets to the maximum – a number of companies are using a form of self-organizing network that we call a *spider's web*. We use this term to avoid confusion with other, more traditional network forms more akin to holding companies or matrix organizations. Typically, a spider's web brings people together quickly to solve a particular problem and then disbands just as quickly once the job is done. The power of such interconnections is so great that even with a modest number of collaborating independent professionals (8 to 10), a spider's web can leverage knowledge capabilities by hundreds of times. (See Figure 18.2.)

Consider Merrill Lynch's mergers and acquisitions group. At the firm's centre, specialists work primarily with others in their own disciplines – for example, acquisitions, high-yield financings or equity markets. But when a large financing opportunity emerges, the project becomes an intellectual focal point and a team of specialists from different locations forms to pursue each individual deal. Such projects are so complex that, as one executive says, 'no one can be a know-everything banker. You can't have only specialists doing their own thing, and the client is not interested in dealing with multiple

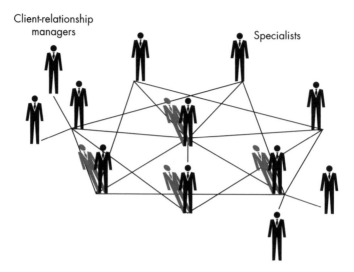

Client-relationship managers

Specialists

FIGURE 18.2 *In a Spider's Web, a Few Experts Team Up to Meet a Specific Challenge. Spider's webs form to accomplish a particular project and disband when the project is completed. They are appropriate when knowledge is dispersed among many specialists, who must provide a co-ordinated solution to a complex customer problem. Many consulting firms, investment banks, research consortia and medical diagnostic teams make use of spiders' webs.*

specialists.' The key problem is focusing Merrill Lynch's rich but dispersed talents on a single customer's problem for a short time. Client-relationship managers, who best understand the customer's integrated needs, usually co-ordinate these teams, but they don't have direct, hierarchical control over team members.

Despite the current popularity of virtual organizations and of networks, few companies understand when and how to use networked forms to leverage professional intellect. As the Merrill Lynch example shows, networks can flexibly combine high specialization in many different disciplines with multiple geographic contact points and a sharp focus on a single problem or customer set. But without the firm's specifically tailored promotion and compensation evaluation processes the system probably would not work.

At Merrill Lynch, individuals work with many different colleagues on a variety of projects over the course of a year. All of them submit a confidential evaluation on everyone with whom they have worked closely. People are willing to share knowledge and co-operate because their compensation is attached to this mosaic of peer relationships, and compensation is a major motivating factor in this business. There are enough close personal team contacts to allow a truly multifaceted picture of an individual's performance. According to one vice-president of the mergers and acquisitions group, 'In addition to profits generated, people are evaluated on how well they throw themselves into various projects, work with different groups to meet priorities and meet clients' needs. The culture penalizes those who fail to be team players or to meet clients' needs. Under these rules, spiders' webs have worked well in our relationship world. In our transactional world, however, we generally win by having the best specialists for that transaction.'

Because each spider's web is unique in its purpose, patterns and organizational power relationships, there is no single 'best way' to manage all of them. For many projects, there may not be a single authority centre. Often if the goal, problem or solution is sufficiently clear, decisions may occur through informal processes if the parties agree. When the various centres of excellence need to operate in a highly co-ordinated fashion, they may delegate temporary authority to a project leader – as when widely dispersed researchers present a contract proposal. In other cases, the organization may designate one person as the lead in order to force decisions or to make final commitments – as when an insurance or investment banking consortium faces a deadline.

How groups communicate and what they voluntarily communicate are as important as the advanced knowledge each centre of excellence may have. For virtually all purposes, however, encouraging shared interests, common values and mutually satisfying solutions is essential for leveraging knowledge in these structures. Research suggests that to accomplish this goal, network managers should force members to overlap on different teams in order to increase continuity of contact, joint learning and informal information sharing; purposely keep hierarchical relations ill defined; constantly update and reinforce project goals; avoid overly elaborate rules for allocating profits to individual nodes; develop continuous mechanisms for updating information about the external environment (for example tax code changes, customer needs or scientific results); involve both clients and peers in performance evaluations; and provide node members with both individual and team rewards for participation. Such consciously structured management interactions can mitigate the most common failures and frustrations.

The other key leverage factor in most spiders' webs is technology. Electronics allow many more highly diverse, geographically dispersed, intellectually specialized talents to be brought to bear on a single project than ever before. Because public telecommunications networks allow interconnection almost anywhere, the key to effective network systems generally lies in software that provides a common language and database for communications, captures critical factual data about external environments, helps players find knowledge sources (usually through electronic menus, web browsers like Netscape, or bulletin boards), and allows interactive sharing and problem solving. Each node will of course have its own specialized analytical software. But networking, groupware and interactive software – along with a culture of and incentives for sharing – are the keys to success in these systems.

Much can be done to leverage professional intellect through extraordinary recruitment, training and motivational measures. But, increasingly, managing human intellect alone is not enough. More radical organizational structures, supported by specifically designed software systems, are essential to capture, focus and leverage capabilities to the fullest. Such systems have become the glue that both joins together highly dispersed service delivery centres and leverages the critical knowledge bases, intellectual skills and accumulated experience in professional organizations. They also bond professionals to the organization by providing them with databases, analytical models and communication power that they cannot find elsewhere. These tools enable professionals to extend their performance beyond their personal limits, allowing them to achieve more inside the organization than they could on their own.

No organizational form is a panacea. In fact, many different forms often coexist successfully in the same company. Properly used, each helps a company attract, harness, leverage and deploy intellect for a quite different purpose. Consequently, each requires a carefully developed set of cultural norms supported by software and by performance measurement and reward systems tailored to the organization's specific purposes.

NOTE

1. Committee to Study the Impact of Information Technologies on the Performance of Service Activities; Computer Science and Telecommunications Board; Committee on Physical Sciences, Mathematics and Applications; National Science Council (1994) *Information Technology in the Service Society: A Twenty-First Century Lever*. Washington DC: National Academy Press.

19
HR and Organizational Structures

*John Storey**

Today's companies are seeking new configurations of organizational structure. They are dissolving internal boundaries and procedures while reaching out to engage suppliers, associates and even competitors in new forms of relationship.

These relationships have taken various forms but most prominent among them are joint ventures, strategic alliances, partnerships, spin-offs and networks. Within organizational boundaries, looser structures are emerging in the move from order, procedure, hierarchy and other classic bureaucratic attributes towards cross-functional teams and even the countenance of 'chaos'.

This chapter sketches an analytical framework for analysing these changes and describes some of their effects on the human resource (HR) function. It draws on the Open University Business School's current research into the management of innovation.

THE ANALYTICAL FRAMEWORK

Conventional organizational analysis generally focuses on internal organizational structures. In the past organizations were seen as systems with distinct boundaries. By contrast, great attention is now being paid to the connections made across organizational boundaries.

Alliances, federations and networks are seen as increasingly important. Information and communication technologies enable managers to transcend organizational boundaries and allow work to be done in new ways on a distributed basis. The past identity of an organization, situated in a particular physical place and associated with distinct products, is becoming less common and less relevant to its success in the new business environment.

Figure 19.1 maps out significant developments in organizational structures with reference to four key dimensions. It indicates a progression towards the

* Reprinted from *Financial Times Mastering Management Review*, Issue 17, October 1998. © John Storey.

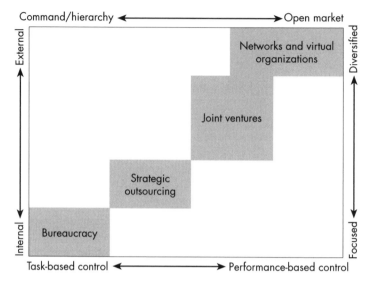

FIGURE 19.1 *New organizational structures and forms*

externalization of relations and towards diversified activities, performance-based control and an open-market mode of regulation. Although it is tempting to infer movement towards the top right of the figure, the evidence is not conclusive – historical analysis of organizational forms would suggest that apparent 'trends' often turn out to be 'cycles'. Nonetheless, in the past few years companies have moved away from conventional and bureaucratic organizational structures.

STRATEGIC OUTSOURCING

'Outsourcing' occurs when a company subcontracts to another supplier work that was previously performed in-house. It is a manifestation of the classic 'make or buy' decision and in recent times has been one of the more popular ways of cutting costs and refocusing on core competencies.

One striking example of this trend is the fact that by the mid-1990s the labour agency Manpower had displaced General Motors as the largest employer in the US. In a study of businesses and government agencies in the US, 44 per cent of the executives surveyed said that they were outsourcing more than they did five years ago and 47 per cent said that they expected to increase the amount of work they outsource in the future. Likewise, IT-related outsourcing revenues are estimated to be growing at 14.4 per cent annually.

In practice there are many different types of outsourcing. Sometimes it is piecemeal and opportunistic with little strategic character. Office cleaning, for example, is usually treated in this way. But for other services outsourcing decisions might arise from a close analysis of the value chain. For example, UK supermarket group Marks and Spencer derives its competitive advantage from a reliable level of quality, which is in turn supported by links between the company and its suppliers.

There are many reasons for the growth of outsourcing. In complex, fast-moving markets it is a speedy way of gaining access to specialist services. It can also reduce costs by using low-cost producers – many of whom are unlikely to be unionized. Advances in information and communication technologies have also contributed to the popularity of outsourcing. Companies headquartered in high-wage cosmopolitan areas, for instance, can outsource such tasks as routine billing to remote stations almost anywhere in the world.

Considerations for HR management

Since organizational hierarchies are much flatter in outsourcing organizations there is less scope for inter-functional activity and therefore a reduced need for managerial co-ordination. The priority for managers shifts from handling physical and capital assets to handling processes and staff who are not direct employees of the company. The negotiation of contracts with providers affects the HR function, extending into issues of confidentiality and risk sharing. Even when opt-out clauses for non-compliance are clearly denoted and formalized, occurrences of non-compliance may prove difficult to manage in practice.

A critical HR management issue is the potential loss of expertise in certain areas, which may be difficult to recover. Outsourcing may 'hollow out' the organization, threatening any aspirations towards organizational learning, corporate culture and shared vision.

Likewise, the sources of innovation that are needed to keep pace with rapidly changing markets may be threatened if a company is heavily reliant on strictly delineated services from a host of outside suppliers.

HR departments currently play a role in 65 per cent of outsourcing selection cases in the US (an increase of 30 per cent in the past five years). While the search-and-selection team ideally includes a senior executive, the respective department manager and a legal expert, HR managers often become centrally involved as facilitators and co-ordinators of the overall process.

Many contracted staff enjoy high levels of pay but in general, levels of inequality have increased as the outsourcing company's remaining permanent staff enjoy higher earnings, fringe benefits and better access to training. This presents a further challenge to the maintenance of organizations that are low on formal control structures but are supposed to score highly on shared values.

JOINT VENTURES AND ALLIANCES

Joint ventures and strategic alliances have become a common feature of the business world. They are especially prevalent in high-technology sectors such as telecommunications and pharmaceuticals. For example, British Telecom has more than 70 joint ventures and overseas distribution arrangements. Their popularity has been driven by increasing complexity and the accelerating pace of change in many industries. No single company can hold exclusively the intellectual resources and unique capabilities necessary for market domination. Hence many form alliances and joint ventures.

The need for innovation prompts many companies to reorganize. This strategy does not preclude the use of acquisition; many of the companies most active in joint ventures and alliances also engage in outright or partial acquisition. Large pharmaceutical companies, for example, use a repertoire of strategies in relation to small biotechnology enterprises: outsourcing, partnering and acquisition.

Organizations use joint ventures to achieve a number of objectives. First, large companies – using their marketing expertise and production and distribution systems – can bring products developed by smaller companies to market faster than a small company could by acting alone. Second, large companies may also gain a foothold in new product areas and acquire new expertise rapidly. Third, joint ventures enable the partners to reduce their cost base by allowing them to pool their resources. Fourth, certain countries may forbid inward investment that is not tied to some form of joint venture with a domestic concern.

Considerations for HR management

Companies usually neglect the impact of new alliances, acquisitions and joint ventures on HR management. There are, however, a few exceptions. US company Merck, for example, has a reputation for using HR in the management of joint ventures. Its HR staff are involved in the earliest stages of a prospective alliance or venture and become proactively involved in new staffing arrangements – for example, by devising new procedures and policies for the joint venture. Communication and education are given a high priority to ensure that partners not only understand each other but can learn from each other.

In the case of acquisitions, the HR role is usually assumed to involve the blending of corporate cultures and the harmonization of compensation schemes, job grades and HR procedures. However, in the case of joint ventures and strategic alliances, HR considerations are not generally thought to be relevant. The participating partners are assumed to be intent on preserving their own separate identities and the relationship is regarded as primarily commercial.

This is arguably a short-sighted, outdated and inappropriate response, especially when cross-boundary learning in modern corporations is increasingly recognized as vital. Alliance and joint venture partners may co-locate joint project teams and ring-fence their terms and conditions. They may actively seek to learn from each other and to institute a new variety of HR practices. IBM has recently been to the fore in experimenting with several kinds of employment arrangements.

On the other hand, it should be noted that even in the case of full acquisition, HR harmonization is not necessarily the best option. For instance, the UK division of Hewlett-Packard has traditionally incorporated acquired businesses into the corporate fold and imposed the corporate culture known as the 'HP Way'. Recently, however, some successful acquisitions have sought to maintain the independence of the separate unit.

A variant on the joint venture is an arrangement whereby companies enter into co-operative arrangements to invest in and share common services, such as a local training facility. This is exemplified in a more formal way by the Shared Service Centre established for the BBC by a joint venture company formed by Coopers and Lybrand and EDS, a US computer systems group. The new company will provide routine accountancy and financial services. Staff employed in the centre will be located on BBC premises and will eventually be able to sell its services to other customers. Similar shared service arrangements have also been initiated by other companies, such as General Electric and Whirlpool.

NETWORKS AND VIRTUAL ORGANIZATIONS

A 'network organization' is an economic entity that operates through a cluster of compact business units and is characterized by relatively few levels of decision making and a willingness to outsource whatever can be done better elsewhere. Organizations that have moved in this direction have found that new managerial roles are required.

Free-flow across organizational boundaries can cause a situation in which the organization *per se* becomes indefinable – a state of affairs sometimes described as a 'virtual organization'. Such an organization has a permeable and continuously changing interface between its core, its suppliers and its customers. In traditional organizations clear demarcation lines separated 'insiders' from 'outsiders'. Roles were relatively clear. The virtual organization, on the other hand, constantly reforms according to need. Job responsibilities shift, as do lines of authority – even the notion of the 'employee' becomes problematic as some suppliers and customers spend more time on company premises than do some of the firm's permanently contracted employees.

Considerations for HR management

Co-operative relations between organizations should be given high priority in network and virtual organizations. Instead of developing strategies independently, planning details need to be co-ordinated and shared with other

353

participants in the network. Information should be shared to allow joint problem-solving and auditing systems co-ordinated across the network.

Most of the computing and telecommunications companies in the OUBS research project collaborate with key suppliers and customers. They share 'road maps' so that product and service plans, sales, specification and scheduling data can be co-ordinated. Data packages are regularly shared with main suppliers and customers.

As for the management of resources and capabilities, a new emphasis on shared resources is emerging in the areas of technical and financial expertise, management skills, information systems and training and development.

As many employees as possible should become involved in the company's plans so that they can respond appropriately to customers' and suppliers' needs. One way of setting this process in motion is to invite customers and suppliers to meetings at which outlines of plans and their potential problems can be discussed. Employees can also be sent on customer and supplier field trips to experience their day-to-day operations.

In network organizations, employees tend to collect and collate more customer and supplier information than in conventional organizations. A more advanced network organization might even share technical information and services with customers and suppliers. Technical managers may end up spending more time with people 'external' to their organization than they do with internal colleagues. Under these circumstances, HR managers should be concerned with the well-being of the whole value chain.

CONCLUSION

The scale of these challenges has led some corporate chiefs to revert to old-fashioned command and control solutions. For example, Lord Simpson, Lord Weinstock's successor at GEC, has said that he wants to move away from 'the joint venture culture' towards direct investment and control by GEC managers.

Over the past decade, partnership with rivals and others has been one of the central pillars of GEC's strategy. Now it appears that this strategy is being largely abandoned in favour of attempts by the group to build global businesses on its own. Microsoft is another interesting case: business might seem suited to virtual operation, yet it has 20,000 employees focused on developing its own software products and a Chief Executive who maintains direct control. Where gaps appear in his company's expertise, he prefers to buy a specialist company and the expertise of the people in it.

It seems unlikely that just one of the three models will triumph. Market segmentation will continue to find reflection in markedly different organizational forms. Nor, perhaps, are the contrasts between them as great as we have been led to believe. Even 'knowledge-centred' organizations want to externalize as many costs and risks as possible. Thus it would be simplistic to categorize the 'new' forms as good or bad.

Nevertheless, changing business environments will continue to throw up challenges for managers charged with the task of finding appropriate structures for their organization, and some organizational forms will be more attractive than others. Raising awareness of the range of possibilities and of the ways of achieving the desired outcome is a worthwhile mission for the organizational analyst.

20

Quo Vadis Nunc: Where Does an Innovative Company Go Next?

*David Straker**

OUR CURRENT DILEMMA

Hewlett-Packard's whole 59-year history is based on constant innovation. From our first successes with oscillators for Walt Disney's *Fantasia*, we have grown into a $43 billion, 121,000 person company where 65% of our 29,000 current products were developed within the past two years.

But the rest of the world has not stood still. Where HP was once the only choice in many of its marketplaces, we now face hordes of vigorous and aggressive competitors who are relentlessly nibbling away at our lead. Like an elephant that has learned to dance nimbly, we face both ants that foxtrot as well as other global elephants who can quickstep to the same tune. We are also aware that other companies who have grown to our size have subsequently either stopped growing or had their growth radically reversed.

So where do we go? How can we avoid a 'Decline and Fall' of our much-admired empire? How can we dance faster or differently to leave the marauders behind again? Where are the next steps? How do we get onto them without stumbling? We know that innovation is the key, but how do we get even more innovative? How do we extract and use the full creative juices from our people?

THE ANSWER IS UNDER OUR NOSES

In 1979, Philip Crosby[1] introduced the idea of five levels of maturity, which an organization might ascend as they get better at quality management. Although we did not adopt the strict definition of the stages that he proposed, we did, ten years later in 1989, adapt the principles of maturity and five distinguishable stages for our 'Quality Maturity System'. The HP QMS is an internal Business

* Paper presented at MKIRU workshop, 'Building and maintaining the capability to innovate workshop', The Open University, Milton Keynes, 30 September 1998. © David Straker.

Excellence model, the content of which was based on the Japanese Deming Award and the US Malcolm Baldrige National Quality Award, along with our own experiences of successful business practices.

The QMS has proved to be a robust model, which has enabled us to consistently improve our internal business processes and practices. In 1997 we tested this against an external standard in the UK by applying for the Business Excellence award. At our first attempt and simply by describing what we already did, we scooped the top honours.

In the true innovative style of shamelessly stealing, adopting and adapting models and methods (we also won the first European Benchmarking Award), we can take the maturity model a step further by applying it to innovation.

Using an already accepted and proven conceptual framework makes change easier and faster, as the arch-innovator Edison demonstrated as he replaced the gas main with the electricity main, and the gas lights on the wall with electric lights, plus switches, in the same place. The maturity paradigm is well understood and using it to frame innovation should help speed us on our way.

THE FIVE LEVELS OF INNOVATION MATURITY

This chapter describes five levels of innovation maturity (shown in Table 20.1) which can be used both to assess the current position of a company and to show the way forward. The transition from each level requires a cultural shift to create and sustain the change in behaviour that is implicitly required for the next level of innovation maturity. Each of these maturity levels is described in the sections below.

Level 1: Suppressed

Frederick Taylor both advanced and froze management thinking with his 'scientific management' that focused solely on the task, relegating the worker to the machine. It is perhaps not surprising that Taylor was himself psychologically stunted with all the hallmarks of a disturbed, neurotic, anal-compulsive personality.[2] His very focus on efficiency blinded him to the inhumanity of many of his proposals, which were deeply unpopular even in his own day.

TABLE 20.1 *The Five Levels of Innovation Maturity*

Level no.	Level name	Management style	Individual approach	Critical domain
1	Suppressed	Fear	Displacement	None, product
2	Enabled	Ignoring	Skunkworks	Near
3	Encouraged	Supporting	Analytic/Intuition	Process
4	Educated	Training, structure	Tools, skill	Distant
5	Enlightened	Deep understanding	Appropriate	Strategic

Yet Taylor's legacy persists, despite the real and well-publicized concerns highlighted by people such as Douglas McGregor (Theory X and Theory Y)[3] and Hertzberg (Motivation-Hygiene theory).[4] Perhaps it is because it appeals so much to our deep need for control that many managers still stubbornly resist the notion that people can successfully think for themselves. It is also alluringly attractive for managers to assume that they have greater wisdom and creative ability than their charges. The notion of their subordinates having greater intelligence can be perceived as a threat to be suppressed rather than a skill to be encouraged.

Going further back, the blame might even be laid at the door of the Christian Church, where the constraints of the scriptures and their interpretation by a controlling clergy forbade innovation for many centuries. In 1634, Galileo was forced to recant his heresy about the place of the Earth in the firmament thus:

> I Galileo, being in my seventieth year, being a prisoner on my knees, and before your Eminences, having before my eyes the Holy Gospel, which I touch with my hands, abjure, curse and detest the errors and the heresy of the movement of the earth.[5]

This 'Management by Fear' results in creative abilities being displaced either towards disruptive activities such as strikes and other unhelpful actions or in hobbies outside the workplace which range from flower-arranging to fly fishing. W. Edwards Deming's exhortation to management to 'Drive out fear'[6] is a critical first step towards bringing innovation into the workplace.

What official innovation there is in such companies, is very largely product-oriented, contained and focused inwards. Individuals using innovation of any kind are also likely to keep it to themselves, for fear of punishment for stepping outside the rules.

HP has never really been at this level (although, being a large multinational, there have no doubt been occasional pockets of suppression). Brought up in the austerity of the Great Depression, Bill and Dave (Hewlett and Packard) founded the company with a spirit of family care for its employees. The people they employed were mostly like themselves, engineers with a passion for invention and technology and who clearly worked for far more reasons than bread alone. They also ensured that managers understood and applied these principles, thus building the foundations of an innovative culture.

> Another requirement is that a high degree of enthusiasm should be encouraged at all levels; in particular, the people in high management positions must not only be enthusiastic themselves, they must be able to engender enthusiasm among their associates.[7]

Level 2: Enabled

In an organization where innovation is enabled, the basic culture contains rules that give permission to be creative, but provide limited assistance or direction with the task. This seems a small step, but it can have a powerful effect on the innovation within companies. Many significant innovations have come from unofficial projects where people were simply allowed to continue work on pet projects.

The 'skunkworks', popularized by Peters and Waterman, is an example of enabled 'official unofficial' work, where people are allowed to work on projects either in their own time or outside of the main research activity.

> Last year a major corporate product bombed. A skunk works member asked for and got permission to take two samples home and set them up in his basement. He used one as a benchmark. He tinkered with the other for about three weeks and corrected virtually all of the flaws (with nickel and dime items), actually improving performance over original design specs by a factor of three. The president visited the basement and approved design changes on the spot.[8]

Skunkworks and indeed most innovation in the Enabled organization seem to work largely through intrinsic motivation. As Kohn has shown,[9] promised reward is neither a motivator nor any guarantee for innovative success. The impoverished conditions of the typical skunkworks seems to be an important ingredient for creativity. Finke et al.[10] report on increased creativity when conditions are restricted and Fritz describes the power of creative tension as internally generated desire pulls people forward.[11]

For such private projects to work, the domain of innovation needs to be close to the skills and interests of the people working on them. Innovating to order in more distant fields is neither of interest nor practical at this maturity level, where managers studiously ignore much innovation activity, allowing people to come up with ideas on their own.

The original HP culture was largely based at this level, with a principle of 'hiring bright people, pointing them in the right direction and letting them go'. Our basic values as embodied in the HP Way are characterized by Dave Packard's comment:

> It has always been important to Bill and me to create an environment in which people have a chance to be their best, to realize their potential and to be recognized for their achievements.[7]

We also allow people to work on private projects; there is a company story about Bill Hewlett walking around a lab at night and finding an electronic component stores cupboard locked, presumably because engineers had been pinching parts for home projects. He got a pair of bolt cutters, cut off the padlock and left a note to the effect that the cupboard was never to be locked again.

Whilst official skunkworks do not exist in HP, we, as well as several other companies (eg. 3M, DuPont), have policies that give space for people to work on their own ideas. In HP there is a loose rule that 10% of an individual's time can be used in areas of personal interest. This is often not specifically encouraged, but when people have ideas, the culture is forgiving enough to allow them to work on their project, at least in some form.

A typical story of enabled development was in the original work for the inkjet printer, where a curious and enthusiastic engineer fought hard for resources and support to develop it into a full product. Only persistence overcame several management attempts to cancel his project.

In our early years, we were electronic engineers creating electronic equipment for use by other engineers. This simplified innovation in that we simply made equipment that made our own jobs easier. The 'Next Bench' principle was to show an idea to the engineer at the next bench and ask him if it would help him with his work. When we started making products for use outside the electronic test arena (such as medical equipment), the pressure to move to another level of innovation was increased.

Level 3: Encouraged

At the level of Encouraged innovation, the creative skills of most people in the organization are actively sought as the viewpoint around innovation has expanded from a primarily product focus to wider work processes.

Many companies reached this level in the late 1980s and early to mid-1990s, when the recession of the time, along with increasing need to offer quality as a basic essential, forced serious work in changing the culture to a more humanistic, empowered environment. Total Quality Management[12] was the 'fad' that triggered many such change efforts. It really was a great effort for many organizations as they tried to vault directly from a Suppressed organization to the Encouraged level of maturity.

Innovation at this level often follows analytic work. The classic quality improvement project involves measuring the process, analysing to find root causes and then finding an innovative solution to fix the underlying problem (for example as in Straker).[13]

The primary tool that is commonly used here is classic brainstorming – which is often used incorrectly, typically collecting a few logical ideas, rather than being a wide-ranging exploration of creative possibilities. Few people who use or facilitate brainstorming have ever read Alex Osborn's original work,[14] and fewer still abide by his rules. It also comes as a surprise to many people that brainstorming as is commonly practised can be less efficient than individual critical thinking.

> An extensive body of research shows that for both quality and creativity, brainstorming groups seldom are more effective, and certainly less efficient than individuals – even when redundant ideas by individuals are not counted.[15]

Still, the TQM activity has resulted in major gains for a significant number of companies (although there has also been the usual crop of casualties along the path of change). The dilemma that many of these companies now face is that they have done the easy work, having picked the low-hanging fruit amongst their business problems. They are now left with difficult problems and short-lived advantage as global competition continues to escalate.

> The workplace is demanding more innovation and creativity. That's a fundamental shift from five years ago, when the focus was on reengineering and efficiency.[16]

In some ways, it is possible for this level to become a retrogressive step from the previous level, if the intrinsic motivation of the Enabled organization is replaced by reward for improvements made. Well-meaning compensation of a proportion of costs saved has resulted in large payouts and a focus on the immediate reward rather than the longer-term and whole-company benefits.

The transition to Encouraged innovation started in Hewlett Packard in 1977 in our Japanese division, which set and achieved a five-year goal to win the Japanese Deming award. Their enormous improvements along the way attracted the attention of the rest of the company, and the methods started to spread through the company (even today, we tend to use 'TQC' rather than the more Westernized 'TQM').

This activity was accelerated by the internal development of the Quality Maturity System, styled after the Baldrige and Deming awards and including sections on leadership, customers, planning, process management and process improvement. A results section was added for a President's Award, which the UK Sales organization won on several occasions.

Past success is no predictor of the future and we face many of the same competitive problems as other companies, along with some special problems of our own, including having reached a size ($42 billion in annual revenues) where sustaining our 20% growth rate seems almost impossible. We thus are looking for ways of becoming even more innovative, increasing the depth and breadth of ways we can use the talents of our people to sustain and grow our market positions.

Level 4: Educated

At the Educated level of maturity, innovation is a critical agenda in its own right, sufficiently so to warrant direct expenditure on training and for the domain of focus to expand to include other areas of the company's interest. People are now being asked to help the whole company with ideas, rather than just to improve their limited part of it, as in the previous stage, consequently the creative domain might be more distant from the creator than at previous maturity levels. For example, a receptionist might sit in a marketing creative session, adding hybrid vigour with ideas such as how to make customers feel comfortable when starting to use new products.

To increase creative and innovative skills, people are trained on a range of tools and techniques, either to stimulate general creative thinking or for specific use in creative problem solving. There are several schools of thought, each with books and training courses ready and waiting in the wings, including de Bono,[17] Synectics[18] and Osborn's legacy organization, the Creative Education Foundation.[19]

In many ways the transition from Encouraged to Educated is not as difficult as previous transitions as it requires limited cultural change, although being creative may require a more significant change in openness than was previously permissible in the company culture. This is mitigated by the tendency at this level to constrain the creative thinking to specific problem-solving sessions, where the psychological safety and freedom[20] required may be controlled by a trained facilitator.

A problem at this stage is that, when working in groups, people who have not been trained in the approaches are likely to find it difficult to pick up the new methods on the fly, especially where different modes of thinking are required. The trained people may also be inhibited by the presence of the untrained people.

Many parts of HP are currently entering this stage, as evidenced by an increase in the number of and interest in courses in creative problem solving. Lew Platt, our CEO, has also been asking for suggestions to help HP in the broader sense through an intranet-based internal magazine.

The techniques we are using are a combination of Synectics, CEF and de Bono, along with some traditional methods such as morphology and metaphor. A local UK course, which I have developed, starts with structured techniques that generally break down and challenge individual components, eg. with Attribute Listing and SCAMPER and then develops more unstructured methods such as PO and Role-play. Group work aims to improve on basic brainstorming through using warm-up exercises along with some nominal techniques and Synectics-style excursions within the CPS Mess/Data/Problem/Idea/Solution/Acceptance framework.

We are planning involvement on four levels:

- Problem owners, who just want a creative 'fix'. This as the Synectics definition.[21] They will contact a facilitator who will run a creative problem-solving session for them.
- Trained creative problem-solvers, who can act as resources for the above. These people are typically motivated by individual work or personal development needs and will go on the standard creativity course.
- Facilitators who can run creative problem-solving sessions. These are typically business consultants, either from quality or human resource backgrounds, although they may also be individuals with appropriate focus or interests within discrete departments. Facilitators receive additional training on using and facilitating with creative toolsets.

- Trainers who can teach courses on the topic. These are selectively sourced from facilitators and are those with teaching ability and sufficient interests to dig deeply into the subject.

Level 5: Enlightened

To achieve maximally in any activity requires getting back to the fundamentals of how things work. Athletes study physiology, artists study light and materials, and creative people must ultimately study psychology and neurology in order to truly understand how creative thinking works.
   Factors that need to be taken into account include:

- Personal change. It is a difficult task to study and change oneself, as this is first-order change from within. To make a lasting, second-order change to ourselves requires that we step outside and look back in.[22]
- Psychological blocks. Adams and others have listed many internal and external factors that act to reduce our creative potential, from environmental and cultural blocks onwards.[23]
- Deep drivers, such as Maslow's hierarchy of prepotence[24] and Argyris's Model 1 Theory in Use,[25] which tend to make us less creative and the double-loop learning that is required to help us get out of the mire.
- The effects of early childhood and education, and models that help to understand this, such as Transactional Analysis.[26]
- Various other dysfunctional psychological effects around decision making, such as risk bias, negativity bias and confirmation bias.[15]
- Interpersonal psychological effects of working in groups, including groupthink,[27] risky shift[15] and leader dependency.[28]
- Effects of personality type, such as Kirton's Adaptor-Innovator (KAI).[29]
- Internal modes of thinking that result both in creative ideas and ways to carry these through to practical applications. Creative people have been studied in depth and from various angles, and their mental strategies are available for adoption from a number of authors.[30, 31, 32]
- The deeper cognitive effects of various stimuli such as preinventive forms.[32]

Does this mean we all need to become PhDs in psychology? Not really. Psychological principles have long been a part of management training. All that is required is to direct and enhance this education to include those factors which will act to increase the creative ability and application within the organization.
   It is a well-known marketing principle that as you are reaping the benefits of the current marketplace, you should also be preparing for the next. Within our current training, we are laying the foundations for moving up the ladder by including fundamental education on the psychology of creativity. Amongst the subjects covered are:

- a foundation in an equation of creativity as 'problem + stimulus − blocks = idea';
- a focus on perceiving the blocks in the underlying thinking, exposing delegates to a number of models and psychological principles such as those described above;
- a focus on the stimuli in the tools used, resulting in a wide variety of stimuli, from words to sensory experiences (the latter being carefully introduced only when individuals are ready!).

HP is a fertile environment for deep understanding, being full of engineers who will actively seek the underlying reasons of 'how things work'. We have also a long history of careful management of inventive talent:

> Upon first being approached by a creative inventor with unbridled enthusiasm for a new idea, Bill immediately put on a hat called 'enthusiasm'. He would listen, express excitement where appropriate and appreciation in general, while asking a few gentle and not too pointed questions. A few days later, he would get back to the inventor wearing a hat called 'inquisition'. This was the time for very pointed questions, a thorough probing of the idea, lots of give-and-take. Without a final decision the session was adjourned. Shortly thereafter, Bill would put on his 'decision' hat and meet once again with the inventor. With appropriate logic and sensitivity, judgement was rendered and a decision made about the idea.[32]

These hats match closely with Dilts' identification[30] of Walt Disney's three stages of creative management: Dreamer, Realist and Critic. Disney and Hewlett both were perhaps instinctive managers of creative people. To duplicate this ability on a daily basis requires making the 'strange familiar'[21] through deep understanding and careful propagation.

LIMITATIONS OF THE MATURITY MODEL

As W. Edwards Deming said, 'All models are wrong, but some are useful'. Maturity is a useful model, but we cannot simply push an organization into a box marked 'Level 2' without recognizing the limitations that this categorization brings.

The maturity of an organization is an aggregate of the maturity of its individual members. Skills and abilities do not diffuse instantly across a company and individuals are known to accept change at different rates.[33] Innovation diffuses according to a number of factors,[34] such as social position and the ability to understand new concepts. There is also more direct need for innovation in functions such as R&D than in some other areas, resulting in a natural imbalance in the attention to creativity and innovation.

As a result, there is a distribution of innovation maturity across groups and organizations, and the numerical 'innovation maturity' of the organization is an average. If the standard deviation of that distribution is high, then a single numerical maturity level is probably not a good measure of the company in question.

Nevertheless, the model is a useful paradigm for understanding parts of the organization and identifying actions required to transform individual entities to the required level of innovative ability.

DIRECTIONS FOR FUTURE RESEARCH

The maturity model of innovation is proposed as a conceptual framework, with a goal of helping to identify actual innovation style and to guide future activity in this area. How useful this is in practice will only be discovered through active experimentation and research.

The effects of different distributions of innovation maturity distribution in organizations and groups are probably little understood and there may be some merit in investigating this area.

Perhaps the most intractable area for many organizations is in the more general management of change, that is, the *transitions* between the maturity levels. In the academic field we often skip straight to the 'understanding' level, but people organizations are not (perhaps by definition), that clever. This also raises the question of whether organizations *have* to go through each level, and if they do not, how the transition process differs.

Methods for measuring innovative tendencies and abilities have been well researched,[29][35] and there is probably little requirement for further investigation, although one or more of these instruments may be used in the above research.

CONCLUSIONS

'Where next' for HP (and probably a number of other companies) is make the transition from intuitive innovation to deliberate tool-usage and thence to deep understanding of how creativity can be engendered and sustained. There are two parallel activities we are undertaking, as indicated in previous sections:

Short-term skill-building

Explicit tools for individuals and groups, particularly for use in contained, explicitly creative environments:

- training individuals and groups plus facilitators and trainers;
- facilitating creative sessions to ensure they are effective.

Longer-term cultural change

Changing culture and management support/attitude to encourage, support, etc. innovation at a deeper level:

- building 'how it works', 'it is important' and 'how you affect it' into management training;
- coaching and mentoring to help effective encouragement and management of innovation.

Creativity often requires that managers radically change the ways in which they build and interact with work groups. In many respects, it calls for a conscious culture change. But it can be done, and the rewards can be great.[36]

The price of empowerment and freedom at HP is that change cannot be dictated from the top. We are, to use the Boeing metaphor, 'A set of parts flying in close formation'. To become even more innovative will take time as we diffuse the principles of maturity through the organization. But we have the fundamental culture and a predilection for communication and change. With these and taking our own medicine in applying innovative approaches to speeding the change, we will get there.

REFERENCES

1. Crosby, P., *Quality is Free*, Mentor Books, New York, 1979.
2. Morgan, G., *Images of Organizations*, Sage Publications, Newbury Park, CA, 1986.
3. McGregor, D., 'The human side of enterprise', in *Adventures in Thought and Action*, Proceedings of the Fifth Anniversary Convocation of the School of Industrial Management, MIT, 1957, pp. 23–30
4. Hertzberg, F., *Work and the Nature of Man*, World Publishing, 1966.
5. Milsted, D., *They Got it Wrong (The Guinness Dictionary of Regrettable Quotations)*, Guinness Publishing, London, 1995.
6. Walton, M., *The Deming Management Method*, Perigee Books, New York, 1986.
7. Packard, David, Kirby, David, Lewis, Karen (1995) *The HP Way: How Bill Hewlett and I Built Our Company.* New York: HarperBusiness.
8. Peters, T. and Waterman, R., *In Search of Excellence*, Harper and Row, New York, 1982.
9. Kohn, A., *Punished by Rewards*, Houghton Mifflin, New York, 1995.
10 Finke, R. A., Ward, T. B. and Smith, S. M., *Creative Cognition (Theory, Research and Applications)*, MIT Press, Cambridge, MA , 1996.
11. Fritz, R., *The Path of Least Resistance*, Fawcett Columbine, New York, 1984.
12. Oakland, J., *Total Quality Management*, Butterworth-Heinemann, Oxford, 1989.
13. Straker, D., *A Toolbook for Quality Improvement and Problem Solving*, Prentice-Hall, New York, 1995.
14. Osborn, A., *Applied Imagination (Third Edition)*, Scribner, New York, 1963.
15. Beach, L. R., *The Psychology of Decision Making*, Sage Publications, Thousand Oaks, CA, 1997.
16. 'What money makes you do', *Fortune*, 17 August 1988: 79.
17. de Bono, E., *Serious Creativity*, HarperCollins, London, 1992.
18. Ceserani, J. and Greatwood, P., *Innovation and Creativity*, Kogan Page, London, 1995.
19. Isaksen, S., Dorfal, K. B. and Treffinger, D., *Creative Approaches to Problem Solving*, Creative Problem Solving Group, Buffalo, New York, 1994.

20. Rogers, C., *Towards a Theory of Creativity*, in P. E. Vernon (ed.), *Creativity*, Penguin Books, Harmonsworth, UK, 1970.
21. Gordon, W. J. J., *Synectics*, Harper and Row, New York, 1961.
22. Watzlawick, P., Weakland, J. and Fisch, R., *Change: Principles of Problem Formation and Problem Resolution*, W. W. Norton, New York, 1974.
23. Adams, J. L., *Conceptual Blockbusting (Third edition)*, Addison-Wesley, Reading, MA, 1986.
24. Maslow, A. H., *Motivation and Personality (Third edition)*, Harper and Row, New York, 1970.
25. Argyris, C. and Schön, D., *Organizational Learning II*, Addison-Wesley, Reading, MA, 1996.
26. Harris, T. A., *I'm OK, You're OK*, Pan Books, London, 1970.
27. Janis, I., *Victims of Groupthink*, Houghton Mifflin, Boston, 1982.
28. Bion, A., *Experiences in Groups and other Papers*, Tavistock, London, 1961.
29. Kirton, M. J., 'Adaptors and innovators: a description and measure', *Journal of Applied Psychology*, 61, 1976: 622–629.
30. Dilts, R. B., Epstein, T. and Dilts, R. W., *Tools for Dreamers*, Meta Publications, Capitola, CA, 1991.
31. Gardner, H., *Creating Minds*, Basic Books, New York, 1993.
32. Shekerjian, D., *Uncommon Genius*, Penguin Books, New York, 1990.
33. Connor, D., *Managing at the Speed of Change*, Villard Books, New York, 1993.
34. Rogers, E., *Diffusion of Innovations*, The Free Press, New York, 1962.
35. Miller, W. C., *Validation of the Innovation Styles Profile*, Global Creativity Corporation, Corte Madera, CA, 1986.
36. Amabile, T. M., 'How to kill creativity', *Harvard Business Review*, September/October 1998: 76–87.

21

Conclusion: Managing Knowledge in a Global Context

*Stephen E. Little**

Toward the end of the second millennium of the Christian Era, several events of historical significance have transformed the social landscape of human life. A technological revolution, centered around information technologies, is reshaping the material basis of society. Economies throughout the world have become globally interdependent, introducing a new form of relationship between economy, state and society, in a system of variable geometry. (Castells, 1996, p.1)

The notion that something fundamental is happening, or indeed has happened, in the world economy is now generally accepted. As we look around us all we seem to see is the confusion of change, the acceleration of uncertainty, feelings currently intensified by our proximity to the new millennium with all its promises – and threats – of epochal change. (Dicken, 1998, p.1)

The firm is an institution that has evolved to make the most efficient and effective use of the factors of production – traditionally labour, money and materials. These factors of production are being transformed by the increasing importance of knowledge in economic activity. As the factors of production change, so too must the nature of the firm. (Burton-Jones, 1999, p.57)

This concluding chapter provides an opportunity to link the issues identified in Chapter 1 and developed and elaborated in the subsequent four parts of this book to developments in the global economy. It also provides an opportunity to identify issues and concerns which are likely to become more central to knowledge and its management in the medium term. In doing so it makes use of frameworks provided by Peter Dicken, an economic geographer, and Manuel Castells, an urban sociologist.

The framework for managing knowledge that we have set in this book is deliberately broad. Looking at the diversity of its proponents and the claims made for it, Clive Holtham initially predicted the rapid demise of knowledge management as a management innovation. He now argues that, in terms of a

* The Open University Business School

368

biological analogy, such diversity may be a key strength of the emerging discipline (Holtham, 1999). This chapter considers the diversity necessary to provide the variety demanded by a rapidly evolving global economy. It also tracks some of the drivers of change to their origins in the middle of the twentieth century.

DRAWING CONCLUSIONS

We have moved beyond the narrow, technical frame in which the *information* management requirements for knowledge intensive organizations are often presented as synonymous with *knowledge* management. Such a view neglects the broader currents within commerce and administration which have created a sensitivity to the nuances of knowledge in all its forms. Both the present and future of knowledge in organizations and its effective management must engage the breadth of themes we have enumerated. No doubt these themes will themselves need adding to, and we suggest some probable directions of development.

Paths and barriers to globalized knowledge

We start by looking at two barriers to this broader view of managing knowledge. The first is the characterization of knowledge management as simply the current management fad, the second its characterization as a recycled version of knowledge engineering. Each limits our understanding of both the potential and the complexities of managing knowledge.

Maintaining communities of practice

We continue by looking at the issue of the maintenance of communities of practice, the key to the effective application of knowledge within an organization. The speed of change in markets, competition and technology was discussed in Chapter 1. Responses to these rates of change are defining the business model of the new century.

Knowledge creation in a global context

The speed of technical and infrastructural change in business practice together with a new understanding of the centrality of intangible assets to wealth creation has brought the Silicon Valley paradigm of innovation to prominence. We place the very particular circumstances of northern California in the context of institutional innovation, as seen in the dramatic change in the nature of the dominant multinational corporations within the global economy.

Flows of resources, flows of knowledge

The technologies that have facilitated a globalizing economy allow new forms of adjacency and community. We examine these in terms of flows of knowledge and resources. This approach gives us an overview of the current state of global markets.

Chains into networks

Global production has shifted from a chain of material flows from periphery to core, then back as manufactured goods. In the new global production *networks* the management of global brands is becoming more important than the management of specific material resources. Activities once associated with either geographical core or periphery co-exist in interpenetrating spaces, whether in inner-city Manchester or suburban Shanghai.

Life space and knowledge space

Innovation in products, processes and institutions has led to significant shifts in patterns of work, and the nature of participation in the workforce for many individuals. If people are the locus of knowledge, does the fragmentation of organizations into networks and of working life into casualized portfolio employment assist or undermine the development of organizational knowledge? We examine the relationship between social and organizational space in this context.

Inclusion, exclusion and infiltration

Finally some issues of the future of knowledge are addressed though the concept of the digital divide, and inclusion and exclusion from the increasingly networked knowledge economy.

PATHS AND BARRIERS TO GLOBALIZED KNOWLEDGE

Beyond the boundaries of a narrowly defined technical framework and beyond the boundaries of individuals and individual organizations, the current prominent interest in managing knowledge can be seen as just one consequence of a globalizing economy. This situation in turn is a consequence of a related set of technical innovations which have led to a redefinition of the nature of formal organization and of organizing, in Weick's terms (Weick, 1979). The rapidly developing knowledge required to maintain and deliver these information and communication technologies (ICTs) requires conscious attention. Implicit in this global context is an understanding of the spatial and cultural aspects of globalization and of managing knowledge. This in turn leads to consideration of new forms of both work and organization and of broad issues of economic and social inclusion and exclusion.

We need to move beyond two barriers to a full consideration of knowledge and its management. The first is the implicit or explicit assumption that knowledge management, in whatever form, is simply the latest in a line of management 'fads' promising a simple resolution of intractable problems. The second is a lineage that links knowledge management with knowledge engineering and recurrent claims for a central role for artificial intelligence technologies in the management arena.

In an historical catalogue of 'management fads' our current foregrounding of knowledge requirements might appear as the necessary antidote to the excesses of the preceding 'fad' of Business Process Re-engineering (BPR). The BPR model, promoted by Hammer (1990) dominated much Western management thinking throughout the 1990s. Unfortunately, despite claims of high levels of efficiency gain, in practice the only reliable measure of progress for a manager became the number of staff displaced by such re-engineering. Downsizing, or 'rightsizing' in its user-friendly guise, became almost synonymous with BPR. Unfortunately many of the individuals 'rightsized' out of organizations took with them key knowledge. There are plenty of examples of the expensive re-purchase of professional insights only recently deemed disposable by organizations across a range of sectors.

For some observers with longer memories, BPR was simply a repackaged version of the systems analysis introduced in the 1960s. Similarly the related process of outsourcing was regarded as another iteration of the computing bureau that delivered earlier generations of computer technology to business users. Initially outsourcing was concerned with identifying and retaining mission-critical skills and systems within the organizational boundary. Secondary, mainly support, activities which did not need direct control could be outsourced. However, by the late 1990s, outsourcing meant replacing key internal sources with external resources. Only those competencies which were unique to an organization's competitive position should be retained. Often the outsourced activities were carried out by the same individuals whose knowledge and skills had previously been internal resources of the organization in question. Outsourcing in its original guise often meant lower pay and poorer, casual conditions for the outsourced worker engaged in lower-cost and routine activities. In its revised form outsourcing meant that higher-cost and more obviously knowledge-intensive activities were likely to be relinquished, imposing an additional strain on the maintenance of effective communities of practice.

We examine the implications of these changes for the structure of work and employment and their relationship to the broader processes of globalization below. For the present we should note that such resizing or redrawing of organizational boundaries depended on the reduced transaction costs achieved through the use of ICTs. In such a context, a degree of healthy cynicism over the claims of centrality for the novelty of 'Knowledge Management' (KM) is understandable.

The second barrier to overcome is the legacy of the so-called 'AI-hype' of the 1980s. This serves to distract us from the centrality of people as the creators and possessors of knowledge and knowing in organizations. At the end of 2000 a familiar claim emerged once more: intelligent computer programs would in the near to medium future outstrip human intelligence and rightly take their place as the next stage of human evolution (e.g. Menzel and D'Alusio, 2000). Such claims can be traced to Alan Turing's formulation of a test to distinguish whether a conversation over a teletype terminal was being conducted with a human or a computer (Turing, 1950). The issue surfaced in the mid-1950s, alongside the first generations of commercial computers as the research field of 'artificial intelligence'. This reappeared in the 1980s when the fruits of this research offered 'expert systems', applications with a genuine if circumscribed role in business and administration. Goodall (1985) gives a set of definitions of expert systems, the simplest of which is: 'a computer system that performs functions similar to those normally performed by a human expert'.

Knowledge was usually represented as a set of rules that could be operated by the so-called 'inference engine'within the expert system. These 'rule based systems' required either human 'knowledge engineers' to interview expert practitioners, or algorithmic programs which could derive rules from sets of examples of expert judgement. Recently the AI community has proposed the application of these techniques to Knowledge Management (e.g. Weilinga et al., 1997; Milton et al., 1999).

The notions of knowledge engineering and knowledge elicitation and representation have their equivalents in current notions of codification and personalization of knowledge (e.g. Hansen et al., 1999). However, the emergence of commercial expert systems in the 1980s triggered debates over the nature of skill and expertise, and of human versus machine capability. These echoed the equally intense current discussions of the nature of explicit and tacit knowledge and of collectively held and individually held knowledge. The definition of expert versus competent performance developed by Hubert Dreyfus to demonstrate the limits of artificial intelligence still offers insight into the subtlety of human performance. Dreyfus noted that 'Competent performance is rational, proficiency is transitional, experts act arationally' (Dreyfus and Dreyfus, 1986: 36). In this view, integrated expert performance cannot be codified effectively, it can only be experientially developed by an individual who may have been assisted formally to the level of competence. Unfortunately there seems little acknowledgement of these issues in relation to the renewed claims for AI in the context of managing knowledge. Without this perspective, the whole approach confines knowledge to a technicist framework.

The strong claims made for this subset of artificial intelligence applications echo equally strong technical claims made for the much wider range of more general ICT applications. These have transformed the dynamics of commerce and administration in the last thirty years and have had perhaps the greatest impact on the nature of knowledge and of the tasks of management. The key to understanding such impact lies, however, not in the technical realm but in the social and next we examine the implications for the development and maintenance of communities of practice.

MAINTAINING COMMUNITIES OF PRACTICE

Chapter 1 identifies the rediscovery of the role of people as the locus of much organizational knowledge, coupled with the dramatic demonstration of the level of wealth underpinned by knowledge and intangible assets. The notion of social learning espoused by Sproull and Kiesler (1991) in relation to the deployment of information systems allows us to see why certain innovations in both product and process are able to take root while others wither within organizations. Accounts of social learning have been provided for a number of technologies. Marvin (1988) describes the social learning curve associated with the introduction of new electricity-based technologies at the turn of the nineteenth century. The claims for social transformation based on electric light and the telephone seem exaggerated now that we have assimilated these technologies. However, the time taken to reach a general consensus on the appropriate social use of the telephone is a reminder of the importance of the social learning that must accompany any technical innovation. Such learning is an essential part of the concept of the community of practice described by Brown and Duguid in Chapter 2. A shared understanding of the nature and qualities of the media of expression for such a community is a precondition of its robust development.

Sproull and Kiesler (1991) distinguish between relatively short term technical learning, against measurable objectives of efficiency, and longer-term social learning that may lead to a redefinition of organizational objectives themselves. While the original formulations of BPR were intended to achieve both efficiency and effectiveness, practice revealed an ever tighter focus on measurable efficiency gains, as described above. Sproull and Kiesler point out that it is easier to justify expenditure against quantifiable gains in efficiency than against qualitative shifts in the orientation of a business.

However, since the 1970s and the appearance of commercially viable integrated circuits, an increasingly rapid pace of development has challenged our capacity for social learning in organizations. Successive versions of a tool are released before the implications of the previous generation have been fully absorbed. Both individual skills and knowledge and the level of the knowledge requirements of the organization as a whole are altered rapidly. The consequences of the speed of change are manifest at the technical level in the so-called 'productivity paradox'. Landauer (1995) argues for a user-centred approach to computer systems development to overcome this. Such an approach would represent a form of social learning in which the design process is extended to encompass the end users. However, we need to look at contemporaneous changes in the nature of employment and their impact on individuals and work groups to assess the practicality of this proposal.

Meanwhile, the enormous gains in technical and cost efficiency achieved within the technical infrastructure do not seem to be reflected in effectiveness gains at the level of the organization. As a result of continuing rapid change there is an increasing institutional lag between the systems of corporate and social governance and the emerging forms of organization. Perez (1983) identifies such lag as indicative of a change in the basic techno-economic paradigm which underpins an economy and its socio-institutional paradigm.

Reductions in transaction and communication costs have led to the transformation of relationships not just within and between organizations, but across the world economy. Diminished regulatory systems have had to deal with such phenomena as the complex financial products and derivative markets made possible by negligible transaction costs. The volatility of such virtual markets has made real impacts on physical trade. Castells (1996) has pointed out that the vast majority of resources circulating through the world financial systems at any moment are seeking purely speculative gains from relatively minor variations in exchange rates. To appreciate the likely priorities in managing knowledge in the next decades we now look at the nature of the transformation of relationships at the corporate level and beyond.

KNOWLEDGE CREATION IN A GLOBAL CONTEXT

> The conjunction of an immense military establishment and a huge arms industry is new in the American experience. The total influence – economic, political, and even spiritual – is felt in every city, every state house, and every office of the federal government. . . . In the councils of government, we must guard against the acquisition of unwarranted influence, whether sought or unsought, by the military-industrial complex. (President Dwight D. Eisenhower Farewell Address to the Nation, 17 January 1961)

In the final quarter of the twentieth century global economic integration grew rapidly, following the end of the Cold War, and of what Ohmae (1995) terms the 'bi-polar discipline'which constrained relationships between ideological blocs. This accelerating change had its roots in conditions at the outset of the Cold War. J.K. Galbraith articulated Eisenhower's concerns in his book *The New Industrial State* by defining the emergence of the 'technostructure'of the industrial state as the necessary consequence of a change in the locus of power from land via capital to knowledge and technique (Galbraith, 1967). The technical experts delivering the calculative rationality necessary to the industrial state become the new locus of knowledge and power.

Globalization, in its current form, is a consequence of the rapid development of ICTs during the Cold War period. The initial development of both electronic computers and communication technology was driven by military requirements some of which were only revealed by one of the participants after almost three decades.[1]

In the last quarter of the twentieth century there were significant changes in the dominant model of the transnational corporation. In that period the vertically integrated multinational corporation, under unified ownership, was superseded by networks of externalized relationships between associated but often autonomous firms. This paradigm shift is encapsulated in Saxenian's comparison between Route 128 around Boston and its associated high technology industries and Silicon Valley in northern California (Saxenian, 1994). The East Coast paradigm relied upon established companies and a new relationship with universities and central government, the core of Eisenhower's 'military–industrial complex' (the phrase was modified from 'military–industrial–congressional complex', in a late draft).

The closed nature of these large, individual organizations contrasts with the densely networked environment of the more dynamic West Coast firms. Silicon Valley is dominated by companies which grew up with the new technologies they promote. Today's start-up companies can secure both finance and personnel from their environment and draw upon a highly skilled and mobile workforce. However, the highly specialized labour market was originally created by an outflow of personnel from the larger, established companies and from universities, particularly Stanford. These older companies provided a form of internal quarantine, with unstructured and dynamic knowledge creation taking place in customized research laboratories, carefully separated from the routine production of their stable products and services. Such separation was both overt, as with the Bell Laboratories, and covert, as with the Lockheed Skunkworks, where cutting-edge military products were pursued in conditions close to those of the fabled Silicon Valley 'garage start-up'(see Rich and Janos, 1995).

> Silicon Valley is the only place on Earth not trying to figure out how to become Silicon Valley. (Robert Metcalfe, *InfoWorld*, 2 March 1998)

The Silicon Valley model has become an almost subconscious archetype for innovation. Manuel Castells (1989) describes the complex web of relationships necessary to sustain this level of knowledge creation as a 'creative milieu'. Such a milieu extends beyond the boundaries of the high-tech firms themselves into a hinterland of rich knowledge resources, involving universities, appropriate financial institutions and a highly sophisticated labour market. Histories of Silicon Valley plot the genesis of several generations of innovative companies. The trail of innovation leads to pre-World War II electronics spin-offs from Stanford University and the availability of university real estate. There have been numerous attempts to replicate the dynamics of Silicon Valley, through science parks or science cities. Massey et al. (1992) argue that many such attempts fail to take account of the particular historical circumstances of Silicon Valley, and rely instead on simplistic notions of innovative activity in relation to space, and divisions of labour. Castells and Hall (1994) catalogue mixed results, both within the original Anglo-Saxon business culture and beyond, unsurprisingly given that the fundamental conditions which gave rise to the phenomenon are not well understood, even by some of the key participants whose anti-statist, free enterprise rhetoric ignores a key ingredient of the recipe.

Established Silicon Valley firms are as likely to innovate though the acquisition of promising start-up companies as through internal development. Despite its free-wheeling entrepreneurial milieu, Silicon Valley was as dependent upon public sector, defence-related expenditure for its genesis as Route 128 had been a decade earlier. The Internet was derived from the ARPANet, named after the Advanced Research Projects Agency of the US Department of Defense. The intention was to share expensive research resources efficiently, and in a Cold War frame, to ensure the survivability of a fragmented or degraded network under physical attack. The World Wide Web originated in a project to share documentation and other materials seamlessly among the staff involved in basic science at CERN, the European Centre for Nuclear Research. The NCSA, the National Center for Supercomputing Applications at the University of Illinois at Urbana-Champaign contributed the Mosaic browser that underpins both Netscape and Microsoft equivalents. The Silicon Valley paradox is that much of the robustness and ease of use of Internet-based applications, a key to their rapid commercial dissemination in the run-up to the millennium, can be traced to the requirements of large public sector institutions. This was a lesson better learned by the developmental nation states of East Asia, Singapore, Taiwan and Korea in particular.

By the 1970s, multinational corporations were prominent in the economic landscape, and being identified as significant investors in and exploiters of knowledge (e.g. Galbraith, 1967; Tugendhat, 1971; Vernon, 1971) but subsequent developments were poorly anticipated. Tugendhat, for example, does not examine the Third World, arguing that its problems are separate and distinct from those of the developed economies. Thirty years ago Asian involvement in the multinational arena was minimal: Tugendhat's data for 1969 show that Japanese investment in the USA was smaller than that from Belgium and Luxembourg. However, following a variety of state sanctioned developments, East Asia is now considered an integral part of the global economy, a source of markets and resources, and a contributor of innovations in both products and processes.

Yet even informed and sincere imitators of Silicon Valley face the problems of reproducing an adequate or equivalent set of conditions as described by Castells and Hall (1994). Regional and national disparities in access to resources and capabilities still present real problems, as in the case of Malaysia's bold attempt at the creation of a multi-media super-corridor to connect the country to global high technology production (Wilkinson et al., 2001). Next we examine some frameworks which seek to explain how such ICT-driven efforts to overcome the consequences of geographical location might meet with at least some success.

FLOWS OF RESOURCES, FLOWS OF KNOWLEDGE

Castells proposed the Informational City as a space of flows, arguing that access to flows of information and resources was the key to participation in the wider economy (Castells, 1989). We will look at the issue of ICT-based accessibility and related concerns about the 'digital divide' later. First we need to look back a further two decades to Melvin Webber's 'city as communications system' (Webber, 1964: 84). In order to move from the physical bias of established planning conceptions, Webber switched the emphasis of urbanity from physical built form to the quality of interaction in cultural life through the exchange of information. Webber formulates 'non-place community' in terms of interest-communities, accessibility, rather than the propinquity aspect of 'place' being the necessary condition for this form of community (Webber, 1964). He argues that this definition implies that suburban and exurban dwellers enjoy a significant measure of 'urbanity'in terms of diversity of social interaction and of the accessibility of diverse cultural resources and economic services. For Webber, the traditional 'place community'was in fact a special case of a larger genus of association. For Webber individuals are involved in an overlapping set of communities which involve different social and physical spaces.

Webber suggests that emerging institutional changes and technological developments coupled with ever increasing mobility and specialization are likely to involve urban dwellers in increasingly wide area communications. As a consequence, both behavioural models of individual locational decisions, and descriptive models of overall spatial structures would benefit from an orientation to communication patterns. The shifting balance between physical and electronic adjacency facilitated by information and communications technologies exemplified by the web, e-commerce and distance working reflects Webber's formulation of 'non-space realms'.

Webber influenced and was influenced by an orientation towards non-physical aspects of community, and a participatory approach to design which emerged strongly during the 1970s. The result of Webber's arguments is a relationship between urbanity, density and community radically at variance with that being advanced by Jacobs in her influential *Death and Life of Great American Cities* (Jacobs, 1961) in the same period. For Jacobs, richness and density of physical interaction was the key to quality of urban space, and this in turn was under threat from simplistic zoning regulations which threatened the vibrancy and flexibility that typify Castells's 'creative milieu'. Webber prefigures the celebration of Southern Californian urbanism by Banham (1971) and subsequent commentators by arguing that, in his terms, the urbanism of the Los Angeles region may not be that different from that of New York City. He adds that certain approaches to the classification of urban centres were more amenable to the consideration of the range of interactions which he identifies, but that any reconsideration of definitions of centrality in the terms outlined by him would call into question the traditional notions of centre and hinterland. Webber contributed an early appreciation that social and commercial activities take place in both physical and virtual spaces.

Business paradigms for a global knowledge base

The continuing shifts in the relationships between the components of what is still an emerging global economy have already significantly changed our understanding of the nature and role of knowledge and will continue to do so in the new century. Proponents of the 'strong globalization' thesis, typified by Kenichi Ohmae, suggest that there is a coherent and irresistible logic of globalization (Ohmae, 1990). For Ohmae, globalization is dominated by a core 'triad'of economic regions: North America, Western Europe and North East Asia, predominantly Japan. As attention shifted from flows of material to flows of information and knowledge, disparate national and regional cultures became increasingly interlinked within networked and globalized organizations. Production and consumption of goods and services take place in an increasingly complex web, where both sophisticated and commodified products may be produced and consumed at centre and periphery. However, this complexity is far removed from the bland, uniform global culture that is often assumed to be the consequence of top-down globalization. Any flattening of cultural terrain and the erosion of difference is countered by the reverse colonization of the information infrastructures. We will touch on this tension later, in the context of inclusion and exclusion.

In response to developments in organizational technologies, organization theorists have produced a number of descriptions of the new organizational forms that have resulted. The rise of the Internet and e-commerce as a facilitator of transnational commerce has led to a range of formulations of 'networked organization'. The Internet appears to offer an opportunity for smaller players to access resources from and to compete within global networks. Inoue (1998) describes a 'virtual village' in which small enterprises are able to form and reform alliances in order to provide high technology services to larger companies. Their physical co-location across a number of inner suburbs of Tokyo is enhanced by electronic exchange. Such electronic adjacency is stretched further by the London-based supporters of Sohonet. A group of specialized media companies shares high-capacity data links in order to participate in the creative milieu based around Hollywood and West Los Angeles. The high-speed digital exchange of film, video and sound enables post-production operations to be carried out in London, in direct competition with Californian companies. The open, networked nature of the entertainment industry of southern California which permits this remote participation is in effect a lower-tech version of the Silicon Valley networks of northern California.

Such striking organizational innovations undermine our assumptions of the relationship between organizational size and performance. However, the additional accessibility and flexibility available to smaller players also allow larger firms to restructure into networks which can enter niche markets yet still draw on their wider resource base. Castells (1996) describes a form of 'network enterprise'which is composed of components of larger corporations, collaborating in specific spatial and temporal circumstances, while the companies as a whole are still pursuing global strategies of direct competition. Castells is describing a mechanism by which larger corporations can achieve some of the agility of smaller competitors. The larger firms are able to decouple key business units better to target customers and markets traditionally served by much smaller firms. This niche marketing by large corporations presents a formidable challenge to smaller and medium-scale players. However, these interrelated processes can best be understood by reference to a venerable model of the traditional production process: the production chain. This is best exemplified by Peter Dicken's use of it to examine the global shift in economic activity (Dicken, 1998).

CHAINS INTO NETWORKS

Dicken (1998) uses a generic production chain to analyse the dynamics of the global economy by focusing on the globalization of production. In common with Porter's representation of the value chain (Porter, 1990, Figures 2.3 and 2.4), a range of critical support activities is modelled at each stage of this generic model. Dicken separates these into flows of materials, personnel and information on the one hand and technology and research and development functions on the other. Established views of the diffusion of the knowledge and practice involved in global production reflect these essentially linear models. Vernon (1974) developed a model of locational decision making based on increasing product maturity. As technology becomes familiar and routine, production can be transferred away from the centre and its R&D milieu, via overseas subsidiaries to less developed regions from where, in the final stages of product life, the output is sent back to the original source. However, the very success of such approaches to international production has led to a range of imitators. The globalization of productive resources brings new competitors to the markets previously dominated by the most developed economies. The rate of diffusion is no longer a prerogative of the centre, and transnational companies now have to make complex location decisions for each part of their production chain. Dunning presents a more complex model of the choices facing investors seeking to establish international production (Dunning, 1993). This identifies a variety of motives for seeking overseas location, including investment directed at securing natural resources, at securing new markets or at securing synergy with existing assets or activities.

The response of established players in the global system has been to shift their focus towards the end of the production chain. Product differentiation and customer support can maintain demand for goods and services and maintain premium prices for them. Such a shift makes the distinction between products and services less obvious. It also leads to an intensification of knowledge requirements since a focus at the end of the chain requires closer adjustment to cultural variation among users and customers. ICL (International Computers Limited), now owned by Fujitsu, provides an example of such a shift. The company has moved further from its original manufacturing hardware base to position itself as an information services provider that can support the specificities of a European business environment. The service end of the chain is more culturally variable and success reflects specific local or regional knowledge. ICL resulted from a series of mergers in the UK computer industry running from 1959 to 1968. These produced an integrated national champion and these European credentials allow a Japanese company to maintain a convincing presence in a key market and to deliver products and services tailored to regional practices and requirements.

Managing value chains and managing value

Evidence of a 'value chain' approach (Porter, 1990) can be seen in a very different industry. In the production chain linking bulk and specialist chemicals to consumer packaged goods, both ICI and Unilever have been engaged in moving to the area of higher added value. In 1997 Unilever passed its specialist chemical division to ICI in order to concentrate on the delivery of differentiated brands made from chemical feedstocks that could now be sourced competitively, not internally. Unilever went on to concentrate on the management of a subset of its original portfolio of brands, via an extensive culling operation (BBC World Service, 2000). This aimed to reduce 1,600 brands to 400 in order to increase the value of the retained products by developing them into global brands. ICI in turn off-loaded its bulk chemical business to firms content to compete primarily on price at the commodity end of this chain, while retaining its established brands, such as Dulux paint.

Naomi Klein argues that there is a shift in the focus of what were formerly manufacturing organizations from material production to a form of cultural production (Klein, 2000). She argues that the apparent global expansion of high-profile brands is in fact accompanied by a downsizing or hollowing out. Ultimately all functions except the management and development of the brand itself are subcontracted. This represents the apotheosis of out-sourcing facilitated by both a reduction in transaction costs and the alteration of the relative advantages and economies of size. These changes in turn have increased the significance of intellectual capital leveraged by the technologies on which it depends. Ultimately brands may become the carrier of the core values and emotional capital of what were once physically extensive organizations that have been reduced to sets of networked relationships. The global scoping of brands requires the icon branding described by Mary Goodyear in Chapter 11. In a sense leading brands are becoming commodified through being packaged for franchise operators. Brands, and the brand equity discussed by Feldwick in Chapter 8, may represent the core resource of the emergent global networks, the brand identity being the only aspect readily visible to target consumers. The emergence of business-to-business branding along the supply chain suggests that in an extended networked organization, brands also may serve as an internal carrier of organizational values.

The management of organizational values is brand equity and values are likely to become a central issue for the maintenance of communities of practice and the coherence of networked organizations.

Space, location and knowledge

The newer entrants to the global marketplace quickly became aware of the need to maintain value through a knowledge-intensive approach to the delivery and support of goods, and have themselves invested in the established economies. James and Howells (2001) show that Asian companies are establishing or acquiring research and development facilities within the United Kingdom and the United States. There are two motives for this. Knowledge of regional markets can be obtained by the route of partnership or part ownership followed by acquisition, as with Fujitsu and ICL. It can also be captured through R&D focused on local product development, informed by feedback from local customers and incorporated in regionally targeted products, such as the Nissan Primera, a model developed for the European market. At the same time, access to a broader intellectual capital base can be obtained through tapping into regional knowledge which might enhance home-based operations. Both Malaysian and Korean automotive companies have acquired British-based engineering and design companies to further develop their home capabilities. Silicon Valley itself has attracted not just North American but Asian and European entrepreneurs, who seek a point of presence for networks that reach back to their home locations in India, Taiwan or France.

We have used an established model to describe an orderly shift of attention along a linear chain. However, we have also noted that the emergence of transnational production and distribution networks shows that later entrants have already adopted some aspects of the strategy of established players. This reflects a breakdown of the assumptions underlying models of the diffusion of technologies necessary to industrialization and participation in a global economy. The definition of technology accommodates the social technologies of organization structure and human resource systems critical to the effective deployment of knowledge. However, these models imply a diffusion of innovation from centre to periphery along the lines set out by Rogers in his classic treatise (Rogers, 1983). Yet the information and communication technologies that underpin the global system allow the reconfiguring or disaggregation of the production chain into a network. Each activity can be located at its point of greatest comparative advantage, while a degree of oversight and control not previously possible can be maintained. For example, in the 1980s North American automotive manufacturers elected to control production lines in their Canadian component plants through data links from the US side of the border. More significantly from a knowledge perspective, the divergent, creative activities which produce intellectual capital can be disaggregated from the convergent, focused discipline of the production process.

The British government and the European Commission are encouraging companies to seek alliances and opportunities in the opposite direction, in the less developed economies of South East Asia. This is presented both as a means of accessing the market potential of these growing economies and as a means of improving offshore manufacturing resources in relation to both home and export markets (EC/UNCTAD, 1996). In some instances complementary manufacturing takes place at both ends of such relationships. Overseas plants are increasingly selling to both local and home markets. The diffusion path from more to less developed countries is becoming a feedback loop, at least for the economies that operate within Ohmae's 'triad'.

Lipietz (1992) argues that the ability to separate production from consumption signals the end of the 'Fordist compromise' which underpinned the Keynsian social-democratic paradigm. Harvey (1990) points out that Ford significantly increased wages when he introduced his five-dollar, eight-hour day in 1914 in conjunction with his production line. He saw the workers as an integral part of a production and consumption process. Production workers remote from the destination market no longer need to be paid sufficiently well to consume the products of their own labour. The result of these changes is a complex layering of labour markets, both internal and external to the developed economies driving the globalization process. Harvey regards this post-Fordist situation as a regime of flexible accumulation which is tightly organized through its geographical dispersal and flexible responses to labour markets, and which is even more reliant on the creation of scientific and technical knowledge.

LIFE SPACE – KNOWLEDGE SPACE

A key issue in any consideration of managing knowledge is the relationship between individual and the organization. Parts III and IV of this book deal with the human aspects of communicating and the necessary support of human resources. In particular, Chapters 13 to 15 discuss relevant organizational experiences. However, as we have already indicated, the nature of employment is changing in both the established and the newly participating economies in the evolving global system. Castells (1997a) characterizes this as the replacement of organizational man with flexible woman, and Beck (2000) speaks of the 'Brazilianization of the West'. Castells is arguing that the North American 1950s stereotype of the white-collar worker with the Western equivalent of lifetime employment in a large corporation is being replaced by the short-term contract worker, often female, who may gain some advantage from flexible working hours, but who is inevitably on a lower level of remuneration and benefits. Beck goes further to argue that the patterns of employment common in semi-industrialized countries typified by Brazil are the future for developed countries. He bases this judgement on the impact of the current neo-liberal economic policies which deny any developmental role for the national state, relying instead entirely on market mechanisms. Bond, for example, analyses the implications of adherence to such policies in post-apartheid South Africa (Bond, 2000). A minority of waged or salaried full-time workers will coexist with a majority of multi-activity workers following a variety of discontinuous and unregulated sources of income. Such a scenario is far removed from the lifetime employment model of the major Japanese corporations, or even of recent Western practice and assumptions, and renews the challenge to sustainable communities of practice discussed above.

Work and employment must still take place in some physical space, however electronically connected that space may be. Recently the spatial requirements of knowledge creation and management have returned to the agenda (e.g. Holtham and Ward, 2000). Increasingly, however, even in developed economies, that space is the household (Little, 2000). At the micro-level consideration has been given to the physical requirements of creative work, as well as the social needs of group formation and interaction. DeMarco and Lister (1987) identified the environmental obstacles put in the way of productive activity by software development companies.

At the meso-level of space and location, the problems of physical absence for distance workers, and of the split between high- and low-value work into front and back office functions have been recognized for some time (e.g. Nelson, 1988), but at the macro-level communications between front and back office can cross cultural and national boundaries.

The difficulty of achieving effective communities of practice across both spatial and cultural distance is already being identified in studies of attempts by Western firms to capitalize on the resources of the Indian software industry (Nicholson et al., 2000). There were significant changes in the Indian economy during the 1990s, with a change in government policy towards participation in the world economy. Indian firms are successfully providing services in Europe and North America. However, these either have key staff in place in the client culture in order to ensure the alignment that ICL provides for Fujitsu, or operate via partnerships. One Indian software company approaches the North American market under the brand of its Swedish partner, confident in the quality of its own products, but aware of the image of Indian products.

It is clear that careful consideration of space, in each of the senses we have noted, is likely to become a key component of knowledge creation and management in the future. However, re-examination of Webber's work in the light of current information technology offers insight into immediate issues of the redefinition of centre and periphery and the implications for global systems.

INCLUSION, EXCLUSION AND INFILTRATION

ICTs offer the potential for participation in the 'information economy' to peripheral areas. However, in the new context 'periphery' is defined by access to these very technologies. There are disadvantaged regions and localities within developed economies as well as in the so-called 'Third World'. The United States Department of Commerce has expressed its concern over the 'digital divide' in relation to inequities with the US economy. These reflect differential access to the basic technologies of telephony as well as the latest forms of Internet access (NTIA, 2000).

We noted that Castells argues that access to flows of information and resources is the key to participation in the global economy (Castells, 1989). However, with the end of a global ideological divide, the regions beyond Ohmae's 'triad' are no longer seen as potential clients or allies in a global game. They may be seen as offering material resources, or minor market opportunities. Beyond the core of the so-called global economy a high proportion of populations are more than 30 minutes' walk from even a low-quality telephone line (Lamberton, 1995).

More recently Castells has described 'informational politics in action' (Castells, 1997b: 333). He is concerned that one aspect of globalization, the reliance on simplified mass communication, inevitably reduces the complexity of political discourse. However, in the same volume he describes very different and complex forms of electronically mediated communication by dissident minorities: Zapatista rebels in Mexico and militia groups in the USA. In both cases movements premised on the championing of the local and specific and a rejection of the global economy are achieving a presence and a voice in a global arena through the appropriation of the technologies of globalization. The ubiquity and accessibility of the Internet and World Wide Web do offer combinatorial opportunities for the extension and enlargement of multi and parallel cultural voices and visions to inhabit the world of global communication. It is possible to sample voices from geographically disparate locations. Together these reveal the dynamic between traditional cultural practices, modern communication forms and the enrichment of global symbolic life (for examples see Little et al., 2000).

Many discussions of the impact of the Internet and the globalization of communication are concerned with impacts on local culture and material practice. They focus on the 'McDonaldization' of symbolic life (Ritzer, 2000). Global communication is seen as flattening the cultural terrain in the direction of the dominance of the modes and material practices of the global economic leaders, especially the United States. The US ownership of the strategic components of global communication technology, most particularly the dominance of Microsoft, is seen as an important element in this flattening of the terrain. Equally important in this doomsday scenario of the destruction of a rich and varied cultural and symbolic life is the emergence of English as a global language. Some 80 per cent of websites are in the English language, and it would be foolhardy to deny the validity of this scenario as a potential state of the future world of global communications. However, it ignores many of the new cultural capacities of new forms of global communication. Just as Crystal (1997) argues that the global English language is no longer under the control of its original native speakers, so are the technologies of globalization appropriated by users at the margins.

The structure and format of Internet-based communication have created a proliferation of software applications which operate as multivoicing mechanisms. At the very lowest level they permit the intermediation of language through instantaneous translation facilities, enabling many highly detailed views and images of the world to be accessed simultaneously. The richness of a medium that can include image and sound allows cultures and cultural groups more actively to communicate their world views. Equally the consequences of such capabilities and choices for the formation of identity, both at the individual and at the community level, can be seen in the economic practices of cultural marketing now present on the Internet. On-line cultural sites developed expressly with the intent of selling through the net also carry active links to indigenous use of the mode for a range of economic, cultural and social purposes. There is a symbiosis between the use of the Internet for e-commerce purposes and the maintenance of living and differentiated cultures, a pattern which is already evident in Canada, Africa and Indonesia.

In this context, the rise of the portal metaphor as an organizer of web access has allowed countries such as Estonia to provide public access in its own Finno-Ugric language (Abbate, 2000). The use of 'front-end' translation software can now overcome the language barrier. The portal is a home page which provides structured links into resources appropriate to its users. As an organizing device it can reduce search time for newer users. The World Bank recognized the role of knowledge in the 1998–99 *World Development Report* (World Bank, 1998) and is currently rebranding as the Knowledge Bank. Stephen Denning, the Director of the Knowledge Management programme at the Bank, has presented this as a necessary dialogue between all parties concerned with the development process (Denning and Grieco, 2000). A component of this realignment is the development of a web portal for Global Knowledge Partnership. The Bank has opened a web-based debate with non-governmental organizations which has inevitably raised the issue of power relationships. These can be seen in the framing of access pathways by the resource rich on behalf of the resource poor.

Future knowledge and knowledge futures

This chapter has set a range of issues dealt with by our book in the context of an emerging global system. This system is far from complete and far from determined, but it has already had a profound impact on social and working life in the regions included within and excluded from it. Information and communication technologies are driving the processes of globalization. They are also providing avenues of entry for excluded constituencies and the means to refine and develop the management of the knowledge which has been foregrounded by the new relationships.

We have negotiated the barrier of seeing knowledge management as simply one of many fads, but the speed of change in markets, competition and technology means that there is a socio-institutional lag as the new techno-economic paradigm emerges (Perez, 1983).

For example, e-commerce is already mutating into m-commerce: mobile delivery of services. Despite the relative inadequacy of current WAP (Wireless Application Protocol) mobile telephony, the combination of low earth orbit (LEO) satellites with Global Positioning Systems (GPS) in proposed systems such as the European Galileo GPS will allow location-sensitive services to be delivered to individuals and groups on the move (Taplin, 2000). New forms of community of practice may arise, together with a reassessment of the spatial dynamics of knowledge creation and application. With LEO direct satellite systems, the network coverage will of necessity be equally dense and universal across the majority of the planet's surface beneath the hundreds of orbiting satellites.

Whether these and other opportunities lead to robust and effective communities of practice or the reintegration or redefinition of core and periphery will only be discovered though emerging practice. Clearly the appropriate and effective management of knowledge continues to be a matter for fruitful study and debate.

NOTE

1. Winterbotham (1974) described the massive British World War II code-breaking undertaking which at its peak employed 8,000 workers, using state-of-the-art business technology and the specially designed Colossus electronic computer. By the time Winterbotham broke the post-war silence around these achievements, much of the early history of computing had already been framed around the requirements of the post-Manhattan Project nuclear weapons programme of the United States. The von Neumann architecture which specified the relationship of computer hardware and program was formulated with weapons calculations in mind.

REFERENCES

Abbate, J. (2000) 'Virtual nation-building in Estonia: reshaping space, place, and identity in a newly independent state'. Paper presented at Virtual Society? Get Real! Conference, Ashridge House, Hertfordshire, May.

Akin, W.E. (1977) *Technocracy and the American Dream: the Technocrat Movement 1900–1941*. University of California Press, Berkeley.

Banham, R. (1971) *Los Angeles: the Architecture of Four Ecologies*. Allen Lane, Harmondsworth.

BBC World Service (2000) 'Range slashed as Unilever culls brands', *World Business Analysis*, broadcast 24 March.

Beck, U. (2000) *The Brave New World of Work*. Polity Press, Cambridge.

Bond, P. (2000) *Elite Transition: from Apartheid to Neoliberalism in South Africa*. Pluto Press, London.

Burton-Jones, A. (1999) *Knowledge Capitalism: Business, Work and Learning in the New Economy*. Oxford University Press, Oxford.

Castells, M. (1989) *The Informational City: Information Technology, Economic Restructuring and the Urban-regional Process*. Blackwell, Oxford.

Castells, M. (1996) *The Rise of the Network Society: the Information Age: Economy, Society and Culture Volume I*. Blackwell, Oxford.

Castells, M. (1997a) 'An introduction to the information age', *City*, 7: 6–17.

Castells, M. (1997b) *The Power of Identity: the Information Age: Economy, Society and Culture Volume II*. Blackwell, Oxford.

Castells, M. and Hall, P. (1994) *Technopoles of the World: the Making of 21st Century Industrial Complexes.* Routledge, London.

Crystal, D. (1997) *English as a Global Language.* Cambridge University Press, Cambridge.

DeMarco, T. and Lister, T. (1987) *Peopleware: Productive Projects and Teams.* Dorset House, New York.

Denning, S. and Grieco, M. (2000) 'Technology, dialogue and the development process', *Urban Studies,* 37 (10) September: 1065–1879.

Dicken, P. (1998) *Global Shift: Transforming the World's Economy,* 3rd edn. Paul Chapman, London.

Dreyfus, H.L. and Dreyfus, S.E. (1986) *Mind over Machine.* Free Press, New York.

Dunning, J.H. (1993) *Multinational Enterprises and the Global Economy.* Addison-Wesley, Reading, MA.

EC/UNCTAD (1996) *Investing in Asia's Dynamism: European Union Direct Investment in Asia.* European Commission/UNCTAD Division on Transnational Corporations and Investment, Office for Official Publications of the EC, Luxembourg.

Galbraith, J.K. (1967) *The New Industrial State.* Houghton Mifflin, Boston.

Goodall, A. (1985) *The Guide to Expert Systems.* Learned Information, Oxford.

Hammer, M. (1990) 'Re-engineering work: don't automate, obliterate', *Harvard Business Review,* July–August: 104–112.

Hansen, M.T., Nohria, N. and Tierney, T. (1999) 'What's your strategy for managing knowledge?' *Harvard Business Review,* March–April: 106–116.

Harvey, D. (1990) *The Condition of Postmodernity.* Basil Blackwell, Oxford.

Holtham, C. (1999) 'The future of knowledge management', *Knowledge Management,* 2 (9): 29–31.

Holtham, C. and Ward, V. (2000) 'Physical space – the most neglected resource in contemporary knowledge management', Proceedings of KMAC 2000, The Operational Research Society Knowlege Management Conference, Operational Research Society.

Inoue, T. (1998) 'Small businesses flourish in virtual village', *Nikkei Weekly,* 26 January: 1.

Jacobs, J. (1961) *The Death and Life of Great American Cities.* Random House, New York.

James, A.D. and Howells, J. (2001) 'Global companies and local markets: the internationalization of product design and development', in R. Thorpe and S. Little (eds) *Global Change: the Impact of Asia in the 21st Century.* Palgrave, London.

Klein, N. (2000) *No Logo.* HarperCollins, London.

Lamberton, D. (1995) 'Communications', in P. Troy (ed.) *Technological Change and Urban Development.* Federation Press, Sydney.

Landauer, T.K. (1995) *The Trouble with Computers: Usefulness, Useability and Productivity.* MIT Press, Cambridge, MA.

Lipietz, A. (1992) *Towards a New Economic Order: Postfordism, Ecology and Democracy.* Polity Press, Cambridge.

Little, S.E. (2000) 'Networks and neighbourhoods: household, community and sovereignty in the global economy', *Urban Studies,* 37 (10) September: 1813–1826.

Little, S. Holmes, L. and Grieco, M. (2000) 'Island histories, open cultures?: the electronic transformation of adjacency', *Southern African Business Review,* 4 (2): 21–25.

Marvin, C. (1988) *When Old Technologies Were New: Thinking about Electric Communication in the Late Nineteenth Century.* Oxford University Press, New York.

Massey, D., Quintas, P. and Wield, D. (1992) *High Tech Fantasies: Science Parks in Society, Science and Space*. Routledge, London.

Menzel, P. and D'Alusio, F. (2000) *Robo Sapiens, Evolution of a New Species*. MIT Press, Cambridge, MA.

Milton, N., Shadbolt, N., Cottam, H. and Hammersley, M. (1999) 'Towards a knowledge technology for knowledge management', *International Journal of Human-Computer Studies*, 53 (3): 615–664.

Nelson, K. (1988) 'Labor demand, labor supply and the suburbanization of low-wage office work', in A.J. Scott and M. Storper, *Production Work and Territory: The Geographical Anatomy of Industrial Capitalism*. Unwin-Hyman, Boston.

Nicholson, B., Sahay, S. and Krishna, S. (2000) 'Work practices and local improvisations within global software teams: a case study of a UK subsidiary in India', *Proceedings of IFIP WG9.4 Conference on Information Flows, Local Improvisations and Work Practices*. Cape Town, May.

NTIA (2000) *Falling through the Net: Defining the Digital Divide*. National Telecommunications and Information Administration, US Department of Commerce, Washington.

Ohmae, K. (1990) *The Borderless World: Power and Strategy in the Interlinked Economy*. Collins, London.

Ohmae, K. (1995) *The End of the Nation State: the Rise of Regional Economics*. Free Press, New York.

Perez, C. (1983) 'Structural change and the assimilation of new technologies in the economic and social systems', *Futures*, 15 (5): 357–375.

Porter, M.E. (1990) *The Competitive Advantage of Nations*. Macmillan, London.

Rich, B.R. and Janos, L. (1995) *Skunk Works*. Warner Books, London.

Ritzer, G. (2000) *The McDonaldization of Society: an Investigation into the Changing Character of Contemporary Social Life*. 2nd edn. Pine Forge Press, Thousand Oaks, CA.

Rogers, E.M. (1983) *Diffusion of Innovations*, 3rd edn. Free Press, New York.

Saxenian, A. (1994) *Regional Advantage: Culture and Competition in Silicon Valley and Route 128*, Harvard University Press, Cambridge, MA.

Sproull, L. and Kiesler, S. (1991) *Connections: New Ways of Working in the Networked Organization*. MIT Press, Cambridge, MA.

Taplin, R. (2000) 'Perfect guidance for the stars', *The Times*, 3 October: 17.

Tugendhat, C. (1971) *The Multinationals*. Penguin, Harmondsworth.

Turing, A. (1950) 'Computing machinery and intelligence', *Mind*, 59: 433–460.

Vernon, R. (1971) *Sovereignty at Bay: the Multinational Spread of US Enterprises*. Basic Books, New York.

Vernon, R. (1974) 'The location of economic activity', in J.H. Dunning (ed.) *Economic Analysis and the Multinational Enterprise*. Allen and Unwin, London.

Webber, M. (1964) 'The urban place and the non-place urban realm', in M.M. Webber, J.W. Dyckman, D.L. Foley, A.Z. Gutenberg, W.L.C. Wheaton and C.B. Wurster *Explorations in Urban Structure*. University of Pennsylvania Press, Philadelphia.

Weick, K.E. (1979) *The Social Psychology of Organizing*. McGraw-Hill, New York.

Weilinga, B., Sandberg, J. and Schreiber, G. (1997) 'Methods and techniques for knowledge management: what has knowledge engineering to offer?' *Expert Systems with Applications*, 13: 73–84.

Wilkinson, B., Gamble, J., Humphrey, J., and Morris, J. (2001) 'International production networks and human resources: the case of the Malaysia electronics industry', in

R. Thorpe and S. Little, *Global Change: the Impact of Asia in the 21st Century*. Palgrave, London.

Winterbotham, F.W. (1974) *The Ultra Secret*. Weidenfeld and Nicholson, London.

World Bank (1998) *World Development Report, 1998/99: Knowledge for Development*. Oxford University Press, Oxford.

Index

3M, 318
Aaker, D., 175–6, 184, 185
Acer, cellular organization, 288–9, 292
Ackerman, M., 196
action, knowing and, 77-8
advertising: intercultural confusion, 241–2;
    literacy, 248–9
affordance, 81–3; dynamic, 83–4, 87, 91
Alchian, A., 124, 126
Andrews, K., 129, 134
'Answer Garden' project, 196
apprenticeships, 93
'attackers' advantage', 133
Axelrod, J., 178

ba, 17, 49–54, 64; building and energizing,
    59–60; in Japan, 109, 110
Bacdayan, P., 69
Bannon, L., 196, 203, 204, 205–6
Barley, S., 28
Bartlett, F.C., 200
Bateson, G., 222
BBC, 353
Beck, U., 382
Bell, D., 3–4
biotechnology, 131–2; difference between
    scientific and technological knowledge,
    151, 162; organizational form, 285;
    spread of knowledge, 31
Bird, M., 184
Blackler, F., 205
Bode, H., 142
Bond, P., 382
boundary objects, 31, 32–3, 91
bounded rationality, 126–7, 135
brainstorming, 360
brand awareness, 184–5
brand equity, 56, 120–1, 170, 171–3, 186–7,
    247–8, 380; as brand description, 172,
    185–6; as brand strength, 172, 175–85;
    as brand value, 172, 173–5
brand image, 170–1

brand loyalty, 175, 176; attitudinal measures,
    183–4; behavioural measures, 180–3
branding, post-modern, 251–3
brands: confused meanings, 240; marketing,
    245, 251; proportion of goods, 246; role
    of, 247, 252
Broadbent, S., 177–8
brokering, 31, 32
Brown, J.S., 205
BT, 352
Business Process Re-engineering (BPR), 371,
    373
business strategy, human resource
    management and, 314–16

capabilities, 119, 126; knowledge-based, 131
Cartesian epistemology, 72
Castells, M., 374, 375, 376, 377, 378, 382, 384
cellular organization, 285–91, 294–8;
    examples of implementation, 291–3
challenges, for professional staff, 338–9
Chandler, A., 22
Channell, D., 143, 146
Chesebrough, H., 28–9
Clegg, S., 212
Coca-Cola, 175
Cohen, M.D., 69
'collective mind', 69
combination, 45, 46, 63
communication, 11, 221, 296, 377; as
    agreement, 215; behaviour as, 214–15,
    224–5; functions of, 226–36;
    globalization, 384; interpersonal, 217–18,
    222–3; as process, 221–2; as
    understanding, 215; *see also* intercultural
    communication
communications technology, *see* information
    technology
communities of practice, 19, 25, 75, 104,
    373–4, 383; *ba* and, 50–1; boundaries of,
    50; movement of knowledge, 29–30;
    organizations as, 25–7

shared meanings, 129, 134, 203, 260; *see also* genres, organizational
shared service arrangements, 353, 354
Shih, S., 288, 289
Shimizu, H., 49
Silicon Valley, 375–6
Simon, H.A., 75, 126–7, 135
skills, 84, 365
skunkworks, 359
socialization, 44–5, 46, 48, 65, 94
specialization, 281, 378–9
Sproull, L., 373
staff development and evaluation, 338–9
standardization, 281, 294
State Street Bank, 338, 340
'sticky' knowledge, 15–16, 28, 29; in Japanese organizations, 102, 107, 109
stories/story telling, 84, 93, 205, 306
strategic alliances, 352–3
strategic thinking, 122–36
strategy, conventional/knowledge-based, 132–5
Swahili, racial-social categories, 220
synergy and synthesis, 26–7, 30

tacit knowledge, 10, 43, 56, 68, 84, 130–1, 152; of groups, 85, 86–7, 88, 90; interaction with explicit knowledge, 17, 44–8, 53, 63, 72–4; and knowing, 80, 94; and knowledge creation, 69, 94–5; in technological innovation, 144, 146, 149, 155–6, 161, 162
Taylor, F., 357
Technical & Computer Graphics (TCG), cellular organization, 286–8, 292, 295
technological knowledge, 140, 143–4, 162; distinctiveness of, 144–7; typology of, 157–61, 162
technologies: diffusion of, 381–2; organization of, 145; and spread of knowledge, 33–6
technology: heterogeneity of, 145, 162; institutions and, 22–3
Teece, D., 28–9, 308
theory, role of in technology, 146, 151, 157, 160
Tierney, M., 155
time and motion studies, 327
Tobin, J., 308
Toffler, A., 22
Total Quality Management, 360–1

Toyota, 59, 61, 319–20
training, 45, 97, 291, 325–6, 362
transaction costs, 19, 126, 128, 129, 134, 135
translators, 32
triangulation, 287–8, 295
trust, 34, 134
truthfulness, 42
Tugendhat, C., 376
types of knowledge, 157–61, 162

Ungson, G.R., 198
Unilever, 380
United Parcel Service, 327, 328, 329
universities: in Japan, 105, 111–13, 115; and movement of knowledge, 29–30
urbanity, 377
USA: affectivity in, 233; Army Center for Lessons Learned, 270–1; communication in, 226, 227, 229, 235, 236; racial-social categories, 220

value appropriation, 129
value chains, 380
value creation, 129, 132, 335, 340, 345
Vernon, R., 379
Vickers, G., 76
Vincenti, W., 143–4, 144–5, 146–7, 156, 157, 159
virtual organization, 353–4
vision, 57–8, 110, 129, 134

Walsh, J.P., 193
Walsh, V., 142
'war stories', 24, 76, 204
warrants, 27–8, 29
Webber, M., 376–7
Weick, K.E., 69
Wenger, E., 35, 36
Westinghouse, 309
Williamson, O.E., 124, 126, 127, 135
Winter, S., 154, 155, 156
World Bank, 385
World Wide Web, 35, 376, 384
Wynn, E., 205

Xerox, 9–10, 24, 28, 95–6, 306

Yakemovic, K.C.B., 197

Zander, U., 124, 135
Zinchenko, P.I., 201